"The kingdom of God is his primary mission on earth: providing life as he intends—true, beautiful, just, abundant! Dr. Sherman has delivered a masterful tome of how the church has partnered with God in his kingdom work throughout history, along with contemporary examples of this partnership at work and practical strategies and insights for those who want to get in on what God is up to. What a gift, Amy!"
Reggie McNeal, author of *Kingdom Come* and city coach with GoodCities

"Amy Sherman has done it again! Her thesis this time is that the good news is way bigger than we could have imagined. And the church—those who collectively find themselves following Jesus of Nazareth—has the best chance of helping each person flourish in every area of life: spiritually, relationally, economically, educationally, artistically, and vocationally. Throughout history, parts of the church in different parts of the world have gotten parts of this flourishing framework right, which led to the abolition of the slave trade, the adoption of children, care for the sick, the establishment of public schools and public spaces, and job creation for the common good. Today we can see the complete ecosystem of a flourishing community and the role we can play in helping to bring that about. I believe *Agents of Flourishing* can serve as the systematic theology for advancing shalom in every community and will be the go-to source for those who find themselves captivated by Jeremiah's word to 'seek the peace and prosperity of the city to which I have carried you.'"
Eric Swanson, senior fellow with Leadership Network

"Narrowing the perilous Sunday-to-Monday gap may be the most urgent and compelling need for the church in our time. In *Agents of Flourishing,* Amy Sherman brilliantly presses into the implications and opportunities for organizations and local churches that are embracing a transforming vocational mission for the glory of God and the common good. Sherman's theological rigor and storytelling prowess prompt my imagination to soar and my heart to skip a beat in considering the wide-open door of gospel impact available to the church in our time. This is a book every pastor and Christian leader needs to read. I highly recommend it."
Tom Nelson, author of *The Flourishing Pastor* and president of Made to Flourish

"Amy Sherman does it again! She lands squarely on critical issues and practices that should demonstrate what it means to be Christ's people in the world for the common good. She always motivates and inspires me to follow in the Jesus way, to which she so ably points. Don't just read this book, let it guide you to live out its compelling, Jesus-shaped vision."
Mark Labberton, president of Fuller Theological Semina·

T0277209

"When history looks back on the church in America at the start of the twenty-first century, it won't be a pretty sight. Division, scandals, unbelief, materialism, individualism, theological drift . . . the list goes on and on. We've simply lost our way. Fortunately, this latest work by Dr. Amy Sherman provides a road map to help us get back on track. Amy rightly focuses our attention on the central message of Jesus—the good news of the kingdom of God (Luke 4:43)—and provides readers with helpful prompts to improvise this story in their cities and neighborhoods. Miraculously, we are to do this—not by exercising worldly power but from a posture of humility, grace, and sacrificial love. This is the way of King Jesus, and it needs to be the way of the church once again."

Brian Fikkert, president and founder of the Chalmers Center, coauthor of *When Helping Hurts: How to Alleviate Poverty Without Hurting the Poor . . . and Yourself*

"The flourishing of the whole creation, including the entire life of humanity, is the purpose and intention of a good and generous God. Our sin has corrupted and polluted every aspect of creation leading to curse instead of blessing, but one day God will restore that blessing fully. Until then we are called to be agents of God's original intention. Sherman has offered a wonderful blueprint for what that flourishing might look like in our time. What I really laud is her attention to the rich creational diversity of human flourishing—marriage, justice, art, education, business, and more. In a time when idolatry is destroying the witness of the church in America, these words are welcome and timely."

Michael W. Goheen, professor of missional theology at Covenant Theological Seminary and author of *The Church and Its Vocation: Lesslie Newbigin's Missionary Ecclesiology*

"*Agents of Flourishing* offers an expansive, inspirational, and profoundly biblical vision of how churches can contribute to the flourishing of their communities in the name of Christ. This book does what few others do, combining rich theological and sociological reflection with down-to-earth, practical examples of churches acting as agents of flourishing for the sake of their neighbors. I'm delighted to add this outstanding book to the reading list for my DMin seminar on vocation and ecclesiology; I would also recommend *Agents of Flourishing* to all church leaders who are committed to helping their congregations seek first God's kingdom and righteousness in tangible, world-impacting ways."

Mark D. Roberts, senior strategist at the Max De Pree Center for Leadership, Fuller Seminary

"*Agents of Flourishing* is a timely book loaded with expert guidance and amazingly practical insights for local churches (agents of God's inbreaking kingdom) seeking the flourishing of their communities. It presents captivating examples of local churches' engagement with six community endowments—the good (ethics), the true (knowledge), the beautiful (creativity), the just and well-ordered (political), the prosperous (economic), and the sustainable (natural environment)—as congregants carry out their priestly work of restoring shalom: rightness of relationships with God, self, others, and creation."

JoAnn Flett, executive director of the Center for Faithful Business at Seattle Pacific University

"Wanting to seek the shalom of your community is one thing; knowing how to actually go about it is quite another. Amy Sherman's *Agents of Flourishing* offers one of the best operating manuals for the church that I know of. It is at once accessible, scripturally wise, ecumenical, and most importantly chock-full of case studies of actual congregations seeking to answer the call to shalom in real-world contexts. Ever since I developed the Human Ecology Framework as a way to operationalize shalom in practice, I've been hoping someone would translate it for the ministry of local churches. Amy has given us a great gift in doing just that—and she does it as one of the most sure-handed guides to the role of the church in community out there today."

Josh Yates, executive director of the Ormond Center at Duke Divinity School

"In an age of political division and a shrinking Western church, Amy Sherman gives pastors, scholars, and students a comprehensive vision for equipping the saints to work toward the healing of our cities. Sherman bridges the gap from Scripture to praxis and gives readers both theological frameworks and practical examples of how our work and churches once again show our culture what the gospel looks like in the ordinary, everyday movements in our lives. I highly recommend *Agents of Flourishing* for anyone longing to see a reintegration of faith and work, private and public, church and city."

Jeff Haanen, founder and CEO of the Denver Institute for Faith & Work

"Thinking between two worlds, rooted in a life lived between two worlds, Amy Sherman is as comfortable in the academy as she is on the streets, as committed to the good work of think tanks as she is to good lives in the neighborhood. Morally, sociologically, and theologically intelligent, she draws on years of taking the world seriously, listening carefully wherever she goes to the deepest questions that matter for human flourishing. At the same time Sherman insists that her work always be grounded in research-based analysis about what is, what could be, and what should be. She's a unique human being who has embodied a vocation given for the common good."

Steven Garber, senior fellow for vocation and the common good at the M. J. Murdock Charitable Trust and author of *The Seamless Life: A Tapestry of Love and Learning, Worship and Work*

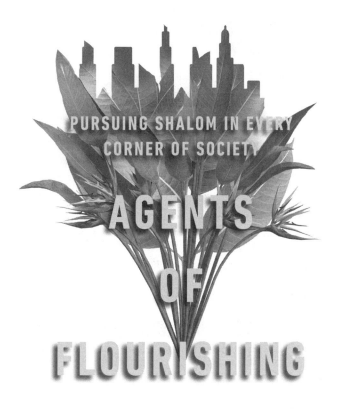

PURSUING SHALOM IN EVERY
CORNER OF SOCIETY

AGENTS

OF

FLOURISHING

AMY L. SHERMAN

An imprint of InterVarsity Press
Downers Grove, Illinois

InterVarsity Press
P.O. Box 1400, Downers Grove, IL 60515-1426
ivpress.com
email@ivpress.com

InterVarsity Press® is the book-publishing division of InterVarsity Christian Fellowship/USA®, a movement of students and faculty active on campus at hundreds of universities, colleges, and schools of nursing in the United States of America, and a member movement of the International Fellowship of Evangelical Students. For information about local and regional activities, visit intervarsity.org.

All Scripture quotations, unless otherwise indicated, are taken from The Holy Bible, New International Version®, NIV®. Copyright © 1973, 1978, 1984, 2011 by Biblica, Inc.™ Used by permission of Zondervan. All rights reserved worldwide. www.zondervan.com. The "NIV" and "New International Version" are trademarks registered in the United States Patent and Trademark Office by Biblica, Inc.™

While any stories in this book are true, some names and identifying information may have been changed to protect the privacy of individuals.

Figure 1.1 adapted from Thriving Cities Group. Used by permission.
Figure 1.3 based on Bob Robinson, 2013. Used by permission.
Figure 7.1, Four Chapters, copyright © by Noelle Stoffel. Used by permission.
Figure 8.1 based on Howard Zehr and Ted Grimsrud, "Rethinking God, Justice, and Treatment of Offenders," in Religion, the Community, and the Rehabilitation of Criminal Offenders *(Philadelphia: Haworth Press, 2002), 259-85.*
Figure 13.1 based on Chuck Proudfit, 2020. Used by permission.
Figure 17.1 adapted from Thriving Cities Group, "Citizen Field Guide," 2016, 11. Used by permission.

The publisher cannot verify the accuracy or functionality of website URLs used in this book beyond the date of publication.

Cover design and image composite: David Fassett
Interior design: Daniel van Loon
Images: green Marian plum leaves: © Bebenjy / iStock / Getty Images Plus
  sun and sunbeams: © Jutta Kuss / Getty Images
  white pearl textured paper: © tomograf / E+ / Getty Images
  bird of paradise flower: © Vac1 / iStock / Getty Images Plus
  watercolor background blue white: © Vesin_Sergey / iStock / Getty Images Plus

ISBN 978-1-5140-0078-6 (print)
ISBN 978-1-5140-0079-3 (digital)

Printed in the United States of America ♾

InterVarsity Press is committed to ecological stewardship and to the conservation of natural resources in all our operations. This book was printed using sustainably sourced paper.

Library of Congress Cataloging-in-Publication Data
A catalog record for this book is available from the Library of Congress.

P	25	24	23	22	21	20	19	18	17	16	15	14	13	12	11	10	9	8	7	6	5	4	3	2	1
Y		37	36		35		34		33		32		31		30		29		28		27		26		25		24		23		22

CONTENTS

INTRODUCTION

MY HOPE IN THIS BOOK is to help pastors and Christian leaders live deeply and wisely into the call of Jeremiah 29:7: "Seek the peace and prosperity of the city to which I have carried you into exile. Pray to the LORD for it, because if it prospers, you too will prosper."

I'm glad whenever I see this notion emblazoned on a congregation's home page. I smile when a Christian businessperson, architect, or artist references the verse as inspiration for their work. In a time when there is much to lament about the church in America, I am encouraged by the city gospel movement that has unfolded over the past couple of decades. This movement embraces Jeremiah 29:7 as something of a theme verse. It is composed of a significant (and I hope growing) portion of the church that has accepted the reality of our exilic position in post-Christian culture. These congregations and their leaders are not trying to wield the tools of cultural warfare or put their hopes in political power. They have recognized the ugliness and failure of this strategy—and, more importantly, have seen how it is a betrayal of the way of Jesus in the world. They are instead seeking (in the phrases commonly deployed) to "engage in gospel renewal in cities," "to be a faithful presence," to "be missional," or to live as a "sign, instrument, and foretaste of the kingdom of God" in their communities.

This is a cause for celebration. The reality of it has helped keep me devoted to the bride of Christ during a season when many media portrayals of the church have highlighted the distortions of a strident Christian nationalism whose visibility has increased in the past few years.

RESPONDING TO EXILE

I've written this book for those Christ-followers who have found in Jeremiah's words a compelling vision for the church in our time and for those who are open to this idea. Like the Israelites in Babylon at the time of Jeremiah's letter, we, too, are in exile.

We are *generally* in exile in the sense that all of humanity has been in exile since human beings were sent out of the Garden of Eden because of our sin. All of humanity longs to be "back home," though some people are more willing to admit it than others. Christ's disciples experience a further dimension of exile. We are members of a kingdom that Jesus taught was "not of this world" (Jn 18:36). We are exiles scattered throughout the nations (1 Pet 1:1). We feel uncomfortable with all kinds of worldliness because we've been made new creatures in Christ. We are trying to obey the command to "not conform to the pattern of this world, but be transformed by the renewing of [our] mind[s]" (Rom 12:2).

As Christians in post-Christian America, we feel keenly a *specific* sense of exile, perhaps similar to the Israelites in pagan Babylon. We're experiencing dislocation because, increasingly, our basic convictions about God, truth, nature, and human nature are unintelligible to our fellow citizens. We feel dismayed by the culture's moral relativism. In our workplaces some of us experience disdain or hostility toward our Christian faith. Older believers in particular remember a time when mainstream culture seemed more in alignment with traditional biblical values. As Bible Society CEO Paul Williams writes, "We live in a generation in which our elders at least can remember a time when Christianity was still a major force in our Western or Western-influenced societies. Thus we feel its declining influence more acutely."[1]

This disorientation has prompted a variety of opinions about how to respond, with some favoring retreat and others attack. I think many Christ-followers in the United States today feel caught. They are disturbed by the aggressive culture-warrior stance of some within conservative Christianity and with this group's seemingly uncritical marriage to right-wing politics. They grasp that Christendom is gone and that the church today must find a new way to be in our current culture. They also sense that it is important to stand up for their moral commitments, to be brave enough to insist on true truths. They don't want to attack, but they don't want to capitulate either, giving in to a version of political correctness that derides basic biblical teachings on such topics as gender or marriage.

Into this context the words from Jeremiah land with freshness and challenge. Rather than trying to conquer the world around us and rather than giving in and accommodating to its values and agendas, we hear God's call to engage this world. It's a call to be, in Timothy Keller's memorable phrase, "a counterculture for the common good."[2] It involves dwelling in the land, not withdrawing from it. It involves maintaining faithfulness to our distinct, biblical convictions while simultaneously laying down our lives for our neighbors—some of whom ridicule and reject those very convictions. It involves trusting God, who showed us grace while we were his enemies, when he says that this path of sacrificial love can bring both us and them true flourishing.

A DISCONNECT BETWEEN VISION AND ACTION

I rejoice that God has raised up a movement of exile-aware Christ-followers who are seeking to enact God's call to seek the peace and prosperity of their communities. At the same time, though, I'm concerned whether the movement has a sufficiently rich understanding of complex society and how to seek shalom in its every corner. This is highlighted when I see congregational leaders pairing Jeremiah's words with a once-a-year "serve the city" campaign engaging their people in a day's labor to clean up parks and paint schools. Don't get me wrong: I'm all for cleaning up parks and painting schools, but there's a disconnect between the depths of the biblical vision to seek the shalom of the community and the shallowness of such initiatives. The actions are rather anemic compared to Jeremiah's robust vision.

I think most congregational leaders are eager for their churches to have a more sustainable, lasting, and comprehensive influence for good in their locales. This is a cause for celebration, for witnessing through our deeds is vital in our current missiological context. Yet even those already making a notable difference through their community outreach say they are still learning. Given the importance of local mission and the difficulties it entails in our cultural context, we need some deeper reflection on what a thriving society looks like and on what the church's theology and practice in seeking to nurture that thriving should be. I offer this book as one attempt to address such concerns. In doing so I am in no way seeking to displace the wise counsel of others who have gone before. My gratitude runs deep toward people like Tim Keller, Ray Bakke, Robert Linthicum, and John Perkins.

In this book I try to bring together a vision of the church's missional identity—including its rich, two-thousand-year legacy of advancing the common good—with a holistic, biblical, and sociological understanding of the dimensions of societal flourishing. I hope to offer a guide for congregational leaders willing and ready to live into God's call to seek their neighbors' thriving. By *neighbors*, I mean their fellow community residents. This book focuses on local outreach, not overseas missions (important though the latter is).[3]

Following the approach to local outreach that I'm recommending will likely feel intense. It requires that congregational leaders learn both their church's and their community's assets. It will require more and deeper thinking and praying than does setting up a food-distribution ministry or writing checks to a few nonprofits. It will likely involve redirecting money or possibly raising more money. It will require greater attention to discipling people for kingdom ministry within their daily vocations. It will mean using a different scorecard for defining "church success." It may involve exploring new ways of being church and of partnering with those within and outside the family of faith. It will involve investing in the kinds of ministries that require a long-term commitment.

Such a pursuit is not a pipe dream: it's what the various congregations profiled in this book have done and are doing. And, importantly, they are not all big, affluent churches. They are diverse in size, resources, denomination, demographic composition, geographic location, and age. I'll grant that they are special; after all, they're the ones I found after several months of looking for strong examples. But what they have done, other congregations—including yours—can do.

HOW TO READ THIS BOOK

This book is long. The good news is you needn't read it straight through. Perhaps you already have a sense of the social arena(s) in which your congregation is well-positioned to work (e.g., because of the particular vocational expertise of your congregants or your church's physical location). If so, I recommend reading chapter one and then skipping to the section on the arena (henceforth called "community endowment") you're most interested in.

Alternatively, you may have a sense that your church's approach to community outreach historically aligns well with one of the three approaches I describe on page nine. You may be looking for examples of other congregations that pursue this approach. If so, you could then skip to the chapter(s) where such churches are profiled.

You might also consider using the book as a text for an adult education class or as a curriculum for small groups. You could ask one individual or subgroup of participants to read the section on one community endowment while others read about other endowments. Then the full class or group could come together for discussion.

Regardless of how you choose to read the book, I encourage you to take it slow. Spend some time in prayer asking Jesus to guide you in the ways he might have you apply the teachings and examples offered in the context of your congregation and community.

SEVEN CONVICTIONS ANIMATING THIS BOOK

My purpose in this book is to encourage and equip congregations to seek the flourishing of their communities—based on a conviction that this is a central mission of the church in our time. Since I'm arguing this is something that churches *ought* to do, I'm coming from a particular perspective regarding what the Bible teaches about the church's identity and mission and how congregations should engage culture. Since this book is already long, I don't spend much time defending that perspective. Others have done that better than I can.[4] This book is not as much about *why* the church should vigorously embrace its calling to be an agent of flourishing as it is about (1) the fact that throughout (most of) its history the church has acted in this way and (2) what living into this calling can look like, now, in our time and place.

Yet the *why* is important. I discuss it in some detail in chapter one by reflecting on the mission of God's people as the "royal priesthood" in and through which Christ's renewing work is unfolding. More generally, the *why* emerges from the following seven core convictions.

What is the story told in the Bible?

1. The Bible is "the story of God's mighty deeds to restore the whole creation with Jesus as the center point of that story. The church finds its identity by participating in what he is doing in redemptive history according to his command and invitation."[5]

2. The Bible is "all about mission." The "whole Bible renders to us the story of God's mission through God's people in their engagement with God's world for the sake of the whole of God's creation."[6]

What is the gospel?

3. "The original preaching of the Gospel on the lips of Jesus was—precisely—the announcement of the coming of the kingdom."[7] Yes, the gospel is about Jesus dying on the cross for our sins—Hallelujah! I'm grateful for that, for daily I know how desperately I need a Savior. But the gospel is also bigger than that. It is an eschatological message about what's coming in the future (a fully restored, purified creation) and what has already arrived in part in the person of Jesus. Salvation is bigger than me getting my ticket to heaven, and it's not about my disembodied soul living eternally in some ethereal realm called heaven. No, "salvation is the restoration of God's creation on a new earth. In this restored world, the redeemed of God will live in resurrected bodies within a renewed creation, from which sin and its effects have been expunged. This is the kingdom that Christ's followers have already begun to enjoy in foretaste."[8]

4. This gospel—Jesus' good news of the kingdom—has profound social, economic, political, and cultural implications. God's saving grace "does not remain outside or above or beside nature but rather . . . wholly renews it."[9]

What is the church, and what is its mission?

5. Three statements from the group of theologians and missiologists who produced the book *Missional Church* do a better job of answering

this question than anything else I've seen: (1) "The church is the sign, foretaste, instrument, and agent of God's inbreaking kingdom." (2) "The church is a messianic community both spawned by the reign of God and directed toward it." (3) The church is "the people of God who are called and sent to re-present the reign of God. This vocation is rooted in the good news, the gospel: in Jesus Christ the reign of God is at hand and is now breaking in."[10] To this I could add Christopher Wright's important observation that the church doesn't have a mission; the church participates in the mission of God.[11]

6. As disciples of Jesus, our task is to "take the Bible and its teaching seriously for the totality of our civilization *right now* and not to relegate it to some optional area called 'religion.'"[12] Put another way: "To be a Christian is to be obliged to engage the world, pursuing God's restorative purpose over all of life, individual and incorporate, public and private."[13]

How should the church relate to the world?

7. As should be clear from the previous convictions, as regards the church's calling in the world I reject reductionist understandings of the fortification, accommodation, and domination paradigms regarding how the church should relate to society. I embrace an *incarnation* paradigm that holds that "the calling of the church is to go into the fullness of the culture, bearing the fullness of the gospel, for the purposes of redemption."[14]

A MAP OF THE BOOK

Chapter one defines biblical flourishing and contrasts it with prevailing secular understandings. Then I review the church's identity and mission as royal priests called to advance flourishing in our communities.[15]

Chapter one also introduces the Thriving Cities Group's "Human Ecology Framework," which serves as the organizing schema for the rest of the book. This framework was developed by sociologist Joshua J. Yates and a group of faith-friendly scholars at the University of Virginia's Thriving Cities Lab.[16] Coupled with serious theological reflection, it offers both the depth of genuine understanding of societal flourishing that Christian leaders need to embody God's call in Jeremiah 29:7 and a set of handholds for our practical action going forward. The framework describes six arenas of civilizational life. These community endowments are *the Good* (the realm of social mores and ethics), *the True* (the realm of human knowledge and learning), *the Beautiful* (the realm of creativity, aesthetics, and design), *the Just and Well-Ordered* (the realm of political and civic life), *the Prosperous* (the realm of economic life), and *the Sustainable* (the realm of the natural environment). Each of these interdependent endowments needs to be healthy and strong if a community is to experience thriving.

The following chapters then take up each of these six endowments. For each endowment I begin with a chapter that tries to do four things:

1. Define and describe the endowment and its connection to biblically defined human flourishing.

2. Reflect on what Scripture teaches about the creational intent of the endowment.

3. Identify ways in which the endowment has been malformed by the fall and some possibilities for how Christians could be engaged in re-forming it.

4. Offer a brief review of the ways the church throughout history has positively influenced the ideas and values animating the endowment, modeled practices in alignment with God's creational intent for the endowment, resisted deformations in it, and contributed to re-formations. This review is, of course, necessarily cursory. I hope that these limited examples and stories will nonetheless provide fodder for imagination and inspiration about the ways we in the contemporary church might imitate the good work of our forebears.

Following this, I offer one to two chapters highlighting how contemporary US congregations are contributing positively to the health and strength of the endowment. Their stories illustrate some specific strategies—by no means *all* of the possible strategies—that churches could take to advance flourishing in that realm of community life. I hope these profiles are instructional as well as inspirational; they typically end with my comments on lessons learned.

In my final chapter I offer some counsel on the kinds of next steps you can take in your congregations to live into the calling of being agents of flourishing in your communities. This is and is not a how-to chapter. It is in the sense that it lays out several key tasks that congregations must take up as they prepare for, design, and implement initiatives aimed at enhancing the flourishing of their communities. It is not, because I do not provide step-by-step instructions for how to execute those tasks. It is best to not learn that from a book but in the setting of a learning community that provides both coaching and networking with other congregations engaged in similar journeys. (One such example is Made to Flourish and the Chalmer Center's Flourishing Communities Incubator.[17])

THREE APPROACHES TO COMMUNITY MINISTRY

The congregations highlighted in this book are not perfect—no church is. In showcasing them I am not endorsing every jot and tittle of their doctrinal or denominational commitments or their ecclesial policies. Some of their leaders hold positions on various subjects I disagree with. All of them love Jesus, are animated by Jesus' gospel of the kingdom, and are seeking to bring foretastes of that kingdom here on earth. Their progress and achievements are varied and proximate. Theirs are the stories I landed on after about eighteen months of research into illuminating examples of churches genuinely and deeply influencing re-formations in the six community endowments. I chose them because their work—deeply thoughtful labor of years—is closer to consonance with the big vision of seeking the shalom of our communities than is typically seen today. No reader of this book is likely to agree with everything these leaders have said and done. All readers, I believe, can still learn much from them.

The approaches to community ministry followed by the churches whose stories I cover in detail fall into three broad categories (see fig. 0.1). The first I label "institutional." That is, the missional endeavor they are engaged in is something conceived of as *whole church* and is driven by senior leaders (e.g., pastors, elders). The congregation corporately understands this endeavor as central to its DNA. Not every single congregant may be personally involved, but everyone is behind the initiative financially (through their general tithes and offerings), understands it is the signature outreach initiative of the

church, and expects it to be showcased publicly regularly. The stories about
Christ Community–Downtown in Kansas City, East End Fellowship in
Richmond, Virginia, and Grace Chapel in Mason, Ohio, fit into this category.
Shorter stories—such as those about Bible Center Church and Marietta
Cumberland Presbyterian Church in chapter five and Colonial Church in
chapter thirteen—also fit this profile.

Institutional	Organic	Partnership-Focused
Christ Community–Downtown (chap. 7)	Church of the Servant (chap. 9)	Churches engaged with Live the Life Ministries (chap. 3)
East End Fellowship (chap. 10)	Resurrection Catholic Church (chap. 3)	Churches engaged with Caring for Kids (chap. 5)
Grace Chapel (chap. 12)	Crosswater Community Church (chap. 3)	Pleasant Hope Baptist Church (chap. 16)
Bible Center Church (chap. 5)		Church of the Redeemer (chap. 15)
Marietta Cumberland Presbyterian Church (chap. 5)		
Colonial Church (chap. 13)		

Figure 0.1. Three approaches to community ministry

The second I call "organic." These are stories about initiatives conceived of
and directed by a group of individual congregants. The initiative aligns
strongly with the church's overall values and priorities. Senior leaders have
decided not to lead the church's outreach ministry from the top-down. Rather,
they teach and preach on whole-life discipleship in ways that encourage
congregants to faith-inspired action in the community. They then listen to,
offer support for, and celebrate the missional endeavors launched by these
commissioned congregants. Church of the Servant in Grand Rapids fits this
category best. Some shorter stories, such as those about Resurrection Catholic
Church and Crosswater Community Church in chapter three, do as well.

The third category I label "partnership-focused." These kinds of missional endeavors come in a few shapes. One is when a church collaborates
with a network of other congregations in a common initiative. Pleasant
Hope Baptist Church/Black Church Food Security Network in chapter
sixteen is an example. Another shape is when a church or group of churches

partners with a faith-based nonprofit organization in a common endeavor largely conceived of and directed by that nonprofit. The stories about churches engaged in the marriage-strengthening initiative in Jacksonville led by Live the Life Ministries in chapter three and those partnering with Caring for Kids in Kansas City in chapter five are examples. Church of the Redeemer in Los Angeles in chapter fifteen offers another dimension of the partnership approach. This congregation is wedded to a sister nonprofit, Redeemer Community Partnership (RCP). RCP enjoys volunteers and financial gifts from other congregations but is closely tied to the Church of the Redeemer through its leaders. Congregants view RCP as the church's "outreach arm."

A BEWILDERINGLY ATTRACTIVE CHRISTIANITY

Christianity weds doctrinal convictions with social responsibility. The best part of working on this book has been discovering the stories of Christ-followers of today and of yesteryear who have embodied this truth with courage and grace. When I was weighed down with discouragement over the state of the American church, these accounts injected me with fresh hope.

The history of the church is checkered, to be sure. Examples abound of churches *failing* to help their local communities flourish. And as David Kinnaman argues in *unChristian*, American Christianity today has "an image problem"—not just among nonbelievers but also among 40 percent of believers ages 16–29.[18] We tend to be known more for what we're against than what we're for. And yet *there is a different story line we can tell from our past and live in our present*. We have the opportunity today to recapture the best of our past missional action. We can reject both a chaplain-to-the-culture accommodationism and an ugly, dominate-the-culture approach that lusts for political power. We can instead embrace our identity as strangers in this world who—in ways that are bewilderingly attractive to nonbelievers—honor our King through holy lives of wise, sacrificial love. In today's disenchanted culture, it is vital that the church prioritize such an embodiment of demonstrated, gospel truth. *This* is the witness that stands a chance of being heard by neighbors trapped in our age's "immanent frame";[19] it is a key to our own spiritual revitalization, and an essential path to nurturing our communities' genuine flourishing.

1

ALL ABOUT FLOURISHING

It is the task of the Christian minister to keep before the public an
understanding of when human beings are well-off and when not.

DALLAS WILLARD,
"ECONOMIC WISDOM AND HUMAN FLOURISHING"

Those who belong to Jesus the Messiah are now to be "rulers and priests,"
serving our God. . . . Jesus is the one true "living stone"; and his followers
are the "living stones" by which the true Temple is to be built, bringing
the presence of God into the wider world, carrying forward the mission
of declaring God's powerful and rescuing acts, and beginning the work
of implementing the messianic rule of Jesus in all the world. This is what
it means to be a "royal priesthood."

N. T. WRIGHT, *AFTER YOU BELIEVE*

MY FRIEND G'JOE told me a while back of an encounter he had with a
young clerk at the Speakeasy Clothing store in San Diego. He was killing
time for a few minutes before a meeting, and she was friendly and chatty.
Given G'Joe's winsomeness and wit (not to mention his good looks), it's no
surprise she was ready to talk. The conversation ranged from work to race
to religion—the latter prompted by her inquiry of whether G'Joe was a Buddhist. He replied that he was a follower of Christ.

Thinking of C. S. Lewis, G'Joe responded, "I actually believe that my God
has given us desire and wants us to know him through enjoying and de-
lighting in his gifts." Taken aback, the young woman exclaimed, "I've never
heard anyone talk about Christianity like that!" To G'Joe's glee, she asked,
"Could I come to your church sometime?"

The clerk's reaction reveals an important reality. Like all of us, she desires. God designed us as desiring creatures. We are hungry for relationship, for beauty, for pleasure. Our desires are typically a mix of the noble, the mundane, and the sinful. Our desires are complicated.

But that doesn't mean we should avoid using words like *pleasure* or *beauty* or *delight* when talking about our Christian faith. Jesus was too much a lover of a human life fully lived to justify that. Moreover, the creation, though marred, shouts these words. Simply think of the most recent time you enjoyed a fantastic meal, a stunning sunset, or good sex with your spouse.

Desire isn't the problem. The problem is wrongly ordered desires and desires pointed toward the wrong objects. The problem isn't that we want to flourish. God wants that for us too. The problem is our definitions of human flourishing fall short of God's.

SHALOM: HUMANKIND'S DEEPEST DESIRE

We fallen humans need an expanded imagination to help us understand our deepest longings and desires. Augustine, that great theologian of desire, famously reminded us that our hearts are restless until they find their rest in God. All the food, natural beauty, and sex in the world won't truly satisfy us because we are made for more. We are made for God and others. Made in the image of the triune God who exists in blissful, loving friendship between Father, Son, and Holy Spirit, we, too, are relational beings.

Indeed, the Bible teaches that we are made for four foundational relationships: with God, ourselves, others, and the creation itself. The Hebrew word *shalom* captures the notion of peace in these four relationships. Shalom signifies spiritual, psychological, social, and physical wholeness. And shalom is God's normative intention for us. Shalom is what we find in his original creation, and shalom is what will characterize the new heaven and new earth in his consummated kingdom. Put another way, God designed us for flourishing. This is because, as Art Lindsley has said, flourishing is simply "shalom in every direction, personal and public."[1]

WHAT IS GENUINE FLOURISHING?

This book seeks to urge and equip congregations to seek the flourishing of their communities. The first task in doing that is defining what *true* flourishing is. Helping people see the difference between genuine flourishing and false flourishing is one of the most important things followers of Jesus can do to serve the kingdom of God and the common good.[2]

A short history lesson from Yale theologian Miroslav Volf will help us get started on this task. In a 2013 essay on human flourishing, Volf describes three dominant definitional paradigms.[3] To simplify, the first is essentially Augustinian. It argues that since God is the source of the True, the Good, and the Beautiful, human flourishing arises out of communion with God. We flourish when our lives are centered on the love of God and of neighbor. The second is an Enlightenment/humanist paradigm that reoriented the focus from God to humans. Here flourishing was defined without reference to a higher authority, yet there remained a sense of human community—the belief that our flourishing is tied to the flourishing of others. The third, now-dominant, late-twentieth-century paradigm argues that human flourishing is all about an individual's *experiential satisfaction*.

For our purposes here, it's important to highlight the progression in these definitions of human flourishing. Volf explains:

> Having lost earlier reference to "something higher which humans should reverence or love," it now lost reference to universal solidarity, as well. What remained was concern for the self and the desire for the experience of satisfaction. . . . [Other humans still matter but] they matter mainly in that they serve an individual's experience of satisfaction.[4]

Western Christians today swim within this cultural water. Thick in our imagination is a view of flourishing that assumes the highest goods are individual freedom, happiness, and self-expression.

SIX MARKS OF TRUE FLOURISHING

To dislodge this prevalent view, we need to examine several images of human flourishing provided by the bookends of Scripture's grand narrative: creation and new creation.[5]

The first mark of true flourishing is *communion with God*. In the ancient past, human beings enjoyed the profound goodness of God's fellowship as he walked in the Garden. Our great future hope in new creation is that we will "see the goodness of the LORD in the land of the living" (Ps 27:13) and live eternally with God, who promises to dwell among us (Rev 21:3).

The second mark of flourishing involves *beauty* and *creativity*. God is the source of all beauty and creativity. Made in his image, we experience deep joy when encountering beauty and in creatively crafting beauty.

The third feature of flourishing involves *learning* and *discovery*. God designed human beings with intelligence and curiosity. He made us thinking beings. He gave us brains to exercise and placed us in an intricate, complex, wonder-full, awe-inspiring cosmos. He commanded us to cultivate and develop his good creation. That command includes a call to pursue knowledge of the world—to observe, study, contemplate, investigate, experiment, and learn.

Wholeness is the fourth feature of biblical flourishing. In the Garden we enjoyed total physical and psychological health. In the garden-city of the new Jerusalem, we will again delight in bodies free from all disease, depression, and distress. This wholeness will extend to the creation itself. Many of the biblical passages that give us previews of the coming consummated kingdom speak of the healing of the natural world as God restores everything that was once barren. Isaiah 51:3 is representative: "He will make her deserts like Eden, her wastelands like the garden of the LORD." God will one day set his beloved creation free from all its groaning.

Fifth, in the consummated kingdom we will experience deep, rich, satisfying *unity in diversity* with other people. We will experience peace and harmony as richly diverse members of Christ's body from every "nation, tribe, people and language" join in common worship of King Jesus (Rev 7:9-20). This unity will be expressed in *peace*. In the new Jerusalem we will enjoy complete security and safety. All violence, injustice, and war will cease.

Finally, when we consider the flourishing of creation and the new creation, we observe *prosperity* or *abundance*. In Genesis, God creates a virtually endless array of plants and animals; the original creation "teemed" and "swarmed."[6] Prophetic glimpses of the new earth speak of "showers" of blessing (Ezek 34:26), reapers overtaking sowers (Amos 9:13), and mountains flowing with wine and milk (Joel 3:18). The new heaven and new earth will be a place of economic bounty.

FLOURISHING IN THE TIME OF NOW AND NOT YET

It is delightful to meditate on creation and new creation. But we live in the time in-between. Is flourishing possible *now*? Is flourishing something God wants for us *today*—or only in the sweet by-and-by? Our gracious God says yes to both queries. Indeed, much of his instruction in his Word is aimed at helping us to experience a measure of shalom even in this fallen world. This comes about in two ways.

The first involves God's faithfulness and presence. These enable us to be resilient even in tough times. Consider the image of flourishing provided in Psalm 1:3. There, the righteous person is depicted as a tree whose leaf never withers, which bears fruit in *every* season. In biblical terms flourishing and difficulties can exist simultaneously. In this fallen world we're not guaranteed a pain-free life. In a more delicate phrasing of the popular contemporary bumper sticker, "Drought Happens." But the righteous person can still thrive amid drought and trouble—and in "trouble or hardship or persecution or famine or nakedness or danger or sword" as the apostle Paul puts it in Romans 8:35—because God's love and presence sustain them.

The second emerges from living in conformity with God's wisdom. He instructs us in the path of life. Imagine you're driving on a twisting mountain road. You see a speed limit sign warning you of a dangerous curve ahead. The posted speed is 25 mph. If you try zooming around it at 65 mph, the serious consequence is not so much that you might get a speeding ticket (though this is possible as a punishment for breaking the law). The serious consequence is that by ignoring the laws of physics, your car will likely go careening off the road and you could end up dead.[7] God has given all kinds of instructions about life that are like the posted speed limit. Obeying these commands offers the prospect of greater health.[8]

THE KEY DIFFERENCE BETWEEN REAL AND FALSE FLOURISHING

God created a world of flourishing, and even now, in the age before the final kingdom, he desires that people experience a measure of shalom. God created us with legitimate desires (e.g., for sufficient nutrition, warm and safe shelter, meaningful work, and physical health) and delights in giving good gifts to his children. God knows that we want to play, to read, to connect, to belong, to matter, to feel, and to rest. In short, we want to live and to live fully. Jesus has no problem with that; in fact, he says he came to bring us abundant life.

The Bible teaches us to find abundant life in communion with God and conformity to his ways. Our secular society believes we can achieve the good life by satisfying all our natural desires devoid of any connection to or dependence on supernatural intervention.[9] Flourishing is defined in a way that shuts out the satisfaction of our deepest, truest desires: for God, for his kingdom, and for his righteousness.

Further, the secularist sees flourishing as achievable through human actions alone in a society that has cast off the strictures of orthodox religion, with its (allegedly) outdated view of a God who has a claim to our obedience. In our hubris we imagine that we can build a society that will fulfill all our human desires, principally by embracing a radical enthronement of the self. We think we can create a community free of fear and free of want, a welfare society that meets at least minimal standards of well-being—*but without reference to God*.[10] Our flawed definition of human nature (extracting as it does our soul) then leads to a fundamental misconception of genuine pleasure and happiness. We think such treasures are achievable apart from a relationship with our Maker and Sustainer. We want, in Mark Sayers's memorable phrase, "the kingdom without the King." Our post-Christian culture, Sayers explains, "intuitively yearns for the justice and shalom of the kingdom, whilst defending the reign of the individual will."[11]

WHO WE ARE: ROYAL PRIESTS CALLED TO FLOURISH OTHERS

You and I were made to flourish—in two senses. We've been looking at the first. We were created for a certain state of being. God's normative desire is for us to live as whole people in a world of shalom. We will not fully experience this genuine, holistic flourishing on our still-broken planet. But God desires that in an intimate, obedient relationship with him, we will discover even now some foretastes of the full, future thriving we'll enjoy in the new Jerusalem.

The second sense in which we are made to flourish is that we are made for a purpose, for a vocation. Though this isn't an exact, grammatically correct way to put it, a huge part of that purpose is *to flourish* others. Jesus called this loving our neighbors. True biblical flourishing involves the good of others as well as our own good. Flourishing is meant to be a shared experience. We are blessed *to be* a blessing (Gen 12:2). "You will be enriched in every way," said the apostle Paul, "*so that* you can be generous on every occasion, and through us your generosity will result in thanksgiving to God" (2 Cor 9:11, emphasis added).

This is opposed to how flourishing is defined in the kingdom of darkness. In a fallen world unbridled human desires and the demand that they all be fulfilled creates brutal power struggles as people compete for resources.[12] In this context so-called flourishing bends inward: it's about me getting my desires satisfied— and the heck with you. This is the exact opposite of biblical flourishing.

ROYAL PRIESTS FLOURISH OTHERS

Throughout the Scriptures this vocation of flourishing others is described as the work of the royal priesthood. If the first task in pursuing the shalom of our communities is understanding what true flourishing is, the second is understanding biblical teaching on who we are as royal priests. Unfortunately, this is not a very familiar concept to many Christ-followers, despite its prominence in Scripture.

Our identity as royal priests: From Genesis to Revelation. First, I must emphasize that royal priests are what human beings were originally *meant to be*. That's how deep this identity runs. When God created Adam and Eve, he created royal priests.

In Genesis, God commissions the first humans with a mandate to rule and fill the earth (Gen 1:28) and to tend and develop the creation (Gen 2:15). God gives humankind this commission in a particular setting, namely, in the Garden of Eden. This matters greatly for our discussion on the royal priesthood. This is because the Garden was a kind of temple. A temple is a place where humans and the divine meet.[13] The setting where God gives the cultural mandate must shape our understanding of that mandate. As Kelly Kapic and Brian Fikkert explain in *Becoming Whole,*

> The garden of Eden was far more than just a place where Adam and Eve watered plants and cared for animals. *It was a temple-garden in which the first humans served as priests and kings.* As priests, they were to protect the "temple" from any corruption and lead others into worship of the one true God. As kings, they were to promote the welfare of others and the rest of creation by ruling as God's vice-regents, his assistant rulers. As priest-kings, then, humans were to lovingly serve God, others, and the rest of creation.[14]

From the very beginning of our story we were created to be royal priests. Not surprisingly, in the book of Revelation, which reveals the end of our story, we find the same thing. Revelation tells us that human beings are re-created in Jesus to (again) be priest-kings—for all eternity. As N. T. Wright describes in *The Day the Revolution Began*, four places in Revelation speak of this vocation.[15]

Two of those texts (Rev 1:5-6; 5:9-10) teach us something astounding and rarely heard in our churches today: *Jesus died to (re)make us as a kingdom of priests.* Meditate for a moment on Revelation 5:9-10:

> You were slain,
>> and with your blood you purchased for God
>> persons from every tribe and language and people and nation.
> You have made them to be a kingdom and priests to serve our God,
>> and they will reign on the earth.

Being the new humanity, living as the royal priesthood of God, is the church's telos. It is the point of life for every Christ-follower, its central objective. "This is the goal of human existence," Wright sums up. "Forget 'happiness': you are called to a *throne*."[16]

I'd encourage you to stop here and linger on this profound (and perhaps somewhat unfamiliar) idea. If you are a pastor, think for a moment about how a liturgy like this might influence your flock.

LEADER	Who has God created us to be?
CONGREGATION	*The royal priesthood of God.*
LEADER	What is God's given purpose for our lives?
CONGREGATION	*To live as his royal priests, being the presence of God to and for the world. We bring the praises of creation before the Creator and we reflect God's wisdom and justice into this world.*[17]
LEADER	What is our telos as the people of God?
CONGREGATION	*To reign on earth with King Jesus in the consummated kingdom.*

The context in Revelation where these truths about the human vocation are affirmed echoes the context where they were proclaimed in Genesis. As we saw, there the setting was the garden temple. In Revelation the setting is the new Jerusalem, the garden-city wherein God dwells with redeemed humanity.[18]

So, the narratives at the Bible's bookends—creation and consummation—affirm our foundational calling to be a royal priesthood. What about the in-between parts? As we will see, the theme of the royal priesthood remains prominent.

The royal-priestly vocation. At the heart of the sin of the first humans, Wright contends, was *a failure of vocation.* We were made for a purpose. Humans were created to image God in the world, offering up our worship to him alone, and to reflect his character in the world. We were made, in short, for worship and mission. *We* flourish when we inhabit this vocation (since it connects us in an intimate relationship with our heavenly Father and engages us in the life we were designed for), and *others* flourish when we discharge it in God's strength and according to God's ways. We were made to be with God and to work in the world as his royal priests, bearing his image.

Our human forebears turned away from this vocation. They didn't want merely to *reflect* God in the world; they wanted to *be* God. Their fundamental sin was idolatry, turning away from the true worship of God. This quickly expressed itself in humankind's turn to self-preoccupation instead of the royal-priestly job of flourishing others.

The biblical story does not run immediately from this vocational failure in Genesis 3 to Jesus' life, death, and resurrection in the New Testament. The story of God's response to the fall is much longer and more layered. There is a very long interlude between the fall chapter and the redemption chapter, namely, the rest of the Old Testament. It tells us about God electing a certain group within the human race, the Israelites, to take back the human vocation. The Old Testament matters because it tells the story of how God chose and called Israel to be the people through whom he would redeem the world. As Wright says pithily, "The call of Abraham is the answer to the sin of Adam."[19] We won't fully understand Jesus' work—or our call as his disciples—if we don't pay attention to Israel's story.

The fall of humankind began in Genesis 3 but continued circling in a downward spiral. In Genesis 11 the same kind of human arrogance found at the base of that infamous tree in the Garden of Eden—that of wanting to be like God—is repeated at Babel. There, all the peoples of the earth decide to build a tower that will reach the heavens so that they could "make a name" for themselves (Gen 11:1-4). The right-side-up vocation, the original royal priesthood vocation in the Garden, involved humans making *God's* name great. At Babel humans turned this calling upside down, seeking instead to make their *own* name great.

God's response to this is one of both judgment and mercy. The judgment involves confusing the people's language and scattering them throughout the earth (Gen 11:8-9). The mercy is that following this, God calls a single human family back to the image-bearing, earth-blessing, royal-priesthood vocation (Gen 12:1-3). Through Abraham, God now promises to undo the mess humankind has made. In this gracious covenant, God will bless the world through Abraham as his family takes up the original call to worship and to work, to be in loving, obedient relationship with God, and to live as his image-bearers bringing flourishing to others.

Tragically, as we know all too well, neither Abraham nor his descendants end up doing a very good job.

Indeed, the story gets so far off course that Israel ends up enslaved by pagan Egypt. Humankind's exile from the Garden is echoed in Israel's exile in the land of bricks, lashes, and tears. Exile is the consequence of vocational failure. When Israel chooses to love other gods instead of YHWH, when Israel refuses to live as a blessing bringer, "a light to the Gentiles," this brings slavery and death.

Exodus: Presence and recommissioning. And yet faithful YHWH remembers his covenant and acts mightily to rescue the people chosen to be his conduit of blessing. In great mercy God unleashes judgment on the gods of Egypt and brings his people out in the exodus. It is a marvelous story of rescue and provision. It is also—vitally for our review of the royal-priesthood idea—a story of recommissioning.

In Exodus 19:4-6, God instructs Moses to restate the human vocation given at creation and to apply it specifically to his chosen people Israel, whom he has just rescued from oppression:

> "You yourselves have seen what I did to Egypt, and how I carried you on eagles' wings and brought you to myself. Now if you obey me fully and keep my covenant, then out of all nations you will be my treasured possession. Although the whole earth is mine, you will be for me a *kingdom of priests* and a holy nation." These are the words you are to speak to the Israelites.

God here gracefully chooses (or elects) Israel for a purpose. This recommissioning is—again—given in a temple setting, that is, in a place where God is present with his people, where heaven and earth meet. The recommission is given in the wilderness, where God himself has traveled with the rescued Israelites by day as a pillar of cloud and by night as a pillar of fire.

Tragically, despite God's continually and graciously giving his presence to his people, they continually turn away from him to idols and away from the vocation God gave them. Even a cursory read through the Old Testament offers a picture of this repeated reality. Unlike royal priests who serve God alone and spread flourishing to their neighbors, Israel persists in idolatry and oppression. The prophets repeatedly exhort Israel to turn from such grave sin, but the people refuse to heed their words. The result is both the exile of the Jews into Babylon and the shekinah glory's departure from the temple.[20]

The Israel chapter and the redemption chapter. This story of Israel is the backdrop to the redemption chapter of the Bible's big story. We miss critical insights about Jesus' mission and our mission in that chapter when its Jesus story is delinked from the Israel story.

Jesus not only came to be God in the world in his divinity. *He also came, in his humanity, to be the perfect fulfillment of a royal priest.* He faithfully takes up the vocation that we sinful, selfish, idolatrous humans abandoned. Through Jesus flows the Abrahamic blessing that Israel failed to bring to the world. The blessing of God runs into and out from Jesus: the Spirit descends on him like a dove, and "power comes out" from Jesus even to those who merely touch his garments (Mk 5:24-35).

Through the life and death of Jesus, the perfect royal priest, full redemption comes. Through Jesus, sin—not just the breaking of individual moral codes but the whole deviation of humankind from worshiping the Creator to worshiping idols—is conquered. In Jesus, sin—humankind's failure to be the image-bearing, royal priests we were created to be—is conquered. In Jesus, sin—Israel's failure to be the chosen royal priests through whom God would remake the world—is conquered. In Jesus, our sin is forgiven, and as a result the greatest, fullest return from exile is made possible. Indeed, in Jesus, rescue from the ultimate exile—our captivity in the kingdom of darkness—comes.

THE CHURCH AS A THIRD ISRAEL

This brings us to the next big point about royal priests: that Jesus commissions his followers, the church, to live into this identity.

Missionary-theologian Lesslie Newbigin speaks of "three Israels" who are elected and commissioned by God "to be a sign and instrument of God's redemptive purpose for all humanity."[21] First, God chooses Abraham and the nation that comes from him to be his royal priests in the world, living in true, single-minded devotion to God and being a blessing to the nations. This Israel failed.

Second, God chooses Jesus to act as a kind of second Israel, "faithfully doing what Israel did not do—disclosing and effecting God's renewal for the whole world."[22] Jesus reenacts the Israel story in a variety of ways. He spends forty days for Israel's forty years in the wilderness. He calls twelve disciples, reminiscent of the twelve tribes. Like Moses on the mountain with the Ten Commandments, he gives his new commandments in his Sermon on the Mount. He calls and commissions the Twelve to both be with him and to join him in the work of bringing blessing—shalom—to the peoples (Mk 3:14).

King Jesus' unique redemptive work is all-sufficient: his death atones for the sin of the whole world and his resurrection accomplishes the defeat of all the demonic forces of sin and anti-shalom, everything that sets itself up in opposition to God's kingly reign. Yet the story of the King's work in our world is not finished, for the kingdom inaugurated by Jesus is not yet completely revealed or consummated. *Jesus still has work for his followers to do.* Those followers, the "third Israel"—the church—are commissioned to live as royal priests, spreading the good news of the kingdom throughout the nations.

For the church to understand fully our commission as a third Israel, we must see its link back to the original charge given to the first Israel (Ex 19:6). This is precisely what the apostle Peter does in 1 Peter 2:9, where he writes: "You are a chosen people, *a royal priesthood*, a holy nation, God's special possession, that you may declare the praises of him who called you out of darkness into his wonderful light." Peter's reference back to the Exodus text is vital to our Christian identity and our Christian mission. Consider the similarities between these two Scriptures. The Exodus text speaks of God's choosing a people to be his treasured possession and commissioning them to be a kingdom of priests. The 1 Peter text repeats this idea of a chosen people, a treasured possession, and their commissioning as a royal priesthood to declare God's praises.

This "declaring" is meant to happen through both words and deeds, since Peter continues in verse 12: "Live such good lives among the pagans that, though they accuse you of doing wrong, they may see your good deeds and glorify God on the day he visits us." Peter, in short, understands that Jesus' commission to his disciples is that they be a royal priesthood. The vocation is now for Gentile as well as Jewish followers of Jesus.

To sum up, living as the royal priesthood is central to the church's identity and mission.

Following Wright, Newbigin, and other lesser-known theologians, I believe that *the chief end of man (and woman!) is to be God's royal priesthood.* My choice of words here is deliberate. Having been in Reformed congregations for the past thirty-five years, I've heard the Westminster Confession aplenty. We are indeed made to "glorify God and enjoy him forever," but that may not be the fullest and best way of expressing the Bible's teaching on the human vocation.[23] It certainly isn't when it's interpreted to mean some kind of 24/7 worship service or to suggest that *only* the "being" part of our human purpose (to be with God) and not the "doing" part of our purpose (fulfilling the role God scripted for us as royal priests) is what truly matters. And given the ascendency of what Fikkert and Kapic call "Evangelical Gnosticism" in America, these are too often the very ways this statement is interpreted.

What are we made for? Flourishing. How has God designed that to happen? By giving us the vocation of the royal priesthood. When we live in Christ as the priest-kings we were always meant to be, we experience flourishing ourselves and we contribute to the flourishing of others.

HOW DO WE DO THE WORK OF ROYAL PRIESTS?

Having explored what genuine flourishing is, and having reviewed our identity and mission as royal priests, we can now ask, How do we do the practical work of flourishing our communities? What does that look like in action?

The rest of this book takes up this question. I organize my discussion using Thriving Cities Group's "Human Ecology Framework." As noted in the introduction, this framework asserts that community flourishing occurs when there is strength and health in six arenas of civilizational life: the Good, the True, the Beautiful, the Just and Well-Ordered, the Prosperous, and the Sustainable (see fig. 1.1). Thriving Cities Group calls these "community endowments" to highlight the fact that these arenas are dynamic. Their health can fluctuate up or down. As royal priests committed to neighbor love, one of our key tasks in our communities involves assessing the relative health of these endowments and making strategic investments in selected ones in ways that contribute to their strength.

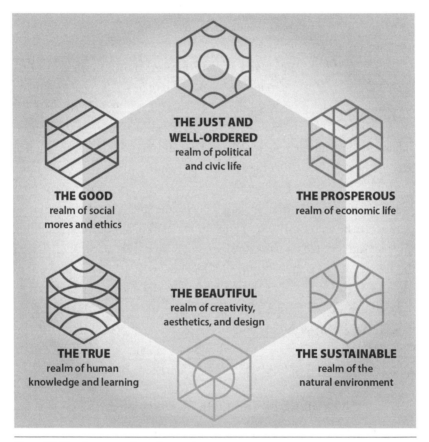

THE JUST AND WELL-ORDERED
realm of political and civic life

THE GOOD
realm of social mores and ethics

THE PROSPEROUS
realm of economic life

THE BEAUTIFUL
realm of creativity, aesthetics, and design

THE TRUE
realm of human knowledge and learning

THE SUSTAINABLE
realm of the natural environment

Figure 1.1. The six community endowments

I've chosen the Human Ecology Framework over other definitional models of community flourishing for three reasons.[24] One is that it covers well the many aspects of our common life, such as family, religion, education, government and civic life, commerce, finance, the natural and built environment, arts and media, the justice system, and public health and safety, among others. Another is its recognition that the six endowments are highly interrelated and interdependent. Third, and most important, it corresponds well with the marks of genuine biblical flourishing I highlighted in the introduction (see fig. 1.2).

Marks of Genuine Flourishing	The Six Community Endowments
Communion with God	The Good
Beauty and Creativity	The Beautiful
Learning and Discovery	The True
Peace, Justice, and Unity in Diversity	The Just and Well-Ordered
Wholeness and Health	The Sustainable
Prosperity and Abundance	The Prosperous

Figure 1.2. Comparing biblical flourishing and the six community endowments

With its attentiveness to the dynamism of human society and its comprehensive and holistic approach, the Human Ecology Framework is an excellent resource for Christ-followers eager to promote the shalom of their cities. At the same time, to this sociological approach we need to add theological reference points. Theologian Albert Wolters's notion of *structure* and *direction* can help.

STRUCTURE AND DIRECTION

In *Creation Regained*, Wolters explains that God is the maker and designer of not only the physical cosmos but also of families, social institutions, beauty, and "an almost unimaginable variety" of objects and relationships.[25] And God rules over his creation via both "laws of nature and norms."[26]

The idea that there are given norms for human behavior is highly suspect in our postmodern culture. But it is a foundational part of a biblical worldview. Through general and special revelation, Wolters argues, human beings can "discern the creational normativity" of created things.[27] He labels this created normativity *structure*. "Structure," he says, "denotes the 'essence' of a creaturely thing, the kind of creation it is by virtue of God's creational law."[28]

All created things have been tainted by the fall, and all are being renewed through the work of Christ—a work yet to be fully completed in the consummation of the kingdom of God. Wolters uses the term *direction* to denote these two opposing movements. As depicted in figure 1.3, direction "refers to a sinful deviation from that structural ordinance" or toward "renewed conformity to it in Christ."[29] Created things, in other words, are either aligning with their original intention (structure) or moving away from that intention.

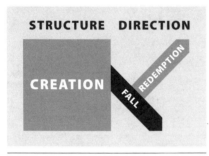

Figure 1.3. Wolters's "structure and direction"

However, in the places and ways that created things are pulled and distorted by sin, they can be brought back in the proper direction by the quickening power of the gospel. Referencing Jesus' teaching in Matthew 13:33 about yeast in dough, Wolters says that "the gospel is a leavening influence in human life wherever it is lived, an influence that slowly but steadily brings change from within."[30]

As we seek to promote the flourishing of our communities, our task involves

- seeking to understand the "structure," that is, the creational intent of things (e.g., marriages, business transactions, artwork, communications systems, agricultural practices, architecture, and everything else from A to Z)

- recognizing and resisting where those things have been deformed by sin

- praying for and working for their re-formation in Christ

Although it is sobering to observe the many deformations in every sphere of social life, Christians have hope because of the power of the gospel. As Michael Goheen writes in the postscript to *Creation Regained*, "the gospel is a redirectional power . . . it is the renewing power of God unto salvation. The gospel is the instrument of God's Spirit to restore all of creation."[31]

The chapters ahead seek to illumine a biblical vision for the True, the Good, the Beautiful, the Just and Well-Ordered, the Prosperous, and the Sustainable. They also offer descriptions of how the church today, and in years past, has pursued various strategies to cultivate flourishing in each of these realms. The stories told are by no means comprehensive. They showcase one or two strategies for how congregations can contribute to the health of that particular endowment—but there are many other possible strategies. I hope that these stories will inspire congregational leaders to imitate their strategies or try additional ones.

2

THE GOOD

FLOURISHING IN THE REALM
OF SOCIAL MORES AND ETHICS

In 2018 Timothy Keller was invited to London by members of Parliament to address their National Prayer Breakfast. He was asked to speak on the topic "What Can Christianity Offer Our Society in the Twenty-First Century?" His answer—drawing from Christ's teaching that his followers are to be the salt of the earth—was that Christ-followers could be "salty" in ways that bring out the best in society while also preserving it from decay.

"Christianity," Keller asserted, "has been massively 'salt' in our society and it still is operating today."[1] This is because of how Western society has been built on Christianity's "other-regarding ethic" rather than the shame-and-honor culture, which prizes strength over love. This foundational shaping of the West's "moral sense" has had tremendous ripple effects for good. Quoting Jürgen Habermas, Keller reminded the Brits that "the ideals of freedom, of conscience, human rights and democracy [are] the direct legacy of the Judaic ethic of justice and the Christian ethic of love."[2]

It is impossible to overstate the importance of the other-regarding ethic Keller notes. This ideal has been the foundation from which Christians individually and corporately have shaped the social mores and ethics of Western culture. Christianity has put certain ideas into the water we swim in. Innumerable good actions and decisions have been carried out by innumerable people in history shaped by those ideas. Gerhard Lenski, the reputed sociologist of religion from Yale University, captured this notion when he argued that we should not measure the influence of religious organizations on society only based on their particular successes in bringing about institutional reforms. Even more important than the achievements of such campaigns, Lenski explains, are the "daily actions of thousands (or millions) of group members whose personalities have been influenced by their lifelong exposure" to the religious impulses.[3]

THE GOOD AND HUMAN FLOURISHING

In this chapter we will consider the contributions the church has made in the realm of social mores and ethics, which the Thriving Cities Group calls the community endowment of the Good. Marriages, families, religious organizations, nonprofit social service organizations, philanthropic foundations, and schools are important institutions within the realm of the Good.[4] These are the institutions in which moral education, character formation, training in good citizenship, and service of others occur. These are the places in which we learn and practice compassion, empathy, integrity, and responsibility. These institutions "facilitate the formation of underlying social bonds and civic commitments" required in healthy communities.[5]

The endowment of the Good "plays a defining role in determining the vibrancy of community life," say the scholars at Thriving Cities.[6] This realm includes nonprofit organizations, congregations, and civic organizations, and it concerns the level of social trust and care in a community. The Good "highlights the important role these institutions and social attitudes play in strengthening community ties."[7] Joshua Yates, director of the Thriving Cities project, further emphasizes the irreplaceable nature of this endowment for a flourishing community:

> A concern with thriving reminds us of the benefits and obligations that come with belonging to a commonwealth. From cradle to grave we rely on countless others—people and institutions—in order to flourish. . . . *[T]hriving is a holistic endeavor that is impossible outside relationships of reciprocity, interdependence, shared contexts of opportunity, and impossible without strong sources of moral concern.*[8]

Through the institutions and practices in the realm of the Good, community members experience and express the reciprocity and interdependence Yates speaks of. The Good—the realm of social ethics—is the arena in which we negotiate the definition of our aspirations and the boundaries of acceptable conduct.

CREATIONAL NORMS AND OLD TESTAMENT RE-FORMATIONS

Following Albert Wolters's framework, we can ask, What is God's creational norm for the realm of social ethics? What deformations have arisen within this realm? To start to answer we begin in the Genesis creation account. It provides us with a handful of foundational insights. But because in the world before sin God didn't need to articulate detailed instructions for how people were to live together, we will also need to look beyond the creation chapter of the Bible's big story.

Insights from the creation chapter. One insight from the doctrine of creation is that human beings are designed as social beings. God himself is a relational being existing eternally in fellowship within the Trinity. Made in his image, we, too, are social creatures. We are designed for relationships with God, others, and nonhuman creation. The relationship with God is primary; we were created *for* him (Rom 11:36; 1 Cor 8:6). Given this design it's plausible to think that God's will for how people should treat each other is by an ethic of mutual, generous love since that is what characterizes God's own relationships within the Trinity. Just as God the Father, Son, and Holy Spirit are bound together in love, so human beings should understand themselves as connected in a deep sense. We are none of us islands unto ourselves. We have claims on each other and responsibilities toward one another. The great potential deformation here emerges from a philosophy and practice of radical individualism that denies these obligations.

A second insight is that all human beings have great dignity because each is made in God's image. From this we can presume that honoring the basic human dignity of each person is foundational to any conception of Christian social ethics. The obvious deformation here is the claim that certain groups lack this inherent dignity.[9]

A third insight is that God gives the commission of the cultural mandate to both men and women. God invites us to participate with him in his work in the world. This work is designed by God for men and women to undertake together cooperatively. God's blessing and God's invitation are given to both Adam and Eve: "God blessed them and said to them, 'Be fruitful and increase in number; fill the earth and subdue it. Rule over the fish in the sea and the birds in the sky and over every living creature that moves on the ground" (Gen 1:28).

From this we can posit that God desires men and women to respect one another's equal share in the creation mandate and to seek to find ways to cooperate in fulfilling their stewardship roles. The deformation here is the claim that only one gender has the dignity of God's commissioning.

In addition to these general norms about mutual love and cooperation, the other foundational key to how God wants humans to live together relates to his sovereignty. *We are designed by God to live under his benevolent, all-wise rule.* Put another way, we are designed to live according to what our all-knowing and all-wise God defines as the Good, not what we limited human beings define it as. God designed the first humans to trust that he knows what is best for us, to trust that his desire for us is life, not death. Adam and Eve were supposed to demonstrate this trust by submitting to God's command not to eat from the tree of the knowledge of good and evil. God in his goodness even gave them the reason for why he didn't want them to do this (as opposed to just saying that phrase that all children hate: "Because I said so"). He told them that eating from this tree would bring them death. The obvious and deadly deformation here is the contention that human beings rather than God are on the throne. This is the very root of sin.

Old Testament social ethics. Not surprisingly, after the fall God's instructions for how people ought to live in human society get a lot more specific. In his great wisdom God anticipates the many possible varieties of human sinfulness and brokenness. In his great goodness he gives instructions to his people Israel to show them how to live in ways aligned with life and flourishing—for their own good and as a witness and blessing to the rest of humanity.

The Old Testament law and prophets tell us volumes about God's will for how he wanted the Israelites to live together in community. Not everything God commanded of them then is normative for us now (e.g., the ceremonial law). Yet, since "all Scripture is God-breathed and is useful for teaching, rebuking, correcting and training in righteousness" (2 Tim 3:16), plumbing the Old Testament for insights on social ethics is a fruitful labor.

A big-picture survey of the Old Testament shows God's passion for *life*. Having given human beings the gift of life, God desires that we experience— to the fullest extent possible—that which gives us genuine life. This is why the psalmists and the poets of Scripture proclaim that God's words *are* life. We live not by bread alone but by every word from God's mouth. Walking in alignment with God's ways is what brings true life. The law's instructions on how the Israelites were to live together should not be seen so much as a long list of moral dos and don'ts. Rather, it is a body of teaching directing people in the path conducive to life and flourishing.

Old Testament social ethics are like a multilayered symphony of multiple movements. I can mention only a few of the prominent melodies. One is *justice*, which we will consider in more detail in chapter eight. For now, suffice to say that justice in the Old Testament involved both fairness (giving each person their due) and openhandedness (recognizing the rightful claims that others have upon us). These are rooted in the creational norms of *imago Dei* and the beloved community.

A second melody is of *grace*. The Old Testament covenant ("I will be your God and you shall be my people") emphasizes the connection between how God dealt with the Israelites and how they should deal with one another and with outsiders. On many occasions God tells the Israelites to remember his dealings with them in grace; this is the reason why he wants them to extend grace to others.

For example, in Deuteronomy 5:15, the Israelites are told to provide sabbath rest for their slaves (indentured servants) because they themselves were once slaves in Egypt, and God rescued them. In Deuteronomy 26:1-11 God commands that when the Israelites bring their offerings—some of which will be used to provide for the poor—they must recite their own history. By recalling how they were once poor and oppressed, they will be able to offer charity rightly, with a humble attitude that does not disdain the poor.

These texts reveal that not only *right actions* are important to God but also a *right heart*—a heart of mercy that humbly understands it has been the recipient of mercy. This principle remains binding on Christ-followers today, for we also are told to love because he first loved us (1 Jn 4:19).

A third major melody in the symphony concerns *holiness*. God called the Israelites to be holy because he is holy (Lev 19:2). What does this holiness consist of? One phrase used to describe it is "clean hands and a pure heart" (Ps 24:4). Holy people gratefully delight in God's law (Ps 1:2). They trust that God's words are life. They understand that life is best lived within the creational norm of obedience to God's ways. Holy people revere the Lord.

Multiple texts in the Old Testament provide specific examples of holy living. Holiness is about moral purity in terms of honesty and the absence of any kind of corruption or bentness. Holy people hate all that is false (Prov 13:5). They have a blameless walk and speak the truth from their hearts. They keep themselves sexually pure (Ezek 18:6). They do not swear deceitfully (Ps 24:4). They maintain just weights and balances; they do not defraud (see Lev 19:36). In brief, holiness is about the kind of virtuous personal character that does right by one's neighbor out of reverence for God. Here again these ethical standards are relevant to us today, even as we have to apply them under different social and economic circumstances than those that marked ancient Israel.

Holiness is also about being set apart for God. The Israelites were called to be ethically distinct from the people around them. This was both for their own and their neighbors' good. *There is a missional quality to ethical living*: it is both a sign of God's presence and a foretaste of his coming kingdom of righteousness. Old Testament scholar Christopher Wright emphasizes that ethical distinctiveness was key to the Israelites' vocation of being a blessing to the nations.

> The clearest expression of this combined ethical and missional role of Israel is Genesis 18:19, where God, speaking about Abraham, says, "I have chosen him *so that* he will direct his household and his children after him to keep the way of the LORD by doing righteousness and justice so that the LORD may bring about for Abraham what he has promised him."[10]

Israel was to live as a distinctive community as a way of glorifying God *and* pointing the nations around them to God and God's goodness. "In the midst of a world characterized by Sodom whose evil is causing an outcry," says Wright, "God wants a community characterized by his own values and priorities. . . . [S]uch ethical distinctiveness is put forward here by God himself as the very reason for the election of Abraham. . . . Election means election to an ethical agenda in the midst of a corrupt world of Sodoms."[11]

Put another way, living in alignment with God's intended design for social ethics (Wolters's "structure" of the Good) was vital to Israel's calling—for its own sake and the sake of its role in God's mission. This principle remains true today for the church.

NEW TESTAMENT: KEY THEMES OF KINGDOM ETHICS

The New Testament is also voluminous in its teaching regarding social ethics. I cannot cover much beyond the tip of the iceberg. It seems sensible to look briefly at Jesus' teaching on the ethics of the kingdom of God (mainly in the Sermon on the Mount) and at his actions as depicted in the Gospels. This reliance on the Gospels seems permissible in a short survey since echoes of Jesus' teaching are heard throughout the rest of the New Testament and the deeds commended in the Epistles are those modeled by Jesus.[12] In the following paragraphs I highlight five key themes of Jesus' teaching that inform social ethics.

Agape love. First and most important is the theme of love. This is at the center of Jesus' teaching and of all New Testament teaching. All the Law and the Prophets, Jesus says in Matthew 22:36-37, can be summed up in the Great Commandment to love (Greek *agapaō*) God and neighbor. Agape love is the highest form of love. It is the kind of love God has shown to humans. John Piper describes it as "characterized by sacrifice in the pursuit of another person's good."[13] Here we have the root of Christianity's other-regarding ethic noted by Keller in his speech in London.

Agape love is referenced over two hundred times in the New Testament, including in Matthew 5. This is a generous, self-giving love. It includes, but goes beyond, justice (Hebrew *mishpat*, giving someone their due). Jesus' way of love expounded in the Gospels includes love even for one's enemies.

With this teaching we find that Christian social ethics far surpasses even the most demanding forms of virtue ethics and duty-based ethics. Living according to agape love requires both right internal motivation (pure, other-centered love) and righteous external actions of great sacrifice. Such a life is impossible by human effort alone. This kingdom-of-God living requires nothing less than supernatural power. It requires a new heart; it requires new creation wrought by the Spirit. It is the life of the new humanity Christ came to create. It requires formation by the Spirit. New City Commons has defined this spiritual formation as "the ordering of the whole person toward love through daily habits by the power of the Spirit."[14] Were Christ-followers to actually live like this, our ethical distinctiveness would be shocking, jaw-dropping to those around us. We would indeed "shine among [a crooked generation] like stars in the sky" (Phil 2:15).

The call to agape love undergirds Jesus' teachings concerning how Christ-followers should negotiate money, sex, power, and tribe—four huge realities of life in society. With each the way of the kingdom contrasts starkly with the way of the world.

Money: Sacrificial stewardship. The way of Jesus' kingdom requires recognizing that we are *not* the ultimate owners of what we possess. This contrasts with both secular teaching on the rights of private property and on much *functional* teaching in the contemporary church, wherein we can largely do what we want with the 90 percent of our money left over after tithing. Jesus' view of money truly involves turning around (repenting) and walking in the opposite direction of the worldly-wise. In this new direction the Christ-follower then eschews greed (Mt 6:24; Lk 12:15), practices sacrificial generosity toward those in need (Lk 12:13-21; 16:1-13; 16:19-31), and invests enthusiastically in kingdom priorities (Lk 19:11-27). It all sounds radical to our Western ears. And yet the rest of the New Testament writers take it as normative (and echo Jesus' teachings). Some New Testament Christians followed this radical way: sharing their goods (Acts 2) and giving in deeply sacrificial ways to others (2 Cor 8). This is agape applied to money.

Sex: Honoring marriage and family. In the kingdom we are not our own. We're bought with the precious price of Jesus' blood. Our bodies are not our own but temples of the Holy Spirit (1 Cor 6:19). In contrast to the ancient world's (and our world's) sexual promiscuity, Jesus warned of the dangers of lust and called for self-control. He also held up the institution of marriage. Referencing Mark 10 and Matthew 19, Bible scholars Van Pelt, Blomberg, and Schreiner write, "the overall impetus from Jesus is to noticeably tighten up what, in His day, were very loose standards with respect to divorce (much like is true in many parts of the Western world today)."[15] For Jesus the call in marriage is to agape love. The apostle Paul's writings later reinforce this, teaching that the love between the married couple is to imitate Christ's own self-sacrificing agape love. Jesus' family values also emphasize unselfishly honoring one's parents (as the Pharisees were failing to do; see Mk 7:9-13) and cherishing children (see Mt 18:1-7; 19:13-15).

Power: Servant leadership. Jesus recognized the power dynamics of his day within both Jewish and Roman cultures. In the face of this he modeled a radically different way of exercising power. While the Romans ruled by force, Jesus preached peace and turned the other cheek. While Herod showed his power by throwing a sumptuous banquet for the rich in his lavish palace, entertaining them with John the Baptist's head on a platter, Jesus demonstrated his power by providing a miraculous supper in the wilderness for more than five thousand poor people. Jesus taught his disciples not to lord authority over others but rather to lead with a sacrificial spirit that puts others' needs ahead of their own (see Mt 20:25-26; Mk 10:35-45; Jn 13). The apostle Peter repeats the theme of servant leadership in his first epistle (1 Pet 4:10; 5:3) and Paul beautifully discourses on it in Philippians 2.

This is the kingdom's countercultural way of power. In Jesus' way we recognize power as a gift to be used in the service of love. As Andy Crouch writes,

> Power is not given to benefit those who hold it. It is given for the flourishing of individuals, peoples, and the cosmos itself. Power's right use is especially important for the flourishing of the vulnerable. . . . Power is not the opposite of servanthood. Rather, servanthood, ensuring the flourishing of others, is the very purpose of power.[16]

Tribe: Including the excluded. Christ-followers are charged to love those beyond their own tribe. We see this theme exemplified in at least four ways in Jesus' ministry. First, Jesus demonstrated compassion toward the outcast, the marginalized, and the *other* (non-Jews). He moved toward lepers, demoniacs, and prostitutes—and Samaritans and Gentiles. Though his ministry was primarily to the house of Israel, Jesus did not build a wall shutting out those from a different tribe. He affirmed the humanity of all. Second, Jesus included women—who were oppressed in Jewish, Roman, and Greek culture—among his followers and elevated their status by entrusting them as the first witnesses to his resurrection. Third, Jesus invited Matthew, a despised tax collector, to be a member of his band of twelve disciples. Fourth, Jesus included the poor within his own self-concept. Jesus profoundly identified with the poor. He taught that his followers would be judged by how they treated him in his mysterious disguise of sick, hungry, thirsty, naked, and imprisoned people (Mt 25:31-46). All of this is agape in action applied against the narrowness of tribal identity. It is a love that risks reputation and the approval of one's own group by welcoming the stranger to a place at the table.

THE CHURCH'S HISTORICAL CONTRIBUTIONS TO THE REALM OF SOCIAL ETHICS

The church is not and has not ever been perfect. Indeed, it has been far from that on far too many occasions. We could spill much ink describing the church's shortcomings today and of old. Nonetheless, by God's mercy his people have sown ideas into the cultures of their day that aligned with biblical social ethics and they have acted to reform institutions and practices that violated those ethics.

Throughout history Christians have influenced notable changes in social policy, literacy, living conditions, and education—many of which we will be examining throughout this book. But their most important influence has come through millions of decisions and actions carried out by citizens in their daily lives who adopted new attitudes and customs as a result of their faith. As historian Herbert Schlossberg has argued,

> The importance of Christianity in the history of the West [lies] in the constant preaching to the multitudes . . . of love and humility week after week in such a way that how people feel, think, and behave is vastly different than it otherwise would have been, a phenomenon that has tended "greatly to alter the quality of life and the very texture of human history."[17]

There is of course no way to count or exactly quantify this influence—but it has been massive. But we can identify some key ideas that historic Judeo-Christian faith infused into the water of Western society with effects far beyond measure. Here I look at four such ideas and offer some illustrations of how these ideas were embodied in transformative actions.

Idea 1: **Imago Dei.** The first is the doctrine of the *imago Dei*: the notion that every person, regardless of race, gender, ability, ethnicity, or social status has inherent value because they are made in God's image. This revolutionary idea is the font of Western civilization's notion of inalienable human rights. Cornell University historian Brian Tierney roots the concept of all human beings having equal dignity and worth in Christian and biblical teaching.[18]

The early Christian formula of "in Christ there is no slave or free, Greek or Jew" reiterated the truth of the *imago Dei* with a particularly counter-cultural edge amid hierarchical Roman culture. In a society based on inequality, the apostles' message was radical. Now, it must be quickly admitted that the *practice* of the church has often and woefully fallen short: consider the demeaning ways some of the church fathers spoke about women or the shameful support of American slavery by many Southern Christians. But this doesn't change the fact that the belief that all people possess inherent dignity because they are made in God's image has had massive influence on the history of Western civilization.

As Keller noted in his speech before Parliament, the earliest account of someone protesting that slavery was wrong per se (because human beings, being of infinite worth in God's eyes, could not be sold) was the church father Gregory of Nyssa in the fourth century. Over thirteen centuries later one of the most effective artifacts of the campaign to end the British slave trade would be a medallion crafted by Christ-follower Josiah Wedgewood showing an African man in chains with the caption, "Am I Not a Man and a Brother?"

Action: Promoting the sanctity of life. Given the early church's embrace of the *imago Dei*, it's no surprise that it was active in promoting the sanctity of life. Believers resisted four commonly accepted practices in Greco-Roman culture that demeaned human dignity: abortion, infanticide, pederasty, and the gladiatorial games.

The *Didache*, a Christian treatise from the first century, enjoined Christ-followers from practicing infanticide. Church fathers Clement of Alexandria and Tertullian strongly denounced the practice. Early Christians rescued infants left to die from exposure. "They frequently took such human castaways into their homes and adopted them. Callistus of Rome gave refuge to abandoned children by placing them in Christian homes."[19] Christian bishops successfully pressed Roman leaders for reforms to respect human life and dignity. Under the influence of bishop Basil of Caesarea, for example, the Christian emperor Valentinian outlawed infanticide, abortion, and child abandonment in AD 374.[20]

Pederasty was socially accepted and common in Roman society. The early church, however, condemned it. Summing up Kyle Harper's *From Shame to Sin: The Christian Transformation of Sexual Morality in Late Antiquity*, Kevin DeYoung writes, "The Christian sexual revolution became codified in law under the reign of Justinian (527–565). Sex between males was a crime, and pederasty was outlawed. Christian laws under Justinian also vigorously opposed coerced prostitution."[21]

Early Christians also opposed the gladiatorial games as inhumane. The church father Tertullian lobbied against them in his book *de Spectaculis* (*Concerning Shows*) and spent an entire chapter admonishing Christians not to attend the games. Eventually the Christian emperor Theodosius I outlawed the gladiatorial contests.[22]

Other reforms influenced by the idea of the *imago Dei* included the outlawing of branding the faces of criminals (by the Christian emperor Constantine the Great in 313) and introducing segregation of male and female prisoners so that women could be better protected (by Constantine's son Constantius).[23]

Action: Elevating the status of widows. The doctrine of the *imago Dei* also had profound implications for the treatment of widows.

Roman culture countenanced the abuse of widows because they were considered second-class citizens. For example, widows without property were at the bottom of the Roman social order. Roman culture also exerted tremendous pressure on widows to remarry. Emperor Augustus even decreed that widows should be fined if not remarried within two years.

By contrast, fueled by the conviction of the widow's inherent worth (and by recollection of God's ancient instructions in the Mosaic law), the early Christians demonstrated special concern and practical care for widows. As Rodney Stark explains in *The Rise of Christianity*, "Among Christians, widowhood was highly respected."[24] While pagan widows lost all control of their husband's estate when they remarried, Christian widows who chose to remarry were allowed by the church to maintain their prior husband's estate.[25] Poor widows were also supported financially by the church. Historian Peter Brown reports that by the middle of the third century the church at Rome cared for fifteen hundred widows and other poor persons.[26]

Beyond that charitable practice, though, were other elements of the church's engagement with widows that were even more notable in dignifying this group. For example, the church's "Order of Widows" recognized the contribution that widows "could make to the well-being and spiritual growth of their fellow believers."[27] This order was composed of older widows of strong character whose duties involved intercessory prayer, visiting the sick, and instructing younger women. Widows in the order were positioned in a place of honor during the liturgy, "sitting in front of the assembly along with the bishops, priests, and deacons."[28] Reflecting on the order, one scholar comments that "the true innovation in early Christian communities was not in coming to the aid of the widows" but rather "in discovering genuine ways in which the widows could aid others, thereby creating an innovative form of social unity."[29]

In more recent times Christians have been engaged in two important efforts to protect widows. First, Christian missionaries in nineteenth-century India played a vital role in outlawing the practice of *sati* (the Hindu custom by which a widow is burned alive on her husband's funeral pyre). *Sati* was supposed to be a voluntary act. In reality widows often faced extreme pressure from family to participate and in some cases were forcibly set up on the pyre. The well-known missionary William Carey and his friends engaged in a tireless twenty-five-year campaign to raise awareness of the practice and see it banned.[30]

Second, in the past few decades Christians have engaged in efforts, primarily in Africa, to fight the scourge of land theft against widows. International Justice Mission (IJM), a Christian human rights organization, reports that when widows refuse to leave their home, they and their children are sometimes chased out violently, often by the husband's relatives. Although such practice is against the law, local police are often unwilling to intervene, viewing the circumstance as a family matter. IJM combats the problem through legal representation of widows, prosecution of land grabbers, and educating and training police and local leaders on the effective enforcement of land theft laws.

Action: Expanding women's rights and roles. The doctrine of *imago Dei* and God's commissioning of both men and women in the cultural mandate have positively influenced the status of women. At the same time it must be quickly said that individual Christians and the church have frequently oppressed women. I cannot review the long history of the Christian church's complicated and ambiguous relationship to women's rights. Suffice to say that the topic is contested. There is certainly plenty of evidence detailing discouraging accounts of the ways women have been and continue to be constrained in the use of their gifts and of abuse of married women rooted in false interpretations of male headship. It is also the case, though, that as already evidenced, early Christianity brought a new dignity—and practical new protections—to women.

Moreover, in the nineteenth and twentieth centuries revivalist activities produced both theology and practice that enlarged the spheres of women's engagement and leadership within the church. These activities and the self-confidence and practical skills they nurtured subsequently contributed to the broader social movement for women's equality.

The Second Great Awakening, for example, fueled several social reform movements, including those concerned with protecting and expanding the rights of women. Clemson religion professor Nancy Hardesty goes so far as to argue that "the nineteenth-century American woman's rights movement was deeply rooted in evangelical revivalism. Its theology and practice motivated and equipped women and men to adopt a feminist ideology, to reject stereotyped sex roles, and to work for positive changes in marriage, church, society, and politics."[31] Other scholars agree. Speaking of the women associated with Charles Finney's revivalist movement, Keith Melder writes,

> Their sisterhood in faith helped these women to achieve an attitude of self-confidence and a sense of mission that infected many of their later activities. Surely it is no coincidence that the areas where Finney's revivals and women's religious education flourished—New England, upstate New York and northern Ohio—were early centers of women's reform work and feminism.[32]

In more recent decades Christians for Biblical Equality has played an important role in celebrating women's giftedness and the history of women's contributions to the advance of the gospel around the world. The organization provides rich scholarship and is active in advocacy work to eliminate gender-based violence and human trafficking and to promote girls' schooling.

Idea 2: Sexual ethics. A second groundbreaking idea of the early Christians concerned their teaching on sexual ethics. Drawing on the work of

Kyle Harper, Keller told the British parliamentarians that believers introduced into Roman culture the revolutionary notion that sex must be con-
sensual and covenantal. Such a stance challenged the Roman free man's
belief that as a person of high social status he could have sex with whomever
he wanted—regardless of whether he was married—and that women of
lower social status could not deny his sexual demands.[33]

Action: Elevating the status of married women. Christian teaching on
sexual ethics had the effect of elevating the status of married women. Against
God's norm of treating men and women equally and calling both to live in
the world as royal priests, many societies have oppressed women and treated
them as second-class citizens. Thus the teaching of Saint Paul in Ephesians 5
that a husband should love his wife as Christ loved the church and that "he
who loves his wife loves himself," would have sounded very strange in the
ears of the ancient Greeks and Romans.

Greek wives were not permitted to leave the home unsupervised or to eat
or interact with their husband's guests. According to the second-century
Greek essayist Plutarch, Spartan men kept their women under lock and
key.[34] Greek girls were not permitted to go to school and Greek women were
not allowed to speak in public.[35] In both Greek and Roman cultures a wife
could not divorce her husband, but a husband could his wife. The Roman
law of *manus* placed a married woman "under the absolute control of her
husband, who had ownership of her and all her possessions."[36] Roman law
also gave a father the exclusive right to choose his daughter's husband and
some used this power to marry off their daughters as child brides (ages as
young as 11 or 12) to older men.[37]

Both Jesus' good treatment of women and the early church's inclusion of
women as evangelists and missionaries contributed to the appeal of Christianity for women and helps explain why women outnumbered men in the
early church. Moreover, as Stark notes in *The Rise of Christianity*, "there is
virtual consensus among historians of the early church as well as biblical
scholars that women held positions of honor and authority within early
Christianity."[38] Christian women "married at a substantially older age and
had more choice about whom they married."[39]

For both Romans and Christians, "love and affection between spouses
was common and the procreation of children was a central expectation" of

marriage.[40] However, as historian Susan Mobley explains, the Christian view of marriage "was distinct in two significant ways."

> In Christian marriage, the spouses were moral equals and held to a single standard of fidelity (unlike the double standard in Roman marriage) and marriage represented a lifelong, indissoluble bond (i.e., divorce was not permitted). These differences impacted the spread of the Christian ideal of marriage in the Roman world.[41]

Idea 3: Children as persons. A third revolutionary idea that Christianity advanced was a countercultural view of children. In his book *How Children Became Persons*, historian O. M. Bakke poses two questions: "What did early Christians think about children and about the nature of children?" and "What did they say about the treatment of children, and how did they treat children de facto?"[42] He concludes that "Christian theology and ethics protected children's life in a way not found in the Greco-Roman world, and in this sense we can speak of Christianity as a 'child-friendly' religion."[43]

Bakke argues that "Christianity introduced new anthropological viewpoints" on childhood.[44] These were rooted in Jesus' teaching on the importance of becoming like a child (Matt 18:1-4). Jesus held up children as a "positive paradigm" for adults. This idea is picked up by the patristics, who spoke of the innocence of children and their lack of worldliness. John Chrysostom, for example, spoke of how children, unlike adults, are not grieved at the loss of money or overly concerned about physical beauty.

Bakke also shows that, in contrast to the normal practice of wealthy Roman citizens who left child-rearing to servants, Christian leaders encouraged Christ-followers to prioritize parenting and children's education. He again cites Chrysostom, who urged those in Constantinople to "let everything take second place to our care for our children, our bringing them up in the discipline and instruction of the Lord . . ."[45]

Action: Caring for orphans and foundlings. Christianity's embrace of the personhood of children led to vital actions on behalf of orphans and foundlings. With adult life expectancy under thirty years of age—and in the context of warfare, inadequate health care, and the chances of mothers dying in childbirth—there were many orphaned children in ancient Rome. They were highly vulnerable to murder and slavery. Instead of seeing such orphans as dispensable or as commodities, the church taught that they were precious children needing homes.

The *Apostolic Constitutions* (eight treatises by early Christian leaders dated from 375 to 380) included encouragement of adoption. Christian households were urged to take in boys and treat them as sons and to marry their sons to young women who had been orphaned.[46] In *Dirty Faith: Bringing the Love of Christ to the Least of These*, author David Nowell adds:

> In the growing Christian movement, the Church fathers consistently and conspicuously called upon followers of Christ to be faithful to Scripture's demand that we care for the orphan. Virtually every early writing on Christian conduct stressed the importance of caring for children without parents. Eusebius, the Apostolic Constitutions, Lactantius, Ignatius, Polycarp, Justin Martyr . . . the list goes on and on, but every one of them called on the early church to care for orphans.[47]

Over time, networks of church organizations worked to meet the needs of orphans. During medieval times, Catholic hospital orders, such as the Order of the Holy Spirit, began accepting abandoned children and caring for them.[48] The Catholic Church operated foundling homes through the 1400s–1700s.

By the time of the Reformation, foundling homes run by or in close consultation with the church were part of the urban landscape in Italy, Spain, France, and Portugal. In northern Europe, more dominated by Protestant churches, fostering and adopting orphans was more common than institutional care.[49]

Since the early 2000s, Evangelicals have been "one of the most powerful forces in international adoption."[50] Moreover, increased attention to the needs of orphans abroad laid the groundwork for reinvigorated engagement by US churches in domestic foster care. After decreasing for many years, around 2012 the number of children nationally who needed foster care began to rise. One reason, reported officials at the federal Department of Health and Human Services, was the opioid epidemic.[51] The economic fallout from the Great Recession also played a role. Today, churches are playing a significant role in addressing this crisis.

Arizona's story is a good example. There, rising numbers of children taken from their parents combined with a declining number of families willing to foster them created a huge crisis. In response, three pastors from Phoenix gathered to brainstorm how churches could respond. The result was a new Arizona chapter of a nonprofit organization called Project 1.27 (for Jas 1:27) that had launched five years earlier in Colorado. The Christian nonprofit builds relationships with state child welfare agencies and trains and connects church families with fostering opportunities. In Colorado, Project 1.27 has contributed to a dramatic decrease in the number of children needing placement. In Arizona over ninety churches have worked with Project 1.27 to foster over 2,100 children. Today Project 1.27 is "the biggest recruiter of adoptive and foster families in Arizona."[52]

Action: Ending child labor. With a conviction that children are persons, Christ-followers have acted at various times and places to protect youngsters from labor exploitation. One of those times and places was nineteenth-century England.

In his magisterial *History of the English People in the Nineteenth Century*, historian Élie Halévy discussed the movements that led to significant labor reforms in the 1830s–1840s. "The historian of the movement which produced the factory acts [which outlawed labor for children under age nine] must not forget the many tributaries which swelled the stream," he wrote. "But the source of the river was the piety and Christian sentiment of the Evangelicals."[53]

Richard Oastler, an Evangelical, led the way in publicizing the harsh conditions of child labor. According to the UK National Archives, in 1821, approximately 49 percent of the workforce was under twenty.[54] In cities boys and girls as young as seven worked in textile factories for fourteen hours a day while in rural areas they labored in the fields and the mines. Although a law against using children as chimney sweeps had been passed in 1788, they continued to be used in this role into the nineteenth century. Oastler wrote editorials in newspapers decrying child labor and lobbied members of Parliament to end the practice.[55] He mobilized "Ten Hour Bill" committees to lobby for factory reform. He even went severely into debt funding their efforts.

Lord Ashley, the Earl of Shaftesbury, picked up the fight in the 1830s, eventually succeeding in passing a bill prohibiting children under nine from working at all and reducing older children's daily work hours to twelve. During the following decade Shaftesbury helped establish the Children's

Employment Commission, whose 1842 report revealed that children were employed as miners and caused a significant public outcry.[56] Oastler's dream finally came true in 1846 when William Wilberforce's "Bettering Society" won the campaign to pass the Ten Hours Bill.[57]

Idea 4: Clean living. Church leaders have long urged followers of Christ to live morally pure, upright lives free from excessive indulgence in sensual pleasures. The writers of the New Testament Epistles, for example, enjoined Christ-followers to eschew the debauchery of their surrounding culture. The Epistles command believers to avoid drunkenness, coarse language, and sexual promiscuity. The early church fathers warned the faithful about the corrosive influence of Roman spectacles, theaters, and gladiatorial games. They ridiculed the excessive drinking and gluttony of the Romans, commanding the faithful to be moderate in drink.

Christians have certainly been guilty of extreme asceticism on the one hand (consider Origen's self-castration) and hypocrisy on the other (such as when clerics do not match their preaching on sexual purity, greed, or alcohol abuse with their behavior). But it is also true that Christian leaders have consistently taught clean living as a corollary of faith and that such instruction has often led to a better quality of family relationships and living standards.

Improvements in family life in nineteenth-century England. Consider, for example, the effects of the Evangelical revivals of the 1800s on the working-class household in England. Though Victorian respectability has often been the object of satire and ridicule, its cultural triumph (for a season) in the nineteenth century, as one historian argued, was an important "part of the history of the battle for refinement and civilization, and above all the better protection of women, against the promiscuity, animalism, brutality and grossness which had been common even in the eighteenth century."[58] Moreover, Evangelical encouragement of the virtues of self-control, frugality, and—especially—sobriety, played a significant role in improving a family's economic prospects.

SUMMING UP

Just as the Israelites were called as part of their mission to be an ethically distinct people, so too are we as the new Israel. In the apostle Paul's poetic phrasing in Philippians, followers of Jesus are to seek to "become blameless and pure, 'children of God without fault in a warped and crooked generation.'" In this way, we will "shine . . . like stars in the sky" as we embody the life of the Word (Phil 2:15).

For Jesus, who came to fulfill all the Law and Prophets, there was no separation of personal morality and passion for social justice. Both are vital components of following the One who is good. And since both are very difficult to pursue, we will never reach perfection in our attempt to be a community of virtue. As we try, we will undoubtedly face opposition. These realities can tempt congregational leaders to neglect an emphasis on personal morality in favor of ever-increasing encouragements to engage in works of social justice. Though getting people to create space in their lives to attend a protest, tutor a kid, or invest in a social enterprise may be challenging, for some church leaders these things are easier than talking about divorce or insisting on the "old-fashioned" idea of no sex before marriage—or even telling the sheep to sabbath from their cell phones. The call to pursue the Good, though, must always involve an effort to become people of greater humility, integrity, purity, kindness, faithfulness, and self-control. Just because personal piety is not 100 percent synonymous with Christlikeness does not suggest it is unimportant. Clear preaching and consistent discipleship efforts that help Christ-followers grow in holiness, submitting to biblical injunctions on gluttony, greed, sexual immorality, marital infidelity, and drunkenness, must never go out of style—even as they are increasingly incomprehensible in our degenerating culture.

Promoting the Good by strengthening marriage. If nurturing the Good involves embodying a godly ethical distinctiveness and working to uphold the dignity of persons, then labor by churches to strengthen marriage seems a particularly apt strategy. After all, if Christian couples can model what a healthy, enduring relationship looks like, they will indeed "shine like stars" in a culture where family is disintegrating. Moreover, as churches help couples outside their walls to heal and restore their unions, they can prevent the toll divorce frequently takes on children. In chapter three we will see how a collective effort by congregations in Jacksonville strengthened the Good in their community by remarkably lowering their community's divorce rate.

3

A STRATEGY FOR CULTIVATING THE GOOD

STRENGTHEN MARRIAGE

In 2016, Chris and LaCresha Hannah's marriage was on the rocks. The Jacksonville, Florida, couple, in their late thirties with three children, was not communicating well—or much. Chris was working long hours, defending his absences with an "I've got to provide" mantra. LaCresha was withering emotionally. Looking back, Chris realizes that the everyday stresses of life, work, and kids had led him to "start neglecting the most important person." LaCresha struggled to communicate her needs. "You could feel the division in the house during that time," she says.

Things got so bad that she turned to another man. The affair went on for months but wasn't fulfilling. "I was looking for help. I felt like nobody could relate to how I felt," she says, her voice catching. During the crisis Chris turned to his faith. He prayed, read Scripture, and tried to pursue his wife. Feeling ashamed, LaCresha remembers "waking up" and realizing that this was not how she wanted to live, that it was her destiny to be with Chris.

The Hannahs started marriage counseling. They learned of a class being offered by their congregation. The "Adventures in Marriage" course at Celebration Church taught Chris and LaCresha practical skills to get them back on track. They learned new ways to communicate and problem solve. They learned to be far more intentional in how they treated one another and to regulate their emotions.

These days the Hannahs are thriving. They're even giving back now by serving as marriage coaches in Celebration's premarital ministry. "Without the church support, these classes, a great group of friends, my marriage wouldn't be possible," says Chris. "They saved our marriage."[1]

EXCEPTIONAL IMPACT

The Hannahs are just one couple out of thousands who participated in the nation's largest privately funded marriage-strengthening project ever implemented at a city level.[2] Philanthropy Roundtable's "Culture of Freedom Initiative" (COFI) targeted Jacksonville for an ambitious divorce prevention effort from 2016 to 2018. The city had been called by *Men's Health* magazine the sixth worst in America for marriage.[3]

JP DeGance, a devout Catholic, led the $5 million project. COFI was implemented in partnership with Live the Life Ministries, an Evangelical nonprofit organization in Florida that had been focused on promoting healthy relationships for years (see livethelife.org).

At the heart of the COFI was a network of nearly fifty local churches that provided a variety of marriage-related programming: premarital counseling, marriage enrichment, and intensive interventions for struggling couples. By 2018, the end of the three-year initiative, nearly fifty-nine thousand residents in Duval County (which is nearly synonymous with the city of Jacksonville) had participated in some kind of marriage-related program of at least four hours' duration. That represented a massive increase: in 2013, about three hundred local residents had availed themselves of Live the Life's programs.

Even more impressively, the divorce rate in Duval County dropped 24 percent over the three-year period. That 24 percent decrease is significant for a variety of reasons. First, it marked the first time that Duval County had a divorce rate lower than the state average. Second, in forty of the forty-four years before 2014, Duval County had the highest divorce rate among all large Florida counties. But, after the project, Duval had the lowest rate among all large counties in Florida.[4]

Third, the 24 percent drop in Duval County beat out by far Florida's 10 percent decline and the nation's 6 percent decline over the same period.[5]

W. Bradford Wilcox, director of the National Marriage Project at the University of Virginia, Spencer James, an assistant professor for the School of Family Life at Brigham Young University, and Wendy Wang, a researcher with the Institute for Family Studies, conducted a rigorous evaluation of the COFI. They concluded that the project had "an exceptional impact" on marital stability in Duval County.[6] "We have rarely seen changes of this size in family trends over such a short period of time," Wilcox told *Newsweek* magazine.[7] The report noted that "the increase in family stability in Jacksonville during the years of the Culture of Freedom Initiative was larger than the increase in family stability witnessed in the vast majority of other large, comparable counties across the U.S."[8]

What happened in Jacksonville was extraordinary. Summing up, Dennis Stoica, board chair at Live the Life Ministries and a key player in the project alongside DeGance, said, "It was believed that the divorce rate is this intractable problem." But Jacksonville achieved "a huge shift."[9]

And the church was the major factor in the initiative's success. As DeGance told a reporter in 2019, "Churches were the heroes of Jacksonville."[10]

GENESIS OF A BIG, HAIRY, AUDACIOUS PROJECT

DeGance says the Jacksonville project was motivated by a desire to find "replicable philanthropic strategies that could strengthen families, marriages, and faith."[11] Often philanthropy seeks to ameliorate problems that arise from family breakdown. DeGance and his colleagues thought, "What if we got upstream of that and found ways to boost marriage and family stability and religious observance? And what if we could actually use [dollars] more effectively . . . by getting upstream of the problems before they manifest themselves in other ways?"[12] In Jacksonville, they achieved that.

The COFI was originally focused on three cities: Dayton, Phoenix, and Jacksonville. Early on, though, the team realized that in the other two cities problems of scale and distribution made it impossible to do the work at a reasonable cost. So, they focused their energy on Jacksonville.

"In Duval County, there were different indices we wanted to move: increasing marriage, decreasing divorce, decreasing out-of-wedlock births, and increasing regular church attendance," DeGance explains.[13] Live the Life leaders looked at that list and recommended paring it down to what they had the most experience in trying to do: lowering the divorce rate.

Jacksonville was a good location for the experiment for at least three reasons. First, its divorce rate was comparatively high. Second, some religious leaders there were familiar with Live the Life's solid track record of marriage-strengthening work in Tallahassee.[14] Third, Jacksonville boasts a high level of religious affiliation (56 percent of residents claim some connection to a religious congregation), but many of these individuals do not attend church regularly. This familiarity with religion likely reduced apprehensions individuals may have had about participating in a church-hosted program.[15]

THE PROBLEM: NEGATIVE EFFECTS OF DIVORCE

The well-known statistic that "half of US marriages end in divorce" is wrong. While it may have reached that level at its height around the 1980s, the divorce rate has been declining. It dropped significantly between 2008 and 2016. That's the good news. The bad news is that the divorce rate is still high—around 40 percent. In fact, the United States has the third-highest rate in the world. Moreover, many divorcées remarry, and a very high number of those marriages (estimates reach 60 percent) end in divorce.

Several years ago a study sponsored by the Institute for American Values and three other nonprofits concluded that the financial costs of divorce on our society are tremendous. This research estimated that divorce and unwed parenting cost taxpayers some $112 billion annually. The costs arise from increased public spending on antipoverty, criminal justice, and education programs and because of the lower levels of taxes paid by individuals in poverty.[16]

For Live the Life's Dennis Stoica, though, the real bottom line for the COFI was kids' well-being. Decreasing the number of divorces in the community meant increasing the number of children who'd be spared the suffering that arises when marriages fall apart.

Substantial social science research has concluded that children in intact families do better on a wide range of metrics.[17] Marriage increases the likelihood that moms and dads have good relationships with their kids. Children in intact, two-parent families are physically and emotionally healthier and less likely to be abused. These children are less likely to commit delinquent behaviors or to use drugs or alcohol. They are less likely to become pregnant or to impregnate someone as a teenager, and they have a decreased risk of divorcing when they get married. Marriage also reduces poverty for disadvantaged women and children. By contrast, divorce often increases child poverty. Moreover, research by Raj Chetty at Harvard, Wilcox's team at the University of Virginia, and Penn State's John Iceland has shown that "family structure is one of the most powerful predictors of economic mobility, incarceration, and racial inequality in America." There is, in short, a "consensus in scholarship that marriage matters, that kids are most likely to thrive when raised in an intact family."[18]

Preventing the harm of divorce on children is a moral good and provides sufficient motivation for churches to be engaged in marriage ministry. But there is also a practical reason for clergy to care about marriage ministry, says Wilcox. "Stable marriages generate many more people in the pews in the short and long term," he explains. "There's a strong correlation between family stability and church attendance. When divorce happens, often the man leaves the church. Also, children of divorce are less likely to remain in church. So, pastors and priests have a big, long-term incentive to try to strengthen marriage."[19]

THE SOLUTION: MOBILIZE CHURCHES

Live the Life was founded by Richard and Elizabeth Albertson in 1998. What started in the back of their townhouse is now a nationally recognized marriage/relationship education ministry headquartered in Tallahassee with three regional offices. The nonprofit had been working in Jacksonville for three years before it joined up with DeGance on COFI. Staff had begun building relationships and credibility and had learned the local landscape. Their success in recruiting churches into COFI likely stemmed from two factors. First, they started with their support base, churches—like Celebration—with whom they had already been working. They invited these congregations to partner with them in even more vigorous marriage ministry activity and promised the support and training to help them make that a reality. Second, they particularly targeted efforts on the two largest faith communities in Duval County, the Southern Baptists and the Catholics. Live the Life hired a Southern Baptist minister and a Catholic couple with long experience in marriage ministry as the organization's main recruiters. Having coreligionists approach each community respectively facilitated a more rapid buy-in on the initiative than might have happened otherwise.

Eventually, nearly fifty congregations of diverse sizes and denominations joined the effort. They implemented a wide variety of programs. Some offered Dave Ramsey's "Financial Peace University" program to help couples address money problems. Others sponsored date nights featuring clean comedians. Some hosted weekend retreats or multiweek classes using Live the

Life's "Adventures in Marriage" curriculum. Others ramped up premarital counseling and still others implemented marriage intervention type programs to serve couples on the brink of divorce. Altogether over the course of the initiative, fifty-nine thousand Jacksonville program participants completed at least four hours of education related to marriage or family life during the COFI.[20]

Why churches? Churches aren't the only ones trying to strengthen marriages. A variety of secular nonprofits work at this too, some with government funding. But churches bring some unique assets to the table.[21] Stoica came to Florida after leading California's Healthy Marriage Initiative. This federally funded program offered couples a variety of skills-based marriage programs: learning how to communicate better, resolve conflicts better, and so on. Stoica recognized limitations in this approach because it was not tied to a larger ecosystem of supportive relationships. Couples benefited from the instruction in relational skills offered in the classes. But when the courses were over, they didn't enjoy any ongoing system of support.[22]

Richard Albertson from Live the Life agrees. He values what his parachurch organization has been able to accomplish and acknowledges that it can do some things that most congregations cannot—such as put on an intensive weekend serving couples in crisis. But, he quickly adds, "We can't be a church. Our Hope Weekend can't be a church. The church hands us their couples and we handle them very tenderly, but then we hand them back because we can't provide that ongoing support."[23]

Churches are "sticky in a way that nobody else is sticky," explains DeGance. A person attending a church program about marriage could be invited over by a congregant for a meal, asked to join another couple at a Sunday service, or welcomed into a small group. Congregations, he says, are eager to help people connect. At churches, "You've got a deep reservoir of your membership passionate about forming one-to-one, life-changing relationships, which produces the stickiness that churches have over other NGOs," DeGance explains. "So, in Jacksonville, churches made the difference."[24] John Stonestreet of the Colson Center agrees. Churches are "scattered, de-centralized, and localized" social institutions, he notes. They are positioned to identify and connect with specific couples that are struggling in their marriages.[25]

Moreover, Stoica says that religious communities provide couples with a beautiful vision about what marriage can and should be. They support couples in their relationships and teach and encourage healthy marriage skills.[26] Congregations can also be places where younger married couples rub shoulders with older ones. This provides access to mentoring for younger adults by more experienced couples.

Live the Life's Mieko Paige adds that by laboring with churches, para-church ministries like Live the Life "piggyback on the credibility of the church leaders." The congregation is a "built-in audience" for the content and programs a nonprofit like Live the Life has to offer. Another important reason her ministry works with churches, she says, is because that is a sustainable approach. "If we can help equip the leaders, teach them, train them, and they are serving couples in their community, then if Live the Life closed its doors tomorrow, the work would still continue."[27]

A data-driven strategy. Stoica explains that COFI's strategy was threefold. First, increase demand for marriage-related programs and ministries. Second, increase the supply of church-based marriage programming. Third, condition the landscape to be receptive to these kinds of programs.

DeGance partnered with marketing data firms to develop a predictive model that could identify individuals in Jacksonville most at risk for divorcing. The analytics could also identify individuals open to an invitation from a church.[28] This information was then used to create microtargeted advertisements via social media to these individuals about the importance of marriage, the need for intentionally nurturing relationships, and the availability of marriage-related resources and programs in the area. The digital advertisements were complemented by radio spots and billboards, often using Live the Life's slogan that "It's never too early or too late to invest in your marriage." At the height of the initiative, targeted individuals were receiving about a dozen advertisements per month. The huge investment in advertising worked: interest was stoked, and the initiative achieved its goal of dramatically increasing demand for marriage-related programming.

All the project's advertising directed county residents to a single website, JAXMarriage.org. On this platform, users could search for resources or programs according to their particular interest or need; for example, to find a premarital counselor or a class on communication or a weekend retreat for struggling couples. Churches, nonprofits, and denominations all promoted their programs through this one site. DeGance explains that the strategy was about catalyzing churches to "work alone, together." That is, rather than trying to get everyone to co-create programming or coordinate activities—which takes a lot of time and energy—the idea was that everyone shared the overall goal of preventing divorces but was free to offer the particular events they wanted to do.[29]

The data-driven approach also helped accomplish the COFI's goal of "flooding the market" with church-based marriage programming. DeGance's team developed instruments to create estimates of the percentage of congregants in individual congregations with the propensity for divorcing and the number of children that would be affected by that. Essentially, DeGance told John Stonestreet on a *BreakPoint* podcast in late 2019, "we were leading with a diagnostic, not a content resource."[30] Historically there has been a wide range of content resources available to churches; lack of a curriculum to try hasn't been the problem. The need has been to get busy clergy to focus on this issue. "We illustrated to churches that this [was] a gap in ministry and that they need to fill that gap," explains DeGance.[31] This also worked, galvanizing pastors to action.

A MINI CASE STUDY: COFI AT CELEBRATION CHURCH

Pastor Wayne Lanier from Celebration Church, a megachurch of around fifteen thousand members with campuses on Jacksonville's west and south sides, is a good example. Wayne says his research into how Celebration was falling short in helping married couples motivated his enthusiastic involvement in COFI.[32] Around 2015, he and his assistant Rachel Grogan had examined the extent to which Celebration was reaching its congregants with marriage-related ministries. They determined that under 10 percent of married couples were participating. So when Wayne was asked by DeGance's team to be part of a pastors' group meeting in Washington, DC, to hear about the proposed COFI project, he eagerly accepted.

At that meeting Wayne agreed to help with COFI's efforts in Jacksonville. He also accepted an invitation from COFI partner Leadership Network (LN), a Christian nonprofit that equips megachurches, to join a new learning community composed of pastors from each of COFI's three target cities.

During the first eighteen months of the initiative, LN facilitated group re-treats three times, once each in Jacksonville, Phoenix, and Dayton. The pastors swapped stories, brainstormed programming ideas for marriage-strengthening ministries, and worked on customized action plans for their churches. "We learned a ton through that process," Wayne says. "It gave us a strategy and we formed a plan and put it to work."

Initially, Celebration sketched out a four-pronged strategy for a robust marriage ministry. First, they would focus on premarital counseling and classes. "We were a very young church [demographically] and we had tons of people getting married, so that was a good place to get going," Wayne says with a laugh. Next was programming for newly married couples less than eighteen months into their journey. The third area was marriage enrichment, and the fourth was care for struggling couples. Wayne's team determined that they were strongest in this final arena since they had a system in place for responding to couples in trouble. They were already partnering with Live the Life Ministries in supporting their Hope Weekends—intensive interven-tions for couples in crisis. "Their Hope Weekends were the most fruitful thing I'd ever come across as a pastor for helping turn the tide for couples that were already in the divorce process or about to go into it," Wayne says.

After the first year the Celebration team modified their approach. The marriage ministry still focused on four arenas, but the first became "Healthy Relationship Development," with various classes directed to high school and college youth and single young adults. The second area merged engaged couples seeking premarital counseling and young couples in their first year of marriage. The marriage enrichment and care foci remained unchanged.

The changes came because Wayne had realized through many conversa-tions with single young adults in their twenties that there was a big desire for guidance on dating and healthy relationships. Celebration's "College and Career" ministry was booming, with six hundred to eight hundred young adults showing up weekly. The format involved some large-group worship and instruction, followed by smaller group classes—with many topical of-ferings to choose from. They talked over potential curricula with Live the Life and other ministries and eventually created a new class called "Relation-ships 101." They decided to offer it as part of the college and career ministry. By week three, even without any promotion, the class boasted standing-room-only attendance. "They loved it," Wayne recalls. The next semester his team offered the course in two large classrooms and both "were packed out."

Rachel's husband, Scott, a staff member with Live the Life, began teaching a class at Celebration called "Preparing for Forever" in COFI's second year. At the time, Julian Cano, a young millennial, was living with his high school sweetheart and wasn't interested in pursuing marriage. He felt like they were practically married anyway—living together, going on vacations together. "Marriage was just like a ceremony," he says.[33] But then the relationship grew flat. "The energy wasn't there. We were in the same room, but we weren't really there," Julian explains. "And then obviously the expected outcome happened: we went our separate ways."

"During this time, I was at the lowest of my lows, and the only thing I could do was get my butt to church," Julian continues. He says he was drawn into Scott's class "from the very first two minutes." He credits the course for reigniting his faith and transforming his view of marriage. "The way I see marriage now," he explains, "it's not just a ceremony. Looking at how my life was before, and how it is now, I feel like I'm in a totally different space."

"Julian now has this awesome support system," says Scott. "He's surrounded by people who are doing the same things and headed in the same direction he's going in. And it's so important that you have that in this world."[34]

In the premarital and marriage enrichment areas, Celebration increased its focus on marriage mentoring. Each semester the church offered different programs at its three campuses, often using Live the Life's curriculum "Adventures in Marriage." The multiweek classes would be capped off by a special Date Night event. Twice during COFI, Celebration partnered with the nationally known ministry "Marriage Today" and hosted its XO Conference. At the end of each semester Wayne's team would contact participants and ask if they wished to volunteer in the marriage ministry in some way. This enabled the team to identify couples with a passion for helping other couples. Live the Life then trained those couples to become marriage coaches.

One joy along the way for Wayne was seeing lay leaders grow. "Coaches started to own things," he reports. "Some empty nesters were so enthusiastic about coaching engaged couples that they ended up working with as many as four couples at a time." Mieko and her husband volunteered as marriage coaches at Celebration for over a year before Mieko took her position as Live the Life–Jacksonville's marriage and family program manager. They also hosted group meetings gathering other coaching couples so they could encourage each other and share ideas. "We're passionate about marriage because God is passionate about marriage, and we're passionate about him," Mieko says.

Through its success in offering highly relevant programming and recruiting motivated volunteers, Celebration was able to reach many more of its own couples as well as attract couples from outside the church into its classes and special events. At the end of COFI in 2018, Wayne and Rachel repeated their research and found that 25 percent of Celebration's married households were now engaged in some kind of marriage-related programming. The church had more than doubled the number of couples who were being actively served.

Today Wayne Lanier has a new role at Celebration, as the campus pastor at its Orange Park location. Across all its campuses Celebration's programming has been reorganized, with a stronger emphasis on family. Currently, marriage ministry falls under Celebration's care department and centers primarily on engaged couples. The church continues to attract a young demographic (more under their forties than over forties), and leaders see premarital preparation as an effective community outreach strategy. At the city agency where couples apply for a marriage license, Celebration is listed as a provider of premarital classes and coaching. Couples who participate in at least six hours of such programming earn a certificate from the church that enables them to receive a discount from the city on the cost of the marriage license.

Pastor Patrice Brier, who oversees the care department, reports that anywhere from thirty to fifty couples participate annually. A team of volunteer coaches from Celebration, trained by Mieko, uses curriculum and questionnaires from Live the Life with the couples. Coaches meet individually with couples, and if they spot any red flags, Patrice says, they alert clergy, who then meet with them. Couples attend two group classes lasting two hours each and also meet with their coaches outside of class for two hours. Those who wish to can continue meeting with their coach throughout the engagement period and up to a year into the new marriage.

A consultative model. With Celebration and other partner churches, Live the Life took what Stoica calls "a consultative approach." The idea was to help church leaders develop the kinds of marriage-related resources and activities they were most interested in and best suited to provide. "It wasn't about Live the Life coming in to do a bunch of workshops" at the churches, Stoica explains. "That would be a 'give them a fish' model. Instead, we used the 'teach them to fish' model, where we're actually empowering the churches to develop self-sufficient marriage ministries."[35]

Mieko says that most churches don't have an official, organized marriage ministry with leaders and consistent programming. It's not that churches don't value marriage or care about struggling couples, she says. "They just don't tend to make it a priority in light of everything else the church is doing." When Mieko offered Live the Life's free consulting to pastors and told them she would "do the heavy lifting" of identifying lay congregants who could be trained to lead a marriage ministry, they were motivated to join in.

Meanwhile, in churches with small marriage ministries overseen by volunteers, participation in COFI brought welcome support. At Crosswater Community Church in Jacksonville, for example, deacon Mike Adams and his wife, Karen, had been trying to get a marriage ministry going and even spearheaded special weekend intensives two different times. "We've had a heart for doing this," Mike explained, but little help or supportive structure. COFI offered them both. Live the Life helped them host a major marriage conference at the church in 2018, trained five couples from Crosswater in leading the six-week Adventures in Marriage class, and trained another eight couples in the "Start Smart" curriculum that helps engaged couples prepare for marriage.

Resurrection Catholic Church was a highly active participant in COFI and continues its robust marriage ministry today. Since 2016, says lay leader Barbara Handzel, marriage ministry activities have been "very visible and highly verbally promoted" at the church. Resurrection's pastor, Father Peter Akin-Otiko, is an enthusiastic supporter. Chuckling, Barbara reports that Father Peter "will announce the availability of marriage ministry activities and then say, 'This is not optional.'"[36]

With help from Live the Life, Barbara and her team of about twenty volunteers have hosted a marriage enrichment program called *Choice Wine,* which focuses on the sacrament of marriage. The church has hosted special dances, a ministry fair highlighting multiple resources for couples, a four-week marriage-strengthening class called "Every Day in Love," and a monthly Marriage Building Sunday when couples celebrating their anniversaries are honored. Live the Life has also trained some of the ministry team in the Adventures in Marriage curriculum. "For young people especially," Barbara says, "I think many marriages could be saved by this course."

CHURCH-BASED DIVORCE PREVENTION: WHAT'S DOABLE?

The Culture of Freedom Initiative was a unique project, well-funded, with an experienced and trusted local partner, and its accomplishments were impressive. Whether or not other philanthropic foundations will choose to invest millions of dollars in a single community to take aim at the divorce rate remains to be seen. But the kinds of programming the involved churches executed in Jacksonville are not beyond the reach of other congregations in other cities. As Richard Albertson jokes, "We're not building a space shuttle. This is not a complicated, extremely difficult thing to do. There are couples in your church that would be outstanding at this, and they just need to be encouraged to go and do it." Pastors don't need to see this as something *they* need to do, he emphasizes. Rather, pastors need to bless the effort, identify the people in their congregations who have healthy (if imperfect) marriages and invite them to share what they've learned with other couples.

Live the Life has found that a church can be effective in marriage ministry if it has three things: vision, skills, and support. Churches first need to affirm marriage, talk about it as God's institution, and have a "vision that it is sacred and holy," Albertson says. Many churches, he reports, do have this. At the same time, though, vision alone is insufficient. Too many congregations "don't have [the] skills and they're not ready to provide support." Churches need to think through how to provide a support system for couples "at different ages and stages of the marital life cycle," Albertson explains. That certainly means providing some programming—like premarital counseling or marriage enrichment events. But it also means thinking through ancillary questions like how to provide the childcare couples might need to avail themselves of such programming or taking time to identify older married couples who can be matched to younger ones to provide advice and support.

To this support system the church must add skills-based training. Most churches focus instead only on knowledge, Albertson says. "They talk about how the Bible says this or that about marriage." But knowledge only goes so far. The good news is that parachurch organizations like Live the Life can come alongside congregations to train laypeople in marriage-strengthening skills. There are also curricula like Adventures in Marriage that emphasize skills.

THREE MARRIAGE-STRENGTHENING PROGRAMS FOR COMMUNITY FLOURISHING

Based on Jacksonville's experience and research into the effects of marriage programming, it appears that a combination of premarital programming, marriage mentoring, and specialized intervention efforts with couples in crisis by trained personnel are the three initiatives with the greatest promise. Every church need not focus on all three. But if a group of congregations can each do their part and ensure that all three are available in a specific locale, marriage can be strengthened in a community.

Premarital programming. Investment in premarital counseling is a wise bet; research has shown its effectiveness. Professor Scott Braithwaite from BYU has been studying divorce prevention for nearly fifteen years and is a strong advocate of premarital counseling. "Premarital counseling is a great way for people to do their homework about the most important decision they are ever going to make so that they can go into it armed with skills that are going to be very helpful," Braithwaite told a Utah journalist in 2017.[37] Wilcox at the National Marriage Project points to research suggesting that couples who get premarital counseling are on average more likely to report happy marriages a few years into their marriage compared to their peers who did not do premarital counseling.[38] University of Denver research psychologist Scott Stanley led a large study of three thousand couples from four states and found that those who had participated in premarital counseling had a 31 percent lower divorce rate.[39]

Marriage mentoring. Some marriage experts report that marriage mentoring is an especially effective programming strategy for churches. Interestingly, one of the pioneers of the idea was a clergyman from Jacksonville. In the 1990s, Father Dick McGinnis at St. David's Episcopal Church in Jacksonville was feeling overwhelmed by his knowledge of couples in trouble. After

praying, he got the idea of matching them up with couples who had been
through rocky times but made it. He announced in church one Sunday that
he'd like to meet after the service with any couples whose marriages had
been endangered but were now healed. Ten came forward. He listened to
their stories and with them came up with several lessons learned and key
principles for keeping the relationship healthy. He asked each couple to meet
weekly with a troubled couple.[40] Seven agreed to serve as these marriage
mentors. It worked. The pairs shared stories, listened, and learned. Over the
next five years, McGinnis's mentor couples saved thirty-eight out of forty
crisis marriages.[41]

Mike McManus, the founder of the nonprofit Marriage Savers (and
author of a 1993 book by the same name), is a big fan of marriage mentoring
because he has seen it work. For over two decades Marriage Savers has been
partnering with clergy in local communities to encourage them to adopt a
"Community Marriage Policy" (CMP). Signatories agree to utilize marriage
mentoring with both engaged couples and struggling couples, as well as to
provide some annual marriage enrichment programs and to establish step-
family support groups (stepfamilies divorce at a rate of about 70 percent). A
formal study of the effectiveness of CMPs in reducing divorce rates in
112 counties published in the journal *Family Relations* concluded that they
contributed to an average decrease of 17.5 percent.[42]

Crisis care. In Jacksonville, Albertson believes that the "flagship reason"
for the 24 percent drop in divorce was the effectiveness of the numerous
"Hope Weekends" that Live the Life hosted with church partners. These in-
tensive weekends for couples in crisis occurred monthly throughout the
three-year COFI. Typically, six to ten couples participated each time.
Couples gathered together for teaching on specific skills and then went into
individual breakout rooms with an assigned coach to practice the skills.
"The couples have a volunteer holding their hand the entire weekend,"
Albertson says. The Hope Weekends "operationalize the gospel," he says.
Couples receiving help are overwhelmed by the loving investment of their
volunteer coaches.

Live the Life keeps records on the two hundred-plus couples who participated in Hope Weekends during COFI. "We have their evaluations,"
Albertson reports. "We were able to document . . . the saved marriages."

CONCLUSION: A CALL TO ENGAGEMENT (PUN INTENDED)

Marriage ministries are good for the church. According to Communio, family structure is the key to passing on the faith to children. Millennials from married homes are 78 percent more likely to attend church than peers from unmarried homes.[43] When marriages are strengthened, churches are strengthened.

Offering help to married couples is also a good outreach strategy for increasing attendance in worship services and exposing community residents to congregational life and the good news of the gospel. During the three years of COFI, participating churches saw an average increase in church attendance of 23 percent.[44] Wilcox says that's because marriage ministries are "a real drawing card for people outside the church."[45]

The church has something deeply good to say about relationships, something that counters our current culture's often nihilistic and destructive messages about relationships. Christ-followers know that healthy relationships are at the center of human flourishing. We have a big opportunity to make a difference in pushing back the disintegration of families. If the church does become engaged in marriage ministry, DeGance predicts, "strategically and over time [we] will see major transformative renewal in our communities."[46]

4

THE TRUE

FLOURISHING IN THE REALM OF HUMAN KNOWLEDGE AND LEARNING

We have corrupted the earth through folly and sin, but God means
to restore all things in the harmony, justice, and delight of shalom.
This is a sign to us: On the third day Jesus Christ rose again from
the dead, the pledge that one day all things shall be renewed. And
God has called the followers of Christ to become agents, witnesses,
and models for the restoration project that is already in process.
These agents need to be educated.

CORNELIUS PLANTINGA, "EDUCATING FOR SHALOM"

IN 2017 GRACE POINT CHURCH in Lancaster County, Pennsylvania, hired Katie Beiler. Her job wasn't to lead worship at the church or to run the youth ministry or keep the books. She was hired to visit homes in the community to help preschool kids in the Pequea Valley School District get ready for kindergarten.

Out of sixteen Lancaster County school districts, Pequea Valley ranked thirteenth in 2017 on the percentage of third graders passing the state's English language arts exam. School district officials said they needed teachers to make in-home visits to parents of toddlers to encourage reading aloud and other activities aimed at building vocabulary and intellectual curiosity.

Beiler's salary is paid by Grace Point, but she works for the school district. "Our church doesn't just exist for ourselves," explains lead pastor Tim Rogers. "Our vision is being a transforming presence in the town square."[1]

Grace Point's action was sacrificial. The 250-member congregation had been talking for some time about their need for an additional pastor. But then Rogers found out about the district's need to have kids better prepared for school. He asked a staffer in the school superintendent's office if there was anything his church could do to help. Informed about the need for home-based literacy outreach, Rogers had an idea. He knew from a conversation with Beiler, a teacher in his flock, that she was hoping to spend more time with preschool children. He talked with the church elders about his idea to hire Beiler and second her to the school district. They agreed with the plan, seeing it as a concrete way to live into Grace Point's vision of advancing the common good in the community. When he brought the idea to church members for a vote at a congregational meeting, Rogers said he didn't just ask whether they thought it was a good idea. He told them, "This might cost you."[2]

The idea won unanimous support.

HUMAN FLOURISHING AND THE REALM OF HUMAN LEARNING

Grace Point's action may raise some eyebrows. Is this what churches ought to be doing with their money? Should promoting literacy be part of the church's mission? Should congregations support their public school districts so generously?

This Pennsylvania congregation believes they are called to contribute to their community's common good. Hiring Beiler was an investment in strengthening what the Thriving Cities Group calls the community endowment of the True. As defined by Thriving Cities, this endowment concerns "the realm of human knowledge and learning."[3] A community's education system—institutions including universities, research centers, primary and secondary schools, libraries, and educational associations—is at the center of this endowment. (It also includes things like book clubs, museums, publishing companies, newspapers, teachers' colleges, and more.) As we will see in the second half of this chapter, the church has a rich history of contributing to education.

It is not that difficult to understand why the realm of human knowledge and education is vital to human flourishing. As social beings humans are "wired to connect."[4] Daniel Goleman, author of *Social Intelligence*, explains, "Neuroscience has discovered that our brain's very design makes it sociable, inexorably drawn into an intimate brain-to-brain linkup whenever we engage with another person."[5] As believers in the Trinity, a Godhead of three separate but deeply interrelated beings, we know this truth at a gut level. Made in the Trinity's image, human beings are built for connection and communication. *Literacy*, by definition, is the ability to "read, write, speak and listen in a way that lets us communicate effectively and make sense of the world."[6]

Illiteracy and ignorance fundamentally hinder human flourishing because they inhibit that connection and communication. Without education we risk profound social isolation or seek the very poor substitute for genuine connection offered by social media.

Moreover, human beings are intellectual creatures. We look for creative outlets for our mental energies. When people lack opportunities to express their intelligence and curiosity, a stifling of personhood occurs. As the scholars at the Barbara Bush Foundation for Family Literacy argue, "Literacy gives a person the ability to navigate the world with dignity. . . . When people aren't equipped with [skills of reading and writing], they're left with limited options in life."[7] Illiteracy can also produce feelings of shame.

There are additional ways that literacy and educational efforts are connected to human flourishing. Numerous studies show that child development, for example, is stimulated by being read to. This fosters cognitive development, cultivates empathy, and accelerates young children's language acquisition. Scholars argue that "toddlers who have lots of stories read to them turn into children who are more likely to enjoy strong relationships, sharper focus, and greater emotional resilience and self-mastery."[8]

But what happens when the parent is not able to read?

Illiteracy also prevents people from accessing information and making use of technology such as the internet. This can be a mere inconvenience (think about being unable to read street signs). It can also be downright dangerous when, for example, a person is unable to comprehend the vital instructions on a medicine bottle or when a worker's failure to understand safety directions on the job leads to a workplace accident.

Moreover, education is connected with economic prosperity. Generally, less education means worse job prospects. Students who do not read proficiently by the third grade are four times more likely to leave high school without a diploma.[9] High school dropouts generally earn low wages and are more likely to experience unemployment or incarceration than are high school graduates.

Illiteracy can also make people vulnerable to others' abuse or to making unwitting mistakes with costly penalties. Illiterate peasants in the developing world, for example, are regularly defrauded by unjust public bureaucrats in part because they are ignorant of their rights or cannot read official documents. Here in the United States the National Center for Educational Statistics reports that 21 percent of Americans are functionally illiterate.[10] These adults lack the necessary literary skills to effectively navigate bureaucracies, the health care system, and many workplaces. I have personally worked with low-income adults in my city whose inability to understand written communication from public agencies (e.g., courts, the DMV, the tax assessor's office) has led to negative consequences.

In this chapter and the next I argue that churches should be vigorously engaged in education, including via partnerships with public schools. In so doing I am not asserting that public schools do a wonderful job teaching truth. Often they do not. Nor am I necessarily arguing for Christians to send their children to public schools, though I believe that can be a good missional choice.

I'm also not saying that supporting public schools is the *only* way to strengthen the realm of human knowledge and learning. That is certainly not the case. A huge part of living into the creational norm of the endowment of the True is "educating for shalom": cultivating believers who will be agents of justice and wholeness, working for the repair of this fallen world. Christian schools and universities have a great opportunity to do just that, assuming they keep that vision front and center. Thus, establishing and strengthening Christian schools is a powerful way of contributing to the True. Churches can also promote the True by hosting excellent libraries and bookshops or by contributing human and financial resources to public libraries. Establishing publishing centers that produce excellent books and magazines are additional ways that denominations have contributed to this endowment in the past, and some still are.

Because the realm of human knowledge and education is crucial to human flourishing, the church must be an active participant in it, seeking to increase people's opportunities to pursue learning. Furthermore, in light of God's passion for justice and the realities of educational inequities in our society today, there is a pressing need for agents of shalom to give themselves to strengthening public education.

In keeping with the approach of this book, I will now reflect on some insights we glean from Scripture that give us clues into God's creational intentions for the realm of human learning. Then I will note some malformations in this community endowment. Following that, I offer some examples from church history of ways Christ-followers have served as royal priests enhancing flourishing in the realm of the True.

CREATIONAL INTENT: THE REALM OF HUMAN LEARNING

At least six principles from Scripture indicate the importance of education and the role it plays in the world God has designed.

1. God designed human beings to be learners. God made human beings with brains and gave us curiosity. By design we are inquisitive. We possess "a God-given capacity for apprehension," an ability to discover.[11] God's command to human beings to cultivate and develop his good creation embedded within it a call to pursue knowledge of the world—to observe, study, and experiment. The fall darkened our understanding and twisted our motivations for gaining knowledge. But it did not eliminate our intellectual abilities.

Education is a form of cultivating the mind. The cultural mandate calls us to this, as does our responsibility to steward all that God has given us—including our minds. Our labors of culture making in God's glorious world should be breathtakingly broad. They should include (just to name a few of innumerable examples) writing books of history and poetry; developing science experiments; organizing and categorizing the plant world; plumbing the depths of both the ocean and the human brain; composing symphonies; using physics to construct bridges, buildings, and bioshelters; and reveling in how the beauty of pure mathematics gives us glimpses into the ineffable treasures of God's wisdom and knowledge.

2. The goal of pursuing knowledge and wisdom is to know God and to embrace his mission of shalom in the world. The Bible enthusiastically affirms the pursuit of knowledge and wisdom. Proverbs 18:15 is perhaps one of the best succinct statements of this: "The heart of the discerning acquires knowledge, for the ears of the wise seek it out." God is the source of all knowledge. His understanding has no limit (Ps 147:5). According to Jeremiah 10:12, he "founded the world by his wisdom and stretched out the heavens by his understanding." Strong education programs awaken us to fresh ideas and new discoveries. They can help develop in us a sense of wonder about the world and about the diverse peoples and cultures God has placed in it. Pursuing knowledge is one avenue for learning more about God, his multifaceted creation, and his present work in renewing all things.

This pursuit, though, must be informed by wisdom. Simply learning a bunch of facts or gleaning information from the internet does not lead us inexorably toward God and his purposes. Knowledgeable people may know some facts about a wide variety of topics. But wisdom refers to a deeper sense of understanding about the world. It perceives the connections between things. Wisdom involves having the perspective to apply one's knowledge appropriately in the right settings and times. Wisdom helps us put our knowledge to good use, to direct our labors in alignment with God's mission of shalom for the world.

In reflecting on the purposes of Christian education, Cornelius Plantinga argues that it is "to form students into agents of shalom, models of shalom, witnesses to shalom."[12] To repeat myself, God's vision for the world is shalom—universal flourishing. He has called us to join in his mission. Consequently, Plantinga explains that the overarching goal of Christian education is "equipping young people with the knowledge, the skills, the practices, and the attitudes that can be thrown into the battle for peace, the battle for universal wholeness, justice, and delight. . . . [I]t's folly to expect our sons and daughters to serve and help transform a world they have not studied."[13]

3. Scripture affirms the place of parents as the principal agents of transferring wisdom. Human learning takes place first and foremost in the family. Scripture indicates that parents have a responsibility to pass on wisdom to the younger generation.[14] In Deuteronomy 6:7, God commanded parents to diligently teach their children "when you sit at home and when you walk along the road, when you lie down and when you get up."

Proverbs 1–7 offer a description of how a parent puts into practice this command. Proverbs 4:20-22 is illustrative of the theme of all seven chapters:

My son, pay attention to what I say;
    turn your ear to my words.
Do not let them out of your sight,
    keep them within your heart;
for they are life.

Wisdom is of inestimable value (Prov 4:5-9). "Get wisdom," the father urges the child, "though it cost you all you have."

4. The story of Jesus affirms the educational process. In the incarnation God did not come to earth as a man but as a child. This dignifies childhood and the very human process of development, including intellectual development.

God in his providence set Jesus on earth *as a learner*. It's a mind-boggling idea, given that the second person of the Trinity is also the Logos through whom the whole world was made and the one who is the Truth. But Jesus came not as an already all-knowing divine man. He came as a baby who had to grow up and in the process be educated.[15] We know very little about his actual education. We can surmise that in accordance with Scripture and Jewish custom, his parents, particularly his father, were his first educators.

Given the importance that the Jewish people put on instruction, they also built schools to complement the educational role of the family. As the *Holman Bible Dictionary* notes, after the return of the Israelites from captivity in Babylon "the synagogue spread rapidly and . . . the elementary school system among the Jews developed in connection with the synagogue. Even before the days of Jesus, schools for the young were located in practically every important Jewish community."[16]

According to Shmuel Safrai's *Jewish People of the First Century*, there were more rabbis in the Galilee district than in Judea, which suggests the likelihood of a school in Nazareth.[17] Thus, in addition to what he learned from Mary and Joseph, Jesus may also have attended an elementary school attached to the local synagogue.

Whether or not Jesus was a student at Nazareth Elementary, we know that he "grew in wisdom and stature, and in favor with God and man" (Lk 2:52). And, as the story of Jesus remaining in Jerusalem "in the temple courts, sitting among the teachers" (Lk 2:46) suggests, he was an eager learner.

At some point Jesus learned to read well enough that he was able to read aloud from the scroll of Isaiah in the Nazareth synagogue (Lk 4:16). This set him apart from most Jews: though basic schooling provided rudimentary skills, the ability to read from Torah scrolls was uncommon.[18] Jesus had also learned to write, as indicated in John 7:53–8:11. He was not merely doodling in the sand; the term *graphō*, writing words, is used here.

5. In his word, God teaches us about many things beyond religious matters. The Bible's scope is not limited to discussions of theology, religion, or religious rituals. Apparently, God wants us to learn about a lot more things than just those topics. Consider, as one example, all that the Old Testament law has to say about public health, earth keeping, conflict resolution, and economics. (This is not to say that Scripture is the definitive, comprehensive word on such subjects, as though the Bible could replace all our botany, biology, architecture, medical, or business textbooks. I'm simply noting that God's instructions to the Israelites covered many subjects.)

The broad-ranging nature of biblical teaching is on grand display in the books that are collectively known as the Wisdom literature. The ultimate aim of these books is to point readers to the truth of God, specifically to the insight that God himself is the fount of all knowledge and truth. True wisdom, these books argue, comes from recognizing that "the fear of the LORD is the beginning of wisdom" (Prov 9:10). At the same time, these books do not confine themselves to teaching solely about God or salvation or religious rituals. They celebrate God the Creator and the intricate and vast cosmos he made. The Bible certainly teaches much about God the Redeemer, but the Redeemer is also the Creator. This is the fact that explains the Wisdom literature's place and role within God's kingly rule.[19]

The Wisdom writers have comprehensive interests, offering an amazing breadth of commentary and instruction:

> The range of topics addressed by Old Testament wisdom is remarkable: acquisition of knowledge, epistemology, family, speech, politics, work, business, law, education, government, and so on. . . . Wisdom serves as a reminder that kingdom life embraces every aspect of the creation as God has made it and that Christians are called to serve God in all areas of life, including farming, politics, architecture, winemaking, marriage, eating, etc.[20]

The Old Testament's wise man, Solomon, is depicted as possessing a wide range of knowledge. We read in 1 Kings 4:33 that Solomon could speak with authority about all kinds of plants, from the great cedar of Lebanon to the tiny hyssop that grows from cracks in a wall. He was also learned about animals, birds, small creatures, and fish. Because of his gifting from God, Solomon's knowledge was "as measureless as the sand on the seashore" and his wisdom exceeded that of "all the people of the East" (1 Kings 4:29-30).

6. God's gifts of common grace and general revelation show he desires that nonbelievers, as well as believers, gain broad-ranging knowledge and insight. In his graciousness God supplies common grace to humankind, enabling even those who have turned away from him to possess insight and creativity. This is depicted well in Genesis 4:17-22. This text describes the lineage of Cain, who murdered his brother, Abel. From Cain arose people who became knowledgeable in the fields of animal husbandry, music, and metallurgy. Human beings who worship God *and* human beings who fail to do so both contribute to the advancement of civilization.

Because of common grace, Christians can humbly anticipate that nonbelieving scholars may be helped by God to discern and articulate beautiful truths about the world. All truth—including that discovered by nonbelievers—is God's truth, after all. In *On Christian Doctrine*, Saint Augustine urged believers to plunder the pagan classicists, particularly Plato, because of their wise insights. Even Reformed theologians who embrace the idea of total depravity recognized the genius God has given to scholars who do not serve him or who even worship other gods or no god. John Calvin references a host of secular authors—Homer, Aristotle, Plato, Cicero, Juvenal, and Ovid to name a few—in the *Institutes*. And as Abraham Kuyper once mused, "Precious treasures have come down to us from the old heathen civilization. In Plato you find pages which you devour. Cicero fascinates you and bears you along by his noble tone and stirs up in you holy sentiments."[21]

God's grace is further displayed in what theologians call general revelation. This refers to the ways that God reveals himself through "the creation, preservation, and government of the universe" (as the Belgic Confession puts it). "The heavens declare the glory of God," the psalmist sings in Psalm 19:1. God has revealed his character and his ways through his creation. The apostle Paul explains in Romans 1:20 that "since the creation of the world God's invisible qualities—his eternal power and divine nature—have been clearly seen, being understood from what has been made."

As believers we can enthusiastically advocate for the education of those who do not yet know Christ or who have no interest in pursuing him (i.e., whose motivations for study are different from ours). We can do so because God himself is generous in supplying the gifts of both common grace and general revelation to *all* people, not just believers. Moreover, because of general revelation believers can hope that by assisting nonbelievers in all manner of studies into this world they will be contributing to opening the eyes of their students to the glories of God hidden within nature.

MALFORMATIONS IN THE REALM OF EDUCATION

Many volumes could be written on the ways that our culture, institutions for learning, and philosophies about education have strayed from God's intentions. Indeed, there's already a book on just about every contemporary problem said to be plaguing education. I'll simply mention in cursory form two major malformations. The first has to do with truth and the second with justice.

Malformations of modernity and postmodernity. Christians believe that God himself is truth and the fount of all truth. As the nineteenth-century Dutch theologian Herman Bavinck explained, God is "the primary, the original truth, the source of all truth, the truth in all truth. He is the ground of the truth—of the true being—of all things. . . . God is the source and origin of the knowledge of truth in all areas of life; the light in which alone we can see light, the sun of all spirits."[22]

Christ-followers hold tightly to the idea that an overarching, absolute truth exists and is knowable. Francis Schaeffer coined the phrase *true truth* to connote the idea of the unchanging truth that is rooted in God.[23] To repeat Proverbs 9:10, the Scriptures teach that "The fear *of the* LORD is the beginning of wisdom" (emphasis added). Reverencing God, seeking to learn about and know the One who is the Truth, is the way to find life and wholeness.

The New Testament reiterates this. It teaches us that truth has been incarnated. The Truth is a person: Jesus, the Son of God. Jesus himself tells us plainly: "I am the way and the truth and the life" (Jn 14:6). In other words, the triune God—not human beings—possesses the ultimate wisdom in discerning the True, the Good, and the Beautiful. And the Truth that is God is not a collection of propositions. This Truth is a living, loving being who has called us into fellowship with himself. Followers of Jesus acknowledge his moral authority: he is the shepherd; we are the sheep. *His* voice alone can lead us to the shalom of green pastures. The telos in the pursuit of wisdom and learning is to gain God and his kingdom.

The philosophies or movements that have come to be known in shorthand as modernity and postmodernity have both nurtured malformations in the realm of the True. Modernity's main malformation is its naive and idolatrous conviction that human reason and rationality alone are sufficient for plumbing and comprehending the world. This sensibility leads to the idea that truth consists of only whatever science can empirically confirm. The atheist of modernity is arrogant, disputing not that some truths may exist but that we do not need the power of God (or God's Word) to discover them.

Relatedly, modernity distrusts any authority outside the self. As Tim Keller writes, "In the 18th century, European Enlightenment thinkers insisted that the modern person must question all tradition, revelation, and external authority by subjecting them to the supreme court of his or her own reason and intuition."[24] Modernity claims that humans "are our own moral authority."[25] What matters is the individual's happiness and autonomy.

The main malformation brought into the realm of human learning by the sensibility of postmodernity is its "incredulity toward metanarratives," to use the words of Jean François Lyotard.[26] While modernity was naive in that it supposed human reason could discern ultimate meaning, postmodernists are often hypercynical about the possibility of the existence of ultimate meaning.[27] At the same time, though, much postmodern critique claims that traditional metanarratives are just power plays by dominant groups to continue the oppression of marginalized ones. This implies a moral claim about the injustice of this. But that is incoherent within the thinking of postmodernism since it argues against the possibility of absolute truth. As Keller puts it in regard to postmodern critical theory's ideas about justice, "You cannot insist that all morality is culturally constructed and relative and then claim that your moral claims are not."[28]

With its suspicion of metanarratives, the basic problem with a postmodernist spirit as that relates to the realm of education is its lack of any telos.

The Christian gospel, of course, is a metanarrative—and it holds that God is moving all things toward the future restoration of shalom. Not surprisingly, Christian philosopher Nicholas Wolterstorff titled his reflections on Christian higher education, *Educating for Shalom*. The *for* there is important—and it is what postmodernity lacks.

Educational inequity. A second major malformation in the endowment of the True concerns the substantial degree of educational inequity in our society today. In *Educating All God's Children: What Christians Can—and Should—Do to Improve Public Education for Low-Income Kids*, author Nicole Baker Fulgham summarizes the problems well: "Every urban center and many mixed-income suburban and rural school districts exhibit significant academic disparities between children in wealthier communities and children in low-income areas."[29] Multiple research studies have revealed the problem of educational inequity in the United States. Part of the issue is a funding gap: wealthier school districts can spend far more per student on their schools than can poorer districts.[30] Part of it is unequal access to skilled teachers and quality curriculum.[31] Additionally, poor school districts have "more students in need of extra help, and yet they have fewer guidance counselors, tutors, psychologists, lower-paid teachers, more dilapidated facilities and bigger class sizes than wealthier districts."[32]

The principle of common grace "suggests that equitable public schools are within the realm of God's concern for humanity."[33] God cares enough for unbelieving farmers that he sends them—not just the believing farmers—rain. God cares that *all* children are educated, not just the children of believers. It is not a stretch to assume that God cares about the state of our public schools.

Supporting quality education of all children (believers and nonbelievers) is a matter of justice. This is because of the connections between literacy, learning, and human flourishing that we examined earlier. God desires that all people flourish and that the church play its part in facilitating that. Christians cannot sit idly by while some children receive a poor-quality education and their prospects for flourishing are thereby diminished. In practical terms today, this means that Christ-followers are obligated to respond to the sad realities of educational inequity in our public schools.

It appears that the vast majority of US Christians—eight out of ten church-going believers according to 2014 research by the Barna Group—support the idea of Christians helping public schools. Survey respondents tended to give two reasons for their position. One was that efforts to improve public education were important for demonstrating Christian concern for the wider community. The other was that investment in public schools was viewed as an expression of the Christian responsibility to help the poor and needy.[34]

The same survey, though, also spotlighted some hostility to public schools. Nine percent of respondents said churches shouldn't get involved in public schools because the culture at the schools is contrary to religious beliefs. Sixteen percent said that public schools "need more prayer and religious value, not academic support."[35] At least some believers, it would seem, need convincing that the kind of investment Grace Point Church in Pennsylvania made is appropriate.

Theologian and author Jemar Tisby reports that he was surprised by the anti-public-school attitude of many of his classmates at the evangelical seminary he attended:

> Some contended that it was, at best, neglectful and, at worst, sinful for Christians to surrender their children to the secular humanism oozing from the pages of science textbooks and dripping from the lips of liberal educators. But I never thought inculcating one's children with a vibrant faith in Jesus Christ and concern for public schools were mutually exclusive. More significantly, when I thought about public education, I thought about the children.[36]

Rather than abandoning public schools, Tisby argues that investment by the church in them is a matter of biblical justice. While many middle- and upper-class Christ-followers can choose a different schooling option for their children, many low-income families lack the funds for private education. Tisby does not dispute that a Christian family might choose to place their kids in private Christian schools for good reasons. He just argues that "personal choice about education shouldn't prevent us from doing Micah 6:8."[37]

CHRISTIANITY'S CONTRIBUTIONS TO THE REALM
OF KNOWLEDGE AND HUMAN LEARNING

The following historical scan of how Christ-followers have strengthened the community endowment of the True is necessarily incomplete. By noting five areas of contribution I hope to inspire some creative thinking about contemporary ways believers today can contribute to needed re-formations in this endowment.

Christianity and books. Christianity hastened the movement toward the codex (book) form over scrolls. Like their theological forebears the Jews, followers of Christ revered sacred texts. As the New Testament writings developed, Christians sought to preserve them in book form, often using vellum, a more durable material than papyrus rolls.[38] This form, more than scrolls, allowed for easier comparative studies of sources. That was important to believers as they cross-referenced between Old and New Testament texts and within the New Testament writings.

Moreover, Christianity's evangelizing impulse "produced a stream of books" and commentaries, translations, and polemical pamphlets distributed wide and far to "disseminate and explain" the faith.[39]

When the marauding barbarians of the fifth century toppled the Roman Empire, Christian monasteries preserved libraries. Christian monks toiling silently in scriptoriums copied religious and secular texts, thus preserving irreplaceable treasures of the ancient world. Thomas Cahill tells this tale in a thorough and entertaining way in his book *How the Irish Saved Civilization.*

Christianity and literacy. Early Christians, with Jesus' words from the Great Commission ringing in their ears ("make disciples of all nations . . . teaching them to obey everything I have commanded you"), embraced the vocation of education. In the first few centuries following Christ's death, for example, Christians' desire to practice lectio divina, meditatively reading and studying the Holy Scriptures, engendered activity to teach converts to read.[40]

Later, in the fourteenth century, John Wycliffe, seminary professor at the University of Oxford, translated the Latin Scriptures into English so that those unschooled in Latin could read them. Today, the Bible translating mission named in his honor has translated the Scriptures into over five hundred languages worldwide.

The sixteenth-century Protestant Reformation is credited by many scholars as the driving force for education in Europe. The Reformers encouraged people to learn to read so that they could read the Bible for themselves. Martin Luther led the effort to translate the Scriptures into German. Some scholars credit the so-called Second Reformation—the German Pietist movements in the seventeenth and eighteenth centuries—with having an even greater impact on literacy rates.[41]

The Reformers' view of the priesthood of all believers contributed to increased educational opportunities for women. "The Protestant Reformers' study of Scripture and the resulting conviction of the equality of all believers before God led them to initiate changes in the way education, the church, family, and societal structures were conceived," writes Talbot School of Theology professor Karen Stetina. "As a result of the Reformation, women were given new opportunities to be educated, participate in the church and in the family, and share the Gospel."[42]

Throughout the developing world, conversion to Christianity has been associated with rising literacy rates and expanded educational opportunities, particularly for women.[43] Baylor University sociologist Robert Woodberry has conducted long-term, groundbreaking research on the influence of the nineteenth-century "conversionary Protestants"—missionaries active in evangelism who emphasized lay vernacular Bible reading and were not funded by the state. His careful study over fourteen years, involving extensive historical research on the ground in developing countries, interviews with church historians from around the globe, and a massive amount of statistical analysis, concluded that

> Areas where Protestant missionaries had a significant presence in the past are on average more economically developed today, with comparatively better health, lower infant mortality, lower corruption, *greater literacy, higher educational attainment (especially for women),* and more robust membership in nongovernmental associations.[44]

Christianity has continued to contribute to women's literacy to an extent greater than the influence of other major world religions. A 2016 study of over 150 countries by the Pew Research Center, for example, found that the educational attainment gap between men and women among Christians is just 0.4 years. This was lower than the gender gap among Buddhists (1.1 years), Muslims (1.5 years), and Hindus (2.7 years).[45]

Christianity and scientific inquiry: Renaissance and Enlightenment. In his provocative book *The Victory of Reason*, sociologist of religion Rodney Stark argues that "the rise of science [rested] entirely on religious foundations, and the people who brought it about were devout Christians."[46] Stark discusses how Christian faith, with its emphasis on a rational God who created a coherent world, spurred logical investigation of that world. The early church fathers, Stark emphasizes, embraced reason. In the second century, for example, Tertullian taught that "reason is a thing of God, inasmuch as there is nothing which God the Maker of all has not provided, disposed, ordained by reason—nothing which He has not willed should be handled and understood by reason."[47] In the Middle Ages, Christian monks freed themselves from what Stark calls "the stultifying grip of Roman repression and mistaken Greek idealism," and developed all kinds of innovations: chimneys, clocks, eyeglasses, the water wheel, fish farming, and the three-field system of agriculture.[48]

In Europe many of the leading artists, inventors, and scientists of the Renaissance and Enlightenment eras were Christians. Copernicus, Kepler, Galileo, and Pascal were all practicing Christians who embraced the church fathers' idea of God's self-revelation in nature. Holding a teleological view of the world and worshiping the Creator, they affirmed the earth's material goodness and enthusiastically engaged in the scientific investigation of it.

The seventeenth-century Royal Society of London for Improving Natural Knowledge was founded by a Christian—the famous architect Christopher Wren—and many members were Puritans or other Protestants. Various fathers of the sciences were Catholic laymen, including Roger Bacon, credited as an early advocate of the scientific method, Andreas Vesalius (human anatomy), Gregor Mendel (pioneer of genetics), Antoine Lavoisier (chemistry), and Augustin-Louis Cauchy (calculus).

The Enlightenment, too, was not as secular as many think. Yale professor David Sorkin's 2008 book, *The Religious Enlightenment: Protestants, Jews, and Catholics from London to Vienna*, examined in a case-study method several leading intellectuals of the period—including the German Protestant theologian and historian Siegmund Jakob Baumgarten, the English

churchman and literary critic William Warburton, and the influential
Genevan pastor Jacob Vernet—to support his thesis that "the Enlightenment
was not only compatible with religious belief, but even conducive to it."[49]
One reviewer commented after reading Sorkin's work, "Religion was not
always the object of disapprobation but very often drove and invigorated the
intellectual debates of the time."[50]

Christianity and schools. Early Christian education was primarily about
teaching the ways of the faith to the next generation, but—in keeping with
the tradition noted earlier of the Wisdom literature—it was not limited to
religious subjects. In the second century Saint Ignatius, bishop of Antioch,
encouraged the congregation at Philadelphia to teach their children both
the Scriptures and a trade.[51] The fathers established catechetical schools in
Ephesus, Rome, Alexandria, and elsewhere. These schools emphasized theological education but eventually added grammar and at times mathematics
and medicine to the curriculum.

Notably, Christians engaged in teaching men and women together in the
same setting. This coed model was revolutionary. Moreover, Christian education was not limited only to the wealthy.[52] Between the fourth and tenth
centuries, Christian bishops maintained schools for girls and boys from all
different ethnicities and socioeconomic backgrounds. These schools taught
Christian doctrine and the seven liberal arts (grammar, rhetoric, logic, arith-
metic, music, geometry, and astronomy).[53]

With the advent of the Reformation, Christian engagement in literacy
and education dramatically increased. Leading Reformers such as John Hus,
Martin Luther, Ulrich Zwingli, John Calvin, and John Knox all contributed
to the expansion of Christian schools. Calvin and Luther advocated universal education, and it may be that Luther was the first to suggest the idea
of compulsory, tax-supported public elementary education.[54] Luther even
favored schools for girls, quite a progressive idea for his time. Luther's principal coworker, Phillip Melanchthon, successfully persuaded German authorities to implement a public school system there.[55]

Under Calvin's urging and leadership, Calvinists in Switzerland, France,
England, Hungary, Holland, Scotland, and America established thousands
of elementary and secondary schools.[56] Writing about the English Puritans,
for example, literacy historian Harvey Graff notes that "Puritan strongholds

were among the most education-conscious and literate centers in England. . . . Household and schoolhouse, as well as pulpit and chapel, were centers of schooling. Puritans were for their day a reading people. . . . To an impressive degree, they effected an educational revolution."[57] In Massachusetts, Puritans pioneered the idea of public schools in the colonial period. The Massachusetts School Law of 1647 required that "every town with 50 households or more hire someone to teach the children to read and write."[58] This public education was paid for by property taxes.

In England the indefatigable Evangelicals of the Victorian period launched a variety of educational efforts, including so-called Ragged Schools for the poorest children. These schools were established in the districts of the working poor and provided basic education in reading, math, and the Bible. British Evangelicals were also highly active in starting Sunday schools. In addition to religious instruction, these schools taught reading, manners, sanitation, and punctuality. According to historian Herbert Schlossberg, during the first half of the nineteenth century the number of Sunday schools grew from 2,290 to 23,135 and involved over two million children.[59]

Christ-followers were responsible for many achievements in education.[60] The British Evangelical James Kay-Shuttlesworth was arguably "the main influence on the direction of teacher training" in England.[61] A Lutheran layman, Johann Sturm, conceived of the idea of graded education. Sturm introduced the gymnasium—a secondary level of education—to France. The German Christ-follower Friedrich Froebel was the first to introduce formal education to very young children. He used a structured, activity-based learning method, establishing the first kindergarten in 1840.[62]

Christianity and higher education. While ancient Greece produced brilliant philosophers still read and studied today, men like Plato and Aristotle did not found permanent *institutions* of higher learning. They did not build libraries, engage in empirical research, or certify their students. The roots of the modern universities are found instead in early Christianity.

In the fifth and sixth centuries some bishops established cathedral schools to provide an educated clergy for the churches. Some of these schools ultimately became the West's first universities. In the early medieval period, monasteries were the center of intellectual culture, learning, and libraries.[63] The church-supported universities grew throughout Europe in the eleventh and twelfth centuries. The university at Salerno became a leading medical school while Bologna University specialized in canon and civil law. Ignatius Loyola's Jesuit missionaries brought both Catholic faith and Western learning to the Far East as well as to Central and South America, establishing schools and colleges as well as churches.

In the seventeenth and eighteenth centuries in the United States, many universities began as Christian schools. Harvard University (1636), for example, was established by the Congregational Church. The Episcopal Church launched the College of William and Mary (1693). Presbyterians established Princeton University (1746), Washington and Lee University (1749), and Hampden-Sydney College (1776). The Methodists founded Brown University (1764), and the Dutch Reformed Church founded Rutgers University (1766).

Indeed, writes American historian George Marsden, "until the Civil War era, the vast majority of American colleges were founded by churches" and these were seen not only as "church colleges, but also public institutions."[64] The Methodist Church was especially active in launching universities, including Emory University (1836), Duke University (1838), Boston University (1839), and Northwestern University (1851). Baptists founded Mercer University (1833) and Wake Forest University (1824). By 1881, 80 percent of all colleges in the United States were church-related and private.

Christian churches and denominations continue to be vibrantly involved in higher education today. The Council for Christian Colleges and Universities counts over 150 schools in its ranks. Altogether there are over 900 colleges and universities with a Christian affiliation.[65]

Secondary and university education in the Black community. The Black church in America has a long and rich history of engagement in all kinds of social welfare and economic development activities, including involvement in education. Many of today's historically Black colleges and universities (HBCUs) have strong religious roots.[66] In 1867, for example, Springfield Baptist Church, the oldest independent African American church in the United States, established the Augusta Institute in its basement. Today it is known as Morehouse College.

The African Methodist Episcopal Church (AME) is illustrative of the efforts of Black churches in promoting education. The AME founded a variety of universities, for example, Ohio's Wilberforce University, in the 1860s. By 1880 the denomination operated more than two thousand schools, chiefly in the South, with 155,000 students. Drawing from research originally conducted by W. E. B. Du Bois, sociologist John Sibley Butler found that just in the period 1897–1903, the AME invested $1.6 million in education.[67] In the twentieth century and particularly during Jim Crow, the AME utilized church buildings for schoolhouses, many pastor's wives became schoolteachers, and congregants sacrificially pooled their resources to keep education alive for Black children when segregated public schools were starved of funds.[68] Today, eighteen colleges and seminaries operate in conjunction with the AME denomination.[69]

WRAPPING UP: TWENTIETH-CENTURY CAVEATS AND A TWENTY-FIRST-CENTURY VISION

The picture I've painted in this chapter is true: the church has played an impressive role throughout the centuries in strengthening the endowment of the True. But two shadows have to be mentioned briefly to be fair to the full history.

One concerns the strain of anti-intellectualism within evangelical and fundamentalist Christianity. Some scholars see this as rooted in the populist awakenings in the eighteenth and nineteenth centuries.[70] Mark Noll, author of the landmark book *The Scandal of the Evangelical Mind*, offered this list of evangelicalism's "built-in barriers" to careful and constructive thinking:

> an immediatism that insists on action, decision, and even perfection right now, a populism that confuses winning supporters with mastering actual existing situations, an anti-traditionalism that privileges one's own current judgments on biblical, theological, and ethical issues (however hastily formed) over insight from the past (however hard won and carefully stated), and a nearly gnostic dualism that rushes to spiritualize all manner of bodily, terrestrial, physical, and material realities (despite the origin and providential maintenance of these realities in God).[71]

Ten years after publishing *Scandal*, Noll wrote in *First Things* that he was heartened by some positive developments within evangelicalism. These

included "a renascence of Christian philosophy," the move in many evangelical colleges to "season their sectarian certitudes with commitment to
'mere Christianity'" and "to promote the academic life as a legitimate
Christian vocation," "the multiplying Christian presence in the nation's plu-
ralistic universities," and the establishment of Christian Study Centers at
several top-notch secular universities.[72]

Still, as Baylor University professor Alan Jacobs (author of the 2017 book
How to Think) told an interviewer, "There's no question that conservative
evangelicalism—within which I include fundamentalism—has been an
overwhelmingly activist movement that has had little time for scholarly, or
more generally intellectual, reflection."[73] Evangelicals' anti-intellectualism
baggage is lighter these days but still there.

The other deeply troubling phenomenon that must be mentioned is the
shameful story of some White Christians' withdrawal from public schools
in the wake of the 1954 school-integration decision, *Brown v. Board of Education*, to avoid mixing their children with Black children. Many Whites—
northern, southern, Christian, and non-Christian—were disturbed by the
Supreme Court's ruling and moved to found private academies for White
children only or transferred their children to existing private schools.[74]

Facing these realities from the twentieth century is painful. But it can
provide the impetus for moving ahead in fresh ways. Christianity's history in
the story of the spread of education is largely a positive one. Christ-followers
have opportunities now to live into that legacy as well as to redemptively
repair the harm that has been done in more recent decades. The stories in
the next chapter illustrate a variety of ways this is being attempted.

5

A STRATEGY FOR CULTIVATING THE TRUE

PARTNER IN PUBLIC EDUCATION

GRACE POINT CHURCH in Lancaster County, Pennsylvania, is not the only one to hire an employee dedicated to serving the public schools. Southlake Church in West Linn, Oregon, placed member Heather Huggitt full time in an office at Roosevelt High School so she could help address students' needs for food, clothing, and school supplies and coordinate a mentoring program.[1]

The relationship between the affluent megachurch and the low-income school twenty-six miles to the northwest began in June 2009 with a massive one-day school cleanup and landscaping day. Southlake's senior pastor, Kip Jackson, had encouraged a strong turnout, but even he was surprised when nearly fifteen hundred of the church's two thousand members showed up.

Southlake's outreach pastor, Kristine Sommers, divided the crowd into small teams tackling different aspects of the project. One leader enthused that a punch list that "would have taken three years to complete" was finished that day.[2] School personnel estimated the volunteers had saved the school about $250,000.

Given that initial success, school leaders invited Southlake volunteers to consider helping in other ways. Members responded, returning to serve as tutors despite the long drive. "The needs were so great," Jacob says. "We just filled gaps and met needs, and they kept inviting us in to do that to the point where they invited us to have a staff person with an office in the school to help coordinate volunteers."[3]

Over time the church set up a clothes closet at the school, where students could grab needed items. Church volunteers met with students to help them with speech lessons and mock job interviews. When the school established an onsite daycare center to enable teen moms and dads to stay in school, church members came and babysat for free.[4] Neil Lomax, a former NHL quarterback from Southlake, offered to help out the Roosevelt Roughriders football team. The football coach snapped him up, making Lomax his offensive coordinator. Within two seasons the team broke its fifteen-year losing streak and made the playoffs.[5]

"One of the things about the suburbs is, we're nice," says Jackson. "And I did a study of the word 'nice' once. It comes from the Latin word 'to ignore.' And we are good at ignoring a lot of things." Seven years after partnering with Roosevelt, Jackson says, "We're not as nice now. . . . When you come out of ignorance and become aware of needs that are real-life needs in the community, it helps you come out of your own self-interest and be able to make a difference in the world."[6]

PUBLIC EDUCATION: BIG CHALLENGES

Over fifty million kids are educated in the US public school system. Many receive a good education, do well, and enjoy a healthy, safe school environment. But many don't. Education statistics paint a worrying picture of academic performance. According to data from the National Center for Education Statistics' May 2020 report, "The Condition of Education," about a third of fourth graders nationwide score below basic proficiency in reading, as do just over one-quarter of seniors.[7] Elementary school kids fare better in math, but older students struggle. In 2015, 38 percent of high school seniors were below proficiency. Nationwide, the high school graduation rate is 85 percent. But the rate is ten percentage points lower for Black students.[8]

The quality of the school environment also matters to kids and parents. Here, too, there are concerns. In the 2019 "Indicators of School Crime and Safety" report from the US Department of Education, researchers reported that 71 percent of schools reported one or more violent incidents occurring during the school year.[9] There were sixty-six school shootings in 2018–2019.[10] Twenty-eight percent of middle schools reported having bullying incidents at least once a week.[11]

Added to this is the persistent inequality of education in the United States by race and class. Decades after *Brown v. Board of Education*, US schools remain highly segregated. A 2019 study by EdBuild, for example, found that "More than half of the nation's schoolchildren are in racially concentrated districts, where over 75 percent of students are either white or nonwhite."[12]

Meanwhile, leading scholars argue that reform efforts have largely been ineffective. Criticism comes from both liberals and conservatives. University of Chicago professor Charles M. Payne laments, "We have too often been more invested in our paradigms than in solving the problems they address."[13]

PARTNERSHIPS FOR EDUCATION: SIX APPROACHES

Education matters for a strong, healthy, democratic society. Education woes, then, must concern all citizens. Education matters deeply for human flourishing; not caring about it isn't an option for Christ-followers. Some may give themselves to the beautiful work of explicitly Christian education. In so doing they push back against the malformations in the realm of the True that we just examined. Others can invest in public education, thus reforming the True in God's creational intent to see all people develop their God-given intellect and curiosity. Today many congregations are taking up the cause of loving their neighbors by strengthening their local K–12 schools, bolstering higher education, and supporting various forms of adult education. The rest of this chapter examines six ways churches are engaged as partners in public education in their communities.

1. Partnering with principals: Caring for Kids, Kansas City. "Local schools offer a window into the community like no other," says Reggie McNeal, author of several books about church-based community engagement. "Many church leaders have found that working with schools offers them a robust way of engaging with their communities."[14] Whatever the issues in a community—poverty, gangs, mental illness, homelessness, hunger—you will find them in the schools.

Throughout the country, churches of every size and denomination have shown they can make a significant contribution to strengthening schools and helping children and youth to thrive. Some congregations have gotten engaged in their local schools with the help of an intermediary organization that plays a brokering role between schools and community organizations. Caring for Kids (CFK) in Kansas City is one such intermediary (see caringforkidskc.org).

CFK has helped to build multisector partnerships involving civic agencies, faith-based organizations, businesses, and nonprofits around some eighty-plus schools, mostly elementary, from seven different area school districts. Hundreds of churches, businesses, and nonprofit organizations are engaged.

The CFK partnerships at each school are driven by specific goals established by the principal. A designated school liaison works alongside a staff member from CFK to facilitate the collaborative involvement of churches and community organizations. Representatives from these partner organizations typically gather monthly at the school for meetings with the principal and school liaison.

The principals' goals vary from school to school. Nonetheless, a few common themes are noticeable. Most are looking to improve student attendance, academic achievement, and parental engagement. The principals also usually desire to implement activities that tangibly demonstrate appreciation for teachers. Sometimes school leaders hope that community partners will assist with physical plant improvements, such as installing gardens onsite. Others are looking to churches to help with material needs in poor students' families, such as help with food or utility bills.

Mitchell says that churches "are involved in greater and lesser degrees. Some simply participate in backpack drives while others have congregants and even senior pastors serving in the schools as reading buddies."[15] However, as relationships and trust build, so does the investment in the partnership. The churches and other community partners, such as local businesses, collectively have invested over $841,000 in the public schools.

Churches of different sizes and assets have participated fruitfully in school partnerships brokered by CFK. For example, Christ Church Mission, a congregation of about two hundred attendees, joined the CFK partnership at Rushton Elementary School in Mission, Kansas, in 2017. It participates alongside the other CFK partners in teacher appreciation activities at Christmas, providing gift bags to teachers. Once a week two different families from the church sign up to supply and deliver perishables like milk, cheese, and fresh produce to the school's food pantry. Many families are also involved in the annual fall backpack/school supplies drive. The church's most important contribution at Rushton, though, is its afterschool program.

About sixteen congregants run a series of five-week sessions, each of which offers kids the chance to join a different club—basketball, crafting, cooking, music, board games—that meets once a week. Rushton's school social worker, Cathy Lorino, enthuses that the students "really wouldn't have had an opportunity to engage in extracurriculars without these clubs."[16] She also credits them with encouraging social-emotional learning among the students.

Vida Abundante Church is an eighteen-year-old Spanish-speaking congregation of around 130 members. It partners with Frances Willard Elementary School, primarily by providing a robust afterschool program in a community center located just two blocks from the school. The center offers homework help and arts-oriented enrichment activities for children. Most of the volunteers are teenagers from the church. Raquel Lara, volunteer youth pastor at Vida Abundante, explains that this is a positive way for the teens to express their artistic gifts and to gain leadership skills. Church volunteers also serve as translators at the school's quarterly Family Engagement Nights. The congregation is visible to school families through the various activities of the CFK team. That familiarity has led to an increased number of parents enrolling in night classes—cooking, fitness, ESL (English as a Second Language)—at the church's community center. The congregation has also mobilized a crew of volunteers to do grounds maintenance and beautification at the school, planting rose bushes and other flowers. Principal Cesar Alvarez is passionate about gardening, and so the CFK partners helped to establish a garden on ground that is used for educational purposes with the kids. Volunteers from Vida Abundante help with maintaining it.

2. Supplementing public education through out-of-school programming. Parents, kids, and educators want and need strong afterschool programs in their communities. Already it's estimated that about six in ten children participate in afterschool activities, with another nineteen million parents reporting that they would enroll their children in such a program if one were available to them.[17] Meanwhile, a survey for the National Association of Elementary School Principals found that 77 percent believe afterschool programs are "extremely important."[18] The enthusiasm is understandable given that several meta-analyses of afterschool initiatives credit structured afterschool programs with at least modest success in improving academic performance, school bonding, and positive social behaviors.[19]

Complementing classroom education with STEAM. In the Homewood neighborhood of Pittsburgh, Bible Center Church (BCC) has been operating an afterschool initiative called the Maker's Clubhouse since 2011. Before the coronavirus pandemic, the Maker's Clubhouse (TMC) was serving over one hundred children after school on Mondays through Fridays. The kids come from the community's two public elementary schools: Lincoln Elementary and Faison Elementary. The student body at both schools is roughly 95 percent African American. The vast majority of these kids are from low-income families.

TMC's effectiveness and creativity stem in large part from the fact that BCC's pastors—John and Cynthia Wallace—are both educators. John is a college professor at the University of Pittsburgh. Cynthia served as a principal for seventeen years. They believe education is a game-changer in kids' lives, and their congregants agree. In 2019, church leaders held strategic planning meetings with staff, board members, and congregants, discussing the things they most value and their biggest priorities. "The work that we do with children and the Maker's Clubhouse was number 1," reports Cynthia.[20] "We think there's promise in children."

TMC runs a STEAM-focused program. Children work on highly interactive enrichment activities around five foci: science, technology, engineering, agriculture, and math. Cynthia explains that with the advent of the federal No Child Left Behind legislation, schools increasingly focused on reading and math, the main subjects tested. This meant that science got short shrift. Many local schools taught a total of only nine weeks of science during the typical school year. Bible Center Church leaders knew they needed to try to supplement that. "We're not trying to *be* the school," Cynthia emphasizes. "We're trying to partner with them. I think we do a good job of working collaboratively, providing things that in the school's curriculum haven't been highlighted as much as they should have been."

Another reason for the church's emphasis on STEAM was the Wallaces' insights about the connections between schooling and the work world. "The world is changing, and the problem is that schools have not kept up," Cynthia says. "There are so many jobs that children in our community, even coming out of high school, will not be qualified to do. They don't have the prerequisite STEM knowledge. They have not been taught to be problem-solvers and innovators."

Kids at TMC, though, are exposed to robotics, aquaponics, and all manner of science and engineering projects. TMC's special science and engineering festival on Martin Luther King Jr. Day in January 2020, for example, featured kids playing Pac-Man using handheld apples and oranges with embedded electronic circuits connected to laptops. Kerri Clauser, a former BCC staff member who played a key role in developing TMC, remembers how leaders started using the creative design process with students in 2015. "It teaches kids to walk through forming a hypothesis, identifying action steps to take, [and] if you failed, what you will do different next time," she explains.[21]

The *A* in the church's STEAM program stands for agriculture. BCC started an urban microfarm in the neighborhood in 2016. Called Oasis Farm and Fishery, it produces herbs and vegetables for local vendors, including a coffee shop called Everyday Café that the church launched as a social enterprise in 2016. Farm manager Tacumba Turner teaches seventy-five-minute lessons for around fifty kids. On any given day kids might be touring the farm's bioshelter, learning the basic chemistry undergirding its hydroponics system, or harvesting kale. Kids in the "Better Food, Better Me" elective learn where their food comes from and the importance of nutrition. They also cook healthy meals using ingredients from the farm. "We're providing experiences that shift their perceptions," Tacumba says. "We're showing them that science and technology is a cool thing."[22]

TMC is also addressing educational inequities. As Clauser says, "We [had] to address the opportunity gap. We knew that our students didn't get access to science or art all the time. Kids in wealthier schools in the district were having opportunities our kids weren't. We wanted our kids to have those same opportunities as well, to set them up for success."

Not every congregation enjoys the educational expertise resident at Bible Center Church. But any congregation that adopts the same attitude BCC has taken can make a difference in serving their community's kids. Cynthia sums up that attitude well: "We are servants to the community. We are not a Sunday-only church."

Filling the gap: Music education. Since 2008, 80 percent of public schools have experienced budget cuts.[23] And when money is tight, according to Jessica Hoffmann Davis, author of *Why Our Schools Need the Arts*, the arts are "the single discipline that's always on the chopping block."[24] Additionally, kids in poorer school systems typically have less access to the arts and music than students in wealthier districts.

That is particularly troubling in light of research suggesting connections between arts engagement and academic performance among lower-income students. A study by the National Endowment for the Arts, for example, found that 74 percent of eighth graders from poor households who were involved in the arts from kindergarten through elementary school showed higher scores in science and reading. High school students who had high levels of arts engagement were more likely to say they were headed to college.[25]

Most people agree the arts enrich our lives. Increasingly, research seems to indicate they also help make kids smarter.[26] That's two good reasons to work to ensure that all students have access to arts and music.

Churches have a great opportunity to step in here. Many already have youth music programs like choirs or handbell groups. Churches often own musical instruments like pianos, guitars, and drum sets. Some have special practice rooms for their choirs. Some have talented musicians on staff, and most have at least some musicians sitting in their pews. Some congregations have dance programs or drama clubs. Others have visual artists and ceramists on their membership rolls. The question is whether all these arts assets are being used only for the benefit of the church or also for the good of the community.

David Goins, director of music and worship at First United Methodist Church in Frankfort, Kentucky, started the Wesley Academy of Music as an outreach ministry for low-income students in 2017. The church raised the start-up funds for the new initiative by producing the musical *Joseph and the Amazing Technicolor Dreamcoat*. The performances attracted over one thousand people. Proceeds from ticket sales went toward providing free or reduced-cost music lessons for children in the church and community who could not afford such lessons.[27]

The academy operates out of the church building. Kids receive private lessons for thirty minutes using their own instrument or one provided by the academy. In its second summer the academy hosted a week-long band camp and a week-long strings camp. The church has continued to support the academy through ticket sales to special concerts and theater productions put on by their talented members.

3. One-on-one mentoring: Kids Hope USA. In 2011 a team of social scientists published a meta-analysis of seventy-three mentoring programs serving children and adolescents. The researchers found that "active mentoring as an intervention helped to improve children's school achievement and helped to counter poor behavior, drug use, and depression compared to young people who did not receive the help."[28] A 2013 study of the impact of mentoring on youth involved in Big Brothers Big Sisters in Canada also found positive results. Among the nearly one thousand youngsters studied, "children with mentors were more confident in schoolwork and had better behavior and less emotional turmoil."[29]

Pairing elementary students one-on-one in mentoring relationships with caring adults is what Kids Hope USA (KHUSA) has been doing for twenty-five years. Currently, the ministry is active in thirty-seven states, engaged in some twelve hundred church-school partnerships serving about ten thousand children each week.[30] The largest faith-based mentoring program in the United States for elementary school students, KHUSA was the brainchild of Virgil Gulker. Gulker is a trained social worker and Christian social entrepreneur passionate about engaging churches in the lives of vulnerable children.

The KHUSA model is simple: one church adopts one school and provides volunteer mentors who work one-on-one with a student recommended by school officials. The volunteers are screened by the schools and visit on campus for one hour each week. A small evaluation of the program by a doctoral student at the University of Houston found that mentored kids performed better academically and had better school attendance than compared with a control group.[31]

Churches of many different denominations, locations, and sizes have implemented KHUSA mentoring programs. Fielder Church in Arlington, Texas, is one of the larger ones. This three thousand-plus member, racially diverse Southern Baptist congregation has been active in school-based mentoring since 2014. The partnership began after Fielder's lead pastor, Jason

Paredes, contacted the superintendent of the Arlington Independent School District to ask how the church could support the local schools. The superintendent's reply was, "mentor students." So, church staff reached out to Kids Hope for training.

Connie Holland, a retired high school teacher who's been at Fielder since 1988, serves as the volunteer KHUSA program director. She says the ministry aligns well with the church's DNA. "We're very missions-minded here," she says. The church also counts "radical generosity" as one of its five core values.

Notably, nationwide and at Fielder, around 90 percent of the KHUSA mentors stick with their assigned children for more than one year. Typically volunteers only step away if they have a job change or a health issue.

Pastor Paredes himself serves as a mentor as does missions pastor Jared Yates. Paredes and other clergy talk about the mentoring initiative from the pulpit "often," says Holland. The church's 2026 vision document calls for Fielder to be active in ten schools by then, providing five hundred mentors. Asked why she thinks Paredes is so enthusiastic about this particular form of community outreach, Holland laughs and says, "Maybe because he has six kids of his own." She adds, "He has a big heart for our community, . . . and if you don't take care of the kids in the community, you know, that's the future." The church office is "just a parking lot away from the administration building of our school district," Holland says. "Everybody knows about our desire to have mentors in our schools. Everybody knows about Service Sundays. The school district knows who they can come to for help."

Last year the church fielded 192 mentors to nine public schools, six in the Arlington Independent School District. Those six are Title 1 schools, with many students whose parents are working two or three jobs "just to put food on the table." These kids love the one-on-one attention they get from their Kids Hope mentors. Their teachers, Holland says, report that they see changes in mentored kids' self-confidence and self-esteem, and sometimes in their attendance too.

KHUSA says that due to the simplicity of their model, churches of any size can operate a mentoring ministry that makes a genuine difference. In Knoxville, Tennessee, Marietta Cumberland Presbyterian Church has fielded up to thirty mentors annually at Hardin Valley Elementary School for the past eleven years—and its congregation is composed of only around one hundred members. In addition, nearly fifty members of the flock are signed up as prayer partners. The program's volunteer director, Lisa Douglas, says, "You are truly talking about a congregation where everyone is involved on some level, even if they're not a mentor or a prayer partner."[32]

At the beginning of the school year the church brings in a catered lunch for all the teachers. They celebrate them again on Valentine's Day by providing free donuts. The church "adopts" students for the Angel Tree program and provides food and gifts at Thanksgiving. Congregants throw a huge party at the school at the end of the year, inviting all the Kids Hope children, their families, and teachers. "We're extremely involved with the school," Douglas sums up.

Asked if the program is visible at the church, Douglas laughs. "Kids Hope is the topic of conversation every Sunday." The relationships forged in the school have continued outside. Before the pandemic, ten mentors were inviting their students to Sunday morning worship services. Their energy enlivens the services, Douglas reports with a smile.

Marietta Cumberland has also integrated the KHUSA kids into their normal summer activities. The "FROG Days of Summer" program (Fully Reliant on God) occurs over five Sundays starting in mid-June. Children participate in the church service, stay for lunch, and then enjoy special activities—learning tennis, doing arts and crafts, going on special field trips.

Kids Hope USA is a great fit for the church. Asked about Marietta Cumberland's core values, Douglas replies, "Our church has always been about being outwardly focused." The flock includes a high number of educators: twelve teachers, a school counselor, a youth speech therapist, and three college professors. The pastor's wife was formerly a special education teacher at Hardin Valley. Douglas thinks all this played a role in how quickly and well the KHUSA program was adopted and supported. There is a conviction among the flock about the importance of education.

4. Rites of passage mentoring programs. As noted in chapter four, God intends for elders to instruct the next generation in life lessons. The transfer of knowledge occurs not only in formal schools but also in nonformal settings. Consider, for example, the ways that young people can learn wisdom from their sports coaches. Another way that churches can strengthen the realm of the True is to offer out-of-school programs for adolescents through which they can gain wisdom from their elders.

Jewish congregations have long done this through their bar and bat mitzvah practices. Fuller Youth Institute's Brad Griffin explains that these ceremonies help adolescents enter into new levels of responsibility to God and to the community.[33] He believes that the Christian church needs to do better in intentionally providing programs and rituals that assist adolescents transitioning to adulthood. "Ritual *teaches* us," Griffin argues, in ways underestimated by the church.

African American churches have done better at this than many others by instituting rites of passage programs and mentoring. Abyssinian Baptist Church in New York City, for example, developed the Blue Nile Passage rites of passage program in 1994. The Christian, Afrocentric program combines eight months of Saturday teaching sessions with mentoring by mature Christian women and men. The ministry continues today and has served over one thousand youth.[34] On the other side of the country, Allen Temple Baptist Church in Oakland, California, offers the Boys' Rite of Passage program to youth ages thirteen to seventeen from inside and outside the church.[35] The program meets weekly for a few hours on Saturdays. Led by mature men from the church, the ministry aims to instill biblical wisdom and life skills into adolescent males. By doing so it hopes to reduce these young men's engagement in risky behaviors and to "take seriously the need for achievement in school and to gain the understanding of how excellence in educational achievement will positively impact every aspect of their lives."[36]

Not all of these initiatives are for boys. Rev. Richelle White wrote a curriculum for a girls' rite-of-passage club called Daughters of Imani and ran the program for years at First Community AME Church in Grand Rapids, Michigan. One of the main activities completed by the participants was a cultural history program through which the teens videotaped interviews with "senior church women."[37]

5. Partnerships for higher education. Most churches engaged with public school students focus on children and youth. But churches can also consider partnering in higher education initiatives with local colleges and universities. Such collaboration could address two key problems.

The first concerns race and class gaps in college enrollment. According to the National Center for Education Statistics (NCES), 42 percent of White adults between eighteen and twenty-four enroll in college compared to 37 percent of similarly aged Black adults.[38] Family wealth also has a large influence on college enrollment. A 2019 report by the NCES found that young adults from the highest quintile of socioeconomic status were 50 percentage points more likely to be enrolled in college in 2016 than were their peers from the lowest quintile.[39]

The second concerns college completion rates. While about two-thirds of White and Asian college students complete their degree programs, that rate is only 46 percent for Hispanic students and 38 percent for African American students.[40] In addition, roughly 60 percent of community college students fail to complete their degrees.[41]

Churches can play a positive role in addressing both problems by exposing more low-income students to college opportunities and helping them apply for financial aid as well as by providing wraparound support to college students to help them persevere and finish their degrees.

In Florida, for example, Rev. Emery Ailes III of Pristine Spring Hill Baptist Church oversees the Linking in Faith and Education (LIFE) initiative. LIFE connects local congregations, particularly African American churches, to Pasco-Hernando State College. LIFE sponsors monthly summits at local churches that address a variety of subjects. It also hosts workshops on career development and operates a mentoring program. When people enroll in college, they are met by LIFE ambassadors who greet them and help acclimate them to the campus and their college journey. Mentors "walk them through the journey, so they don't do it by themselves," explains Ailes.[42] Because of its mentoring programs, says PHSC president Timothy Beard, "We've had a number of students get a diploma or GED and enroll in [a four-year] college, and some have graduated."[43]

Refine Church in Cleveland partners with Northwest University in a program Pastor Luis Vizcarrondo dubbed "Refine U." It seeks to help Hispanic college students to persevere and graduate. Vizcarrondo and his wife, Sarah, were motivated to start the program because they were aware of the problem of college dropouts among Latino students. Nationally, Hispanics are half as likely as non-Hispanic White adults to hold a college degree.[44] Jill Barshay of the *Hechinger Report* (a national nonprofit newsroom that focuses solely on education) explains, "As [Latinos] enter adulthood, many are supporting their families and don't have the luxury to focus on schoolwork."[45] Refine U encourages Hispanic students to stay in school and provides mentors who offer strong emotional support. "We just take these students and we say, you can do this, and we continuously call them," says Vizcar-rondo.[46] The church also aims to offer students hands-on experiences that complement their studies. As he told a local journalist in 2019, "Let's say you're going for your Bachelors for Information and Technology at Northwest University, we're going to put you in the Sound and Tech program at the church."[47]

6. *Education for Immigrants.* Another creative way for churches to invest in public education in their communities is by offering English classes for immigrant and refugee families. Based on Census Bureau data for 2018, the Center for Immigration Studies reports that 67.3 million residents in the United States—about 22 percent of the population—now speak a language other than English at home.[48] English proficiency helps immigrants and refugees navigate the marketplace, government bureaucracies, schools, and the health care system and improves their prospects for employment. Churches offering English lessons for these newcomers not only provide a vital service, but they also demonstrate concretely the biblical virtues of hospitality and neighbor love. Developing friendships with non-English speakers can also be an avenue for more holistic ministry, including intro-ducing those unfamiliar with Christianity to the love of Jesus.

CrossPoint Christian and Missionary Alliance Church in Akron, Ohio, has offered a robust English teaching ministry since 2014. Bruce Lyman, pastor for international ministries, reports that the church has served hun-dreds of students from a total of fifty-nine countries.[49]

The ministry runs from September to May following the local school dis-trict's calendar. Conversational English classes at five different levels are of-fered on Tuesday mornings and Thursday evenings at the church. Volunteers from the church provide free childcare. Additional private tutoring is offered at ten dollars per hour. Each semester about twenty-five to thirty volunteers are involved. They come from CrossPoint and a large number of other churches whose members hear about the ministry through word of mouth.

It wasn't long before local school officials learned about the vibrant program at CrossPoint. During the first year the ESL director from a public school on Akron's north side called Lyman. She told him there were several children from Uzbekistan enrolled. She wanted to know if the church could help their mothers learn English. "She told me, 'They won't come to your church because they are Muslim. And you can't teach them because you're a man. Do you think you can help?'" Lyman laughs. "I said, sure!" He told the congregation about the need for female teachers for these women and God provided. Now a group of women from several churches has taken ownership of that ministry. From 2017–2019, after being approached by the ESL specialist for Akron Public Schools, CrossPoint also mobilized volunteers to teach English classes to immigrant parents at Jennings Middle School. The forty or so parents who participated were primarily from Nepal, though refugees from the Congo, Burma, and Afghanistan were also involved.

Desiring to find ways to deepen the relationship with the students in the English courses, Lyman encouraged volunteers to start cooking classes and painting and knitting groups. "All of those helped [students] with their English acquisition, but also [provided] time for more personal interaction." Then he mobilized volunteers to help with fifteen-week citizenship classes and tutoring for immigrants who wished to take the Test of English as a Foreign Language (TOEFL) exam (a requirement for anyone from a foreign country who wants to enroll in college classes in the United States).

Lyman says his congregation's enthusiasm for the ministry stems from their commitment to global missions as a member of the Christian and Missionary Alliance denomination (CMA). Congregants hear much about missions through regular weekend missions conferences. "So much of it is 'over there,'" Lyman explains. "I began telling people, 'the mission field is *here* now—you can get involved with people from all of these different countries who are desperately in need of help to navigate life in the US and they want American friends.'" That message has resonated strongly, Lyman says, and is the biggest reason for the ministry's vibrancy. "They are excited about being able to do missions work right here in the local church."

CONCLUSION

Of all people, Christ-followers should be passionately committed to and engaged in education. We serve a God who is the fount of all wisdom and knowledge. We bear the image of a God whose wisdom is unfathomable. He set us in a magnificently designed and complex world and invited us to explore it, develop it, and care for it. To enable us in that commission, God gave us intelligence, rationality, curiosity, and imagination. To grow us in our understanding of himself and the world he created, God breathed into Holy Scripture. Christians are a people of the *Book*: we have sacred Scripture to read, study, memorize, and meditate on. We follow Jesus, the God-Man who was known as Rabbi, "Teacher." And we hear from him the command to love God "with all our minds."

Education is vital for individuals to flourish. Christians believe that God designed human beings to be learners and teachers. How can we not be deeply committed to seeing that all of our neighbors receive a high-quality education? We believe God made human beings "a little lower than the angels" (Heb 2:7). We therefore understand just how fundamentally true the famous statement from the United Negro College Fund's advertisement in the 1970s was: "a mind is a terrible thing to waste."

Christians' support of high-quality education for all is also rooted in our mandate to create healthy communities. Education is critical if we are to enjoy a thriving economy. Future generations must be well-prepared to take up their myriad occupational callings skillfully. Education matters as well for a healthy democracy. Education prepares citizens with the knowledge and skills required for responsible participation in collective decision-making.

Today, too many precious young minds are not being lovingly cultivated. Too many adolescents are not receiving training in character or practical skills for jobs. Too many adults failed by our school systems are being left behind in a state of functional illiteracy. Too many newcomers are struggling to thrive, lacking the language skills necessary for navigating daily life effectively. In short, too many neighbors do not have access to quality education. Congregations can do massive good by stepping into this breach, contributing in the various ways described here—and in many additional ways—to the strengthening of the True.

6

THE BEAUTIFUL

FLOURISHING IN THE REALM OF CREATIVITY, AESTHETICS, AND DESIGN

Beauty has a way of sneaking past defenses and speaking in unique ways. To a generation suspicious of truth claims and unconvinced by moral assertions, beauty has a surprising allure. And everything about Jesus Christ is beautiful!

BRIAN ZAHND, *BEAUTY WILL SAVE THE WORLD*

IN 2012, three professors published the surprising results of a study they had completed based on a statistical analysis among residents of New York City, London, Paris, Toronto, and Berlin. They were trying to determine factors of city living that contributed to individuals' happiness. The main factor they found wasn't wealth, or career, or even health. It was beauty. As a writer in the *Atlantic* summarized, the researchers discovered that

> happiness is most easily attained by living in an aesthetically beautiful city. The things people were constantly surrounded by—lovely architecture, history, green spaces, cobblestone streets—had the greatest effect on their happiness. The cumulative positive effects of daily beauty worked subtly but strongly.[1]

Beauty and happiness go together.

The most remarkable place I have seen this idea made visible is in urban slums in the developing world. These were certainly locales of ugliness and despair, marked by garbage on dirt roads and dilapidated hovels composed of discarded cardboard and tin. Yet on many of those shacks, residents had pasted colorful sheets torn from magazines, plastic flowers, or bits of bright cloth. They were hungry for more than food or jobs (as vital as both those are). They were also aching for beauty and apparently found some small measure of solace in the bits of color they added to their mud-spattered homes.

In *Philosophy in the New Century*, philosopher Anthony O'Hear notes that

even in the poorest of circumstances people have a yearning for order and beauty. This yearning will reveal itself in the ways they organize their shelter, prepare their meals, dress themselves and respond to natural sights and sounds. Aesthetics pervades human life, even at its most basic level and even in fulfilling the most basic physical needs.[2]

FLOURISHING AND THE COMMUNITY ENDOWMENT OF THE BEAUTIFUL

Scholars with the Thriving Cities Group define the community endowment of the Beautiful as the realm of creativity, aesthetics, and design. It includes "the visual aesthetics of the built environment and the artistic, cultural, and historic life of a community."[3] Institutions in this endowment include art patrons and artists, architecture and engineering firms, community planning boards, and public art, among others. This endowment also includes the practice of "placemaking," which the Project for Public Spaces defines as "a collaborative process by which we can shape our public realm in order to maximize shared value."[4]

Though eager to demonstrate the importance of aesthetics for community flourishing, scholars with Thriving Cities acknowledge that this endowment seems to require more defense than some of the others so easily associated with thriving. They write, "When 'The Beautiful' is ranged against other Endowments, especially those that seem to more directly address fundamental aspects of thriving—education, justice, prosperity, and the like—its significance recedes from view."[5]

But the realm of art, design, and aesthetics is indeed vital to community flourishing, for at least four reasons.

First, *the places people inhabit matter and have a significant influence on human flourishing.* We live amid the natural environment (trees, grass, plants, animals) and the built environment (homes, streets, sidewalks, buildings, parks). As indicated in the beauty-happiness connection referenced earlier, both affect human well-being. Those who study animals easily discourse on the ways one habitat lends itself better than another to a species' quality of life. The same dynamics are true for humans. As Eric O. Jacobsen argues, "When [human] habitats are lacking in certain key characteristics, humans tend to languish. And when habitats are in an optimal state, they tend to thrive."[6]

Thriving Cities notes the complementary links between "structural" placemaking through intentionality in the design of the built environment and "creative" placemaking through artistic endeavors.[7] Just as a well-designed built environment contributes to community flourishing, so too do the arts. A second reason the arts are important for community flourishing is that *they can be a means of strengthening social relationships.*

For example, they can promote empathy and understanding of others, helping to break down dividing walls between different cultural groups. The arts bring people together for meaningful discussions on universal topics. As one observer notes, "arts events are one of the best ways to gather individuals and build communities around a shared experience."[8] Public art installations like the I Am a Man Plaza adjacent to Clayborne Temple in Memphis or the National Memorial for Peace and Justice in Montgomery are particularly powerful vehicles for potentially transformational conversations and learning. Additionally, community-development practitioners have found the arts to be an effective means of engaging otherwise disengaged youth in positive activity. Music and song also play important roles in social reform campaigns (think of the role of congregational singing in the US civil rights movement). And on the lighter side the arts offer people numerous avenues for wholesome communal recreation and entertainment, such as live theater, musical concerts, and art exhibitions.

Third, *art and beauty are educative.* Art "illumines something about the world's depth and reality. . . . It shows us something we can learn in no other way," writes William Dyrness in *Visual Faith.*[9] Art can slow us down and force us to consider, to ponder, to think. Art can stimulate our intuitive side, causing us to reexamine, to consider from a new perspective, to "try on" a different way of understanding something. This aspect of art causes Makoto Fujimura to argue that "the arts in some ways are fundamental to even scientific research and mathematics. We talk about needing math and science education all the time, but we don't realize that they start with an intuitive process."[10]

Fourth, *art can be cathartic and therapeutic, bringing a sense of peace, healing, and well-being.* Artists from painters to poets, musicians, and dancers speak of losing themselves in the process of artistic creation. (If only writers of nonfiction could enjoy such experiences.) As people create art, they can forget at least for a little while their sorrows and stresses. Meanwhile, the act of experiencing art can also be healing, as the music heard or art contemplated speaks to our souls. It's no wonder the discipline of art therapy has arisen in the mental health field.

CREATIONAL INTENT: THE REALM OF AESTHETICS

God *is* the Beautiful and the ultimate source of all beauty. Scripture speaks frequently of this, noting that beauty and how it is intertwined with God's splendor, majesty, and glory (e.g., Ps 27:4; 50:2; 1 Chron 16:28-29; Is 4:2; 28:5, 33:17). It is not only his truth and goodness that draw us to God. We are attracted as well by his beauty.

Contemplation. We are made for God; thus, we are made for beauty. And we were designed to delight in, dwell upon, and meditate on that beauty. Indeed, it may be that *contemplation* is the core principle of God's intention for the realm of aesthetics. In Psalm 27:4, David—the man after God's own heart—prays,

> One thing I ask from the LORD
>   this only do I seek:
> that I may dwell in the house of the LORD
>   all the days of my life,
> *to gaze on the beauty of the* LORD
>   and to seek him in his temple. (emphasis added)

Kyle Strobel, author of *Embracing Contemplation*, writes,

> In a Christian sense, the word contemplation is broken up into two parts. You have the first part, *con*, which just means with. And *templem*, which means temple. You have "with God" in his temple. And so in the Christian sense, all contemplation is exactly what Colossians 3 said. It's setting your mind on things that are above where Christ is, seated

at the right hand of God in the temple of the Lord, where we can gaze upon the beauty of the Lord.[11]

In Matthew 4:4, Jesus says that people cannot live on bread alone. He was referring to the fact that we are more than physical beings; we also have a spiritual nature. The same text could be used to convey the truth that God made us *aesthetic*, not just physical, beings. He designed us to find joy and satisfaction in our meditation on his great beauty.

God also provided additional sources of beauty to delight in. He gave us five senses and set us in a world created to be more than just functional. God's creation was filled with the beauty of color and texture. The Garden of Eden's trees and fruits were not only good for eating but also "pleasing to the eye." Repeatedly, God calls his creation good. The Hebrew word there is *tov* and, importantly, it can also be translated "beautiful."[12]

The nourishment of beauty. God designed humans with a desire for the beautiful; our large appetite for it "comes inscribed into every soul."[13] When that desire is unfulfilled we experience something less than what we were created for. Beauty—God's and the creation's—nourishes us in ways that are real but mysterious. It can reorient our fears and distresses. The beauty of his natural creation is a means of directing our minds to contemplate God's beauty. Notably, Jesus encourages us to "consider" or "behold" the lilies of the field in all their splendor since that verb is often used in conjunction with the worship of God. Jesus understands that our beholding will not only bring us pleasure but also remind us of God's intimate care and soothe our worries. Beauty can be a means through which God consoles, calms, and heals his children.

God designed humans not only to be able to experience beauty but also to craft it. He, the greatest Artist, made us in his image as creative beings.[14] Since God calls us to bear his image in the world, we do this in part through our creative endeavors. As we craft beauty, we tap more deeply into our God-given identity.

The power of beauty. All of this indicates that beauty is neither frivolous nor an optional add-on in the Christian life and witness. This is important to remember, for the church has been guilty in the past of forgetting it. Perhaps no one articulated the value of beauty better than Hans Urs von

Balthasar in his magnum opus *The Glory of the Lord*. There Balthasar warns of grave consequences when beauty is not put on its proper pedestal alongside truth and goodness:

> Our situation today shows that beauty demands for itself at least as much courage and decision as do truth and goodness, and she will not allow herself to be separated and banned from her two sisters without taking them along with herself in an act of mysterious vengeance. We can be sure that whoever sneers at her name as if she were the ornament of a bourgeois past—whether he admits it or not—can no longer pray and soon will no longer be able to love.[15]

Beauty has power. It can awaken and transport us. It births wonder. It can take us outside of ourselves and our petty concerns. Balthasar recognized that this decentering of self that beauty can accomplish is a pathway toward the love of others.

Beauty, incarnation, and revelation. A major purpose of aesthetics is to reveal the ultimate reality (God) that lies behind beauty. We've been discussing this so far with the doctrines of creation and human nature in mind. But we can also speak of the importance of the incarnation in like manner. The incarnation, like creation itself, is an act of God's artistry. Jesus is God in the flesh, the invisible made visible. The incarnation is God speaking to us through the language of the aesthetic. Peter Enns writes, "the incarnation, God in human flesh, is not a debate or argument about the nature of God that appeals primarily to the intellect. It is a vivid—and true—demonstration, a portrait, of a radically new and mysterious way of thinking about God, the world, and our place in it."[16]

In the early eighth century, Saint John of Damascus pointed to the incarnation along these lines in his defense of Christian art and icons. John acknowledged that in the Old Testament God prohibited the making of graven images. But once Christ had come in the flesh—God made in visible form and substance—depicting the Lord in artwork as a means of worship and veneration (think *contemplation*) was now legitimate: "When you think of God, who is a pure spirit, becoming man for your sake, then you can clothe him in a human form. When the invisible becomes visible to the eye, you may then draw his form . . . and show it to anyone who is willing to contemplate it."[17]

Beauty and worship. Not only are the arts to reveal ultimate beauty; they are also meant as a vehicle for worship. God enjoys his people communicating back to him in more than just simple prose. The Psalms enjoin disciples to sing and make music as a way of adoring God. Singing was part of the Israelites' formal worship. In King David's day there was a professional class of temple musicians (1 Chron 6:31-32). David himself danced enthusiastically before his Lord as a way of expressing his praise and thanksgiving. In the New Testament we observe Jesus and his disciples singing hymns. The apostle Paul urged the Colossian believers to sing "psalms, hymns, and songs from the Spirit" with gratitude (Col 3:16). And according to Scripture it is not only humans who sing in worship to God. So do the stars (Job 38:7). In the consummated kingdom, so will "every creature in heaven and on earth and under the earth and on the sea" (Rev 5:13).

So, the realm of art and aesthetics exists in part for religious or devotional purposes. God himself made religious art—think about the tabernacle. He gave his Holy Spirit to enable the craftsman Bezalel to implement his elaborate designs (Ex 31:2-3). Among the materials Bezalel and his fellow artist Oholiab used were precious metals. The tabernacle involved intricate ornamentation. Similarly, God's highly specific guidelines for the priests' garments were aimed at crafting something "for glory and for beauty" (Ex 28:2 ESV). God's concern was not limited to functionality. It was "not enough for the tabernacle to be laid out in the right way; it also had to be beautiful," writes Philip Ryken in *Art for God's Sake.* "There was beauty in the color of its fabrics, the sparkle of its gems, the shape of its objects, and the symmetry of its proportions."[18]

But this is *not* to say that the only art that counts as real art is explicitly religious—in the narrow sense of being about those things we humans tend to categorize as spiritual. There is a broad sacredness throughout creation; God's fingerprints are everywhere. So-called secular art—the landscape painting, the still life of a bowl of fruit, the abstract sculpture depicting fortitude, the poem about romantic love, the novel celebrating the resilience of community health workers in Appalachia, the musical *Les Misérables,* Beethoven's Fifth Symphony, your child's coloring of his pet turtle, and untold millions more examples both profound and mundane—also has a role in God's design for aesthetics. This is for at least two reasons.

Beauty and imagination. One reason that secular art has a role in aesthetics is that God created the realm of aesthetics to be a playground for our imagination, which is a vital part of our given nature. God gave human beings the capacity for fantasy, for conjuring up nonliteral ways of articulating and depicting the stuff of both the created world and the wonderful wanderings of our minds. This ability is derived from God, whose art similarly engages in flights of fancy. In *Art and the Bible*, Francis Schaeffer notes God's instructions in Exodus 28 for the pictures to be embroidered on the priestly garments.[19] These included blue pomegranates. In nature, pomegranates are red. Apparently, though, God also likes to imagine them as blue. Celebrating this aspect of who we are Schaeffer enthuses, "The Christian is the one whose imagination should fly beyond the stars."[20] Those who have been particularly gifted by God with artistic talent have been entrusted in a special way with stewarding the imaginative realm.

Beauty and stewardship. The other reason is that God designed the realm of aesthetics to be one means for our stewardship of the created world. Though we cannot make things *ex nihilo* (out of nothing) human beings nevertheless imitate God every time we live into the cultural mandate to take the raw materials of creation and organize or combine them in ways that make music, pictures, textiles, stories, sculptures, and poems that depict all manner of things in creation.

Put another way, art and aesthetics were created as a vital means for expressing and experiencing the delight that is part and parcel of shalom. (Cornelius Plantinga defined *shalom* as "the webbing together of God, humans, and all creation in justice, fulfillment, and *delight*."[21]) We create art of all kinds to delight one another, which—importantly—is a wonderful, meaningful way of expressing *love*.

Beauty and truth. It also seems fair to assume that God created art as a means of communicating his truth. I've already said that art is meant to be revelatory of ultimate Beauty (God). God is also ultimate Truth. God's truth concerns not only his own being but also the nature of human nature and the nature of the world he created. Before the fall, then, we could imagine that all art told the story of glory, beauty, harmony, delight, joy, love, purity, community, health (i.e., the story of unsullied shalom). After the fall, artists are still meant to convey truth, though now that truth will involve not only the glories of shalom but also the realities of sin and evil. In light of Jesus' redemption and the in-breaking of the kingdom, artists today are meant to depict those realities as well. And in light of God's promise of new heavens and new earth, art that is true will also point to the hope beyond today's pain and suffering.

Not every piece of artwork, of course, bears the burden of telling the whole truth of creation and fall and redemption and restoration. (Palpable sigh of relief from artists reading this.) Yet within the world of art all these themes should be present if art is to be true to the task of communicating truth.

THE REALM OF AESTHETICS: MALFORMATIONS

This brings us to the topic of the deformations within the community endowment of the Beautiful. There are far too many to cover in this one chapter. I'll mention three salient ones in our time and one from the church's past.[22]

Brutalism. Perhaps the most significant of these days can be summed up under the heading *brutalism.* I cannot make the point better than does N. T. Wright. He writes specifically of British artists, but his point holds well beyond England's shores:

> The last generation of British artists has been notorious for its portrayal of ugliness, of life's sordid realities. . . . The whole movement is sneering at the pretensions of today's world. In reacting against sentimentalism, against dreamy fantasy, our culture has swung around to embrace brutalism, whose concrete-tower blocks trample on our romantic visions of fairy castles and cozy cottages. . . . We have been shown the seamy side of life so often that our cultural clothes now appear to be nothing but seams.[23]

Brutalism fails to tell the truth about the world because it focuses solely on evil and gives no attention to the realities of God's work of common grace and renewal.

Self-centeredness. A second malformation in the realm of aesthetics occurs when art is solely about the artist. "Today's art tends to be very self-centered," laments Joshua LaRock, an internationally recognized portraitist. "It's all about me."[24] We saw earlier that art is designed to be a vehicle for expressing human creativity and imagination, but it is also meant to be *more* than that. It is designed to point (ultimately) to truths about the world and to offer something to the viewer. Even some secular art critics have agreed that contemporary art's "willful and exclusive focus on self" actually "sidetracks" or "slows down" the artist's creative growth.[25] Theodore Wolff observes:

> In art, as in every other dynamic area of human experience, to see creativity mainly as an extension of our own accrued experiences and perceptions, as merely a projection of our individuality and personality, is to miss its point entirely. . . . To fulfill his task, the artist must engage himself with realities beyond those of self-gratification and self-expression, and interact with the larger issues and realities of his culture and society—as well as with those dimensions of being traditionally described as "universal."[26]

Art without ideas. A third deformation is the notion of art without ideas. Jeremiah Enna, founder of the Kansas City-based arts nonprofit Culture House, explains that the dominant philosophy in today's art world is that "the goal is merely personal expression. The artwork . . . doesn't have to have any specific meaning [in it]. In fact, the less specific the better, because then we can all pour our own meanings into it."[27] The problem with this relates to accountability, Enna says:

> All art is saying something. If I write a song, you can ask me questions about it. You can try to discover whether the result was consistent with the idea I had for it. Part of the responsibility or stewardship of art is thinking about your audience. When I create, I should consider who I am creating for, because *they* matter in the equation.

Neoplatonist iconoclasm. In discussing malformations in the Beautiful, we must acknowledge one the church itself has been guilty of: iconoclasm. The iconoclastic movement against representational art, which began in earnest in Constantinople in the eighth century and then resurfaced "with a vengeance" during the Reformation, was at times even violent in its campaigns.[28] Movement members raided churches and destroyed paintings, sculptures, and murals. The average sixteenth-century Protestant zealot may have been motivated by anger over Catholic excesses or disdain for the distractions of ornamentation. But the underlying problematic philosophy of iconoclasm was its Neoplatonic inclination to view the material world as inferior, something to be abandoned or transcended to achieve communion with God. This is a view biblical Christianity rejects. Orthodox Christianity understands the physical world as considered good, though broken—and a means through which divine transcendence can be experienced.[29]

THE CHURCH'S HISTORICAL CONTRIBUTIONS AND RE-FORMATIONS IN THE BEAUTIFUL

Contributions to the arts. Art expresses cultural ideas, priorities, convictions, and sensibilities. It provides clues to what a people value at any particular point in time. It either embodies and celebrates those values, seeks to nuance them, or protests them. Christianity was the dominant worldview in the Western world for hundreds of years and as such powerfully shaped Western representational art, architecture, and music. Christian thought—and some notable Christ-followers—have also influenced the field of city planning and designing the built environment.

Ideas and contributions: The visual arts and architecture. The earliest Christian art was directly didactic in purpose: it sought to connect followers of the Way with their Hebrew roots. The most common type of artistic works were paintings on the walls of the catacombs and house-church meeting places. According to curator Jeffrey Spier, who brought together a significant collection of the earliest Christian art for the Kimbell Art Museum in 2007, the earliest paintings tended to depict Old Testament figures like Abraham, Isaac, and Daniel.[30] Later, images of the fish, the anchor, and the Good Shepherd appear. In her review of Spier's collection, Annemarie Weyl Carr explains that the early church understood the teachings of Jesus and the apostles as the fulfillment of the Hebrew Scriptures. "The visual images exemplified by the catacomb paintings literally 'picture' the Bible as early Christians read it."[31]

The volume, significance, and influence of Christian art grew steadily from the time of the legalization of the faith in the fourth century onward. Christians of means commissioned religious-themed murals and frescoes for their homes. Ivory sculptures began to be used as decorative elements in places of worship. Churches began to be built in the Constantinian era, often situated at places identified with the life of Christ or the apostles.

In the Middle Ages the church was the leading patron of the arts, followed closely by emperors (and later, aristocrats) whose Christian affiliation ranged from nominal to meaningful. Initially following the fall of the Roman Empire, it was the Eastern Orthodox Church and the Byzantine emperors who were the most active in commissioning a diverse range of art. These included church buildings, mosaics, murals, and small-scale devotional icons.[32] Emperor Justinian I, for example, commissioned the building of four major basilicas at Constantinople.[33]

Later in the Middle Ages, Christian rulers in the Western part of the old empire commissioned great cathedrals and abbeys. The styles varied over time, from Romanesque to Gothic. One scholar calls the church's investment in the great Gothic cathedrals "the most holistic, magnificent, and extensive example of [arts] patronage in history."[34]

The Christian contribution to architecture in the fifteen centuries following Christ's life goes beyond just the commissioning of numerous religious buildings, though, as important as that was. Christianity also affected the form and design of those buildings. For example, to allude to Christ's redemptive sacrifice, architects added a design element called the transept to rectangular Romanesque buildings. This created cathedrals in the shape of the cross. Gothic architecture further sought to reinforce Christian ideas. The height, grandeur, light, and vertical orientation enabled by the new technique of the flying buttress encouraged people to raise their eyes to the heavens and contemplate the glories of a majestic God. Invariably the Gothic cathedral was the tallest structure in the town, signifying its importance. Frequently employed trifold arches and windows were meant to remind observers of the Trinity. Stained-glass windows on cathedral walls served as pictorial Bible stories for the illiterate.

Similarly, the church "developed its own iconography," expressed in decorative art like mosaics and illuminated manuscripts, and in sculpture and paintings.[35] The church commissioned murals, sculpture, and altar decorations. In the fifteenth and sixteenth centuries the Catholic establishment supported grand masters like Michelangelo, Brunelleschi, Bramante, Raphael, Fra Angelico, Donatello, and da Vinci, plus a host of lesser-known artists. Despite the rise of humanist thought during the Renaissance, much art of the period continued to be devoted to Christian subjects.

The Catholic Church's massive investments in the arts became a point of controversy in the Reformation, as people like Martin Luther criticized religious leaders for selling indulgences and raising taxes to pay for these commissions. More than this, though, a new kind of aesthetic emerged accompanying Protestant thought. The impulse was toward a more austere religious experience and an emphasis on simplicity. Protestants wanted the Word at the heart of things. John Calvin was concerned about the idolatry and veneration of Mary and wanted to rid sacred space of images of the saints and the Virgin. "Ever since, there has been a strong tendency within some—but not all—streams of the Reformed tradition to build sanctuaries that are very plain in their adornment."[36] Luther was less strict and allowed the use of a restricted range of religious images in the churches in Lutheran churches in Germany.

The Reformers commissioned far less art than their Catholic brethren. Nonetheless, this was not a period devoid of creative expression. Protestants were keen on using the printing press to get more copies of the Bible—and eventually other Christian books and tracts—into more laypeople's hands. In time these religious publications began to include illustrations.

Reformers like Luther broke down the sacred-secular divide, seeing all realms of life and work as important. He famously said the work of the rustic laborer and the domestic servant girl differed not one whit in God's sight from the work of the monks and priests. Protestant art thus included a wide range of ordinary, this-worldly subjects celebrated in landscape and still life paintings. This is not to say that all religiously themed art went by the wayside. Rembrandt, for example, became the greatest painter of Dutch Protestantism and is well known for his religious works, such as his paintings of Christ's passion.

While the descendants of the Reformers built simple, unadorned worship spaces and retreated from art patronage, they were not indifferent to beauty. Perhaps as an extension of their focus on the Word, Puritans in Europe and the United States turned to poetry and valued beauty through this art form. Indeed, one of the greatest English-language poets, John Milton, was a Puritan.

Protestant religion's influence on American literature continued into the 1800s. Surprisingly, even the feminist and self-proclaimed atheist Camille Paglia admits that

> The Bible, in its poetic and indeed Shakespearean King James translation . . . had a huge formative influence on the language, imagery, symbolism, and allegory of such major writers as James Fenimore Cooper, Nathaniel Hawthorne, Ralph Waldo Emerson, Emily Dickinson, Walt Whitman, and Herman Melville.[37]

The waves of immigration in the nineteenth century brought both Eastern European Orthodox believers and Irish, Polish, and Italian Catholics to the United States. The newcomers soon made their aesthetic preferences known. While the white-steepled buildings of traditional Protestants continued to dominate, the architectural landscape began to include the Gothic-Revival styles of great Catholic cathedrals (think St. Patrick's in New York City, for example) as well as Byzantine influences.

Ideas and contributions: Music. The sixth-century pope Gregory the Great is credited for his substantial influence on music. He "brought all the music of the Western church for the first time into a systematic and well-proportioned whole."[38] Monasteries and abbeys were the greatest musical centers of the mid-to-late medieval period. The plainchant, a single, clear line of vocal music used to convey the meaning of religious texts, dominated the early style.

A vital innovation in music arose when an eleventh-century Benedictine monk named Guido of Arezzo introduced the staff of four lines for writing the pitch of musical notes.[39] This meant that music could now be notated. Guido's achievement is considered "one of the most significant in the history of music."[40]

During the Renaissance, music in the church evolved toward polyphonic a capella singing. Over time innumerable commissions were made for various musical settings for the Catholic mass. In *Music in the History of the Western Church*, music historian Edward Dickinson reports that

> The period from the twelfth century to the close of the sixteenth was one of extraordinary musical activity. . . . In quality as well as quantity the mediaeval chorus music was not unworthy of comparison with the

architectural, sculptural, pictorial, and textile products which were created in the same epoch and under the same auspices.[41]

This polyphonic music, like Gothic architecture, was imbued with Christian ideas, such as diversity in community.

Polyphony symbolized harmony and unity where different and independent melodic lines worked together to create a total that was bigger than the separate elements, as if it reflected the different peoples all over Europe who nonetheless were united under one, single and sublime vision of the world.[42]

The music's beauty was meant to be a sublime expression and experience of the trinitarian divine. Christianity's themes of suffering and hope also found expression in the dissonance and consonance of liturgical music. Affirmations of both individualism and community are expressed musically in Western classical compositions through a repeated, central melody that is experimented on and embellished by additional vocalists or instruments. In *A History of Music and Musical Style*, authors Homer Ulrich and Paul Pisk write that liturgical music "continued for over a thousand years to illuminate the sacred texts and carry their meanings deep into the hearts of all who heard them."[43]

The Reformation introduced new musical forms and texts. While the intricate, sophisticated musical settings for the Catholic mass aimed to stir the soul to an emotional reverence, Protestant hymnody with its simpler style and carefully crafted texts communicated a wealth of "tightly packed, doctrinal and devotional thought."[44]

Martin Luther was an enthusiastic singer and borrowed popular melodies as settings for new texts communicating Protestant ideas. He composed many new hymns for the movement and set in motion "a great age of the writing of hymns, or 'chorales' in the German Lutheran tradition."[45] For Luther, these were "sermons in sound," serving to communicate Scripture and doctrine in intelligible forms.[46] This more restrained musical style developed in time within Anglicanism as well.

Christianity's influence on serious music in the Western world continued into the eighteenth and nineteenth centuries; consider, for example, the sacred music composed by Bach, Vivaldi, and Handel. Churches were major patrons of composers and musicians. St. Thomas Church in Leipzig, for example, supported J. S. Bach. In Venice, the Church of Pity operated the city's major orphanage in which Vivaldi served as music master for years. Churches commissioned all manner of motets, madrigals, and sonatas and held performances of them.

The built environment: Christian contributions to urban planning. The phrases *built environment* and *urban planning* are modern. But the concerns behind them about the role our physical surroundings play in our lives and the ways that communal spaces are organized are age-old. Christian theology and individual Christ-followers have influenced these discussions in some important ways from medieval times to the present day. Following are a few brief examples of how Christian ideas have been adopted in city planning.

Faith and the medieval city. Historians of architecture have argued that the ways medieval cities were designed are further evidence of the "Christian belief [that] was all-pervading and boundless" in Europe during the Middle Ages. "Outward expressions of this belief were to be seen, felt and heard everywhere," writes Keith Lilly, author of *Urban Life in the Middle Ages.* "It was made visible by the multitude of religious buildings in both town and country, and in the countless shrines and wayside crosses placed along roads and streets."[47] Medieval "urban forms . . . conveyed Christian symbolism," Lilly continues. For example, "the city was understood as a scaled-down world—a microcosm—linking city and cosmos in the medieval mind."[48]

Philip Bess, architect and professor at Notre Dame, agrees with Lilly. Each year he takes graduate architecture students to the ancient Flemish city of Bruges to show them the influences of the Catholic faith on the city-states of the medieval period. Bess argues that this city, like others of the high Middle Ages, "aspired to model itself upon the ideal of the New Jerusalem, the heavenly city envisioned and described by St. John the Evangelist." By pursing that aspiration, he says, "Bruges, over time, made itself the enduringly beautiful city it remains today."[49]

The British Evangelicals. The social agenda of the reform-minded nineteenth-century Evangelicals in England included attentiveness to what we now call the built environment, as that affected the urban poor and working classes. The reformers worked to institute safer and healthier housing for the poor, to improve public sanitation, and to ensure access for the working classes to healthful green spaces. Architect Henry Roberts, physician James Kay-Shuttleworth, and urban property manager Octavia Hill are illustrative of their faith-inspired efforts.

Roberts's passion for improving housing for the urban poor led him to serve as the honorary architect for the Society for Improving the Condition of the Labouring Classes. Roberts designed some model buildings and lodging houses for it. His blueprints featured fire-resistant construction, excellent insulation, better air circulation, and improved drainage.[50] Over time Henry's designs became influential in the United States and across Europe.

Kay-Shuttleworth grew up in a Nonconformist (Protestant, non-Anglican) household. He developed a reputation as a dedicated doctor treating the poor in the slums of Manchester during its cholera epidemic in 1832. From his experiences the doctor wrote the influential book *The Moral and Physical Condition of the Working Classes Employed in the Cotton Manufacture in Manchester*. The book played a major role in the adoption of a series of city sanitation reform measures.[51]

Octavia Hill's work in nineteenth-century London would likely today be described as Christian community development with an emphasis on quality housing. Though best known for her housing management, her faith also led her to be a strong advocate for open public spaces for poor people. In 1883 she wrote, "There is perhaps no need of the poor of London which more prominently forces itself on the notice of anyone working among them than that of space." From her personal knowledge, she argued that the poor wanted "places to sit in, places to play in, places to stroll in, and places to spend a day in."[52]

Hill campaigned against development on existing woodlands and helped to save London's Hampstead Heath and Parliament Hill Fields from being built on. She argued that all people want "quiet. We all want beauty . . . we all need space. Unless we have it, we cannot reach that sense of quiet in which whispers of better things come to us gently." Hill was also one of the founders of the National Trust in England, which was established to preserve places of historic interest or natural beauty for the public's enjoyment.[53]

Christian progressives in the United States. In the United States several Christian architects, urban planners, and mayors in the nineteenth to early twentieth centuries played key roles in city reforms to the built environment that brought greater flourishing to residents.

Horace Bushnell, a Congregationalist clergyman, can only loosely be called an urban planner as that was not his primary vocation. Nonetheless, it was his pioneering vision and advocacy that get credit for the building of the first city-funded public park. He pitched his idea and design to the city council of Hartford, Connecticut, in 1853. He was motivated in part by concern for the urban poor, who needed green space and a place where their children could safely play, and all could feel closer to God. In his speech to city officials Bushnell explained that the park could be

> A place where children will play and the invalid go to breathe the freshness of nature. A place . . . where high and low, rich and poor will exchange looks; an outdoor parlor opened for the cultivation of good manners and a right social feeling. A place . . . that will make us more conscious of being one people.[54]

The City Council was persuaded and what eventually became known as Bushnell Park was constructed over the next several years.

Bushnell's influence spread beyond Connecticut as a variety of reformers adopted his theological commitments. One of his protégés was his fellow Congregationalist Frederick Olmstead. Olmstead was the landscape architect who became famous for building New York City's Central Park. Like Bushnell, Olmstead believed in the power of "unconscious influence." By this Bushnell meant the subtle but powerful nonverbal ways in which the Christ-follower sheds lights abroad through his God-given character. Olmstead thought the concept could also be applied to natural surroundings; indeed, that a person "is most influenced by God through 'unconscious influences' from . . . [the] natural environment."[55]

The Chicago architect and reputed urban planner Daniel Burnham was also one whose faith shaped his designs. Burnham grew up in the Church of the New Jerusalem and attended college at a New Church–affiliated school. These denominations were outgrowths of the theology and practices of the nontraditional Swedish Lutheran theologian Emanuel Swedenborg. A central characteristic of Swedenborgians is their deep commitment to the service of others.

Burnham believed in the power of the urban environment to provide positive, transformative experiences for inhabitants. As a result, his designs sought to bring beauty, light, green space, and street patterns that would minimize traffic congestion. Burnham was the director of works for the first world's fair in 1893. The exhibition's so-called White City inspired the "city beautiful movement" of the 1890s and early 1900s. This urban planning reform movement emphasized beautification through systems of city parks and monuments as well as a network of diagonal roadways for traffic efficiency, among other features.

Christians and the New Urbanism. In the aftermath of World War II increased reliance on the automobile and the development of the interstate highway system contributed to the rise of the now ubiquitous suburban housing development. In response to the urban sprawl the New Urbanism movement arose to try to revive what Eric O. Jacobsen calls "the ancient practice of civic art."[56]

In the suburban model, geographic space is divided by function: housing here, shopping over there, businesses somewhere else. The New Urbanists focus instead on mixed-use development—places for "working, shopping, playing and worshiping" are together in walkable distances. They give priority to public places (e.g., sidewalks, parks, and plazas). The emphasis is on design elements that foster "human connection and community."[57] The experience of community, of course, is contingent on the behavior of people who live in these more traditional neighborhoods. That is what Jacobsen calls the software of community development, something largely beyond the control of practitioners of the built environment. But what planners can do is create the kind of hardware that encourages social interaction.

New Urbanism is not a Christian movement per se. Its intellectual and philosophical roots, though, can be traced back to cultural soil influenced by religious dissenters whose political economy was communitarian in character. New Urbanism's design principles draw significantly from the pioneering city planner and landscape architect John Nolen. Nolen, in turn, was a devotee of the Garden City movement in England.[58] Its originator was Ebenezer Howard. Howard was influenced and embraced by the Christian socialists of his day. And Howard's biographer Robert Beevers argues that English Puritanism was "the source of Howard's imagination."[59]

Today some Christians, Protestant and Catholic, have embraced the New Urbanist philosophy because of the ways it resonates with biblical concepts of human dignity, wholeness, and community. Jacobsen is one of those voices, as is Philip Bess (the architect quoted earlier). In *Till We Have Built Jerusalem: Architecture, Urbanism, and the Sacred*, Bess explains that the built environment is an expression of particular values and conditions. Suburban sprawl is an expression of commercialism and individualism. "The more architects and planners have turned their attention to building up the City of Man, apart from some vision of the City of God," Bess laments, "the meaner and uglier the City of Man has become."[60]

The New Urbanism, by contrast, rests on an understanding of human nature that affirms "the whole human being" rather than building environments that reduce people to "*homo economicus* or *homo privatus*."[61] These things matter greatly for human flourishing, Bess says, because "an incorrect understanding of human nature has detrimental consequences for the making of our cities. If we misunderstand human nature, we will surely not make good cities."[62]

CONCLUSION

It must be acknowledged that contemporary Christians have sometimes ignored or even disdained the realm of aesthetics and design.[63] In *Surprised by Hope*, theologian N. T. Wright offers this plea for Christ-followers today to take seriously the responsibility of contributing to the realm of aesthetic life, based on both a historical and scriptural argument:

> Part of the role of the church in the past was—and could and should be again—to foster and sustain lives of beauty and aesthetic meaning at every level. . . . The church, because it is the family that believes in hope for new creation, should be the place in every town and village where new creation bursts forth for the whole community.[64]

We are creation and new creation people, and we are called by a beautiful God to create and extend beauty in God's world. We can do so both inside and outside the four walls of our churches.

What we do inside the four walls matters for at least two reasons. First, research by sociologist Mark Chaves shows that "congregations are one of the most important venues in which Americans experience art or participate in its production."[65] For example, in any given year, nearly two-thirds of American adults hear live music in a worship service. That is far, far more than experience live pop music, jazz, opera, or classical music. Given this reality, Richard Hays from Duke Divinity School urges church leaders to take seriously the artistic crafting of worship services. "If the church is one of the primary places where the arts are actually practiced," Hays says, then we ought to evaluate our worship practices with great thoughtfulness.[66] Second, we live in a world permeated by images. If we are going to take seriously the New Testament's charge to take every thought captive, we will need to intentionally and critically reflect "on the artistic media that profoundly shape the consciousness of our culture."[67]

Outside the four walls, an attentiveness to the arts and the built environment matter for Christian witness. For one thing, Christ-followers must encourage cultural expressions that seek to promote and protect human dignity. For another, "evangelism in a postmodern world must include a concern for image and beauty."[68] Traditional evangelism has been centered on words, on the intellectual defense of the faith. But the younger generations are less interested in such media and more engrossed in the world of images and the imagination. They are looking for an "imaginative vision" of life and reality "that they can see and feel, as well as understand."[69]

Engagement with the arts is needed because the church must show the alluring beauty of Jesus Christ alongside his goodness and truth. As pastor and author Brian Zahnd sums up,

> A Christianity that is deeply enchanted by Christ's beauty and thus formed and fashioned by this beauty has the opportunity to present to a skeptical and jaded world an aspect of the gospel that has been too rare for far too long. Where truth and goodness fail to win an audience, beauty may once again captivate and draw those it enchants into the kingdom of saving grace.[70]

7

A STRATEGY FOR CULTIVATING THE BEAUTIFUL

INVEST IN THE ARTS

Figure 7.1. *Four Chapters* by Noelle Stoffel

CHANCES ARE IF YOU'D WALKED INTO a Sunday morning service at Christ Community Church–Downtown Campus (CC-Downtown) on Baltimore Avenue in Kansas City between 2013 and 2020, you'd notice a large abstract painting just inside the front door. You might also have heard the church's young pastor, Gabe Coyle, reference the painting. It's called *Four Chapters*. Like any piece of abstract art, digesting it takes some effort and contemplation. Gabe likes to tell his parishioners, "In coming here, you are walking into a story. You can see something of it in this painting, but it only gets clearer the further into the community you come."[1]

Four Chapters refers to the grand biblical narrative of creation, fall, redemption, and consummation. The church commissioned it from local artist Noelle Stoffel. Gabe explained to her that the Bible is a story with four chapters and provided her with numerous Scriptures to read and meditate on for inspiration. "To this day I think it's still my favorite painting," he says.

Stoffel's abstract wasn't the only painting you'd have seen at CC-Downtown. Much more art adorned the walls because for seven years in that space on Baltimore Avenue, the church was also an art gallery.

In late 2020, the congregation purchased a new building. Still within the downtown Crossroads arts district, it is now located in a two-story at West 19th Street. The first floor contains the church's art gallery and a worship center seating around 250. The second floor includes offices for church staff and an artist in residence. "The arts have actually become even more integral to who we are as a campus now," Gabe enthuses.

THE HISTORY OF CHRIST COMMUNITY–DOWNTOWN CAMPUS

The roughly 250-member downtown congregation is one of five campuses of Christ Community Church (CCC), an Evangelical Free Church congregation founded in 1988 by Tom and Liz Nelson.[2] From the start it was envisioned as a church-planting church. Its ambitious vision involves planting churches around the Kansas City metro area, with these congregations faithfully engaged in the issues of their locale.

In 2011, church leaders realized that downtown was revitalizing, a place of growing importance. They desired a faith presence there. They initially tapped a veteran leader to oversee the effort, with help from Gabe. About six months in, that older leader took charge of another of the church's campuses, and Gabe was asked to head up the downtown group. He was twenty-six. "I was both thrilled and overwhelmed with the opportunity to shape this," he laughs. "I've been passionate for a while about city center ministry."

Gabe began his new leadership assignment by learning the downtown area, quickly developing connections with residents involved in the city's arts and cultural life. He and others on the team sensed God leading them toward a plant in the Crossroads arts district. The city's visitor's bureau gushes that the area is "home to a cornucopia of hundreds of one-of-kind gallery spaces and art studios."[3] The little congregation of about twenty—mostly young singles, some living downtown, others commuting in—officially launched in October 2011. It has always met in the arts district, though its address has changed a few times.

Within a few years CC-Downtown had grown to about 120 and was gathering at 1708 Baltimore Avenue. Several members were artists. The congregation still leaned heavily toward twenty- and thirty-somethings, with a smattering of empty nesters who'd moved into downtown lofts to be closer to the city's cultural opportunities.

While Kansas City isn't the Big Apple, it boasts a sizable arts community and several arts districts around the metro area. It is home to the Nerman Museum of Contemporary Art, the Spencer Museum of Art, the Nelson-Atkins Museum of Art, and the Albrecht-Kemper Museum of Contemporary Art as well as the Kansas City Art Institute, located downtown. The four-year private college was founded over one hundred years ago and enrolls close to seven hundred students.

CCC's leaders talk often about seeking the common good of the city. For the downtown campus that came to mean "doing something in the arts," though Gabe admits they didn't know exactly what that would be. Whatever they did, though, they wanted to be "a faithful and contributing presence."

To discern how to achieve that, Gabe—a musician, poet, and preacher—reached out to local leaders in the Kansas City arts scene. "I told them that we wanted to be a good neighbor and that means listening first." The counsel these leaders gave was consistent. They encouraged the young pastor to do three things: lead his congregation to be engaged in the arts, use their beautiful space as a gallery, and buy a building in the neighborhood later on where the fellowship could "put down permanent stakes and invest in artists in really meaningful ways." It's been a long journey but by 2020, CC-Downtown had done all three.

Gabe gathered an arts team that included a few of his young congregants and Jeremiah Enna, founder-director of Culture House, a leading arts-based nonprofit. Jeremiah wasn't part of the downtown campus, but he and his wife were members of CCC.

The team brainstormed about the role CC-Downtown could play in the local arts world, given the particular assets it had. The funky, beautiful, light-filled space where they gathered for worship services was their most significant asset. They soon settled on establishing an art gallery in that same space. Four Chapter Gallery, a joint venture between the church and Culture House, opened officially in 2013. The early years were mostly spent "learning the landscape," says Gabe, and discerning where Four Chapter Gallery could fit into the arts ecosystem and make a unique contribution. The group landed on Four Chapter engaging in two main ways.

First, they desired the gallery to offer tangible, loving service to artists—sponsoring shows, elevating artists, hosting art talks. They decided to offer artists a larger commission on sales than is typical (70 percent of the purchase price rather than the usual 50 percent). Gabe says that, plus the fact that "the space was just gorgeous," created favor for the gallery among artists. It appears the church has done well in its mission to love and serve artists. Former gallery director Leigh Ann Dull reports, "Every artist we've had in the space has always said to us, 'You guys have really gone above and beyond to help my show succeed.'" She says that this good treatment has opened up opportunities for her to have "a lot of spiritual conversations with these artists."[4]

Second, the downtown campus leaders wanted to contribute by curating important conversations. This goal eventually got articulated as showcasing "art with ideas." To those unfamiliar with the contemporary art world, the phrase may sound strange. I know the first time I heard it I thought, *What? You mean there's art* without *ideas?* But Four Chapters' approach is genuinely countercultural in today's art world.

The next phase in the gallery's development began when Leigh Ann, who for years had been mentoring Christian artists in New York City through the initiative she started at CRU[5] called "Transform Art," joined CC-Downtown and the arts team in 2015. She had moved to Kansas City a few years before and had been trying to find a church that took aesthetics seriously. She believes the arts play an indispensable role in helping people be truly human. "To be fully flourishing in God's design," she argues, "the arts and beauty must be a part of our lives." CC-Downtown was a great fit.

Leigh Ann says she "fully bought in" to the task force's art-with-ideas vision. The group was still trying to define its particular niche, though. She urged the group to focus especially on emerging artists. This has been her niche with Transform Art. The emphasis on young artists seemed to fit well with a young congregation with plenty of members who were also in their twenties. The arts team was also more interested in the gallery truly serving artists than they were in it making a big name for itself. The most important reason they settled on this focus, though, was because of the potential influence they could have on these young adults at the beginning of their careers. "We thought it would be a powerful story if artists ten, twenty years into their career looked back and said, 'The church invested in and helped form me into the artist I am today,'" Gabe says.

When Leigh Ann arrived, the small group was stretched from trying to oversee the gallery alongside all their other commitments. Jeremiah knew Leigh Ann from her work with Transform Art and trusted her. So, within three months he'd asked her to organize a gallery show.

"Leigh Ann brought an extraordinary show," Gabe recalls. "Mako [Fujimura] was here for it, along with several well-known local artists. It was the biggest show Four Chapter Gallery had done up to that point. After that, we really started to have some momentum."

Several months later, Leigh Ann assumed the role of gallery director. She hosted "artist dinners" in her home every one to two months. During one meeting, the group would talk about art and faith. During the next, one attendee would volunteer to be on the hot seat, showing their artwork and receiving feedback from attendees. Downtown, Leigh Ann expanded on the gallery's cooperation with street musicians and local artisan craft makers and worked on building relationships with local gallery owners. She signed up Four Chapter Gallery as a participant in First Fridays, a monthly gallery hop with a festival feel. "We tried hard to show the community that we wanted to be a part of it, pursuing its good," says Gabe. "We weren't interested in an us-versus-them style of church."

With Leigh Ann's extensive contacts, Four Chapter was able to begin booking serious artists to show their work and give talks. In 2016, Tyler Chernesky joined CC-Downtown's staff as a pastoral resident. One of his key duties was helping Leigh Ann grow Four Chapter's presence. By 2017 the gallery was hosting a new show about every month. Over time its reputation for contributing to the local arts scene grew stronger and more artists were seeking out Four Chapter to host their showings.

THE ARTS: FOR DISCIPLESHIP AND WITNESS

The church's arts focus has two main audiences: Christ-followers (within Christ Community Church and from other local congregations) and people in the local arts community. Four Chapter Gallery's art-with-ideas mission advances discipleship among the first audience and is introducing a new way of thinking about art to the second.

Discipleship for whole people in an image-saturated culture. For Christ-followers uninitiated in the arts, the gallery shows and artist talks nurture thoughtful engagement about the realm of aesthetics and the role it plays in human flourishing. Jeremiah says that congregants are also "learning how to reflect on specific kinds of works, particularly nonrepresentational art."

This discipleship is happening as congregants interact with both explicitly religious art (about 30 percent of what gets displayed) and what Gabe calls "art about reality; art that tells stories and ideates philosophies."

The gallery displays art by believers and those of no known faith. Gabe estimates that a little more than half of the artists are fellow believers. Kelly Kruse, for example, has held two shows in the gallery. Her 2017 show "My Iron Heart" showcased Kruse's mixed-media illuminations of John Donne's nineteen *Holy Sonnets* from the early seventeenth century. "These gorgeous poems wrestle with darkness, turmoil, confusion, devotion, the character of God, and the consequence of sin," Kelly explains.[6] Her aim in painting illuminations for them was to grapple visually with the questions that arose as she meditated on the poems. She hoped her illuminations would help Donne's readers ask their own questions about and interact deeply with his work. Her second show, "Let the Bones You Have Broken Rejoice," was on display during Lent 2018. It featured paintings done of Christ's Passion on canvases 5'4" tall (the estimated height of Jesus).[7] The canvases depicted various aspects of human pain (e.g., anxiety, shame, injustice) to show how Christ's suffering in the Passion corresponds to "practically any kind of human suffering imaginable."[8]

A good number of CCC congregants (from the Downtown campus and others) attend the various talks and gallery shows. On many of the Sunday mornings following the gallery's monthly First Friday display, Gabe or another arts team member interviews the artist whose work was showcased. "We take maybe eight to ten minutes to interview the artist, whether they are Christians or not," explains Gabe. "We talk with them about their influences, what they were hoping to see come out of this particular artwork, and what some of their struggles have been. We ask how we can be praying for them and we tell them thanks for their amazing work and how it made us a better church."

Commenting on this practice Jeremiah says, "It's a wonderful opportunity for the congregation to learn how someone different from them is communicating, using their gifts. It opens up a conversation, it opens up the artwork, and it stimulates discussion and relationships."[9]

The group of CC-Downtown leaders who've been behind its arts emphasis explains that attending to the aesthetic is necessary both because of our human nature and our modern setting. Regarding the first, Tyler emphasizes that humans are whole beings, not just brains. Therefore, discipleship cannot be only cerebral or word-based. "I love the life of the mind," Tyler says, "but I know that people don't make decisions based only on being persuaded intellectually. We are affected deeply by beauty. Our decisions are often formed by our intuitions or our emotions. And that is the world of the arts."[10] He adds, "The arts play a huge part in shaping how people perceive and interact in the world." To avoid being in the arts, to abandon thought on how people are being formed in this way, he says, "just feels negligent."

Jeremiah agrees and adds that a solely word-based approach to discipleship is insufficient because of the ways modern people are shaped by technology. "In Evangelical culture, and to an extent Protestants more generally, we've relied on the sermon to get the job done," Jeremiah says. "But in this day and age, with the internet and superfast everything, how many people do we really think are still truly engaged after ten minutes of a forty-minute sermon?" Words are important, Jeremiah acknowledges, but "God also speaks through arts and nature and not just the Bible."

It's also the case that we live today in an image-saturated culture. "If we're serious about the New Testament's charge to 'take every thought captive,' then we have to disciple people on this, engage with this," says Gabe.

These leaders also contend that the arts and beauty are powerful things God has used throughout history to draw people to himself. "Beauty has always been one of the compelling factors that causes people to worship God or follow Jesus' example," Tyler notes. "Beauty and the church have gone together for a while; they go hand in hand." On a practical level, church leaders report that congregants have been more willing to invite their nonbelieving friends to CC-Downtown because they can tell them the church is also an art gallery. That piques interest and draws people in.

Witnessing to a redeemed way in the world of art. For the artists Four Chapter serves, the gallery's approach to "art with strong ideation" is fresh. Tyler explains that believers are used to "everything being laden with meaning." By contrast, many trends in modern art are away from there being any inherent meaning behind a work. "Essentially what [art] students are invited to do is create something that seems good to them at the moment and then let people take from it what they will," explains Tyler. "The idea of art having a point—a story to tell or a case to make—is less and less common."

Jeremiah says that many emerging artists have a desire to be activists through their art but are reluctant to tell people what their art means. Into this dilemma, Jeremiah says, Four Chapter tells them, "If you do want to say something, that's not evil. Say it! Paint something meaningful."

Jeremiah says the gallery's approach also pushes against another idol in the contemporary arts sphere: a "hyperimbalance toward the self" in which the other is seen as insignificant. "In the art world the self is the center," he says. Artists are taught not to "sully themselves with concerns for the viewer." The problem with this is that it lacks a sense of accountability. "Part of the responsibility or stewardship of art is thinking about your audience," Jeremiah argues. "When I create, I should consider who I am creating for and that they matter in the equation."

Jeremiah explains that art is designed to create relational connections in a world where the fall has brought alienation. Art is to be communicative. "The visual arts, the performing arts, literature—these are some of our highest forms of expression," he emphasizes. "The arts are one of the things that God gives us to—on this side of heaven—start to repair and heal those relationships because it brings us together to share in something, to question things together, to get us talking and thinking and trying to understand together."

The gallery's approach is stretching established artists too, Tyler says. He says they feel as though professional art critics expect them to be ever more provocative and avant-garde. But the patrons of Four Chapter Gallery are not part of that professional arts community. So these artists are having to learn new ways to communicate. The gallery is accomplishing something redemptive by "letting established artists see that there are other ways to gain and shape an audience."

CC-Downtown's investment in the arts has also created a context for non-believers in the arts community to consider the claims of Christianity. Tyler reports that the gallery's events—and the conversations and relationships they have stirred—have "created plausibility for faith." He says that people in the art world are now recognizing that "faithful people can be intelligent, engaged in the city, caring for things beyond their own church. We're showing them that the Christian worldview is more robust and engaged than a lot of these urban folks often think."

CC-Downtown: Striving toward arts patronage. In a modest way CC-Downtown is trying to live into the legacy of the church as a patron of the arts. Jeremiah says the congregation is still early in that journey. Nonetheless, he believes that by making gallery space a priority, the downtown church is "reintroducing the idea to church-going people that the arts are important and meaningful."

Leigh Ann is encouraged by what she has witnessed in the congregation over the past few years. More congregants have gotten involved in assisting with the setup and take down of gallery shows. In addition, she says, "I think the initiative is teaching congregants why it's valuable to buy original art." Leaders talk about how "Christians should—of all people—be patrons of the arts because we know what God has given to us in creation and beauty." Churchgoers are very familiar with the concept of supporting a missionary, Leigh Ann adds. Now congregants are learning how art patronage can also be missional because of the vital ways artists influence culture.

This is a change in perspective Jeremiah is eager to see advanced. "The arts are a megaphone into the culture," he explains. Society's philosophers and thinkers come up with ideas. Then, it's the artists who "write the songs and paint the paintings inspired by these ideas, whether the ideas are good or bad." They get the ideas into circulation. He believes that the church's neglect of the arts over the past several decades is a major reason why Christianity's ideas are not spreading into the culture.

Moreover, Jeremiah sees how Christian leaders who lack a genuine engagement with the arts are failing to recognize the ways that cultural trends influence their churches. "Too often," he laments, "we are just baptizing the world's ideas." Church leaders uncritically adopt cultural forms and think they can simply pour in Christian content. As a result, Jeremiah says (quoting Ellis Potter from L'Abri), 'The world is the salt of the church.'"

Church and gallery leaders are excited about the ways the new church building will expand the CC-Downtown's art patronage. The gallery now has its own, large, dedicated space. It will feature rotating displays of artwork. Leigh Ann enthuses, "Our credibility in the community has risen due to the building and the galley having its own dedicated space. Opportunities for more excellent art abound."

The main worship area, Gabe describes, will feature permanent art commissioned by the congregation. The plan is to ask individuals to create art "that will combat the false narratives of our local context and show how the gospel pushes against those narratives." He reports that, increasingly, congregational leaders are understanding "how the aesthetic forms us as human beings." The presence of these artworks will become "a part of our regular liturgy," Gabe says, "constantly informing our imaginations."

The church also provides studio space for one artist in residence. Jeremiah believes this is a particularly important form of patronage. "We don't know which artists today are going to create legacy art," he explains. "We just have to invest in good artists. Their work may end up being the kind that has that staying power."

Collaborating for community flourishing. The church and Four Chapter Gallery have been engaged in some fruitful partnerships with local organizations in arts-focused initiatives. For example, from its early days the gallery has forged a strong relationship with the Kansas City Arts Institute (KCAI). Students in the fiber department submit their senior proposals to Leigh Ann and Kelly, who choose one to showcase at Four Chapter Gallery.

"We're trying to give these students a wonderful first experience with a gallery that will go above and beyond to serve them," says Kelly (who now serves as Four Chapter Gallery's Curator). She adds, "We take the time to really understand the KCAI student's work and to try to communicate the ideas behind their work to the broader public and our congregants, so they can find resonance in our audience."

Four Chapter gives patronage to the young artist in multiple ways: displaying their art for a full month, providing private tours for the student's family and friends, helping the student craft an artist statement and send out invitations, and often helping the student prepare an artist talk. "We send them away not just with a solo show under their belt but with the tools to share that work with prospective collectors and future galleries," says Kelly.

Four Chapter Gallery has also partnered with the Kansas City public library. In 2017 they worked together on an initiative called "Indisposable." The library provided digital cameras to members of the homeless community, encouraging them to document the city as they saw it. CC-Downtown paid for their photos to be enlarged and matted and displayed in the gallery. The church hosted a dinner there during which Tyler conducted interviews with some of the homeless people, asking them to talk about the subjects they'd chosen and the perspectives they were trying to share through their photography. "There was just a lot of cool stuff happening in that show," Tyler enthuses. "It was so affirming of human dignity. It highlighted people whose creativity isn't often highlighted."

The gallery has also hosted a February show each year that coordinates with Störling Dance Theater's annual production of *Underground*. (Störling is an initiative of Culture House and is led by Mona Enna). The nationally recognized dance troupe performs this show about the Underground Railroad annually at Kansas City's premier venue, the Kauffman Center for the Performing Arts. It tells the story of Whites and Blacks coming together to work toward freedom, justice, and equality. "It's a premier event bringing the African American and White communities together," says Jeremiah. "It has created the energy for the UNITE KC racial reconciliation movement that now involves about one hundred city leaders."

In 2019, Four Chapter's February show was titled "Black Wall Street." In an imaginative assemblage of archived photos and journalistic findings, African American artist Dawn Tree brought to life the history of the massacre of Black citizens by White Oklahomans in 1921. White residents murdered hundreds of Black residents and razed the thriving Greenwood neighborhood of Tulsa, which had been known as Black Wall Street, within hours. As part of the show Four Chapter hosted two events at which Tree and Mechelle Brown of the Greenwood Cultural Center spoke. Sara Forsythe, a former CC-Downtown congregant, attended. "[Tree's] talk was brutally honest," Sara recalls.[11] "It was really uncomfortable, but also good and right."

The event was well attended and, says Kelly, "hugely successful in bringing Whites and Blacks together for fruitful dialogue."

CC-Downtown has also partnered for three years with Mission Adelante, an urban ministry among Latino immigrants and Bhutanese refugees in the city, in offering a summer arts camp for youth ages eight to fifteen. The week-long arts camp was Sara's brainchild. After completing Christ Community Church's discipleship program, she started volunteering with Mission Adelante. Simultaneously, she was teaching music lessons to kids in a wealthy suburban neighborhood. Sara recognized a big gap in available opportunities for the two sets of youth. "The upper-class kids were participating in lots of arts activities—music, drama, dance," she says. "At the same time, I saw these immigrants and refugee kids whose parents were working two or three jobs, maybe didn't have a car, and couldn't take their kid to piano lessons. So, I saw this really stark contrast in access to the arts."

Sara pitched the idea of the arts camp to Gabe and the head of the church's outreach ministry. They loved it and offered to fund it. Sara and a team of about fifteen volunteers from the church hosted the first camp in 2017. Congregants taught a variety of art classes like music, drums, dance, painting, and sewing, and church small groups signed up to bring in lunches for the kids and crew on different days. Some congregants offered special one-time master's classes. The camp was a big hit with Mission Adelante staff, the kids, and the parents. After its first year a staff member launched a weekly arts-oriented program during the school year. In it kids can choose to focus on one particular art activity each trimester. CC-Downtown has continued the summer camp, which most recently boasted forty-five participants.

Sara loves how these activities have created avenues for the youth to express their own stories, sometimes drawing on their native cultural traditions. Meanwhile, the outreach offers a practical way for congregants to live into CC-Downtown's core values about the arts and promoting the common good in the city. "The arts camp has been a fun way for our DNA to come alongside [Mission Adelante's] DNA," Gabe reflects. "It's become a staple outreach initiative that has continued to grow. It's an example of how the arts are just part of who we are, how that emphasis just kind of bleeds into everything."

A rare bird. In making such significant investments in the arts, CC-Downtown is highly unique. It's not the only congregation I found during

my research that gives attention and support to the arts, but it's one of few—
and is more active than any other I found.

Asked why more churches don't engage with the arts, Leigh Ann comments that some just don't know how. Others are "scared of it." She also says
seminaries could do a better job of teaching a strong theology of beauty and
the arts. "The Western Protestant church has tended to value the Word and
been fearful of the visual language," she says.

Gabe thinks part of the issue is that many Christians hold a merely instrumental view of the arts. "Sometimes in the faith community there's a
temptation to see the arts as just an avenue to get people to talk about Jesus
rather than recognizing the intrinsic value of the arts," he says. "They don't
see that the arts bring beauty into the world and can be a catalyst for flourishing." Tom Nelson agrees and is thankful his congregation has gotten
behind CC-Downtown's arts-focused work. "The faithful presence inhabited
in our Four Chapter Gallery is one of our congregation's most important and
enduring expressions of goodness and common grace in our city," he says.[12]

CONCLUSION: CONTRIBUTING TO THE BEAUTIFUL
IN YOUR COMMUNITY

Beauty is a powerful witness. Indeed, as one thoughtful commentator
writes, "Our culture has shut out many Christian messages, but it can still
hear beauty."[13]

Any congregation, no matter its size, denomination, or location, has some
capacity to contribute to the endowment of the Beautiful. Not many will be
in a position to start a full-scale art gallery. But there are many other options
to pursue.

Some congregations may be able to advance the Beautiful by designing
(or redesigning) their public-facing spaces in ways that promote community
building. Sara Joy Proppe, founder of the Proximity Project, consults with
congregations to "connect their mission and their story to their physical
place in the neighborhood."[14] She believes the church has an important role
to play in redeeming the built environment for the common good. Proximity
has helped churches do things like creating public walking paths around
their campuses, establishing outdoor activity centers for children and their
parents, and installing bike racks and outdoor seating. Such positive efforts

to shape the built environment can enhance building relationships, a vital ingredient "for cultivating healthy and restorative community."[15]

Even more churches could contribute to the Beautiful through any number of arts-oriented initiatives. My research, for example, identified churches that had installed panels in an economically distressed community that depicted the likenesses of minority figures who'd made history;[16] partnered with artists to create a new stage for live performances;[17] and offered art classes to youth at a local juvenile detention center.[18] Tyler adds that church leaders could buy local art (instead of mass-produced or commercial art) when decorating their spaces.

LESSONS LEARNED

Tyler thinks the main lesson CC-Downtown has learned over the years is the need to listen well. "It's so, so valuable to hear an artist well, to [understand] their vision, encourage them, [and] partner in a way that's meaningful and authentic," he says. "The church shouldn't try to force the artist to fit into something the church is already doing. When things are more collaborative, an artist will have a better experience, the church will be pushed outside of what it normally does, and everyone wins."

In conclusion, Gabe says that doing ministry in the arts space "is like making really good wine." You combine the ingredients that God has given you—especially the people in the congregation inclined toward this kind of outreach. Then you listen well to the community. You trust in the partnerships developed and you give it time. "Let the flavors marinate and come to fruition," he encourages. "God will make something delicious."

8

THE JUST AND WELL-ORDERED

FLOURISHING IN THE REALM
OF POLITICAL AND CIVIC LIFE

BOB LINTHICUM, an expert in the world of Christian community organizing and community development, tells a story of how he got into this work in his 2003 book *Transforming Power*. As a college student in the late 1950s Bob was doing ministry with African American teenagers in a housing project in a US city. A girl named Eva joined the Bible study he was leading. One day she confessed to Bob that a powerful gang of men in the economically depressed neighborhood wanted her to join the ring of prostitutes they ran. She knew doing so would be wrong, but she was facing tremendous pressure. She asked him what she should do.

Bob was in way over his head. What did a nineteen-year-old White, middle-class boy know to say? He admits that "the only thing" he knew to tell her was to resist evil and it would flee from her. He urged her not to give in to their demands.

When he returned to the community after his summer vacation, he learned that Eva had stopped attending the Bible study. He went to her apartment to find out why. She opened the door, saw Bob, and burst into tears. "They got to me, Bob," she told him, "I'm one of their whores!" Bob was not very sympathetic. He asked her why she didn't resist. She replied that she had resisted, but the gang threatened to beat her father if she didn't join. She refused, and they hurt her father badly. They told her that her brother was next. She still refused. Her brother ended up with two broken legs. They warned that if she didn't join, they would next rape her mother. So, she acquiesced.

Bob responded. "But Eva, why did you let them intimidate you that way? Why didn't you get some protection? Why didn't you go to the police?"

Eva responded in disgust, "Who do you think the gang is?"[1]

Few stories are as bone-chilling as those that involve the abuse of power. Injustice is fundamentally about the abuse of power. Justice, by extension, is rooted in the righteous use of power. When we proclaim that God is just and that all his ways are just, we are saying that God always deploys his power righteously. His power is wedded to his goodness, love, and wisdom. He never misuses his power for the advance of evil. He is never unjust.

And this just God is passionate that his followers act justly. Indeed, when the prophet Micah sums up what God requires of us, he states it simply as "to act justly and to love mercy, and walk humbly with God" (Mic 6:8). God's will is that his people deal with one another and with others in justice.

HUMAN FLOURISHING AND THE JUST AND WELL-ORDERED

The community endowment of the Just and Well-Ordered concerns the realm of political and civic life. The institutions of this endowment include government bodies, police and emergency services, neighborhood associations, interest groups, and local activists, among others. This realm is about a community's system of law and order and the practices of political deliberation, civic engagement, and community organizing. Specifically, in the context of the Thriving Cities project (which is interested in urban centers), it concerns the "organized complexity of cities." In an essay for the project scholar Guian McKee explains that the diversity of the urban environment is a potential source of thriving because of its constant stimulation and interplay of ideas and creativity. Yet that same complexity, "if not appropriately organized, can also contribute to conditions of exploitation, severe inequality, deep power disparities, or even violence and repression." As a result, the polity must address, simultaneously, questions of order and justice.[2]

Justice is a central, irreplaceable component of a flourishing community. Genuine thriving for all community members simply isn't possible unless critical institutions of civic life—for example, legislative and executive bodies, the criminal justice system, the judiciary, the media, and law enforcement—act fairly and transparently. A community will not genuinely flourish without a sense of public safety, equitable policies, avenues for peaceful conflict resolution, and fair due process in the legal system (instead of arbitrary or discriminatory treatment). A community moving toward greater thriving is a community with decreasing oppression, violence, fraud, corruption, segregation, discrimination, and dehumanization. A community progressing toward genuine flourishing is one where people have equal opportunities, disputes are settled nonviolently, laws protect people from harm, and trust among diverse individuals and trust between neighborhoods and law enforcement is growing. It is marked by active and respectful political participation, by nonprofit organizations seeking to invigorate civic life, by community organizing, and by all citizens having opportunities to have a voice.

Importantly, from a biblical perspective, a thriving community is a place where its most vulnerable members are protected from abuse by those with greater power. It is a place where every individual's fundamental dignity and humanity are embraced. Moreover, it is a place where the systems that seek to navigate conflicts and crimes are committed to restoring, to the extent possible, social peace.

THE JUST AND WELL-ORDERED: CREATIONAL INTENT

Scripture is replete with teachings about how God desires community life to be ordered. It is impossible to cover this daunting material in a single chapter. Instead, I looked for a core principle in Christian theology that foundationally animates what the endowment of the Just and Well-Ordered ought to be about. That principle concerns the right use of power.

The power principle. God created this world and rules it with sovereign power. His power is wedded to his goodness and used always in the service of love. God's power advances his righteousness, his will for people to experience "the life that is truly life."

In Andy Crouch's words, "power is for flourishing. When power is used well, people and the whole cosmos come more alive to what they were meant to be."[3] God has shared power with human beings, giving us the capacity and the calling to join him in the creative use of power that enriches human flourishing. In giving away this power God has not diminished his own. Indeed, in the right use of power, capacity is expanded. Crouch explains the Christian understanding of power: "All true being strives to create room for more being and to expend its power in the creation of flourishing environments for variety and life, and to thrust back the chaos that limits true being."[4]

In the realm of politics and civic life, this right use of power takes at least eight expressions.

Honoring the sanctity of human life. In the human community as God desires it, every person's fundamental dignity is honored.

A society that denies the humanity of certain groups of people is by definition a deformed version of society. God intends that every person is honored as a partaker in his image. Moreover, the community should be organized in such ways that all people have freedom and opportunity for exercising their God-given creative capacity.

Practicing fairness. Since each person has equal worth, each is due equal treatment. A key Hebrew term for justice, *mishpat*, conveys this idea. *Mishpat* occurs over two hundred times in the Old Testament. Timothy Keller, in *Generous Justice*, explains that *mishpat*'s "most basic meaning is to treat people equitably. It means acquitting or punishing every person on the merits of the case, regardless of race or social status. Anyone who does the same wrong should be given the same penalty."[5]

In short, judicial, legislative, and executive power must not be used to oppress some people while favoring others.

Keller adds that *mishpat* is also about giving people their rights. He notes that the word is used in Deuteronomy 18 regarding the support that is due to the priests from the people. *Mishpat*, then, "is giving people what they are due, whether punishment or protection or care."[6]

Solidarity with the vulnerable. In a perfect community devoid of sin, no member is vulnerable to abuse. God's norm is a world without injustice. But that world did not last long. Following humankind's exile from the Garden of Eden because of sin, human beings became subject to a variety of vulnerabilities—sickness, famine, impoverishment through natural disaster, and exploitation by people committing evil deeds. Since God is committed to the flourishing of every person, he instructed his people Israel to pay special attention to "the quartet of the vulnerable": widows, orphans, aliens, and the poor.[7]

God himself is a protector and defender of the vulnerable. Moses describes God's character in Deuteronomy 10:18, saying, "He defends the cause of the fatherless and the widow, and loves the foreigner residing among you, giving them food and clothing." The psalmist proclaims that God is "A father to the fatherless, a defender of widows" (Ps 68:5). God uses his power to protect and *empower*. He wants his followers to do the same:

Defend the weak and the fatherless;
uphold the cause of the poor and the oppressed.
Rescue the weak and the needy;
deliver them from the hand of the wicked. (Ps 82:3-4)

God hates when power is used to exploit the weak. He warns, for example, in Deuteronomy 27:19, "Cursed is anyone who withholds justice from the foreigner, the fatherless or the widow." God does not want us to forget that the despised of the earth bear his image. God identifies himself profoundly with the poor and vulnerable. Proverbs 14:31 states, "Whoever oppresses the poor shows contempt for their Maker, but whoever is kind to the needy honors God."

This theme of divine solidarity with the poor and oppressed is continued into the New Testament story: Jesus comes to earth as a baby in a materially poor family. He identifies with the oppressed through his own unjust treatment. He emphasizes his close solidarity with the poor in Matthew 25:35-40, teaching that when his followers feed the hungry, clothe the naked, and visit the prisoner, they are feeding, clothing, and visiting him.

Just generosity. A second Hebrew term closely related to justice is *tsedaqah*, often translated as "righteousness" in English. *Tsedaqah*, Keller explains, "refers to day-to-day living in which a person conducts all relationships in family and society with fairness, generosity and equity."[8] This is rooted first in the right relationship with God, which then should issue forth in a righteous life lived among neighbors.[9]

What are our neighbors (especially the vulnerable ones) due in a just and well-ordered community? Clearly, they are due fair treatment. God does not want them exploited, oppressed, or defrauded. But what they are due goes even beyond this (a concept strange to our Western, individualistic ears). God desires not only that we do not harm others but that we proactively seek their good, particularly the good of the poor. Notably, *God commands generosity as a matter of justice, not mere charity*. Drawing on Isaiah 58, Keller asserts that failure to share one's bread with the hungry isn't just a matter of stinginess. It is unjust:

> In the Scripture, gifts to the poor are called "acts of righteousness," as in Matthew 6:1-2. Not giving generously, then, is not stinginess but unrighteousness, a violation of God's law. In the book of Job, we see Job call every failure to help the poor a sin, offensive to God's splendor (Job 31:23) and deserving of judgment and punishment (v. 28). Remarkably, Job is asserting that it would be a sin against God to think of his goods as belonging to himself alone. *To not "share his bread" and his assets with the poor would be unrighteous, a sin against God, and therefore by definition a violation of God's justice.*[10]

Christopher Wright agrees. Discussing the gleaning regulations of Deuteronomy 24:19-21, he explains that the property rights of the landowner are secondary to the needs of the poor:

> To harvest in such a way as to leave no gleanings would be to deprive the alien or the fatherless of justice. . . . The sense is therefore, "Do not pick the forgotten sheaf, the remaining olives and grapes, *they belong* to the alien, orphan and widow." The remainder of the harvest *is theirs*; they have every right to do the final harvesting themselves.[11]

Despite humankind's efforts to draw a line between *justice* as legal fairness and sharing as *charity*, Scripture contends that generosity is a matter of justice because of the rightful claims the needy have on those with resources.

Our brother's keeper. A closely related feature of civic life as God seems to desire it is this: he wants community members to embrace *a sense of responsibility for one another*. A just polity is one where members adopt the posture that we *are* our brother's keeper, where we understand that our flourishing is tied up with others' flourishing. Keller depicts shalom as a healthy social fabric in which everything is woven together and interdependent. Doing justice means attending to those not adequately woven in, "taking the threads of your life—your emotions, your time, your body, your physical presence, your money—and plunging them into the lives of other people through thousands of involvements."[12]

Tsedaqah includes accepting brotherly obligation—where we as individuals recognize that others have claims on us; where we understand that what's *ours* isn't ours alone. This is the mindset that fuels the kind of sharing we see described in Acts 2.

Right ordering of relationships, personal and institutional. God's concern for justice takes several expressions in the Old Testament law, but all of them find a common root in this principle of our moral responsibility to one another. "To act justly" in the biblical sense, Bruce Waltke explains, is less about obeying commandments than conforming to the ideal of the covenant established by God.[13] *Justice is about fulfilling the obligations of particular relationships.* Shalom results when these relational obligations are fulfilled.[14]

Multiple kinds of *personal* relational responsibilities are discussed in the Old Testament law, such as commercial contracts, lender-debtor arrangements, and employer-employee relations. Leviticus 19:13 and Deuteronomy 24:14-15 enjoin employers to pay their hired hands on the same day their services are rendered (since daily wages were needed to buy daily bread). Exodus 22:25-27 sets restraints on lenders and protections for debtors; for example, the lender mustn't keep a pledged cloak overnight, since the debtor needs it for warmth.

God also desires such right relationships (we could call them *well-ordered* relationships) at the *institutional* level. Society is composed not only of individuals but of all sorts of institutions—families, churches, businesses, government bodies, neighborhood associations, schools, and judicial systems, among others. These institutions need freedom to carry out their various tasks according to their particular norms, and the different spheres should respect one another's authority. None carries absolute authority; that sovereignty belongs only to God. Just as it is sinful for one individual to use their power to exploit another, no one sphere should deploy power to gain domination over another (for example, government infringing on the family's sphere).

Diversity in community. Diversity is good and God-ordained. God chose to make many varieties of trees, fish, and animals, not just one. He made humans to be of two genders. At the same time, God loves community. God is himself trinitarian community; yet there is distinctiveness in the three persons of Father, Son, and Holy Spirit. What do these things mean for human community? It seems safe to say that God desires diversity in community. Yes, there are two genders, but there is one humanity. Yes, there are multiple varieties of four-legged animals, but they are all mammals. Yes, there are three persons in the Godhead, but there is one God.

God is beyond all our best attempts at fully comprehending him. No wonder that when he chose to put his image in men and women, he created an endless diversity among them. There is no way that just one culture or color or gender or ethnicity could ever capture the manifold, multifaceted glory of God. God created diversity because only diversity could reflect who he is.

Yet all that diversity is meant to live in community. Given that diversity in eternal community is his own nature and that he is the ultimate good, then diversity in community must be good for his children too. He desires it for us and our societies, and Jesus' sacrificial death brought the power that achieved such horizontal reconciliation:

> For he himself is our peace, who has made the two groups one and has destroyed the barrier, the dividing wall of hostility, by setting aside in his flesh the law with its commands and regulations. His purpose was to create in himself one new humanity out of the two, thus making peace, and in one body to reconcile both of them to God through the cross, by which he put to death their hostility. He came and preached peace to you who were far away and peace to those who were near. (Eph 2:14-17)

The different groups within the human community ought not to think they do not need one another. Yet our sinfulness, prejudices, and fears can drive us to misuse our power by excluding or repressing certain people groups. A right understanding and ordering of power would lead instead to groups seeking synergistic relationships through which, together, they both become more/better than they could be alone.

Restorative justice. We have seen that biblical justice is understood as a relational concept and that the right use of power involves empowering. Not surprisingly, then, the Bible teaches restorative justice as its central paradigm for dealing with crimes and torts. God's vision involves not just punishing wrongdoing (presumably as a deterrent against future bad action by the offender) but repairing the harm done and to the extent possible restoring the relationship—and even the offender.

These ideas are illustrated in the area of civil torts by the Old Testament's instructions regarding public safety. Texts in Exodus 21–22 cover what we might call rules of liability. To promote public safety Israelites were to pen bulls (to prevent them from goring people), to not leave open pits animals could fall into, and to construct a parapet around the roof of their homes to keep people from falling off. When individuals failed to do these things and harm ensued, they had to pay restitution. They had to take intentional action to try to make the offended party whole again.

Similarly, as relates to crime, restorative justice focuses primarily on repairing the harm. Consider, for example, Exodus 22:1. It commanded that a thief who stole an ox must repay the original owner five head of cattle. Here there is a punishment (the offender incurs a significant penalty—the cost of five cattle). But here also there is restoration for the owner: they receive back what was lost, plus extra. Moreover, the ultimate vision in mind is for restoration of the offender too. The power of the restorative justice approach includes its possibility for new creation: reformed offenders restored to the community where they can deploy their God-given capacity and be contributors. This is not part of the vision of retributive justice that focuses solely on punishment.

In a journal article on restorative justice, leading Christian practitioners Howard Zehr and Ted Grimsrud argue that it conforms to four themes of biblical justice. The first is the idea that justice is for the sake of life. "God's justice in the Old Testament is not primarily about retribution but salvation, not primarily punitive but corrective." The second theme is that "justice is part of the created order." That is, creation is an act of the covenant-making God of Israel, and that which God has made "harmonizes with the values of the covenant love, justice, peace, compassion—that which sustains and nourishes life." God created humans as relational beings and since injustice is about the breaking of relationships, justice is about restoring them. Third, "justice is not soft on evil but rather seeks to destroy evil"—as an expression of God's justice. But the way God triumphs over evil is through suffering love that "works to set right that which has been corrupted." Finally, "God's justice is especially concerned with the most vulnerable members of society."[15] Taken together, Zehr concludes, these themes show that "the Bible emphatically identifies God's love with God's justice. . . . The concern for justice is *people*, much more than 'fairness,' 'liberty,' or 'entitlements.' Biblical justice focuses on right relationships, not right rules.[16]

THE JUST AND WELL-ORDERED: MALFORMATIONS

The principal malformation in the endowment of the Just and Well-Ordered is a deformed understanding of power as zero-sum. This is well illustrated by a quote from Friedrich Nietzsche's *The Will to Power*: "My idea is that every specific body strives to become master over all space and to extend its force (its will to power) and to thrust back all that resists its extension."[17] Here we have power used to dominate others rather than to empower others. This is power hoarded, deployed solely for one's gain rather than shared for cooperative ventures.

Tragically, we see this all over the world. Malformations in the realm of political and civic life are numerous. Injustice and corruption in various forms run rampant in nations across the globe. We see political ideologies that endorse one-party, repressive systems (e.g., China, North Korea). These governments deploy state power to dominate over other societal institutions (e.g., the spheres of family, education, religion, business) instead of recognizing their authority. We see certain people groups denied voice and opportunity (e.g., legalized repression of women in Saudi Arabia). This illustrates the unjust use of power by gender. We see cultural belief systems denying the fundamental humanity of certain citizens (e.g., repression of the Dalits in India by some Hindus).

Here in the United States at least three major deformations are readily visible. First, although the equal dignity of all people is rhetorically affirmed, in practice White supremacy remains embedded in many of our social structures. The story of racism is largely one about the abuse of power by White legislatures, White-controlled economic systems, and White-led police forces. Structural racism is the codification of the abuse of power by the dominant group. This structural racism is about the policies and laws—in education, housing, health care, and the criminal justice system—that have in the past and continue in the present to "dispropor-tionately segregate communities of color from access to opportunity and upward mobility."[18]

Second, our civic life is dangerously segregated and polarized. On the surface the United States is becoming more diverse. According to the Census Bureau, we are on track to become a majority-minority society by 2044. But, as Bill Bishop describes in *The Big Sort*, "the places where we live are be-coming increasingly crowded with people who live, think, and vote like we do."[19] Looking at the patterns of spatial geography, Joshua Yates from Thriving Cities has noted that "our most diverse cities are often our most segregated cities."[20] This segregation is not solely based on ideology or race (though residential racial segregation remains a troubling reality in many locales). It is also about the separation of the well-educated affluent from the less well-educated working class, for example, as described regarding White America in Charles Murray's 2012 book *Coming Apart*. There are now "ZIP codes that have levels of affluence and education that are so much higher than the rest of the population that they constitute a different kind of world," Murray says.[21]

Third, rather than being based on restorative justice, our criminal justice system is dominated by a retributive justice paradigm. Figure 8.1 highlights the differences. For example, retributive justice is more rule-centered than people-centered, and it focuses more on punishing the offender than on repairing the harm done to the victim.

Retributive Justice	Restorative Justice
Rule-focused (break law)	People-focused (cause harm)
Focus on infliction of pain	Focus on making right
Rewards based on just deserts	Rewards based on need
Separate from mercy	Based on mercy and love
Seek to maintain status quo	Transforms status quo
Central actors: state versus individual	Central actors: entire community, including offender
State (or God) as victim	People (shalom/peace) as victims
Goal is offender paying debt to society (God); victim is (often) ignored	Goal is restoration of relationships; healing for all parties

Figure 8.1. Comparing retributive and restorative justice

THE CHURCH'S HISTORICAL CONTRIBUTIONS
TO THE JUST AND WELL-ORDERED

It's no secret that the Christian church has been guilty of terrible failures to do justice. Just think of White Christians' justification of Jim Crow or the multiple scandals around the Catholic Church's failure to adequately address the horror of priests sexually abusing children. And our failings are not only in the past but also in the present. Certainly, there is a great deal that we Christians have to repent of and to lament. We desperately need courage and humility to reckon with past and present sins.

As part of the journey toward doing better, though, it is also important to remember that church history includes many examples of ways believers have contributed to bringing greater justice in their societies. We review these things not to boost our pride but to learn from the past.

Contributions: Three core ideas. The church's historical contributions to the structure and re-formational direction of the Just and Well-Ordered include the following core ideas.

Imago Dei and equality. From the earliest days of the church Christians suffered extreme persecution at the hands of Roman emperors. They were in no position to bring about social reform. They were themselves victims of gross violence and injustice. But the early church still made a critical contribution to the advancement of justice through its Bible-based teaching on the inherent equal worth of all persons. The early Christians' embrace of the doctrine of *imago Dei* and the proposition that in Christ there are "no Greek or Jew, slave or free" meant that a countercultural ethic of equality marked their fellowship. We've already looked at the ways this led to better treatment of women and children (see chap. 2).

Additional New Testament teachings reinforce the ethnicity- and class-abolishing divisions the early church sought to embody (though their fellowships sometimes failed). James, for example, insists on equal treatment of the poor rather than favoritism to the rich (Jas 2:1-5). Paul is deeply concerned that the Eucharist demonstrates incarnationally the new humanity Christ has created, one that upends the identities and cliques of the world. The gathering of Jesus' people should never replicate the divisions or dissensions, class or otherwise, of the world (1 Cor 11:17-34). Rather, "the Eucharist is to interrogate, disrupt, and ultimately abolish them, such that the gathered community manifests a unique form of sociality unknown and unavailable to other social bodies."[22]

In this way the early church embodied Jesus' countercultural way of stewarding power. Jesus taught his disciples not to lord their authority over others (Mt 20:25-28) but rather to use their authority to serve and build up others. The equal table fellowship, wherein people of different social statuses in the world (and different levels of leadership in the church) were all brothers and sisters, manifested this mindset.

In the fourth century Emperor Constantine legalized Christianity, putting an end to the worst of the persecution of Christians. During his reign the church father Lactantius, a philosopher-theologian whom Oliver O'Donovan calls the "first Christian thinker to subject the idea of justice to serious analysis," wrote *The Divine Institutes*.[23] Addressing his tome to Constantine, Lactantius "systematically placed the basic structure and fundamental cultural themes of imperial society on trial before the Christian faith."[24] Put differently, Lactantius was arguing for a new way of understanding power. Lactantius advocated "new public law and policy teaching religious tolerance" as well as "a change in imperial mores in the direction of respect for human dignity . . . and consequent justice as equity." Equity, for this church father, was rooted in the equal human dignity of all persons regardless of social class. Lactantius desired to shape in Constantine a Christian conscience that would attend to the plight of the poor and powerless by establishing protections for them from the exploitation of the wealthy.[25]

The rule of law. The historical origins of the idea of the rule of law are not limited to the Judeo-Christian tradition. Aristotle was an advocate, as was Cicero. Nonetheless, scholarly treatments of the subject that neglect to note Christianity's key contributions (such as the *Stanford Encyclopedia of Philosophy*, which jumps from Aristotle to John Locke) are unfair. "Christianity," write law professors David Skeel and Bill Stuntz, "contains the seeds of the rule of law: the ideas that all men and women have dignity in God's eyes, and that all need governing because all are prone to sin." In other words, the Christian understanding of creation and fall implies "the basic protections associated with the rule of law."[26]

The Christian faith acknowledges just limits on state power. While Romans 13 enjoins believers to obey the governing authorities, it also indicates that such authorities are meant by God to uphold the right and punish the wrong. When a governing authority's actions do the opposite, contravening God's moral law (such as when Pharaoh decreed all male Israelite newborns be killed or when Jewish authorities forbade Peter and James from teaching about Jesus), Christ-followers must obey God, not man.

Christianity likewise holds that no one is above just laws. In the fourth century, Ambrose, the bishop of Milan, boldly applied this principle when he held Emperor Theodosius to account for the massacre he carried out in Thessalonica.

Scripture also provides the basis for applying the same law to all persons regardless of their status. Consider, for example, Leviticus 19:15, which commands God's people to "not pervert justice" by showing partiality to the poor or favoritism to the great. This conviction was the basis for Alfred the Great's reforms of law (the *Doom Book*) in the ninth century. Christopher Collins of the University of Alabama law school contends that Alfred's legislation was the foundation of the Magna Carta.[27]

Restorative justice. The restorative justice movement has been one of the most significant contributions to the endowment of the Just and Well-Ordered in the twentieth century. The movement originated in the Mennonite community, and to this day Howard Zehr from Eastern Mennonite University is considered a grandfather of the paradigm. The evangelical organization Prison Fellowship International has also become a major institutional standard-bearer for the movement.

Contributions: Three practices. In addition to the vital contributions in thought that Christianity has made to the realm of civic life, we can note some key practices conducted by the church that have sought to resist deformations in this community endowment.

Limiting violence. In medieval times the church played a key role in promoting nonviolent dispute resolution. Conflicts between families and communities at this time in history sometimes involved blood feuds: if someone in one clan was killed by a person from a different clan, they sought revenge in kind. The church advocated alternative means of settling disputes through mechanisms that today we'd call reconciliation conferences or mediation. During the "Love Day" custom, for example, apart from common law proceedings church officials would arbitrate conflicts between rivals to settle disputes.[28]

Church leaders in the Middle Ages used their influence to promote greater public safety by seeking limits on violence and warfare. The Pax Dei promulgated in 989 by the archbishop of Bordeaux threatened excommunication for anyone who despoiled church property, robbed the poor, or used violence against women and children. The 1027 "Truce of God" edict issued by the Council of Toulouges limited the days of the week and times of year that the European nobility engaged in violence.[29]

In all of this, we see church leaders putting into practice the foundational principle of the sanctity of life.

The Geneva Convention. That principle is also in play in the history behind the Geneva Convention. It marked another attempt by thoughtful Christians to address the ravages of war. The convention was the brainchild of Swiss believer Henri Dunant, founder of the Red Cross. Dunant had witnessed wounded soldiers bleeding to death in Solferino in 1859 because medical personnel could not safely access them (doctors and nurses were considered combatants). His published memoir of the event galvanized public awareness and concern over the practice. Dunant was successful in gathering international delegates in Geneva in 1863 to discuss his proposal that medical personnel be considered neutral parties. This would allow them on the battlefield to treat the wounded and save lives. To mark out the doctors and nurses, a fellow Swiss delegate suggested they wear armbands of a red cross on a white background. This red cross could also be painted on ambulances. Building on the success of this conference, Dunant and his followers organized a second convention the following year. At its end ten nations had signed the first Geneva Convention. It guaranteed neutrality for medical workers and their equipment and also required that soldiers treat their captured enemies' wounds or arrange for someone else to do so.[30]

Prison reform. Christian principles about the sanctity of human life, solidarity with the vulnerable, and restorative justice have motivated the prison reforms Christ-followers have achieved in past centuries. John Wesley and his band of Methodists are an outstanding example. While students at Oxford in the 1730s, the early Methodists embraced the Scripture's imperative to visit the imprisoned. Shocked by the appalling conditions, they soon were advocating for reforms and mobilizing humanitarian relief in the form of food and blankets. They were able to see the face of Jesus in the face of the imprisoned and responded with compassion.

Indeed, Wesley's concerns for humane conditions for prisoners marked the rest of his life. He frequently chastised prison warders publicly for their base treatment of inmates. He urged all Methodist preachers to make a habit of prison visitation. He, his brother Samuel, and other friends were active for many years in ministering to prisoners at the infamous Newgate prison. By 1761, their efforts had born tremendous fruit. Wesley's letter to a newspaper that year described how the prison was now clean, free from brawling and drunkenness, and women prisoners were kept separate from the men.[31]

Wesley also established programs whereby prisoners were furnished with tools and materials to make articles for sale. In this way these men and women could earn money to purchase additional food. Wesley cajoled medical practitioners to provide treatment in the prisons and held worship services and Bible studies behind bars regularly.[32] In all this Wesley and his friends demonstrated their commitment to being their brother's keeper. They also showed through these actions their conviction that people could change, that reformation is possible. In short, they embraced a biblical commitment to restorative justice that believed in trying to help offenders rehabilitate and become contributing members of society once again.

CONCLUSION

There is no shortage of arenas today where the Christian church can seek to encourage needed reformations in the sphere of politics and civic life. For example,

- Our public discourse has coarsened and advocates on different sides of pressing issues have become contemptuous of one another. In the face of this, faithful congregations willing to do some very hard, intentional work can model thoughtful, respectful dialogue, humble listening, and "living with disagreement." Pastor Charles Drew (author of *Surprised by Community: Republicans and Democrats in the Same Pew*) has led Emmanuel Presbyterian Church in Manhattan to do this over the past several years.

- Police-community relations in neighborhoods of color are severely strained by mistrust. But congregations like Victory in Praise, a roughly 550-member congregation in Stockton, California, are proving that better, healthier relationships are possible. Toni McNeil, Victory's social justice minister, has been cofacilitating workshops since 2017 with senior officers from the Stockton Police Department that bring police officers, congregants, and community members together. The workshops cover topics like procedural justice, history of policing, and principled policing. Police Chief Eric Jones has invested enormous personal energy in the work for the past several years. The result is that trust has increased and crime is down.

- The climate for immigrants in the United States has grown increasingly unwelcoming. Members in both the immigrant community and the law enforcement community say they want to see positive change. In Greensboro, North Carolina, churches are helping to lead the way. There, FaithAction International House has sponsored dialogue sessions between the two communities, held at local churches. FaithAction's executive director, David Fraccaro, says, "That sacred space really made this program take off, really solidified the trust in the room."[33] The conversations led to a fruitful new initiative: the FaithAction ID. It's a photo identification card that gives recent immigrants a way to prove their identity. It's especially helpful to those without access to government-issued forms of identification. It allows police to confirm an immigrant's local address—something that can help prevent immigrants from being arrested (and potentially deported) for simply not having identification.[34]

Engaging in the three "heated" arenas noted above obviously takes courageous leadership. There are also easier but still valuable ways churches can be involved. Mt. Vernon Baptist Church in Arlington County, Virginia, for example, has hosted R.E.S.T Stop East, "a secure sanctuary where First Responders may find respite and experience renewal in noncontact space," since 2014. The acronym stands for Restoring Essential Servants Together. Rev. Samuel Feemster says the rest stop (a dedicated space inside the church with an external entrance controlled via a lockbox) "is an expression of our gratitude for the courageous women and men whose repeated exposure to danger and evil during the routine of their vocational lives is our shield from harm."[35]

Westwood Community Church outside Minneapolis also loves to show its gratitude to public servants. It does so in a couple of ways each year. One is that they bring lunch to city leaders. Another is that, as part of the church staff's annual retreat, they visit the mayor at his or her office to hear a "state of the city" presentation. Pastor Joel Johnson says,

> Serving needs [in the city] is great and we should always be about that. But to try to get to be part of the voice of the community, to be intentional about being at the table, that's even a higher calling. It takes intentionality and an investment of a lot of time, but it leads to our voices being instrumental in decision-making that affects the quality of life in the community. There's a place for us if we come in the spirit of humility.[36]

In the chapters that follow I take an in-depth look at two additional strategies: advancing restorative justice and pursuing reconciliation across racial divides.

9

A STRATEGY FOR CULTIVATING THE JUST

ADVANCE RESTORATIVE JUSTICE

THE UNITED STATES has the dubious honor of sporting the world's highest incarceration rate, with 2.2 million people in prison and jails.[1] It's estimated that one in twenty-eight kids has a parent in prison.[2] This mass incarceration disproportionately affects African American and Latino citizens. For example, African Americans are incarcerated at more than five times the rate of Whites.[3]

The US criminal justice system is about retributive justice. Punishment is its signal feature. It is an approach that fails to achieve rehabilitation. According to the US Justice Department, over two-thirds of prisoners re-offend within three years of their release.[4]

In west Michigan a coalition of churches and nonprofit organizations are vigorously seeking to bring reform. They are advocates of "restorative justice," a paradigm rooted in biblical reflection. Church of the Servant (COS) in Grand Rapids is in the thick of this activity. Through a variety of holistic ministries it has brought about significant improvements in the lives of prisoners. It has helped hundreds of returning citizens find their way back into roles as contributors. It has also played a role in advancing specific reforms affecting juvenile offenders and is an advocate of creating greater opportunities for returning citizens.

Michigan houses some forty-one thousand prisoners in its thirty-one facilities. According to the Annie E. Casey Foundation, one in ten children in Michigan has a parent who has been incarcerated. Parents also watch their children sentenced to life in prison, and it's devastating. Thankfully, the story of Rich and Carol Rienstra's family has a happier ending. Despite receiving a life sentence for armed robbery with assault in 1995, their adopted son Troy earned his parole in 2016. Today, as outreach director for the nonprofit Safe and Just Michigan, Troy is a tireless advocate for criminal justice reform. The Rienstras have been the driving force behind COS's multifaceted engagement in restorative justice initiatives. Several factors, though, including ones that long predated the Rienstras, made COS fertile soil for becoming a leading congregation in the restorative justice movement.

A CONCEPT CHURCH FOCUSED ON SOCIAL JUSTICE

COS began in the late 1960s as a concept church, that is, one based not on geography but a set of core commitments. These included avoiding high expenditures on a building, creating equal roles for women in ministry, and social justice. It organized as a congregation in the Christian Reformed Church in America (CRC) denomination in 1973. A commitment to community engagement and social justice runs deep in the congregation's self-identity. As Andrew Mead, one of COS's current copastors, describes, "We're a church that wants to have its Sunday morning liturgy and worship form us . . . for a life of loving service to our neighbors and a life of witness to the kingdom of God and his justice and shalom in the world."[5]

The congregation's actions back up these words. For forty years it has welcomed and helped to resettle refugee families, launching a basic English worship service for them in 2009. Its creation-care team meets every other month, working to make COS more energy efficient and to educate congregants on environmental issues and advocacy campaigns. An antiracism team has been active since 2000.

Today COS gathers about 550 worshipers on any given Sunday. Located near Calvin University, a Christian liberal arts college, the congregation includes multiple professors and students. COS's academic firepower is manifest in the meaty adult education classes it offers. At the time of this writing, congregants could participate in Sunday morning courses on everything from "a theology of disability" to "mental health and faith," alongside opportunities to dialogue about the intersections of faith and science, study Matthew and Luke, take a class on the spiritual disciplines, or join a three-week teaching series on the church in the Middle East. Additionally, on three Wednesday nights each month congregants can participate in a variety of classes and special lectures held at the church.

Given COS's founding commitments and the fact that one of the nation's premier Christian philosophers on social ethics, Nicholas Wolterstorff, counts COS as his home congregation, it is not surprising that congregants have enjoyed numerous opportunities to learn about biblical justice. Wolterstorff, author of *Until Justice and Peace Embrace* and *Justice: Rights and Wrongs*, has taught classes and events at COS that gather hundreds of eager participants. COS has also offered "The Justice Class" during the 2017 and 2018 academic years. Congregant Tom McWhertor, a board member of the DC-based Center for Public Justice, developed the class to explore a range of justice themes.

Peter Vander Meulen, who served as the first director of the CRC's office of social justice, has been a member of COS since 1980. He counts himself as one among many of Wolterstorff's mentees in the congregation. "Nick and his wife, Claire, were among the original church founders," Peter says. "They have shaped just about everything in this church. Not singlehandedly—alongside a few others—but Nick's been the intellectual heart and soul of the church, especially in its early years."[6]

Today, COS's mission statement includes the commitment to "present Christ to others by showing God's love in Jesus for the world and promoting justice and peace for our neighbors near and far." Andrew Mead says, "As Reformed Christians we believe that all things matter and that salvation is about the redemption and renewal of all creation." Simply put, he adds, "the church has long been committed to justice. It's in our DNA."[7]

ORIGINS OF RESTORATIVE JUSTICE MINISTRY AT COS

When Rich and Carol Rienstra joined COS in 2004, its doctrinal soil was fertile ground for a restorative justice initiative. But the talking and thinking had to be made actionable at a practical level. Carol remembers welcoming COS's strong academics but being hungry for the theological insights to be applied to the all-too-real criminal justice system her son was held in.

Around the same time that his parents joined COS, Troy, a new believer, had started a ministry at the Standish Maximum Security Prison, where he was incarcerated. He called it "Prisoners in Christ." It focused on discipling

Christ-followers behind bars. Troy felt that churches' typical jail ministry—usually involving a Sunday morning worship service planned and implemented by outsiders—was inadequate. Too often Christians from outside came into the prisons to convert inmates. Evangelism was fine, Troy says, but this missed the reality that already "there are hardcore, diehard believers in prison."[8] What they wanted and needed was discipleship for their personal lives and equipping in ministry leadership so that they could reach out effectively to fellow inmates.

In 2005, Troy decided to write the leadership of COS to see if the church would formally adopt the Prisoners in Christ (PinC) ministry. Troy recalls, "I told them there were a number of believers here. We're in the body of Christ, but we are overlooked and quite often condescended to. We're not perceived as having that same relationship with the body of Christ as those living on the outside." Troy hoped PinC could change this.

A delegation from COS that included Troy's dad and pastors Tymen Hofman, Jack Roeda, and Naji Umran drove across the state to the Standish prison. Talking with Troy through reinforced glass in the visitors' area, they confirmed his call from the Spirit to engage in ministry and committed the church's support.

COS's decision to adopt the Prisoners in Christ ministry was a visible implementation of the CRC's national denominational resolution in 2005 supporting restorative justice and the restoration of offenders. "Restorative justice," the Synod's resolution proclaimed, "provides a clear path back to the community, which is often not the case in our criminal justice systems."[9]

The Rienstras have been the driving force behind COS's Prisoners in Christ ministry. They came to COS in 2004, attracted in part by what they'd heard about the church's emphasis on justice. They also found COS's worship a balm. "It's a liturgical congregation, and the prayers often included praying for the prisoners. That's somewhat unique. And it felt like it was for us," Carol recalls.[10]

They are joined by a leadership team that usually includes four or five others. Overall, Carol estimates that about twenty-five to thirty COS members are engaged regularly, with more attending or volunteering in special PinC events. In its earlier years the number was higher. "It's a challenging ministry," she admits. Opportunities to serve the community abound at COS, and engaging with PinC is just one way congregants can "do justice and love mercy." Nonetheless, the ministry remains visible among the congregation through its regular updates in the church bulletin and its frequent events. The fact that Carol serves as a deacon at COS also helps "to keep restorative justice on the radar screen."

HOLISTIC MINISTRY TO INMATES

PinC has focused on three areas. The first is engaging in holistic ministry among prison inmates. This includes putting resources into their hands and helping their loved ones. For example, PinC has collaborated with Citizens for Prison Reform in producing a practical resource guide for friends, family, and advocates for the incarcerated. PinC recruits believers to visit inmates and to build friendships via letter writing. It also connects prisoners to educational opportunities. Its work inside the prison is done with the expectation that believers from outside will be changed just as the prisoners themselves will be.

Celebration Fellowship. PinC's first major ministry achievement was developing the state's first prison congregation, Celebration Fellowship. PinC leaders desired to offer worship services that would gather together free and incarcerated Christ-followers. Rich Rienstra researched potential models, learning much from an organization called Prison Congregations of America. Through it he heard about a church behind bars in Sioux Falls, South Dakota.[11] When he visited onsite, he saw outsiders coming in and worshiping with the incarcerated believers, inmates taking theology classes and learning about pastoral care, and prisoners who knew Christ being fully engaged as congregational leaders, assisting in the planning of the worship services. "This is what we need in Michigan," Troy and Rich decided.

In 2007, Rich and his friend Jim Tuinstra, who had experience working with ex-offenders, were successful in negotiating with the Michigan Department of Corrections (MDOC) for starting a congregation behind bars in the Bellamy Creek Correctional Facility in Ionia. Members chose the name Celebration Fellowship and began gathering on Monday evenings with Rich as their pastor. (He had participated in jail ministry back in the 1970s when he was fresh out of seminary.) Initially, around thirty-five inmates attended, joined by as many as fifteen members from Grand Rapids and Lansing congregations.

Today, Celebration Fellowship (CF) is a member congregation of the CRC denomination in its own right, no longer hosted by COS. It is part of the CRC North America's Classis Grand Rapids East. It is a multisite church with two congregations at the Bellamy facility (for offenders in separate units there) and one at the Handlon prison, also located in Ionia. Approximately 180 inmates attend regularly, according to CF's current pastor, Bob Arbogast.[12] Unlike other churches that conduct services at the prison, CF begins with an hour of small group study, with each group composed of Christians visiting from outside and their inmate brothers. This creates a context for mutual discipleship and learning. The study is followed by a prayer and worship service complete with singing and Communion.

True to Troy's original vision, a group of inmates serves as the congregation's leadership council, taking on much of the responsibility for planning and leading the services.[13] CF members inside the prison lead Bible studies and special programs like the twelve-week Alpha Course. When it was first introduced in 2015, nineteen inmates joined the program. "I've experienced an increase in my faith, prayer life, and understanding of the nature and importance of the Holy Spirit," testified one participant. Word-of-mouth reports of the course spread, and Alpha was offered again with a class of twenty-five more men.[14]

CF "insider" Michael Duthler, who grew up in the Roman Catholic Church, says that the volunteers have helped him by affirming him "as a person and not as an inmate. They help you separate from what is going on out there on the yard and in your cell," he adds.[15] At the same time, the learning and growth at CF are not one-way. Dave Koetje from COS has been "hooked" on the mission of Celebration Fellowship ever since he attended one of the services behind bars and found the small group leader to be "thoughtful, articulate and insightful." He recalls, "I couldn't ignore the reality that God was speaking to me through the voices of men whose behavior at one point in their lives ignited the 'criminal' label on each of them."[16]

Barb Leegwater is a COS member who for almost twelve years has been making the weekly trip to attend CF. "I have seen God's love poured out to people so different from me," she says, "and yet I've realized we are all the same and that God loves us because of who we are."[17] Jimmy Erickson, an inmate who spent a short time at the end of his sentence at Bellamy Creek prison, participated in the very early days of CF. He says the large number of people who came to worship with the inside-prison congregation was unique. In other church services he'd attended over the years, there would rarely be more than a few.[18]

For Troy the ministry's physical presence and affirmation of prisoners' human dignity are its most important aspects. "The name Prisoners in Christ reflects our belief that in Christ we all are inextricably bound up together in the web of humanity," says Troy. "Whether imprisoned or free, victim or offender, we are all creatures created in the likeness and image of God."

Calvin Prison Initiative. In 2009 when Troy was transferred to the Handlon prison facility in Ionia, he began corresponding with Professor David Rylaarsdam at Calvin Theological Seminary. Together they imagined a possible correspondence course for Troy and interested fellow inmates to take. Rylaarsdam brought the idea to seminary administrators. Eventually, the school formally invited applicants for a certificate program in pastoral care. Nearly fifty inmates applied. Twenty of these believers, including Troy, were selected for the initiative's first cohort in 2011.

The innovative move by the seminary laid the groundwork for a larger initiative launched by its sister institution, Calvin University, in 2015. The Calvin Prison Initiative (CPI) sends faculty into Handlon prison to teach courses in a formal, five-year degree program in ministry leadership. The program, says Rylaarsdam, "is not based on sentimental feelings that this project seems like a nice Christian thing to do and might do some good. It is based on consistent, striking statistics about the positive effects of higher education in prisons."[19]

A 2013 RAND Corporation meta-analysis of numerous prison education studies, for example, found that inmates who participated in educational programs were 43 percent less likely to return to prisons compared with those who did not take part in such programs. RAND also concluded that investment in such education programs is cost-effective, with a one-dollar investment in prison education reducing incarceration costs by four to five dollars during the first three years postrelease.[20]

Now in its fifth year the program has ninety-five currently enrolled students.[21] Bob Arbogast estimates about 25 percent of them participate in Celebration Fellowship. The CPI has sparked fresh hope for inmates and given them a new lease on life. CPI's director, Todd Cioffi—who is a member at COS—recalls how one student from Handlon prison keeps his acceptance letter from the college in a plastic holder by his bed. "I'm forty-five years old," this man told him, "and this is the only piece of paper that I've ever received that starts out positively about me. It says 'Congratulations, you've been accepted into the Calvin Prison Initiative.'"[22]

Cioffi says he "can't imagine how COS could give any more support [to the CPI]. They're just all in."[23] Individual congregants have been financial donors to the CPI. Leaders of COS's prison ministry have kept the congregation informed about the CPI. Congregants have befriended CPI students through Celebration Fellowship. Six Calvin professors who are part of COS have taught courses within the program. Cioffi says that he and they "see the Calvin program as an extension of the church's mission and an extension of how we are shaped and formed in worship." Nick Wolterstorff and Alvin Plantinga from COS have guest lectured for the program. After spending two and a half hours with the CPI students discussing his book *Lament for a Son*, Nick (then eighty-four) told Todd, "That was one of the most remarkable classroom experiences of my life."

SUPPORTING RETURNING CITIZENS

PinC's second focus is on ministry outside the prison. Its CONTACT initiative (Celebrating Our Network of Trust, Accountability, Collaboration and Training) facilitates returning citizens' reentry into the life of the community. The program emerged from Rich's concerns about reentry and Celebration Fellowship members' desire for ongoing support post-release.

Before their parole inmates can apply for entry into the CONTACT ministry, which offers returning citizens wide-ranging support: connections to housing, jobs, mentors, educational opportunities, meals, rides, and other practical help. Rich says that CONTACT rarely turns down an applicant but that the process enables ministry leaders to ascertain the individual's frame of mind and personal vision for his post-release life.

Rich estimates that CONTACT has served around two hundred returning citizens since its inception. CONTACT partners with Living Water Ministry Network to address housing needs. Living Water operates several homes in the Grand Rapids area. These have provided a structured environment, ongoing discipleship, and employment assistance to dozens of returning citizens. According to a 2018 report, the ministry had achieved an 88 percent nonrecidivism rate over its more than eleven-year history.[24]

CONTACT also collaborates with the nonprofit organization 70×7 Life Recovery to match returning citizens with mentors. A number of these mentors are from COS. The mentoring component has been an important factor in keeping recidivism rates down.

CONTACT meets two Sunday afternoons each month. Typically, around twenty returning citizens, the Rienstras, and occasionally a few COS members, gather to talk through issues, pray, and build friendships. Jimmy Erickson was involved for years.

Jimmy spent twenty-one years behind bars. At age twenty-five he'd been partying with friends, got into an argument, and ended up stabbing one. The man died, and Jimmy later pleaded guilty to murder. Jimmy became a Christian within his first few months at Jackson State maximum-security prison. When he was released, he had no job and was worried about whether other Christians would accept him. His friendship with the Rienstras and participation in CONTACT were huge encouragements to him:

> Just to have people who are established in the community, Christian people who do accept you . . . who are there to walk alongside you and maybe point you in a direction for work and stuff like that, to give you a ride . . . just knowing you have that support system [matters]. Because when you come out, you know a lot of doors are gonna be closed to you. And to know that people are praying for you and encouraging you to do the right thing, it means a lot.[25]

While CONTACT does not currently implement restorative conferencing (when offenders and crime victims meet), group members do offer guidance and support to those who desire to repair the harm of their crimes and pursue relational healing.

COS members have helped CONTACT participants with rides, job leads, and meals. Anytime COS has leftover food at the church from a special event, it is brought to one of the Living Waters group homes. Some inmates who have been involved in Celebration Fellowship attend COS upon their release. "They make their profession of faith before the congregation and become actual members of COS," Troy reports. Peter Vander Meulen says this is a demonstration of COS's core value of inclusivity. "What could be more inclusive than welcoming prisoners?"

PinC's most recent restorative experiment—which has generated considerable interest among COS congregants—is called "Healing Wounds of the Heart."[26] COS elder Ann Kapetyn has led the initiative, which trains laypeople in leading small groups in Bible studies focused on the healing of trauma. The curriculum was originally developed by Summer Institute of Linguistics and the American Bible Society in overseas contexts of war and displacement where there are few professional psychiatric services available.

The church "has close communities and a long tradition of pastoral counseling," says Ann. This makes it a natural place for the Healing Wounds project. Twenty-five COS congregants participated in a January 2019 intensive training (35 hours). They learned the curriculum and were equipped to start leading trauma-healing Bible study groups. The Rienstras were among the trainees. "It deepened our understanding of victims and strengthened our ability to minister to them," Carol reports.[27] She says it has been helpful to draw on the training's insight in CONTACT meetings since many of the returning citizens are not only former offenders but also former crime victims.

In January 2020 COS hosted a follow-up training for the small group leaders. Ann and others involved in the initiative had met with prison officials and were set to begin offering such groups behind bars in Ionia when the global Covid-19 pandemic hit. The plan has been tabled for now, but Ann is hopeful it can move forward in the future.

ADVOCACY: RESTORATIVE VERSUS RETRIBUTIVE JUSTICE

PinC's third main focus is on advocacy. Through its partners Safe and Just Michigan and the Restorative Justice Coalition of West Michigan, COS is contributing to Grand Rapids' thriving by advocating the adoption of restorative justice practices as an alternative to the current system's emphasis on retributive justice.

Michigan spends nearly $2 billion annually a year on corrections. But this reliance on incarceration does not promote public safety, say leaders from Safe and Just Michigan:

> Research shows that Michigan over-relies on incarceration as a public safety strategy. Overuse of our prisons and jails diverts tax dollars from important health and reentry services, weakens family connections, and reduces employment opportunities—all factors proven to be *more* effective in preventing crime than long prison terms.[28]

Carol agrees. "We cannot incarcerate our way to healthier families and communities."[29]

Her views echo those of her friend and mentor David LaGrand. LaGrand is a former prosecutor who leads the West Michigan Restorative Justice Coalition. He is also an elected member of the Michigan state legislature. "We have a penal system that keeps doing the same thing and expecting different results," he laments.[30]

In a 2019 article for the CRC's denominational publication, *The Banner*, LaGrand explained to his fellow believers that restorative justice is a more biblical response to crime and the harm it causes.[31] The current system asks who is guilty and what punishment should be inflicted. Restorative justice asks about who was hurt and how the harm could be repaired. It is focused on the triple aims of accountability, reconciliation, and peace. While restorative justice advocates know it is important to punish wrongdoing, they are committed to placing the primary focus on the crime victim. When that happens, LaGrand argued,

> it can empower the victim and begin the process of healing. Conversations that include a discussion of consequences and amends may serve as a first step along the road to forgiveness. They might also provide a real opportunity for offenders to understand the magnitude of the harm they caused and to develop empathy with their victims. Such empathy is the best hope for preventing the offender from repeating the behavior.[32]

Education. PinC engages in educational efforts to raise awareness about the fatal flaws in the criminal justice system and the hope offered by a restorative justice approach. PinC has hosted a variety of informative authors, activists, and attorneys engaged in restorative justice to speak and teach at COS. For example, The Micah Center Beyond Prisons advocacy group has taught for COS's Wednesday Night adult education program. For the past four years PinC has connected interested congregants to the Christian Community Development Association's annual "Locked in Solidarity" week, which seeks to raise awareness on mass incarceration. PinC has sponsored book studies on key texts like *The New Jim Crow* by Michelle Alexander, *Just Mercy* by Bryan Stevenson, and *Changing Lenses* by restorative justice leader Howard Zehr. It has hosted film screenings on documentaries about prison life and the criminal justice system and invited speakers to teach on bail reform.

As Ann sums up, "There are book clubs that read books about justice, conferences that talk about justice, politicians who come and speak about restorative justice. There are so many of those kinds of things happening here." This emphasis on educating congregants on these topics aligns with the church's mission, Carol says. "Our original priority as a church was founded on the premise that we have to speak to the social issues of the day through word and practice—through preaching, practice, and training/educating our people to be faithful servants of the kingdom by understanding what's going on in our politics."

COS members also have an additional venue for learning about restorative justice. For several years a small contingent of congregants has gone into Handlon prison on Wednesday nights to participate in a book group led by Christian inmates. The Handlon book group has read over seventy-five books together, including *The Little Book on Restorative Justice for People in Prison* by Barb Toews and *Changing Lenses* by Howard Zehr. They have also watched and discussed over twenty-five films and enjoyed guest lectures from Nick Wolterstorff, Brady Middleton (a crime victim who advocates for Restorative Justice), and several others.

Advocacy. Since 2014 PinC has partnered with the all-volunteer organization Citizens for Prison Reform (CPR) in sponsoring an annual Legislative Education Day at the state capitol in Lansing. During this day volunteers meet with state legislators to lobby on specific bills of interest and host special events aimed at showcasing problems in the criminal justice system, as well as potential solutions. For example, every year since 2016, CPR and PinC have set up a model solitary confinement cell to give lawmakers a 3D sensory experience of what segregation looks and feels like.

PinC encourages COS members to attend public hearings for individuals serving life sentences who have the opportunity to apply for parole. Ministry volunteers have also met with Michigan Department of Corrections officials to urge changes in prison visitation policies. Along with CPR, PinC helped to establish a family advisory board to represent families and friends with loved ones in Michigan prisons. The board meets quarterly with Department of Corrections representatives to remind them that people in prison have advocates who want to participate in their rehabilitation.

The Rienstras and other COS members have also provided leadership and support to the Restorative Justice Coalition of West Michigan. The coalition won a major victory in 2018 when Kent County instituted a restorative justice initiative for juvenile offenders. The program focuses on youth who commit malicious destruction of property, larceny, or assault and battery. Instead of going before a judge, offenders meet face-to-face with their victim(s). "The two of them can come together and in essence agree on what the resolution's going to be for [them]," Kent County prosecutor Chris Becker explained to a local TV news station.[33] Actions might include an apology, paying restitution, or completing community service hours. "It's a way to give the victim a bigger voice and it's also a way to show the offender the damage he's done," Becker said.[34] There's another benefit: if the offender meets the various requirements of the plan, the crime is kept off of their juvenile record.

PinC has partnered with the nonprofit Safe and Just Michigan since 2004.[35] In 2019, after years of lobbying, the nonprofit was successful in seeing a new law passed. "Raise the Age" ended Michigan's policy of considering seventeen-year-olds as adults in criminal courts. Currently, Safe and Just Michigan is working with sympathetic state legislators to move forward a package of bills called the Clean Slate initiative. The bills expand access to expungement. "These bills will have a positive impact on hundreds of thousands of people across Michigan," says Barbara Weiland of Safe and Just Michigan.[36]

PinC not only tries to bring the voices of COS members and other citizens into the public discussions on criminal justice reform. It also seeks to share insights that *prisoners themselves* have about why a restorative justice approach will be better for the flourishing of all. As Troy argues, "Most often the solution to the problem is within the problem itself. . . . There are prisoners who once were part of the problem, after undergoing a transformation of the heart and mind, now are able to offer practical and innovative solutions to some of society's pressing challenges when considering the causes and effects of crime and punishment."[37]

LESSONS LEARNED

Church of the Servant's perseverance in the work of promoting restorative justice stems from several somewhat unique factors. Not every congregation, of course, will have the highly personalized passion of lay leaders like the Rienstras. Not every congregation is home to one of the church's most thoughtful philosophers on social justice. Church of the Servant also benefits from its proximity to Calvin University. It is rooted in the rich Reformed tradition of reflection on the church's role in society and can count the wise Christian statesman Abraham Kuyper among its intellectual ancestors.

Nonetheless, congregations without these distinctive elements can also take up the mission of advancing community flourishing by promoting restorative justice. COS has engaged in at least four practices that any other congregation regardless of size, location, history, or theological tradition could imitate.

1. Praying for prisoners. Praying for prisoners may require a prior step: remembering the proclivity of Jesus to move toward the outcast. The truth is that many of us, unlike Jesus, fail to see the humanity of incarcerated individuals. They are literally out of sight and so easy to keep out of mind as well. We've also been swimming in a "lock 'em up and throw away the key" nation that makes empathy difficult. But Christians should be the first to acknowledge the truth of one of Bryan Stevenson's pithy remarks: "Each of us is more than the worst thing we've ever done."[38]

The Bible urges us to remember those in prison. And we do—usually on the Sunday we're thinking about the persecuted church. That's appropriate but insufficient. There are other innocents in prison. We should certainly be praying for them, for justice to reach them and release them. And then there are the many more behind bars who are guilty. Their guilt, though, should not prevent us from praying for them. Some are both guilty *and* fellow brothers and sisters in Christ. We are called to love them with the same New Testament "one anothers" as we love our fellow congregants in the church we call home—and that includes the apostle James's directive to "pray for each other" (Jas 5:16). Moreover, many prisoners are both offenders *and* crime victims. We can pray for their healing. All are human beings made in God's image. We can pray for them to open themselves up to his profound, merciful love—even while acknowledging we often do not know how to manufacture similar mercy.

2. Educating congregants about restorative justice. COS may enjoy several university professors as Sunday school teachers. But graduate degrees aren't required for running a book study, inviting in a guest lecturer, hosting a discussion on a film like *Just Mercy*, or organizing a Bible study examining texts on justice. Howard Zehr's *The Little Book of Restorative Justice* is very accessible as is Timothy Keller's *Generous Justice*. CRU offers a Bible study on social justice.[39] The Gospel Coalition offers an online course on biblical justice.[40] Prison Fellowship offers a small group curriculum titled *Outrageous Justice* that aims to "awaken Christians to the need for justice that restores."[41] There is no shortage of thoughtful, biblically based resources for adult education.

3. Implementing restorative practices in our congregations. Restorative justice is a biblically rooted way of addressing conflicts that arise in all sorts of spheres—families, schools, churches, and communities. Zeal for advancing restorative justice in the nation's criminal justice system can be nurtured by enacting restorative practices in our congregations (surely we can all agree that disagreement is no stranger to our churches).

4. Facilitating personal connections with prisoners and their families. Many people at COS know the Rienstra family and thus had a personal connection to Troy. But the PinC ministry has also cultivated a heart for prisoners by partnering with specialized ministries that connect congregants to inmates and their families. These include Angel Tree (through which congregants reach out at Christmastime to the children of incarcerated parents), summer camp scholarship programs for children of prisoners, and

Crossroads Prison Ministry (through which volunteers are matched with inmates for correspondence Bible study courses). These are all opportunities "to get your toe in the water," Rich says. They make the abstract idea of "the incarcerated" more tangible and personal.

CONCLUSION: PUTTING FAITH INTO ACTION

One in three Americans has an arrest record.[42] We're a nation of people who make mistakes, sometimes grave ones. This is no surprise to Christ-followers, who understand the reality of the fall. All of us—whether we've been arrested or not—have sinned and fallen short. And all of us, at least in theory, believe in second chances. After all, we are living examples of the truth that a loving, merciful God has given *us* a second chance.

Given this, it's not that surprising that a 2019 Barna-fielded survey for Prison Fellowship found that a majority of practicing Evangelicals support a criminal justice system that aims at "restoration for all parties," offers incarcerated citizens safe, humane prison conditions, and has hope that ex-offenders can make a positive contribution to society.[43] The problem is that these convictions (pardon the pun) have not translated into action by most believers or congregations. The same survey found that only 22 percent of Evangelicals reported that their churches had engaged in raising awareness about criminal justice in the prior six months.

We can hope that one result of the 2020 worldwide protests against racism and police abuse will be more advocacy for criminal justice reform and a better, more effective ministry to prisoners and returning citizens. Church of the Servant offers a promising model.

10

A STRATEGY FOR CULTIVATING THE JUST

BE A RECONCILING COMMUNITY

The Eucharist makes the church a public, social body—the body of Christ—and a sign and symbol of the new humanity in Christ.

NICHOLAS KRAUSE,
"JUSTICE AND MERCY CONTENDING FOR SHALOM"

IN SEPTEMBER 2019 things went from good to bad to worse for Iesha. The thirty-eight-year-old mother of two had recently completed a twelve-week nursing internship at Johnston-Willis Hospital after passing her state certification exams. While still celebrating another achievement—buying her first home—she received a devastating phone call from the hospital's HR department. Johnston-Willis, she learned, was not going to hire her into a full-time nursing position, as was customary for interns who'd successfully completed the program. The reason given was the one that had been plaguing Iesha on the jobs front for six years. She had a felony on her record.

"I felt like my three months' work had spoken for itself," Iesha recalls. "I was so tired of trying to prove myself."[1] Then, just a few days after the hospital's bad news, a driver ran a stop sign and totaled Iesha's car. Now she had no job, no car, an uncertain future, and a mortgage to pay.

But then Jehovah Jireh (the Lord will Provide) showed up in the form of her "spiritual family" from East End Fellowship (EEF), a multiethnic congregation in Richmond's Church Hill neighborhood.

"I have never experienced people just coming around one another and loving one another in the way that we try to do [at EEF]," says Iesha. "We really try to live out the gospel in Acts 2, where it talks about 'holding all things in common.' We don't always get it right. But we try and we stay at the table, and we bear one another's burdens together."

East End's lead pastor, Don Coleman, is proud of how his congregation rallied around Iesha and her teenage sons. Congregants paid her bills for two months and collected a love offering to enable her to purchase a car. They made sure the family had food and the boys had school clothes. It was the second time the church had put "love one another" into practical action for Iesha's family.

Iesha had started attending EEF in October 2011. She was incarcerated in January 2012 for writing bad checks. She explains that she was in school and working on an "as needed" basis at a local hospital. "They weren't giving me enough hours and I got behind on my rent," Iesha says. "I got an eviction notice and wrote the checks to try to get money to pay my rent and buy food for my kids."

Because some of the checks were for over $250, her actions counted as a felony. Her sons were sent to live with Iesha's former foster mother while Iesha went to prison. Iesha's new friends Matt and Sherika from EEF visited her nearly every weekend. When she was released in December 2014, people from the church and the Church Hill neighborhood rallied around her. Iesha moved in with an older couple in the community for several months. Then EEF members Alicia and Clay invited Iesha and her two boys to share their home. Six months later, Lawson and Romesh Wijesooriya from EEF invited the boys and her to move into one of the homes they own in the neighborhood and rent at below-market rates. She accepted.

It wasn't always emotionally easy for Iesha to accept the help she was offered. But she marvels at how the church "made sure we had what we needed."

"The church did what it was supposed to do," enthuses pastor Coleman.[2] He delights in EEF's witness of truly loving one another. "People are going to hear the story of what God's people did for her," he says. "And they're gonna say, 'Can I come?'"

Since 2008, EEF has sought to be a reconciling community, a racially diverse congregation reflecting the unity in diversity of the kingdom of God. Its "covenant community" (formal members) numbers around 125 members, 80 percent of whom are engaged in house churches (small groups). Deliberately located in the Church Hill neighborhood of east Richmond, three words are at its center: *shalom, reconciliation,* and *justice.* The principal way it pursues shalom is through racial reconciliation and efforts to address the injustices rooted in racism. Racial reconciliation was placed at the heart of

EEF because, as Don explains, "it is *central* to the Gospel. It's not an add-on or an optional thing." Since God's future consummated kingdom consists of a multiethnic family of worshipers and given that Jesus commanded his followers to pray for the kingdom of heaven to come to earth, Don reasons, a diverse fellowship must be what God longs to see *now*. As he says, "We know what heaven looks like. We're not doing this because it's a fad. No. It's biblical that we as the church model being together in this realm, on earth as it is in heaven. That is the norm; that is who we are supposed to be."

EAST END FELLOWSHIP'S FOUNDING

East End Fellowship has two birthplaces, one in Richmond and one in Charlottesville. Don, an African American native of the Church Hill neighborhood, is its primary Richmond parent. With sixty years in the community, he has lived its story. But his fitness for leading a multiethnic church on a mission to flourish its neighborhood goes beyond his intimate local knowledge. Don likes to tell two anecdotes from his youth that illustrate God's way of preparing him for this ministry.

First, growing up, he recited the Lord's Prayer each night with his foster parents. "In hindsight," Don says, "I see this really impacted my life. One part in there is 'Thy Kingdom come, Thy will be done *on earth* as it is in heaven.' As I grew in the Lord and read Revelation I learned what heaven looked like: every nation, tribe, and tongue together." Years later, when Don began pastoral ministry, he says, "That became one of my primary teaching topics." Second, Don recalls an incident at his newly integrated middle school in the early 1970s. During a softball game a White boy accidentally hit Don with the bat, drawing blood and requiring stitches. The next day Don's Black friends asked whether he was ready to join them in beating up the boy in retaliation. To their surprise Don told them no, that the fellow was his friend. "I've just always had this heart," he says. "Later, when I became a follower of Jesus, I saw it in Scripture."

Don formed a friendship with Percy and Angie Strickland, a young White couple who moved to Church Hill in 2001. They began meeting together for prayer. "We were praying about an intentional church that would be multiethnic and specifically for people in the community and their families," says Angie.[3]

The Charlottesville side of EEF's conception began at the University of Virginia (UVA) in the late 1990s. There, Corey Widmer and Matt Illian, who are both White, and Danny Avula and Romesh Wijesooriya, who are Indian and Sri Lankan respectively, were living together with a few other male believers at the Center for Christian Study. Their friendships deepened in this communal setting, as did their awareness of the ethnic segregation all too common in Christian churches.[4]

During their senior year Romesh led a group of these undergraduates, along with their girlfriends who shared their interest in racial reconciliation, on a spring break trip to serve at Voice of Calvary Ministries in Jackson, Mississippi. There they were able to meet their hero, Christian community-development pioneer John Perkins. The experience planted a seed within them. "We wondered if one day we might move into an urban community together and live out the principles of the Christian Community Development Association," Corey recalls.[5] Their idea was to seek God's leading for their vocations, get whatever further training was needed postcollege, and then settle down together in a place where they could serve the kingdom.

Joining God's work in Richmond. By 2004 God had providentially ordained a variety of circumstances to bring this vision to reality for some of that original group. By this time Romesh, Corey, Matt, and Danny were married to women who shared their dream of living out Perkins's "3 Rs" of Christian community development: relocation, reconciliation, and redistribution. Danny and Romesh had been matched to the medical residency program at Virginia Commonwealth University in Richmond. Matt's work as a financial adviser enabled him to work anywhere in Virginia. Corey was finishing his seminary degree at Princeton, and he and his wife, Sarah, a nurse, were willing to move wherever the others landed.

"We knew we shouldn't start our own thing," Lawson Wijesooriya remembers.[6] Mary Kay Avula adds, "We wanted to be invited into [a] neighborhood, and we wanted to go to a place where God was already at work."[7]

Then God crossed their paths with Don.

Don and the UVA gang all remember the special meeting where Richmond and Charlottesville came together. The couples shared their vision and asked Don for his guidance. Don had already been praying for

God to send him help for his mission of seeing the kingdom come to a greater reality in Church Hill. Laughing, he admits he didn't anticipate that the Lord would bring him a group of predominantly White twenty-somethings. But he recognized God's provision.

"When I think about what motivated me to support these young people," Don recalls, "it was that I saw they really had an intentionality. They'd educated themselves on how to serve in an urban area. They'd been invested with Dr. Perkins. It was obvious they weren't doing this willy-nilly. The one thing they didn't have was actual experience."

Learning and lamenting the community's suffering. The four couples did their best to follow Perkins's guidance. They bought homes in the Church Hill community. They invested in getting to know their neighbors, listening to their dreams, and finding and submitting to the saints God had already placed there. They practiced open-door hospitality and volunteered with the tutoring ministry the Stricklands had begun. Mary Kay and Lawson took jobs teaching at Elijah House Academy, a bootstrap Christian school serving low-income students. In their residencies, Romesh focused on childhood obesity while Danny pursued a career in public health. Lawson starting coaching part-time at a local school. Corey used his influence on staff at Third Presbyterian Church to direct an increasing share of its substantial local missions budget to Church Hill ministries like CHAT, a tutoring ministry the Stricklands had launched, and Urban Hope, a housing ministry run by a neighbor in Church Hill.

The couples took time to learn the history that their neighbors had lived. The former capital of the Confederacy, Richmond was the second city in the United States to adopt a race-based zoning code (in 1910), identifying specific neighborhoods for Whites and Blacks. The discrimination continued long after such codes were declared unconstitutional through the use of restrictive covenants barring Whites from selling their homes to Blacks. Looking back, Angie recalls being struck by how segregated Richmond was. "We felt like there was kind of a line on one side and people looked a certain way there, and on the other side looked completely different."

Discriminatory redlining by banks denied African Americans mortgages and home improvement loans. Commercial enterprises avoided investing in communities like Church Hill. Many occupations held predominantly by people of color were excluded from Social Security benefits or fair labor standards protections.

The legacy of these kinds of systematic discrimination is easily visible today. A 2020 study of Richmond by E Pluribus Unum found that the average White household in Virginia holds more than eleven times the wealth of the average Black household and that White workers are paid approximately $20,000 more per year than Black and Latino workers.[8] Tom Perriello, a former Virginia congressman, says, "None of this is accidental. It's the product of a century of policies designed to lock communities of color out of the American dream."[9]

A VISION FOR A WORSHIPING COMMUNITY

Amid these realities, the Stricklands, the UVA couples, and Don stubbornly held to their belief that "the Gospel has the power to overcome divisions of race and class."[10]

In fall 2007 the group's hero John Perkins came to Richmond. He enthusiastically commended the community-development efforts but also identified an omission. He urged them to start meeting regularly in worship as a public demonstration of their unity and reliance on Jesus. "Without worshiping together," he said, "you will become a loose, disconnected group of social activists rather than a Christ-centered community."[11]

Don had been leading a prayer-and-sharing group of Christians living on mission in the East End since 2005. After Perkins's visit this fellowship began to take on a more formal shape. Don and Corey decided to work together to copastor a church plant. The group started meeting for weekly worship using space at Franklin Military Academy. A year later they moved to Church Hill's Robinson Theater on Q Street and formed a board of elders. That team originally consisted of Don, Corey, Lawson, and David Bailey, a local, highly talented African American musician Don considered a spiritual son. Later, at Don's urging, Percy joined the board. These leaders plus a few others drafted the church's mission statement: "To be a multiethnic community in the East End of Richmond, working for the joy and justice of our neighborhoods out of love for Christ." The leaders agreed that EEF should be marked by a rhythm of weekly, small house-church meetings that could facilitate deep, authentic community and then large gathering worship services at the theater. By February 2009, they were meeting weekly for public worship.

ARTICULATING EEF'S CORE DNA

Around this time Corey led the elders in writing a "Covenant Community" handbook outlining the church's core DNA. They articulated four key values:

- *Local embodiment* (being the church of Jesus in and for a particular neighborhood)

- *Diversity and reconciliation* (seeking ethnic and cultural reconciliation because such reconciliation was "one of the central themes of the entire biblical narrative")

- *Networking with the broader church* (connecting with existing churches and ministries advancing community flourishing)

- *Being oriented toward the joy and justice of the city* (coming together "in order to be dispersed as agents of transformation, to heal as we are being healed")

EEF leaders emphasized essentials and downplayed secondary doctrinal issues (e.g., church-state relations, practices of baptism). As the handbook stated, "for the sake of unity, we need to work hard to distinguish doctrinal essentials versus non-essentials . . . because we put such a high premium on diversity and reconciliation."

Themes of shalom "were a constant drumbeat" in the early days, Corey recalls. "I probably overpreached it," he laughs. "Jeremiah 29:7—seek the peace and prosperity of the city—was basically our theme verse. It was like *shalom* was tattooed on everybody's arm." The congregation's identity was centered on being the diverse body Jesus wanted and contributing actively to the neighborhood's flourishing.

The new fellowship would pursue shalom principally through racial reconciliation and efforts to address tangible inequities rooted in institutional racism. This, EEF's leaders knew, required clear theological conviction. But while that was necessary they knew it was also insufficient. They understood that they would need to put in place several intentional practices if they were to build a multiethnic congregation that served the community in love.

INTENTIONAL PRACTICES

They already had one key practice in place: diverse leadership. To that they added several more. The first was, in Corey's words, "incredible intentionality" about hiring decisions and who would represent the church up front on Sundays. Tiffany Perry, an African American woman, was hired to shepherd the church's youth. After volunteering in various capacities, David Bailey eventually was brought on staff as East End's first worship arts director.

The second concerned the church's home fellowships. From the start the weekly house gathering was commended as the lifeblood of EEF, every bit as important as the weekly large gathering on Sundays. Staff strongly encouraged newcomers to join a group that would connect them to people different from themselves, desiring as many as possible of the house churches to be racially diverse.

The third practice was something EEF leaders came to call the "75% rule." Corey explained it years later in a 2014 article for *Christianity Today*. He wrote that church leaders hoped that everyone would be happy with no more than 75 percent of what happened in the worship service. "If you are happy and comfortable with more than 75% of what is going on, it most likely means that your personal cultural preferences are being dominantly expressed. So we've decided that no one cultural form will be dominant and everyone will be equally unhappy with the worship!"[12]

This deliberate exhortation toward discomfort is hard to hear in our consumer-oriented culture, but the EEF team felt that calling people to sacrifice a degree of personal preference to "make space for the other" was a mark of gospel faithfulness. Longtime EEF member Elena Aronson says the 75% rule reminds everyone that the church isn't "just for me. It allows us to press in to hospitality."[13] Members adopt the attitude that the parts of the worship service that they don't like or that don't personally resonate are meeting their brother's or sister's needs. "Pursuing unity amidst diversity," Elena says, "requires giving up rights and power."

ROADBLOCKS

The first couple years at EEF were heady, filled with excitement as the church plant pursued the countercultural dream of building a multiethnic community. Being part of the congregation was special. But it was also difficult.

In 2020 Lawson Wijesooriya laughingly told me, "I don't really remember if it's ever *not* been hard. It's been amazing and beautiful—and messy—the whole time."

EEF hit its first significant roadblocks around 2011. At a leadership retreat that year, Tiffany told the group: "I'm hungry, angry, lonely, and tired."[14] Corey swallowed hard and asked who else on the team felt that way. All the Black staff raised their hands. They told Corey that they felt he was catering too much to the Whites in the congregation, prioritizing their concerns and not attending to the voices of the African American members. "It was super hard to hear," Corey admits. "But it resulted in us recognizing that happy clapping on Sundays was not real reconciliation. We needed honest conversations."

EEF's leaders made two commitments. One was to study together more deeply and intentionally. The other was to lead the covenant community in focused dialogue and spiritual exercises related to racial reconciliation. The season that then unfolded, Don recalls, "was hard, honest, and real."

Repentance circles. Repentance circles were one of the most powerful, embodied, spiritual practices they deployed in the pursuit of healing. In this exercise, small, racially mixed groups of congregants join together in circles with their arms around one another. Each circle member is invited to offer a short confession of something they have thought, done, or said that failed to honor people of a different race. After each confession circle members say together aloud, "Christ have mercy." Next, a leader instructs everyone who has ever spoken derogatorily of a group of people to take a step backward, out from the circle. Anyone who has ever been on the receiving end of a racist comment is then told to take a step backward. A further series of instructions are given for stepping backward, for example, if one has left others out because of their race or class or done an act that dishonored someone different.

"By the end of the process," Corey says ruefully, "everyone is far apart and crying." But then a leader reads aloud words of hope from 2 Corinthians 5:16-17:

> From now on we regard no one from a worldly point of view. Though we once regarded Christ in this way, we do so no longer. Therefore, if anyone is in Christ, the new creation has come: The old has gone, the new is here!

A liturgy of grace follows. The leader mentions a series of possible ways that circle members may have received grace from Jesus and invites them to step forward for each one that resonates. Also called out are specific actions of goodwill congregants might have taken. "In the end," Corey describes, "everyone is back together in their circles."

Despite the emotional intensity of these activities, "the increased intentionality about talking through stuff and engaging in the practices didn't lead to more racial conflict but less," David Bailey says, because "people started having tools for dealing with it." EEF's covenant community doubled in size during this period in the church's life. Angie recalls, "Some of the most powerful times were when people were on their knees confessing because we know that we don't all get it right and we need to come to a place of healing and forgiveness. And we have to do that again and again. Because, you know, that's what God does with us every day."

Race, class, and the kingdom of God. During this time, EEF leaders and staff read and studied existing books and articles on racial reconciliation. Most of what they found, though, were materials diagnosing the problems. These were beneficial, but few offered prescriptions for action. Eventually, the team concluded that they would need to craft their own discipleship materials. EEF staff member Ashley Mejias, with help from David, Corey, and the elders, created a series of teachings for EEF's covenant community. These members met monthly to interact with and discuss the biblical teaching.

This material became the basis for a curriculum titled "Race, Class, and the Kingdom of God" that David and Elena would begin using later under the auspices of a new nonprofit David founded called Arrabon (arrabon.com). *Arrabon* is the Greek word for "foretaste of what is to come," and the organization's mission is to help the church "be a foretaste of a reconciled heaven to our divided world."

Valuing the biblical word reconciliation. In their teaching back in 2011 and to this day, EEF and Arrabon have held fast to the term *reconciliation*. This sets them apart from some other Christians who in recent years have argued that the term is inadequate.[15] Such critics contend that in a context where one party has enslaved the other, only conciliation can happen. *Reconciliation* implies that there was once a whole where equality reigned and then somehow it got broken and needs to be put back together. In the US context, of course, there was no equality at the beginning. EEF's leaders acknowledge the concern but have chosen to retain *reconciliation* because it is such a powerful, frequent biblical theme. Indeed, they say, it is at the heart of the grand biblical narrative.

God's story is one of cosmic reconciliation. His grand mission involves reconciling people to himself, reconciling people to one another, and reconciling humanity to creation. Scripture teaches that the multifaceted harmony existing in the Garden was shattered comprehensively by the fall. But humankind's fall into sin does not have the last word in the biblical story. Rather, God through Christ is reconciling "all things" to himself, repairing all the damage of the fall in the work of the cross. This is God's mission to restore shalom in all its dimensions.

Reconciliation is *God's* great work, but it's a work he invites humans into. To be a disciple of Jesus, EEF leaders believe, is to be a reconciler who has joined him in his work of advancing shalom. This will inevitably involve the pursuit of justice, David emphasizes, because biblical reconciliation cannot be separated from justice.

In March 2017, David and Elena taught the "Race, Class, and the Kingdom of God" course during an intensive weekend conference attended by all the EEF staff, house-church leaders, and many congregants. The course covers key themes that make explicit the definitions and requirements in the journey toward genuine reconciliation. One key theme is the idea that cultural diversity is *normative* in the kingdom. This is God's desire and it will be a reality in the fully consummated kingdom. "God defines flourishing as unity in diversity," Elena explains. "Homogeneity is less than God's normative intention for us."

REQUIREMENTS OF RECONCILIATION

The work is hard and long. EEF leaders understand reconciliation as spiritual formation. It's a matter of discipleship, first, because the labor of reconciliation among diverse peoples is a means of glorifying God. Second, since no one culture fully understands God, diversity is a necessity for getting a fuller perspective on him. Third, genuine unity in diversity glorifies God; alleged unity through assimilation simply glorifies the dominant power. Fourth, seeing reconciliation as spiritual formation points participants to God as the only adequate source of the strength and endurance the process requires. It commits people to a vertical orientation in the midst of seeking horizontal shalom. Healing the racial and class divides that are so deeply engrained in our culture and institutions is extremely difficult and complicated. It requires supernatural strength; our mere human efforts are insufficient. Reflecting on his own faithful pursuit of racial reconciliation, Don says the key for him has been "prayer, prayer, prayer, and more prayer."

EEF leaders also believe in renewing the mind. Reconciliation requires, David says, increasing the cultural intelligence of the community. This involves teaching the history of racism in the United States, particularly the ways it has been embedded in social, political, and economic systems. And that means grappling intentionally and thoroughly with the reality of the false worldview of White supremacy. Arrabon defines White supremacy as "a spiritual principality manifested economically and legislated politically, that affects us relationally." Renewing the mind must proceed at a slow pace and involves remembrance, confession, lament, repentance, and forgiveness.

Sometimes Whites resist acts of remembering the suffering White supremacy has inflicted. "They'll argue, 'We weren't there and we're not personally responsible for these racist things of the past,'" David reports. He responds by reminding them that remembrance is a biblical discipline. "None of us have to take the *blame* for the way things are today," he adds. "But as Christians we do have to take *responsibility* for seeing how messed up things are. We need a perspective today that is informed by our history. Then we join Jesus in his mission to bring renewal in all things."

As cultural intelligence increases through intentional education, the need for the spiritual disciplines of repentance, lament, and forgiveness comes to the fore. All participants in the reconciliation journey have to repent of the ways they have spoken, acted, and lived to the harm of their neighbors. Lament appropriately follows such confession. Lament is a frequent expression in the Scripture but relatively rare in many American church services. David says, "We need to learn how to mourn with those who mourn."

True repentance involves but goes beyond recognition and confession to changed behavior. David explains, "We can't learn something and then just keep on doing things the way we've always done them." Elena agrees, arguing that we have to recognize our complicity in unjust structures and take deliberate action to turn around and go in the other direction.

When a diverse group of people walks a reconciliation journey together that is honest, individuals will inevitably offend one another or act unkindly out of anger, shame, guilt, or confusion. Abundant grace is required. Don reports that God has given him a special insight into a way of fostering a forgiving posture, and he teaches this to fellow African Americans:

> God showed me that some Whites are just blind; they have these cultural and racial blind spots. How can I be angry with a blind person? Who smacks a blind man for walking into the wall? They're blind. They didn't see. For me, as an African American older person, this helps me stay away from becoming overly angry.

Diversity doesn't guarantee reconciliation, David likes to say. It only guarantees conflict. One practice EEF has learned to decrease conflict concerns the concept of understanding "diverse shared narratives." Quoting Pastor Sandra Van Opstal, David explains that in the multiethnic church context, "what's a *political* issue for one group is *pastoral* for another." He uses the shooting of seventeen-year-old Trayvon Martin in Sanford, Florida, in 2012 as an example. In the wake of yet another killing of a Black youth, the young African Americans at EEF were angry. Meanwhile, there was a White congregant who felt that Florida's "Stand Your Ground" law had justified George Zimmerman's decision to pull the trigger. EEF's worship leaders tried to help everyone recognize that regardless of one's judgment about the shooting, a mother had lost her son—and that everyone could agree that lamenting *that* was appropriate. They then participated in a song of lament that worship leaders had composed specifically for the Sunday service.

THE ARTS AS THE MEANS OF RECONCILING COMMUNITY

Teaching and preaching a solid biblical theology of reconciliation and engaging in intentional practices like sharing power, seeking understanding, and practicing lament helped East End Fellowship move beyond the pain of the 2011–2012 season. Other congregations striving for unity in diversity have deployed similar strategies. But to this mix EEF has added two other potent ingredients that have contributed to the church's endurance:

contextually crafted worship and an arts-focused leadership development program. At East End both are centered on the unique power of music.

The power of music. "People's theology isn't shaped by what they hear preached passively," David states. "It's shaped by what they sing." His argument rests on two key ideas.

The first is the contention that because of the nature of human beings, information alone does not lead to formation. Referencing the work of James K. A. Smith in his important book *Desiring the Kingdom*, David notes that humans are not brains on sticks.[16] The whole of the human self must be addressed in Christian worship. Biblical truth must be heard, experienced, embodied. Since the Reformation, David explains, there has been a tendency in Protestant circles to overemphasize lengthy sermonizing. But for the fifteen centuries before, "The church relied on an oral tradition, making use of iconography, music, and art."

Second, as EEF's leaders note, there's something very special, even divine, about music. "When we tie theology to a melody, it's going to be much more memorable," says Erin Rose, a former church leader. "People tune a preacher out. A good song," though, "will still hold our attention."[17] For many believers, David adds, "their theology of grace is more influenced by 'Amazing Grace' and 'And Can It Be' than it is by the preaching they've heard."

Music in a multicultural setting. David likes to reference a music teacher who once said, "We can't all talk at the same time and hear one another. But we can all sing together at the same time and hear one another." As important as authentic and deep conversations are in the reconciliation journey, David has come to see that worshiping together is equally formative. In a multiethnic context, he argues, "you're going to need discipleship for tough emotions like fear, grief, shame, and anger. Music and liturgies help."

But not just any music works. What's required is music intentionally crafted for that formation purpose. It must be music that resonates in the cultural location where it is employed, music that speaks out of and into the experiences and emotions of those hearing and participating in it.

That realization led David to another one: he saw that the repertoire of contemporary worship music available was limited. It was largely "vertical theology in orientation, created for the soccer mom, the White college student, and the Black middle class." He experimented one day with the

EEF congregation. He asked, "Who's heard of John Stott?" Most of the Whites raised their hands. "Who's heard of James Cone?" Many of the Blacks raised their hands. "Then I asked, 'Who's heard of Chris Tomlin?' and all the hands go up!"

Elena explains that "the sad fact is that a few groups of mostly White people from a few areas of the world are writing the vast majority of the music that gets used in churches."

In its multiethnic, multiclass, urban context, David says, EEF needed a broader variety of music and messages. It needed "music for the horizontal theology." The fact was that EEF "was preaching a certain message but not singing it." And to have something to sing, they were going to have to write the soundtrack themselves.

Beyond conversation to culture making. David's epiphany about the need for contextually situated, formative worship music occurred simultaneously to a growing concern among the EEF leadership team. The congregation's racial balance was skewing toward a lighter hue, in part because of the young White college graduates who had come to Church Hill to serve in its various Christian community-development ministries. Deeply influenced by their experiences, many decided to stay in the community. There was no similar pipeline for young Christians of color to find their way into the life of Church Hill. "We had a leadership development problem," David says.

To address both that reality and the dearth of a soundtrack for reconciliation, David proposed that the church launch an "urban doxology" songwriting internship.[18] The idea was to invite a group of young adults—predominantly though not exclusively people of color—with musical gifts to study, live, and work together in Church Hill for a summer.

Given David's background as a musician, it's not surprising that he suggested an arts-focused discipleship program. But he also genuinely believes that artists bring a special skill set to the work of reconciliation because artists are also "cultural anthropologists." Musicians, for example, know that "in order to make a connection with your different audiences, you've got to know that you're crossing different cultures."

The interns meet once a week with Pastor Don for informal mentoring and prayer. They are discipled using practices common at EEF—listening to

God, solitude, rest—and learning the core values of the church. They also work their way through the Race, Class, and Kingdom of God course. To counter the too-limited world of Christian contemporary music, Arrabon leaders introduce the interns to a broad range of musical styles and unfamiliar composers.

The internship also helps the young leaders to better understand the role of the artist in society. David teaches, "You can't have flourishing without great storytelling and the arts. Every movement in society has always had a soundtrack. The role of the artist in society is to help express the human experience, both the way things ought to be and the way that things are messed up." Artists have a profound influence on society, he continues. "Think about dictators. The first thing they do is try to put controls on the academy and the arts. Then they use the arts to create new narratives."

This is why art is a potent means of addressing racial divides. Racism is deeply embedded in cultural narratives and social structures (institutions). Changing this will require making new narratives, practices, and institutions, as Andy Crouch, author of *Culture Making*, has explained. "If we want to transform culture, what we actually have to do is to get into the midst of the human cultural project and create some new cultural goods that reshape the way people imagine and experience their world."[19]

Arrabon's leaders say the most important part of the songwriting internship is that this group of diverse, young believers makes new cultural goods together. "The magic of the songwriting internship is the cross-cultural collaboration," David emphasizes. "Everything's theoretical until you do stuff together. We're not transformed by relationships alone. Just sitting around the coffee shop talking about ideas is not going to change us. We're transformed by working together to try to create something that lasts, like music."

Making music together for East End Fellowship is a practical way the interns embody the kind of genuine collaboration required on the journey of reconciliation. As Elena explains, "In true collaboration you are embodying the idea that we are better together. The relationship is interdependent, with influence and communication flowing two ways."

The interns serve as the core worship team for EEF's Sunday afternoon gatherings throughout the summer. They craft songs and liturgies aimed at nourishing the fellowship for the labor of reconciliation. "It's an unusual and special thing to have music that's written specifically for your community," Elena enthuses. "When you can say, 'This song identifies us.'"

BECOMING A SPIRITUAL FAMILY

EEF leaders report that resurrection power has been needed for the reconciling journey and especially for EEF's demanding strategy of practicing Acts 2 economics. EEF's covenant community—which today numbers around 125 people—has committed to ensuring that no member lacks sufficient food and shelter. In a context where some members are very poor and vulnerable to job loss, eviction, predatory lending, and hunger, this requires radical, sacrificial generosity. Erin sees this as a positive progression at EEF, a way of going ever deeper into genuine reconciliation. In the beginning, she says, the emphasis was on building diverse relationships, but that "wasn't yet getting into the heart of some of the systemic injustices." David agrees. "We have to understand that race is an economic problem, not just an interpersonal problem."

The key to living out Acts 2's "holding all things in common," says David, is Christ-followers truly seeing themselves as members of one family. When Christians do that, "we're more willing to share at a whole other level." Erin agrees, "When it's your natural family, you absolutely will take care of them," making sure everyone has food and shelter. EEF encourages congregants to do the same for one another, "brothers and sisters in Christ." While "EEF can't fix all the problems of gentrification and economic injustice in the neighborhood," David says, "within the hundred or so people in the covenant community, we can really try to live out the Acts 2 call of being a spiritual family."

This message of economic mutuality has proven too difficult to swallow for some of the more affluent EEF congregants. A handful have left the church in the past few years. But those who left tended to not be involved in a house church, which EEF leaders contend is truly the lifeblood of the congregation. Regardless, EEF's leaders have made peace with the reality that the congregation is likely to remain small. Erin says, "We're a small church . . . because there is such a cost to the way that we do things. We're gonna ask that you share what you have, whether that's spiritual resources or financial resources—and it's going to be sacrificial."

Other parishioners of means have bought into this vision. Erin reports she sees members "putting their money where their mouth is and not just *talking* about, 'Lord, let your kingdom come on earth.' They're writing checks and sharing their assets to make sure that everybody has what they need."

Probably the most impressive example of the practice involves a wealthy couple who inherited $250,000 from the wife's grandparents. As a way of participating in reparations the couple met with the Baileys and Don and members of his family, and asked these trusted Black brothers and sisters to steward the funds. They gave them full decision-making power over the use of the inheritance.

Stories like this pump energy and hopefulness into EEF's leaders. Don says, "I'm excited about the future. We've got a core group of people that get the vision and wow, we could see something really beautiful happen." In the meantime, he says, his flock is "on the road to the Beloved Community." The road is "bumpy and filled with twists," he says, but it regularly results in times of "overwhelming moments of great joy."

11

THE PROSPEROUS

FLOURISHING IN THE REALM
OF ECONOMIC LIFE

THE COMMUNITY ENDOWMENT of the Prosperous is about the realm of economic life. For many, the word *economics* conjures up images of confusing graphs, intimidating mathematical formulas, or boring news reports about the price of oil. For others, economics is synonymous with business, and they assert that church and business are two very separate spheres. In the Thriving Cities paradigm, the community endowment of the Prosperous includes such aspects of society as commerce, finance, investment, work, philanthropy, production, and consumption.[1] It involves innovation, savings and debt, poverty, wealth, and economic opportunity.

Though we are far more than economic creatures, human beings are engaged in economic life daily. It's a huge facet of our lives: just think about how much time we spend working, spending, creating, and investing. "The everyday world we live in is an economic world," pastor Tom Nelson reminds us.[2] To be faithful to the Scripture's command to not be "conformed to the world," Christ-followers must interrogate our culture's economic beliefs, attitudes, and practices.

THE ENDOWMENT OF THE PROSPEROUS AND HUMAN FLOURISHING

Christian teaching is clear that there is more to prosperity than only economic prosperity. Humans beings are far more than economic agents. Systems that reduce people to *homo economicus* do not bring true prosperity.[3] Genuine prospering involves meaningful relationships and physical health. The Thriving Cities paradigm also acknowledges this; it teaches that thriving is a multifold matter involving far more than economic well-being. Its endowment brief on the Prosperous takes time to critique ways of measuring prosperity that revolve solely around economic production.[4]

For the purposes of this book, though, I want to look specifically at economic prosperity. This is because other chapters discuss the vital roles of health, safety, justice, beauty, education, family life (and more) in creating community flourishing. All of these are necessary for thriving. But enjoying economic health is also a big part of what it means to flourish, for three reasons.

First, human flourishing is not consistent with economic destitution. Those who suffer the excruciating pain of hunger, the misery of being without adequate shelter or clothing, or the tragedy of being unable to afford medical treatment for their sick child are not flourishing. Second, human flourishing requires some degree of economic capacity. This is what allows us to delight in giving and sharing material resources. We cannot share what we do not possess. And sharing is something we are wired for: God is a giver and we are made in God's image. Third, human flourishing requires the opportunity to work. Work is not a result of the fall. Work is good and good for us; it was originally designed to be truly delightful and full of meaning. Productive work was never *all* that human beings were created for, of course. But by God's design, work is an avenue for our enjoyment and a means by which we bring flourishing to others. As Nelson explains, "While human flourishing is more than creativity and productivity, it is not less than this. We were made to add value to the world in and through our work, and to love our neighbor in and through our fruitfulness."[5]

THE SCRIPTURES ON ECONOMIC LIFE

God's Word is saturated with economic themes and teaching. Major portions of Old Testament law seek to order Israel's economic life. We find, for example, rules about property management and how to treat employees, about liability, farming practices, and principles for commercial exchange. The Wisdom literature offers all sorts of insight for economic life: about hard work and saving for a rainy day, shrewdness in business transactions, and how generosity often begets generosity. In the Gospels, Jesus insists on just economic exchange and warns of the dangers of reducing life to only economic concerns. The authors of the Epistles address issues of work and bearing one another's economic burdens.

Though some of this biblical material is specific to the agricultural economy of ancient Israel, many principles transcend that context. Stealing is still wrong. Generosity is still commanded. God is still interested in just weights and measures. And he is still profoundly concerned about those who suffer poverty.[6] God is passionate about the community endowment called the Prosperous.

CREATIONAL INTENT: THE REALM OF ECONOMIC LIFE

What do the Scriptures reveal about God's creational intent for the realm of economic life? I suggest we can observe at least five major themes.

First, we see that *abundance is normative*; it is woven into the very fabric of creation. Let's pretend we had Superman's eyes. We look up and what do we see? Some 100 octillion stars (that's a 1 with 29 zeros after it). And even that's likely a "gross underestimation" according to Cornell University astronomer David Kornreich.[7] Now let's cast our Superman eyes down, penetrating the ocean's great depths. We shall find it, as Genesis 1:20 reveals, *teeming* with life. Two verses later God commands even *more* life, blessing the birds and fish and telling them to multiply. Reflecting on this the psalmist exclaims,

How many are your works, LORD!
In wisdom you made them all;
the earth is full of your creatures.
There is the sea, vast and spacious,
teeming with creatures beyond number—
living things both large and small. (Ps 104:24-25)

Now imagine we're standing in the original Eden. As we gaze around, we see a magnificent array of plants and trees. Not just a few kinds; again, profligacy is on display. God gives his children "every seed-bearing plant on the face of the whole earth and every tree that has fruit with seed in it" (Gen 1:29). There's no shortage in the Garden; there's no scarcity and no hunger. And it is not just *sufficiency* that reigns. Abundance reigns.[8]

Christianity is not a religion of asceticism. Yes, it calls for temperance, chastity, and even self-denial. But it is a faith that celebrates the good world and its good gifts. God has richly blessed us "with everything for our enjoyment," 1 Timothy 6:17 says. Caricatures of Christians as austere prigs are just that—caricatures. Our God calls us to fast, to be sure. But our God also loves a good party. The Old Testament law commanded multiple feasts and festivals, usually marked by plenty of food, wine, music, and dancing. Jesus himself enjoyed a good party, so much so that he was accused of gluttony (Lk 7:34).

In celebrating this theme of abundance I am not asserting in any way some kind of prosperity gospel. Christianity does not condone self-indulgence, and there is no place for an arrogant attitude insisting on one's right to material wealth as a child of the King. There is a great difference between what Christianity has historically defined as "the good life" and the acquisitive goods life of Western materialism.[9] Great Christian teachers from the early church fathers onward have consistently spoken out against materialism.

The second theme concerns *stewardship*. God is the sole and ultimate owner of everything. There is such a thing as private property in the Bible, but not in an unqualified sense. Rather, *everything we possess is gift, and we are trustees*. In ancient Israel, God gave the people land and it was distributed by kinship units. Israel did not have a statist economy. Later, when God gives his people the Ten Commandments, one of them is "do not steal." Clearly, there is a genuine sense in which person A possesses something and person B does not possess that thing. In that sense the object is person A's private property. But person A is not the owner. Person A has very real responsibility and genuine authority over the possession—but not unqualified ownership. Person A's job is to steward that possession in alignment with God's purposes.

God grants human beings this stewardship responsibility for our delight. He has given us capacity (intelligence, creativity) and executing stewardship is fundamental to being the humans God created us to be. We need the economic capacity to fulfill our stewardship roles. This is one reason why God provided the first humans with more than just the minimum, barest essentials. Responsibility for actual resources enables us to engage in creating new resources and to practice love of neighbor by participating in mutually beneficial exchanges and charitably sharing our possessions.

Third (and closely related), God's creational intent is that human beings would *develop the raw materials of his creation*. Humans are told to "work"

or "tend" (Hebrew *abad*) the garden (Gen 2:15). We are to cultivate its possibilities; to make something of it. This is a work of economic and cultural
development. Moreover, as Nelson explains in *The Economics of Neighborly
Love*, God's charge in Genesis 1:28 that humans "be fruitful and multiply" is
not only about fertility (procreation) but also about productivity. The
Hebrew word for "fruitfulness" that is used there is also used in various
forms in other Old Testament passages speaking about the productivity of
land and animals.[10]

God embedded productivity into the warp and woof of creation. The
single fruit contains many seeds; when planted these seeds bear a whole crop
of new fruit. In God's world, multiplication is possible. Created in God's
image, human beings are ingenious creators who can cooperatively bring out,
develop, and multiply the world of possibilities that God made. As John Bolt
puts it in *Economic Shalom*, "We were created for creative production . . . for
using the manifold riches of creation to enhance human flourishing."[11]

Now—importantly—Scripture makes it equally clear that humans are not
to pillage the earth in the pursuit of creating new wealth. The same God who
calls us to fruitfully work the land also charges the first humans to "take care
of" of and "guard" his earth (Hebrew *shamar*). As we will see in chapter
fourteen on sustainability, *preservation*, as well as development, is part of the
cultural mandate. The nonhuman order—the plants and trees and seas and
animals—are all called "good" by God. Human dominion over these aspects
of God's creation must not involve their abuse; we have no such license.
Right action in the realm of the Prosperous is connected to wholeness in the
endowment of the Sustainable.

The themes of stewardship and development, alongside the place of work
in the original creation, provide insight into our fourth theme: *God's intentions for the sphere of business*. God loves and delights in the material world
he created (he called it "good" six times). He set humans in this world and
made us stewards with the capacity to work, create, and imagine. The
Garden was good indeed, but also incomplete. God tasks humanity with
classifying and ordering the creation, and "filling" it (Gen 2:19-20; 1:28). The
earth needed people to work it for it to reach its potential (Gen 2:4-5).

In identifying which aspects of the creation mandate the institution of
business—as opposed to other created institutions—is best suited for, author

Jeff Van Duzer identifies two primary purposes.[12] The first is creating wealth (to "work the fields" and "cause the land to be fruitful") and to provide organized opportunities for meaningful and creative work.

The fifth biblical theme is that God desires all community members to be full participants in economic life. God does not insist that everyone's economic status be the same. Some people will have more and some less. But *his normative intention is for a world without material poverty, period.* There was no poverty in the Garden (since we enjoyed perfect peace with creation) and there will be no poverty in the new Jerusalem. In the in-between times, it seems that God desires no one to be permanently destitute. Consider, for example, Deuteronomy 15:4-5. There, the Lord tells the Israelites that "there need be no poor people among you . . . if only you fully obey the LORD your God and are careful to follow all these commands I am giving you today."

In the world under a curse, some people will suffer economic distress. One might be lame and unable to work. Another might be suddenly widowed and left with multiple dependent children. A third might work hard but see his crops fail. In light of this God commands the economically sufficient not to despise the economically vulnerable. *Everyone* in the community is to be valued as a contributor because everyone has been given gifts and talents by their Maker. In God's economic plan each person is to have opportunities to give and to receive. In their book *Practicing the King's Economy*, Michael Rhodes and Robby Holt call this the "community key" in Scripture. In examining how God wanted people of different economic classes to interact, they find an image of a potluck—where everyone brings something to the table and everyone has a place at the table—rather than a soup kitchen, where only the haves provide the food and the have-nots are kept at arm's length.[13] To truly flourish, all people regardless of their socioeconomic status must have the opportunity to meaningfully participate in their communities.

MALFORMATIONS IN THE REALM OF ECONOMIC LIFE

We've seen something of God's beautiful and just design for economic life. Undoubtedly, there will be great rejoicing in the new heavens and new earth when the true prosperity God desires for all people will once again reign.

While we inhabit the time between the original creation and the new creation, though, it's not hard to see that abundance is not, well, abundant. Instead, millions go hungry daily. A few people have far more than enough while others go without. This is not what God desires. It is a result of the fall, a consequence of sin.

Indeed, sin brought about multiple malformations in economic life. One was the *scarcity* that arose because of the curse laid upon the earth. Scarcity arises in part from diseases that afflict plants and animals and the land itself. In the world "east of Eden," there might be a withering fungus that drastically reduces the harvest or sickness that causes livestock to miscarry. In the fallen world, famine and hunger enter in. Scarcity also arises from the sinful hearts of people. Human beings who were designed for cooperation and mutual delight sometimes turn against one another in hostility. They deliberately ruin others' harvests and poison others' wells. Human selfishness manifests itself in countless ways, from hoarding to theft. Moreover, we fallen humans establish all sorts of systems that produce poverty rather than plenty—for example, systems that deny some people the opportunity to work or that oppress one group for the enrichment of another or that feed consumer appetites without thought for the environmental destruction they are wreaking.

As noted earlier, God's creational intent for economic life is that *all* community members would be full participants. With the entrance of sin into the world, economic life began to be marked by a second malformation: the *exclusion* of some human beings from that full participation (e.g., slavery). Though God didn't want Israel to have any poor among them, a poverty class arose. Households found themselves without land and in debt for a variety of reasons including exploitation. Here we see another example of the interconnectedness of the community endowments: without justice there is no true prosperity.

Our contemporary world remains rife with economic exploitation at home and abroad. The International Labor Organization estimates some forty million people are suffering in slavery today. Here at home we see multiple economic injustices such as policies that shut people out from market participation and continued racial discrimination in employment, housing, and housing financing.

A third malformation in the economic realm is seen in *the distortions of business life*. Business, like all institutions, was created good but has been tainted by the fall. Business was designed to contribute to human flourishing by creating jobs and new wealth. Economic exchange was designed to create efficiencies and meet people's various needs in mutually beneficial ways. The production of goods that serve human needs is one expression of neighbor love. But now humans believe that *they* are the owners of the businesses they operate rather than acknowledging *God* as the owner and themselves as trustees. Additionally, greed plagues every economic system, including the free market. Businesspeople, like all people, engage in all sorts of personal sins—fraud, exploitation, dishonesty. And these harm customers, vendors, and employees.

We can also observe *institutional* deformations in business. For example, since Milton Friedman famously argued in 1970 that the only social responsibility of a business was to "engage in activities designed to increase its profits," a narrow shareholder paradigm has dominated the field.[14] This conventional wisdom coupled with the power of investors to demand strong, quick performance by the businesses in which they hold stock has contributed to a detrimental focus on short-term gain. Profit was designed to be a means to a higher purpose—creating needed goods and services and providing meaningful employment—but in the shareholder paradigm profit has become an end in itself. This in turn has blinded some companies from their own long-term interests. It has encouraged businesses to mistreat workers and pollute the environment. Malformations in the endowment of the Prosperous create tragedies in the endowment of the Sustainable.

Critics of our current economic system from a variety of disciplines— philosophy, theology, sociology, and economics, to name a few—have raised a variety of additional concerns. Some worry that the modern consumer economy has deformed us by commodifying nearly everything.[15] Others fear it has corrupted our understanding of freedom and created an unhealthy mindset of detachment.[16] Still others highlight how the US economy has become increasingly marked by inequality and a lack of economic mobility.[17]

In *Practicing the King's Economy*, Michael Rhodes and Robby Holt spotlight a further foundational malformation in economic life. It is the idol of *homo economicus.* This is the definition of persons as being "at their core, solitary individuals whose lives are devoted to increasing pleasure through consuming more material goods and increasing leisure."[18] This view of a human being is, of course, far from the biblical portrait. Yet these authors worry that our modern consumerist economy with its constant bombardment that "shopping will solve our problems" is reshaping us into this *homo economicus* idol.[19] They write:

> We worship material possessions, we cling to them for security, and we are being remade in the image of our gods. Having made material things the measure of our lives, we have become better and better at producing and consuming more and more. Meanwhile, we're becoming worse and worse at connecting, caring, and serving.[20]

TOWARD REFORMATIONS IN THE REALM OF ECONOMIC LIFE

In our fallen world the untold abundance of God's original creation has given way to natural and manmade disasters. Yet God in his lavish goodness and common grace has set limits on the ruin that sin has wrought: the rain still falls and the sun still shines. There is yet some fruitfulness; there is yet the possibility of creating new wealth. We human beings are still granted intelligence, creativity, entrepreneurial abilities, and strength.

How should Christ-followers live now in this world marked by a strange mixture of scarcity and possibility? How can we push back against the malformations in our community's economy and work creatively for positive change? The Scriptures have wisdom for us on this, too, through at least four themes.

Theme 1. Living in alignment with proverbial wisdom. First, we must continue to live into the cultural mandate to work, steward, and produce—but with attentiveness to our new conditions postfall and to God's instructions. God's wise law, which he gives to us that we might find a measure of shalom east of Eden, provides counsel at both the personal and interpersonal levels. For example,

- We are each to work diligently—even though work is no longer the unmitigated pleasure it was in the original garden. Rest is good; laziness is not (Prov 6:9-11).

- Because of the uncertainties of nature, we must manage resources wisely and save for unexpected ills (Prov 6:6-8).

- We must apply ourselves to creativity, entrepreneurship, and productivity since through these we can create new wealth and new value that offers the possibility for improving the human condition (Prov 31:16-35).

- In our economic exchanges with others, we are to obey God's commands, for example, eschewing false weights and measures (Lev 19:13; Deut 25:15) and not oppressing our workers (Deut 24:15; Jer 22:13).

Theme 2. Economic practices to empower and include the poor and oppressed. Second, because of the realities of human sinfulness and human frailty (given the fall, some community members are now weak, disabled, or infirm), humans must implement practices that prevent the vulnerable from becoming a permanent underclass. The gleaning regulation (see Lev 19:9-10), for example, aimed to help the able-bodied poor. Israelite landowners were instructed not to harvest to the edges of their fields but rather to leave some produce so that those without land could gather what they needed. The law also made provision for the non-able-bodied poor through the third-year tithe (Deut 14:28; 26:12). Israelites were not only expected to practice charitable giving. This third-year tithe was a form of tax to fund social welfare for the needy.

Additionally, the law commanded a system of debt forgiveness within the Israelite community, whereby every seventh year there was a remission of debts (Deut 15:1-3). The Year of Jubilee, described in Leviticus 25, further sought to protect the landless poor. As scholars from the Theology of Work project explain:

> Every fiftieth year, all leased or mortgaged lands were to be returned to their original owners, and all slaves and bonded laborers were to be freed. . . . The underlying intent is the same as seen in the law of gleaning (Lev. 19:9-10), to ensure that everyone had access to the means of production, whether the family farm or simply the fruits of their own labor.[21]

In our contemporary context Christ-followers are seeking to engage in the re-formation of economic life through modern-day gleaning and debt relief. For example, investors in the Calvert Foundation's "community investment notes" accept a reduced financial return to capitalize initiatives seeking positive social return. This is an example of "leaving some profit in the field." Today there are a variety of social impact investment funds Christ-followers can support.[22]

Christian business owners have opportunities to practice modern-day gleaning-type practices. Wes Gardner is doing so through his business, Prime Trailer, in Denver. One way he loves his neighbor is by offering work to people who might have difficulty being hired by others, like Benjamin, a recovering alcoholic, and Lauren, a teen mom. In 2011 Prime Trailer launched the Career Partner Program. Through it Gardner hires unlikely job candidates (found through his contacts with local ministries) and pays them above-market wages for at least twelve months, while also investing in them professionally and personally.[23] Gardner says it's messy. Sometimes offering second chance jobs means that training takes longer or difficulties arise—and those things can erode efficiency and shave something off of the company's revenue. That's the sacrifice of following the gleaning regulation today. Gardner says it's worth it. For him success is measured not only in financial return but in people development.[24]

Christ-followers who own rental properties can practice gleaning by pricing their units at below-market rates, thus helping to create a little more affordable housing stock in their communities.

Churches can practice modern-day gleaning too. Downtown Church in Memphis, for example, hires people with criminal records to set up chairs, break down the nursery, and assist the church office staff. The church also encourages its members to hire people in need of extra cash to complete small home repairs, run errands, assist with a move, or cook meals. The deacons surveyed congregants to identify who would be willing to hire people for tasks like these so that they can connect individuals struggling to find work with these opportunities.[25]

By way of applying Old Testament debt-relief practices, some congregations nationwide have established their own lending programs to counter the exploitation of payday lenders. For example, in Springfield, Missouri, University Heights Baptist Church started the "University Hope" ministry to provide small rescue loans to those trapped in the predatory loan cycle.

By working with a local credit union, UHBC can guarantee loans at low interest rates to pay off payday or title loans. Program participants must have a payday loan of $1,000 or less at above 36 percent interest. They agree to join the local credit union and to meet monthly with a mentor from the church.

Other congregations have pooled resources and partnered with RIP Medical Debt, a nonprofit organization that buys medical debt at steep discounts and then sells it to entities like churches to help people be freed from medical debt. Over the Christmas season of 2018, Christian Assembly Church in Los Angeles worked with RIP Medical Debt to pay off $5.3 million in medical bills for more than five thousand local households. It cost the church just $53,000.[26]

Theme 3. Redeeming business. Because of common grace, believers and nonbelievers seeking to operate in alignment with the original purposes for business can do much good. A productive economy can help lift people out of poverty; indeed, the capacity for a for-profit business to do this is greater than that of nonprofit organizations or philanthropy.[27] Worldwide, economic growth has greatly reduced extreme poverty in the past fifty years: the number of people living on a dollar per day or less dropped by 80 percent between 1970 and 2006.[28] World Bank data shows a similar trend: it reports that from 1990 to 2015, the extreme poverty rate globally dropped from nearly 36 percent to 10 percent.[29]

There is a growing movement within the business sector away from Friedman's shareholder paradigm and toward a more holistic and just stakeholder approach. Thought leaders like Michael Porter at Harvard Business School, for example, advocate creating "shared value."[30] In 2019 the Business Roundtable wrote a new corporate purpose statement to emphasize responsibility to stakeholders and not just shareholders.[31] Praxis, a leading Christian organization supporting and discipling start-up leaders, focuses on teaching "redemptive entrepreneurship." Leaders say, "Our endgame is for our ventures to be agents of redemption as we act as the hands and feet of Christ in the world, knowing that He is 'making all things new.' We work for impact that approximates the ultimate restoration that we know is one day coming."[32] Chapter thirteen examines how Grace Chapel, a church in Ohio, has been seeking for the past twenty years to "redeem business."

Theme 4. Living in the King's economy. Finally, we can push back against the idol of *homo economicus* by remembering and practicing our true identities as persons made in God's image. This will require confronting the ways (subtle and not) we have been "conformed to the world." As Rhodes and Holt remind us, Jesus teaches Econ 101 differently. We must eschew the norms, values, and practices that are not in line with those of Jesus' kingdom economy. One great strength of their book is how it compares and contrasts kingdom economics with American economics. It offers numerous ideas for reforming our spending, saving, and investing habits. It also suggests various spiritual disciplines and individual and corporate practices we can begin to embrace.

THE PROSPEROUS AND THE CHURCH HISTORIC

Christians have been influencing ideas and attitudes around economic matters since the birth of the church. For two thousand years individual Christ-followers, congregations, and denominations have taught and written about wealth and poverty, modeled specific economic practices in alignment with kingdom values, and engaged in efforts to bring about economic reforms opening up greater opportunities for the disadvantaged or exploited. Here I provide some examples of these things organized around five themes.

Money is for sharing. We have seen that God desires humans to understand their role as stewards, not owners, and that he is profoundly concerned for the vulnerable. He wants his disciples to lighten the suffering of the poor, sick, and hungry. Throughout church history we see numerous examples of ways believers have aligned their teaching and actions to these norms.

Probably the best-known example of this is the activity of the early church in Jerusalem described in Acts 2:44-45: "All the believers were together and had everything in common. They sold property and possessions to give to anyone who had need." These believers saw one another as family and took responsibility for each other.[33]

Members of the first-century church not only shared their money and possessions with believers in their local fellowship, but they also gave generously and sacrificially to geographically distant brothers and sisters. For example, the apostle Paul writes of collections from Gentile Christians taken up to assist impoverished Jewish Christians during a time of famine (Acts 20:33-35; 2 Cor 8:1-15). This remarkable, organized philanthropy demonstrated both genuine sacrifice and the gospel's power to bridge a centuries-long cultural hostility. This public fundraising was also unique historically. Scholar Phillip Long writes, "The Greco-Roman world had a system of public benefaction, but nothing like a modern fundraiser where people are solicited for money which is then distributed to the poor."[34]

These practices by followers of the Way in the first centuries were seemingly rooted not only in the Scriptures but also in the clear and frequent teaching of the early church fathers on money. The *Didache*, a second-century collection of Christian writings, instructed believers: "Do not turn your back on the needy, but share everything with your brother and call nothing your own. For if you have what is eternal in common, how much more should you have what is transient!"[35] In the fourth century Ambrose warned the wealthy of the dangers of being mastered by their possessions: "[he] who does not know how to give and distribute to the poor, he is the servant of his wealth, not its master."[36] Saint Augustine, too, taught that believers should see their wealth not as private. "That bread which you keep, belongs to the hungry," he wrote, and "that coat which you preserve in your wardrobe, to the naked."[37]

Centuries later in early America the Puritans displayed similar attitudes toward wealth. Leland Ryken, author of *Worldly Saints: The Puritans as They Really Were*, argues that "the key to everything they said on [money] was their conviction that money is a social good, not a private possession. Its main purpose is the welfare of everyone in society, not the personal pleasure of the person who happens to have control over it."[38] Puritan preacher Hugh Latimer even went so far as to say that "the poor man hath title to the rich man's goods; so that the rich man ought to let the poor man have part of his riches to help and to comfort him withal."[39]

Puritans agreed with John Calvin that money in itself is good. Puritan leaders Samuel Willard and William Adams, for example, believed "riches were consistent with godliness" and could be used to maximize the doing of good.[40] At the same time they recognized the danger of riches in leading one toward self-indulgence or trusting in money rather than God. They did not equate wealth with godliness (or view poverty as a sign of God's judgment).

They rejected "the ethic of unconcern that is content to let the poor remain poor" and "looked askance" at luxury.[41]

Changing attitudes toward the poor. According to Princeton historian Peter Brown, Christians were not the only ones who were generous in the ancient world. But the *manner and direction* of the Christians' philanthropy were markedly different from that of their Roman counterparts. For one thing the early Christians were willing to show compassion to those outside their biological and spiritual kin.[42] Romans, by contrast, limited their giving to citizens and ignored the needs of the many poor who were not Roman citizens. For another, well-off Roman citizens considered themselves superior to those citizens who were recipients of their alms.[43] Christians abandoned such notions.

Under the teaching of church fathers like Gregory of Nyssa, Christ-followers were encouraged to view the destitute, the widow, and the sick through the lens of their faith. Gregory preached that Christians must see Jesus himself in the face of the poor.[44] Meanwhile, Saint Ambrose enjoined Christ-followers to see the materially poor not as "others" but as "brothers."[45] Brown contends that this change was nothing short of an "imaginative revolution."[46]

A similar sea change stimulated by Christians occurred in nineteenth-century England, according to historian Herbert Schlossberg. Schlossberg's *The Silent Revolution and the Making of Victorian England* offers a detailed portrait of the innumerable social reforms advanced by British believers from John Wesley to Lord Shaftesbury. We've already heard about some of these in other chapters. Importantly, though, Schlossberg argues that the greatest contribution by the Evangelicals went even beyond their industriousness to alleviate woe. What they accomplished was nothing less than a fundamental shift in people's attitudes toward the poor. Largely as a result of their activities, "in the early nineteenth century economic hardship was taken to be a serious national matter that could not be allowed to persist." There was not universal agreement among these believers about *what* to do, particularly whether the best progress could be attained through private charity or public legislation. But "the growing religious consciousness changed the general perception of the society about the existence of privation and brought it to the forefront of public discussion."[47]

Organized social welfare for the poor and vulnerable. In the church's first hundred years, benevolence activity was highly organic. By the late second and early third centuries the church's social welfare efforts became increasingly organized. For example, Tertullian explained in AD 197 that Christ-followers made voluntary contributions monthly to a treasure chest. Funds distributed by church leaders supported the poor, paid for the burial of the dead, aided prisoners and those shipwrecked, and supplied "the wants of boys and girls destitute of means and parents, and of old persons confined now to the house."[48]

At the Council of Nicaea in AD 325 the church agreed that bishops should take responsibility for administering hospitals in every cathedral city of the empire.[49] Over time the church either built or was charged with the supervision of orphanages, old-age homes, reformatory institutions, and other social welfare services. In the sixth century the Council of Orleans named bishops as "fathers of the poor," who were to devote one-quarter of church revenues to the poor. In rural areas one-third of church revenues were to be so disposed.[50]

During the Middle Ages organized charity was generally administered through the church or parachurch organizations known as confraternities.[51] The medieval period also saw the rise of religious-run shelters, almshouses, and leprosaria.[52]

During the Reformation, in multiple cities in Germany, Luther's followers put into practice his "common chest" policy for meeting the needs of the poor. Luther had recommended that each city establish a common chest, operated largely by secular administrators, to which parishioners could donate. Funds would then be dispersed at the discretion of council officials. Common chest funds were also used to pay the salaries of teachers and to maintain public buildings.[53]

In eighteenth-century England, John Wesley's Methodists engaged in a variety of social welfare activities. One of Wesley's principal congregations gathered in an old foundry. Seeing firsthand the needs of poor people in the working classes stirred Wesley to launch the Foundry Society. It offered basic medical care and schooling and provided housing for poor and elderly widows and their children.[54]

Additional impressive leaders followed in Wesley's footsteps. At a time when the industrial revolution was bringing both prosperity and dislocation to England, certain Christians—William Wilberforce and his Clapham friends, the More sisters, Charles Simeon, Lord Shaftesbury, John Venn, Thomas Chalmers, John Henry Newman, and Thomas Arnold, among others—provided leadership over a dizzying array of social reforms. Schlossberg describes their activities:

> They distributed food and clothing to the sick. They oversaw both Sunday Schools and "ragged schools" for the poorest children and founded libraries. Some societies provided reduced-cost housing and collected money to purchase furniture and fuel for poor families. . . . There were societies established for the help of endless groups of the needy: soldiers, sailors, agricultural workers, laborers, prostitutes, and so on. This was a great age for organizing, and it was hard to find a significant need that did not have its collection of sympathizers forming a society to provide help.[55]

Christians in the United States also demonstrated a history of engaging in benevolence. Marvin Olasky's *The Tragedy of American Compassion* cites a wide body of original-source material to describe the ways early American Christians were highly engaged in voluntary societies. Examples included the Scots' Charitable Society (founded 1684) to aid widows, the Society for Encouraging Industry and Employing the Poor (active in the 1750s), and the Society for the Relief of Poor Widows with Small Children (founded 1797).[56] Moreover, in the nineteenth century American Evangelicals, like their British counterparts, engaged in all manner of social welfare efforts to alleviate the suffering of the poor, unemployed, and immigrant.

Throughout its history, the African American church has been at the center of mutual care efforts within the Black community. Leading scholars such as C. Eric Lincoln and Lawrence Mamiya have long identified the Black church as *the* cultural, social, economic, and political anchor of the Black community.[57] In the wake of slavery, Black churches were continually involved in both the spiritual and material uplift of their members. For example, in 1787 the two ministers who would eventually establish the African Methodist Episcopal denomination, Richard Allen and Absalom Jones, founded the Philadelphia Free African Society. Members paid monthly fees and after one year were eligible for benefits. These included help with funeral expenses and care for deceased members' widows and children. The society provided financial assistance for widows and paid the expenses for orphans' education or apprenticeships.

In the decades following the Civil War, the commitment to mutual aid continued in most Black churches. A study by Benjamin Mays and Joseph Nicholson of 609 urban churches and 185 rural churches from the 1920s found that 97 percent of the Black churches provided community outreach programs. These included health care, hunger relief, childcare, recreation, and financial benevolence programs.[58]

Economic empowerment and inclusion. In addition to benevolence initiatives for the very young, the old, and the infirm, the church throughout the ages has engaged vigorously in efforts to empower and lift the able-bodied poor.

For example, in John Calvin's Geneva, orphaned boys were put to work in each facet of the agricultural sector: on the farms, at mills, and in bakeries. Parentless girls had similar apprenticing opportunities in other fields. All of this work was supervised by the deacons in the church.[59] The deacons also paid quarterly visits to the homes of poor families that had received church benevolence funds. Additionally, the church provided trained personnel to help families with disabled members and gave or loaned funds to refugees to enable them to restart businesses in the trades they had experience in.[60]

In nineteenth-century England, Evangelicals championed political reforms to improve working and living conditions, established schools, and implemented new forms of economic development for the poor.[61] Some of the voluntary societies they established were focused on teaching poor women how to budget, cook, and use cooperative efforts to buy cheap food and build community ovens.[62]

In the United States, following the Civil War, African American Christians established many economic cooperatives that provided both jobs and job training. The cooperative movement brought both financial returns on people's savings and created new opportunities for young people to find work. W. E. B. Du Bois published an in-depth study of the movement in 1907 called *Economic Co-operation Among Negro Americans*. Many of these cooperatives had their roots in the church. For Du Bois, "religious camaraderie was the basis for African American economic cooperation."[63]

Leveraging business for social good. One of the most important sources of the good that eighteenth- and nineteenth-century Evangelicals cultivated economically was their conviction that the gospel had implications for every area of life. They eschewed a sacred-secular dichotomy. This was a hallmark of the eighteenth-century Methodists, who insisted on both personal and social holiness. According to Schlossberg, a similar view animated the Evangelicals of a century later. These believers embraced

> the conviction that the spiritual and material worlds did not exist separately in watertight compartments, that a profession of religious faith carried with it imperatives that went well beyond private morality. . . . The evangelical reformers of the age . . . assumed that their religious convictions had to issue forth in good works; hence the societies without number, the endless visiting and provisioning of the poor, and the legislative remedies for harsh conditions in factories and mines.[64]

Not surprisingly, then, these groups used finance and business operations as a means for social good. John Wesley, for example, started a fund in the 1740s to make small loans, akin to today's microlending. It made loans to 250 people in the first year.[65] In the 1800s Evangelicals "set up businesses specifically to employ the poor, which they thought was a much better way to help them than giving them charity."[66]

The history of the Black church in America is an especially rich source of examples of Christ-followers leveraging business for social good. Like the Methodists, key Black leaders also eschewed a sacred-secular dualism. For example, Elias Camp Morris, founder of the National Baptist Convention, argued that "entrepreneurship and faith went hand in hand."[67] Morris established a newspaper and a publishing business that generated jobs and revenue and enabled the church to publish its hymns. "The solution of the so-called race problem," Morris asserted, "will depend in a large measure upon what we prove able to do for ourselves."[68]

Mutual aid societies—called by one scholar "the handmaiden" of the Black church—invested not only in insurance but also in small business development.[69] As one scholar notes, "The constitutions of several mutual aid societies stipulated that once a certain amount of money, usually in excess of two hundred dollars, was accumulated by the organization, members could borrow funds in rotation to be used as venture capital for the establishment of a business."[70]

As early as its 1892 annual conference in Philadelphia, the African Methodist Episcopal denomination organized a department of extension through which churches would contribute a portion of their receipts and the department would make loans, mostly for capitalizing small enterprises. The department raised almost $105,000 just during 1897–1900 alone and made loans totaling approximately $42,000.[71]

The AME's historical enthusiasm for nurturing economic development continues today. In 2015, for example, the AME office in the second district pledged to come alongside Black-owned businesses with renewed vigor.[72] In 2018 the denomination announced a new partnership with nineteen Black-owned banks aimed at increasing wealth in the African American community. Bishop Reginald Jackson, president of the Council of AME Bishops, explained, "This initiative will strengthen black banks across the United States and increase their capacity to lend to small businesses, to secure mortgages, to provide personal lines of credit, and to offer other forms of credit to AME churches and our members. This, of course, includes enabling members and their families to become homeowners."[73]

The National Baptist Convention also invested denominational resources in business ventures. For example, during the civil rights era Reverend J. H. Jackson led the NBC to purchase a "Freedom Farm" in Tennessee that provided a haven for Black farmers divested of their land during the struggle.[74] In 1984 the denomination established the National Baptist Convention Housing Commission to create affordable housing for low- and moderate-income persons, particularly the elderly. By 2003 it had built over one thousand units of housing at thirty housing sites across twenty-seven cities.[75] In 2016 the denomination partnered with the USDA in an outreach and education effort to increase the participation of socially disadvantaged farmers and ranchers in USDA programs.[76]

Andrew Billingsley's seminal work *Mighty Like a River: The Black Church and Social Reform* shows that churches in other predominantly Black denominations have also been engaged in all manner of efforts to flourish their communities.[77] Moreover, a 1995 study of 635 Black churches in Northeast and North Central United States found that the overwhelming majority, regardless of their particular denomination, considered the provision of practical community services as a central part of their mission.[78] Networks of Black churches have been involved in health care provision (often in partnership with health care agencies),[79] social and civil rights activism, and economic empowerment initiatives,[80] to name the most common activities.

SUMMING UP

Church history is rich with examples of believers influencing thinking about money and the appropriate uses of wealth. Christ-followers at different points in history helped their societies regard the materially poor in new, more compassionate ways. And as seen in this brief survey, Christian individuals, organizations, and denominations have long invested in the work of what we now call "relief" and "development."

As we will see in the chapters ahead, such work continues today—though much more of it is needed to address both the deformational influences of the late modern capitalist and consumerist economy and the ongoing material poverty of millions of our neighbors.

12

A STRATEGY FOR CULTIVATING THE PROSPEROUS

REDEEM BUSINESS FOR COMMUNITY GOOD

IN 2003 PASTOR JEFF GREER of Grace Chapel, a nondenominational congregation in a town outside Cincinnati, was in a meeting with a few church leaders and a large donor who had concerns about the direction the church was taking. Greer had been outlining his vision for creating a for-profit business in Nigeria that could provide ongoing revenue for the congregation's missions work there. One of the leaders, Pete West, recalls that the woman "took out an imaginary pencil and drew two boxes in the air with a line between saying, 'This is the church, and this is business. And never the twain shall meet.'"[1] She was not in favor of Greer's idea.

In response, Greer said, "Take your fake pencil back out, but this time use the fake eraser and erase those lines. In a biblical worldview, there are no lines."[2]

Although the wealthy donor referenced the idea of "the moneychangers in the temple" as evidence for her argument that church and business shouldn't mix, Greer wasn't buying it. For him it made perfect sense to harness the power of enterprise to generate revenue for the community-development efforts the church's Nigerian partners envisioned. The sacred-secular divide, he knew, was an old Gnostic idea, not a biblical one. Looking back, Greer admits he made a mistake by not laying that theological foundation more intentionally before urging the church forward. "I'm a doer," he says. "I didn't do a good job of bringing people along. Some people just didn't understand this approach and they left."

Chuck Proudfit, a longtime Grace Chapel member who heartily embraces Greer's vision, reports that the church lost many attendees over the new concept. Greer stayed the course, with a passion rooted in both holistic theology and practicality driven by the poverty he was trying to alleviate. Proudfit recalls, "Jeff was really steadfast in that season."[3]

Nowadays, Greer regularly reminds his flock that "in God's economy, there is no sacred versus secular. There is only sacred versus sinful."[4] He teaches that the creativity of business could and should be leveraged by the church as an engine to confront poverty abroad and create opportunity at home.

For nearly twenty years Greer, Proudfit, West, and other leaders at Grace Chapel have honed their theology of work and business. With a bent toward action, theirs has never been a strictly philosophical exercise. Gradually, these leaders have crafted and implemented an innovative church strategy for advancing community flourishing by redeeming business. Their vision involves capitalizing on the wealth-creating genius of a for-profit enterprise while simultaneously reforming its norms and processes in ways that operationalize biblical truth. Through this mission Grace Chapel has brought a renewed sense of joy and purpose to the business entrepreneurs within its sphere of influence; helped launch twenty-five new, redemptive businesses locally and seven in Jos, Nigeria; created nearly three dozen new jobs in their locality; discipled thousands of marketplace Christians in integrating their faith and work; and generated sustainable funding streams for a variety of local and global ministries.

BIZNISTRY: AN ALTERNATIVE WAY OF DOING BUSINESS

By focusing on God's purpose for business and assisting Christian entrepreneurs in designing their enterprises accordingly, Grace Chapel leaders are strengthening the community endowment of the Prosperous in their locality. They have coined the term *Biznistry* to capture the idea of "bringing the best of business and ministry together." This involves not simply generating money for ministry through a business but "integrating kingdom principles into business operations," Proudfit explains.

Today, Grace Chapel and the two related nonprofit organizations that church leaders have created to promote its mission of redeeming business— Self Sustaining Enterprises (SSE) and At Work on Purpose (AWOP)—define a Biznistry as a self-sustaining enterprise dedicated to God, commissioned for a redemptive purpose, operating according to biblical principles, integrating ministry at every level, and releasing a flow of funds for further ministry advances.

Pete West, who leads Self Sustaining Enterprises, is quick to admit that this is a high bar. "The full program is pretty challenging even for existing, profitable enterprises let alone a brand-new enterprise starting from scratch." Start-ups, though, do have the advantage of being able to build this ethos and priorities into the DNA from the ground up. "Then the culture of the organization embraces 'this is who we are and what we do,'" West explains.

The Biznistry vision contrasts directly with economist Milton Friedman's famous view that the purpose of business is to make a profit. Biznistries, Proudfit explains, see profit as a means to other ends. They seek to faithfully serve four main stakeholders: customers, employees, the disadvantaged, and the community. Biznistry leaders are also coached to consider the concerns of contractors, suppliers, vendors, regulators, and even competitors. The vision is that Biznistries will provide a valuable product or service with excellence. Wherever possible these ventures will seek to address a social need in the locality, such as job creation for people needing a second chance. Biznistries will become living laboratories where Christian entrepreneurs can "work out their faith" by designing and managing the enterprises in ways that honor and build on such kingdom virtues as honesty, service, generosity, community, and sabbath rest.

"We know we are directly challenging the modern-day assumption about what businesses are here for," says West. This is not to say that the Biznistry model is indifferent to profit. West emphasizes, "there has to be margin before mission. You need stability in the business in order to do ministry." Simply put, without profitability the business dies. At the same time, profit is not the end goal; it is the means to the end.

Living into the Biznistry vision requires an inescapable degree of intentionality and sacrifice. Entrepreneurs must embrace the truth that their companies are not their own but God's—and that they exist to advance God's purposes. Operating with a stakeholder mindset rather than the shareholder mindset demands attentiveness to the ways the business affects the environment and the community as well as one's customers and workers. Focusing on the creation of what Harvard University's Michael Porter calls "shared value" as opposed to only making profits also demands a long-term perspective.[5] The attempt to treat both customers and employees well while still attending to the bottom line guarantees plenty of late-night stress. And the fact of the fall means that ethical decision-making will not always be black and white; sometimes Biznistry operators will have to choose among competing moral goods. All of these challenges mean that entrepreneurs must rely fervently on the Holy Spirit for wisdom beyond their own.

Grace Chapel has learned that two things are necessary to nurture entrepreneurs who live into the ambitious Biznistry vision. The first is significant coaching—typically, weekly meetings for about two years. West does most of it. He has also recruited coaches from Grace Chapel and another local church. Like him, they have many years of business experience. "Coaches help with designing market research, testing the market, refining the idea for the product, setting up financials, and creating revenue forecasts, that sort of thing," West says.[6] The second is a chaplain who can come alongside the entrepreneurs to help them "deal with the emotional and spiritual stress that is the hard work of start-ups."[7] Kevin Schweiger has served in that role since 2018. Formerly his title at the church was associate pastor. Now he's called Marketplace Minister. Schweiger explains, "It just began to dawn on us that if Biznistry is such a big chunk of who we are, then it makes logical sense that we would designate a pastoral presence over it, just like we have a pastoral presence over the youth ministry or the small groups ministry."[8]

As they disciple Biznistry leaders, West and Schweiger use materials that At Work on Purpose has developed. They are aimed at helping entrepreneurs to identify concrete decisions they can make—about product and service offerings, hiring, employee coaching, customer care policies, and community relations, for example—that express kingdom values of generosity, servanthood, community, humility, and integrity. Biznistry leaders must recognize that every resource they have belongs to God and is meant to be invested "in the flourishing of the people and communities around us."

The struggles and choices Biznistry leaders make on the individual level are echoed at the organizational level, says Proudfit. The way that he and other Grace Chapel leaders have come to define Biznistry shows the

AWOP's "CHOICES PROFILE" (individual) *A marketplace Christ-follower*	BIZNISTRY (organizational) *A self-sustaining enterprise that is*
sees work as worship (no sacred-secular divide)	dedicated to God
sees work as a calling not a career	commissioned for a redemptive purpose
is committed to righteousness (versus compromise)	operating at every level with biblical practices
views work as an arena for spiritual formation	integrating ministry throughout its operations
views oneself as a steward (not owner)	releasing a sustained flow of funds for further ministry advancement

Figure 13.1. Individual and organizational expressions of Biznistry principles

correspondences between AWOP's idea of individual kingdom choices and the five organizational aspects of a Biznistry (see fig. 13.1).

Proudfit believes the church and AWOP still have further to go in articulating their kingdom vision. He wants to help Biznistry entrepreneurs "understand [their] enterprises as a redemptive force for change, not just with the people in their immediate sphere of influence but in the industries and cities where they're placed," he says. "I want to develop a way of speaking to Biznistry that approaches that kind of depth, not just practically but theologically."

GRACE CHAPEL'S DNA: A GIRAFFE AMONG THE HORSES

The Biznistry vision and mission arise out of the personality of Grace Chapel and its senior leaders. Three words—*outward, entrepreneurial,* and *integrated*—and the phrase *passion for the poor* well describe the church's DNA.

Proudfit explains Grace Chapel's leanings by using Mike Breen's notion of ministry shapes.[9] Breen visualizes the church as a triangle, having an upward, inward, and outward focus. Proudfit says, "At Grace Chapel, there's a really strong emphasis on the 'out.' It's not that there's not an 'up' or 'in.' It's just really strong on 'out.' As a result of that, you're getting outside the four walls. You're getting outside convention. You're getting outside normal ways of thinking."

"The organizational culture here is very entrepreneurial," he emphasizes. "And entrepreneurs are by their very nature disruptive of the status quo.

We're always dreaming about what's next." He says it's not unusual at Grace Chapel to "hear weird ideas."

"Grace Chapel is like this giraffe among the horses," Proudfit laughs. "Anybody who shows up can feel immediately that we're not a normal church."

Continuing to describe the church, Proudfit says, "If you cut Jeff's wrist, he'll bleed Matthew 25." That text—and James 1:27 and Isaiah 58—are undoubtedly Greer's heartbeat. Spotlighting God's heart for the poor has always been a hallmark of his ministry. Asked where that passion came from, Greer exclaims, "Because I was poor!" He grew up a latchkey kid in a one-bedroom apartment with his mother in a tough section of New York City.

In addition to outward orientation, an entrepreneurial culture, and passion for the poor, this giraffe's DNA also emphasizes work as worship. Proudfit says, "Jeff's done a great job helping every one of us in this congregation to see the sacred call God has for us in our work. He's very demonstrative about that concept as a teaching pastor." Schweiger agrees, noting that Jeff frequently uses business-oriented examples and illustrations.

Avenues of discipleship. Grace Chapel is filled with congregants engaged in business and entrepreneurship, including several of the Biznistry owners who have received help from SSE. Discipling them unfolds through four main avenues. The first is the preaching and teaching at the church itself. As noted, Greer speaks often about work as worship. He also regularly invites business and Biznistry leaders up front on Sunday mornings to share testimonies about the ways their enterprises are expressions of neighbor love.

The second is the teaching, coaching, and peer-to-peer learning available from AWOP. AWOP is closely connected to Grace Chapel, and it is seen as the church's marketplace ministry. It gathers believers for prayer, mutual support, and discipleship, equipping them for ever more robust application of their faith. It has grown exponentially since 2003 and now counts nearly ten thousand members throughout the region.

The third discipleship avenue is SSE, through which Biznistry entrepreneurs receive intensive coaching from West, Schweiger, and others. SSE, like AWOP, is headquartered on the Grace Chapel campus. It is the arm of the church through which entrepreneurs receive start-up capital and mentoring in how—in nitty-gritty practice—to design and operate an enterprise in a redemptive manner.

The fourth avenue is different from the other three: it's the church campus itself. The seven-acre campus is a living laboratory in which Grace Chapel's vision is made visual through the multiple Biznistries—a state-of-the-art coworking center, an indoor-outdoor sports complex, a CrossFit gym, a landscaping service, and a business-consulting firm—operating on the property. "There's an energy here, a vibe," says Proudfit. On these grounds, the idea of Biznistry is given flesh.

From a dump to a living demonstration. After meeting initially in a local school gym, the roughly 240 members of Grace Chapel stepped out in faith in 2006 and bought a former manufacturing compound located on Reading Road, Mason, Ohio's main thoroughfare. Greer admits with a laugh that it was "a dump." Nonetheless, he knew it brimmed with potential. The campus included multiple buildings totaling over 80,000 square feet. With a massive dose of sweat equity, Greer envisioned the campus becoming a hub for all kinds of kingdom activity that could benefit not only Grace Chapel's members but also community residents. He excitedly imagined the church having a "24/7 ministry presence, not just a Sunday presence," on the grounds.

Big vision, (seemingly) small resources. After the $1.8 million purchase, Greer remembers finding himself at the intersection of his big dreams for ministry and a paltry ministry budget. He was frustrated by the gap between the Bible's call to help widows, orphans, and the poor and the resources he felt were available for accomplishing that mission. "I found myself complaining to God. 'Lord, you gave us this vision but how are going to accomplish it without the money?' God's answer went something like this," Greer chuckles. "'Stop whining! You have some of the finest business minds in the country right in your church.'"

Greer turned to those businesspeople for insight. One of them was Proudfit. Chuck and his family had recently begun attending Grace Chapel and were delighted by Greer's emphasis on whole-life discipleship and getting outside the four walls of the church. Proudfit and several other business veterans and entrepreneurs from Grace Chapel started brainstorming with Greer and eventually landed on the Biznistry vision.

Greer points to the parable of the talents as part of his inspiration. In that story, "Jesus illustrates how God expects believers to *invest* the capital he has provided to grow his kingdom."[10] Greer thinks it's no accident that this parable is followed by the parable of the sheep and the goats in Matthew 25.[11] There Jesus speaks of a coming judgment of God's people based on their response to the poor and hungry. "God's heart is firmly centered on 'the least of these,' those who suffer from poverty, disease, and injustice," Greer emphasizes. He believes the proximity of the two parables indicates that a major purpose for the wealth created through business investment is to meet the needs of the poor. He acknowledges that the problems of poverty and injustice are immense but says church leaders mustn't be paralyzed by the scale of the need. Instead, they should take a lesson from the parable of the talents and respond with risk-taking innovation.

BIZNISTRY'S FIRST DECADE

For over fifteen years Grace Chapel congregants have invested untold hours cleaning and remodeling the old manufacturing buildings one at a time. Despite all that toil, blood, and sweat, Greer looks back at the first several years with fondness. "It was a blast," he insists. "I can tell you the hard stories too. But when you walk around the building, and you know who painted the ceilings, and you know who built the walls—it's fun!" He adds, "Everybody's gifts are in these buildings."

From the earliest days Greer was eager to renovate one of the larger buildings into an indoor sports complex for soccer and basketball. He knew that renting this space out to local teams could generate significant money for ministry. And the church needed it. The congregation had taken out two loans to finance the property purchase. Church leaders engaged in all kinds of creative activities to renovate on the cheap, utilizing Greer's horse-trading abilities and volunteer labor from the flock. Some renovated spaces were rented to generate income.

The sports complex became profitable in relatively short order, generating about $65,000 annually. A boon to the church's youth ministry, the arena also serves the Mason community by providing affordable space for indoor soccer leagues.

The largest Biznistry on the campus was New2You, a thrift store in a renovated 10,000 square foot warehouse. It operated from 2007 through 2017. It served a disadvantaged population—the working poor—with a relevant, needed service.

Over time this Biznistry created four part-time jobs for people who needed them, including single moms and an ex-offender. Congregants with a variety of business skills—marketing, sales, and accounting—helped the store to achieve a visible presence locally and run efficiently. Customers were invited to pen prayer requests in a special journal kept at the checkout counter. The huge warehouse also offered free space for a new kind of food pantry, one that sought to protect the dignity of users. The Mason Food Pantry was set up like a grocery store. Customers grab a shopping cart and peruse the aisles, selecting the items their households need.

New2You embodied everything a Biznistry was supposed to be. It took about a year for the store to operate in the black. Then it grew consistently in profitability. By 2012 it was averaging over $5,000 in revenue weekly. Not all the early ventures were as successful. The church owned and operated a screenprinting business selling branded T-shirts. Recognizing it was requiring much energy without consistent profitability, Grace Chapel sold it.

Most of the early Biznistries were new start-ups. But Proudfit demonstrated how to convert an existing business into a Biznistry by doing just that with his consulting company, Skillsource, in 2004. From the start Proudfit wanted to fund AWOP in a sustainable way, not rely on donations. He moved his company into a remodeled house on the Grace Chapel campus. He set a ceiling on his own salary to maximize Skillsource's contributions to AWOP. He also modeled workplace discipleship, holding weekly prayer and Bible study and a Tuesday "Lunch and Learn" discussion time with employees. In his hiring practices Proudfit focused not only on what potential employees could bring to the firm but also on how the firm could contribute to their development. He hired nontraditional candidates other businesses often overlook. Skillsource also invested in green-friendly building improvements that led to energy innovations like solar electricity. This was yet another way for the Biznistry to witness to kingdom values.

BIZNISTRIES TODAY

By 2020 the church and SSE had helped to launch thirty-two Biznistries, seven of which were in Nigeria. Fourteen were owned by nonprofits (with Grace Chapel among those) and eighteen were privately owned. Overall, only five failed to achieve profitability. That compares well to national data indicating that roughly half of new businesses collapse by their fifth year. West reports that overall, the US Biznistries have created thirty-five jobs and generate around $150,000 in annual revenue to support various ministries domestically and abroad.

Today Grace Chapel owns two Biznistries—His Pins Archery and the ORCA Co-Working Center—in addition to the soccer complex.

His Pins Archery. His Pins Archery was Kevin Schweiger's brainchild. An archery enthusiast, he saw the sport as a potential youth ministry outreach. He started an archery club for youth at Grace Chapel, and it grew rapidly as church kids invited their friends from outside the congregation. Soon local schools heard about it and started inviting Schweiger to teach archery lessons for a couple of days in school physical education classes. The exposure led many new kids into the ministry.

Since His Pins was growing increasingly expensive for the church, Schweiger and Proudfit encouraged Grace Chapel to turn it into a for-profit Biznistry, charging participating families a modest membership fee. Though some congregants involved in the youth ministry worried that the change might decrease involvement, youth participation instead expanded. By early 2020 this Biznistry was generating about $8,000 in profits annually to help support church ministries.

ORCA Co-Working. The ORCA Co-Working Center is housed in the building that formerly hosted New2You Thrift Store. "The thrift store was profitable but over time it faced increasing competition by other similar businesses," Proudfit explains. "The only way to stay profitable would have been to expand further." In keeping with Biznistry's openness to adaptation, church leaders pivoted to a new kind of business instead.

ORCA, one of the nation's first suburban coworking spaces, opened in January 2018. It houses small and large conference rooms, a kitchen and snack bar, and a state-of-the-art "ideation center." West reports that it took ORCA two years to achieve profitability. Before the pandemic the center was generating between $3,000 to $3,500 from membership fees per month for investment in Grace Chapel's work in Nigeria.

West says that the product the ORCA Center is offering isn't office space but community. "This is a unique initiative where church, nonprofits, and free enterprise coexist," he says. ORCA's official mission tagline is: "Creating a community of those at work helping a community of those in need of work."

CrossFit SuperFly gyms. Most Biznistries are privately owned, some by church members and some by believers outside of Grace Chapel. One, CrossFit SuperFly gym, illustrates well the principles and components of Biznistries.

In 2013 Brian Miller was running an informal CrossFit training center out of his garage. It was winter and Miller had been trying unsuccessfully to find affordable rental space to continue his work. Miller approached Greer, who had been his youth pastor. He told Greer and Schweiger about his dual passion for fitness and ministry. The church leaders told him it sounded like he was ripe for doing Biznistry.

They offered Miller space in one of the warehouses on the Grace Chapel campus and connected him with West at SSE. West put Miller through the vetting process SSE uses with potential Biznistry owners. "We assess the concept and the market and work with the entrepreneur to create a twenty-four-month financial forecast," West explains. "We're looking to work with ideas that we think can become profitable within those twenty-four months— or better, even sooner."[12] Miller was approved as a new Biznistry entrepreneur. SSE provided him with a $30,000 loan to purchase gym equipment. Miller signed a covenant indicating he'd pursue the goals of Biznistry and agree to give a portion of revenue to a ministry. SSE helped Miller establish an LLC and write a business plan.

Miller named his gym CrossFit SuperFly and opened its doors in spring 2014. He describes the redemptive purpose of this Biznistry as "helping people push beyond their perceived limitation of themselves." Fitness promotes health and Miller says the CrossFit philosophy fits with a holistic vision of life. Lessons learned in the gym carry over into other areas of life, helping people grow in self-confidence. The dynamic opens them up spiritually, he says. "People put limitations on God, or they can't see God going past something that they can't see," he explains. "When they see that one wall can be broken down, then they realize that the Creator can break down many more walls."

That may sound merely aspirational, but several gym members joined a couple's Bible study led by Schweiger, while others are attending another

Bible study led by a CrossFit member. Gym members have been intrigued by the gym's relationship to the church and are aware that some of the facility's revenue supports local ministry. Schweiger enthuses that he can trace thirty people who are now regular attenders of Grace Chapel because of their involvement with CrossFit SuperFly.

In 2016 Miller opened a second SuperFly gym in the nearby town of Lebanon. To help it prosper the church's elders permitted Schweiger to spend about half his time there for the next two years, getting the Lebanon gym on a solid footing.

The experience was strategic for his work as the Biznistry chaplain, Schweiger says. "It gave me real-life business experience. In those two years I not only helped to save one of our Biznistries but also earned the right to be heard in the future. Now when I am talking to business owners, I have been there, done that, and can commiserate." In addition to overseeing operations, Schweiger became a certified CrossFit instructor and led fitness classes—and eventually a Bible study.

Schweiger and Miller brainstormed about how the gym could bless the Lebanon community. Miller volunteered to be the strengths and conditioning coach for the high school volleyball team and gave free memberships to the student athletes. The gym started hosting free classes for Special Olympians. Miller also decided to offer 40 percent discounts on gym memberships for Lebanon's police officers and fire fighters.

Miller says that creating a strong sense of community at the gym is a high priority. He does it by hosting a variety of social events and fundraisers for local causes. Although Miller doesn't use this language, the friendly, relationship-building gyms he runs have created a kind of *third place* (a social venue apart from work and home) for Mason and Lebanon residents. Sociologists, urban planners, and political scientists say third places are important community builders. They build *bonding social capital* as patrons of third places build friendships and trust that can be the basis for mutual aid. This has happened at the Mason gym. There, a participating couple lost their soldier son in action, and other gym members rallied around them with emotional and financial support.

Third places can also build *bridging social capital*, whereby people from different classes and occupational backgrounds get acquainted. This expands people's social networks and can build empathy and under-standing.[13] This, too, has unfolded at the Lebanon facility. Miller says that the gym community has helped police and first responders "get to know the people that they're rescuing or showing up for, and vice versa. It just creates support for each other."

In addition to all the spiritual, physical, and social good the CrossFit SuperFly gyms are doing, they have also contributed to the local economy by creating fifteen jobs.[14]

CONCLUSION: LESSONS LEARNED

Grace Chapel leaders say they have learned many lessons over their nearly two decades of experience with Biznistry. Characteristically, Greer is cheer-fully blunt on the topic. "With our first Biznistries we were initially 'ready, fire, aim,'" he admits.[15] Chuckling, he adds, "There's a fine line between faith and stupidity. I walked across it too often."[16] These days he has learned to slow down and take on new projects sequentially rather than all at once.

Second, Greer, West, and Proudfit agree that they've gained wisdom on the kind of businesses and businesspeople to pursue. West says, "Now we are looking for microbusiness start-ups that don't require a lot of upfront capital. They usually are ventures that have just one to three employees." The team avoids what Greer calls brick-and-mortar enterprises. Instead, they tend to focus on services. The current list of start-up Biznistries, for example, includes a media company and an IT consultant. The team also carefully vets potential entrepreneurs and only works with businesses whose senior leaders demonstrate spiritual maturity.

A third key lesson concerns the importance of establishing and main-taining a culture of risk-taking. Greer explains, "You need to create an at-mosphere that permits outside-the-box thinking. The pastor can't be a control freak. When you create this climate, then people with energy will take the ball and run with it. And sometimes they'll do stuff that might make you uncomfortable." Grace Chapel's ministry campus, with its embodied expression of the church's DNA, reinforces the entrepreneurial culture. The church's elder board also helps maintain it. Greer has been selective in the individuals invited into leadership at this level. Every one of them has market-place experience and appreciates the church's emphasis on faith and work.

Finally, leaders say they have learned to create widespread congregational buy-in for the Biznistry vision via repetitive messaging and public celebrations of the fruit of the initiative. Recalling the church's first decade, Greer says, "We talked about the Biznistry concept constantly, in worship, Sunday school, new members classes, and one-on-ones."[17] Greer showcases positive results as soon as he has them. Congregants hear about Biznistries that have become self-sustaining and learn how much revenue they are generating for various missional endeavors locally and globally. When Greer interviews Biznistry owners during Sunday services, he gets them talking about how their businesses embody kingdom principles and are contributing to the good of the community.

Biznistries have not only increased community flourishing in Mason but also have had positive influences on the congregation. The most important has been the spiritual growth of those involved in the Biznistry model. In their 2014 book *Biznistry: Transforming Lives Through Enterprise*, Proudfit and Greer write, "Church members involved in Biznistry see worship as more than an hour experience on Sunday mornings. Their skills are used to worship God. Marketing becomes worship, sales becomes worship, manual labor becomes worship, finance becomes worship—because the work is centered on God."[18]

In particular, the Biznistry emphasis has created a "natural avenue to connect with people otherwise disengaged in the church," say Greer and Proudfit. "We have heard story after story of people coming alive spiritually who were once only marginally engaged in the body of Christ."[19]

A STRATEGY FOR CULTIVATING THE PROSPEROUS

DEPLOY ASSETS TO BUILD ASSETS

NOT EVERY CHURCH will find itself with a surfeit of entrepreneurs. But any congregation can make strong investments in the realm of the Prosperous. What's needed is intentionality, perseverance, and an embrace of the Bible's view of people and places: that they are all filled with God-created potential waiting to be developed.

With the publication of Brian Fikkert and Steve Corbett's book, *When Helping Hurts*, congregational leaders have made important strides in critically examining their benevolence and missions investments. Many have learned that good intentions are insufficient and that much wisdom is needed in ensuring that benevolence leads to beneficent outcomes. As a result of *When Helping Hurts*'s advice, many churches have matured in their approach to benevolence and engaged in more fruitful initiatives and partnerships. The book has done more than perhaps any other modern resource to help congregations know what things to avoid.

But, as the authors themselves acknowledge, churches also need to know what things to pursue. Congregational leaders need a robust and creative vision of the positive ways their investments can bring healing, empowerment, and new wealth creation for the flourishing of their communities.

This starts with congregational leaders taking a deliberate, 360-degree inventory of their church's assets. *We cannot steward well that which we fail to recognize we possess.* Often when considering what they have to offer the community, leaders note only the volunteers they might mobilize for frontline service and the money in their benevolence or local missions fund. While vital, these are rarely the church's only assets. Many churches also possess land, buildings, classrooms, playing fields, auditoriums, audio-visual equipment, large kitchens and dining areas, parking lots or parking structures, gymnasiums, musical instruments, financial endowments, credit-worthy standing, strong networks with other faith communities or nonprofit entities, relationships with local public officials and decision makers, respect in the community, a reputation for being a safe space, savings and checking accounts, and purchasing power. God has placed much in our hands!

The people power of congregations is their most important asset. Too often, though, this is calculated only in terms of the potential number of bodies to be mobilized. The real value lies in congregants' vocational power and passions: their wide-ranging skills, expertise, experience, and networks. This is power that can offer education, training, and mentoring: power that can mobilize expertise and capital, power that can bring new partners to the table, power that can identify jobs and opportunities and connections.

A 360-degree inventory helps leaders identify latent assets that—with some creativity and planning—can be activated for community good. For example, the church may have lawns that could be converted into community gardens to grow fresh produce for the local food bank. Churches with unused classroom space during the week could consider renting the space at low cost to a daycare provider (or launching their own preschool program to meet the needs of working parents). A church with a commercial kitchen could offer its use for free or at low cost to an emerging entrepreneur looking to operate a catering business. A church filled with gray-haired, white-collar professionals could mobilize that marketplace talent as part of a mentoring effort with young social entrepreneurs. None of these ideas is a pipe dream. I know of churches in Maryland, Virginia, and Connecticut doing each of the first three things. Toward the end of this chapter we will look at a church in Minnesota that did the fourth.

FROM INCOME SUPPORT TO BUILDING ASSETS

To make the most strategic investments in strengthening the Prosperous, church leaders need to not only better understand their own assets, but they also must shift their approach to financial outreach. While there will always be some level of need for emergency cash assistance, *relief* aid that simply helps the poor manage their poverty should take a back seat to *rehabilitation* and *development* efforts that help them to escape their poverty.[1] *What's needed is a stronger focus on helping the poor to build assets.* The Corporation for Enterprise Development defines assets as "tangible and intangible economic resources—a home, savings in a bank account, a college education—that can produce value for their owner."[2] Assets, research shows, are essential to helping households achieve long-term stability and mobility.

In his groundbreaking 1991 book, *Assets and the Poor: A New American Welfare Policy*, author Michael Sherraden put forward a fresh thesis for how best to help poor people: shifting from welfare payments that enabled their immediate consumption toward mechanisms that helped low-income people accumulate assets.[3] Asset accumulation, Sherraden argues, yields a variety of positive behaviors. It helps people develop a future rather than only present-day orientation, take prudent risk, and focus on developing their human capital. Ultimately, he contends, an asset-focused approach would produce sustainable change and nurture a sense among the poor that they had a stake in the economic system.[4]

Sherraden's ideas caught on to a considerable degree.[5] For example, forty states in the United States adopted his notion of "Individual Development Accounts" (IDAs). These were special matched savings accounts that low-income people could use to help fund education, make a down payment on a first-time home purchase, or capitalize a small business.

Government policy has made modest but important shifts toward an asset-based approach in the thirty years since Sherraden's book. By contrast, churches are still stuck in the relief-focused, income-supplement paradigm. National congregational research shows that the most common ways churches offer aid to the poor is through free food and financial benevolence.[6]

A modest number of pioneering churches are demonstrating a better way of contributing to the community endowment of the Prosperous. These congregations are engaging in efforts that build people's human and financial capital. Their asset-building, wealth-building labors are critical in our day not only because of the promise they hold for all poor people but also because they can help us overcome the injustice of the severe racial wealth gap in our nation.[7]

Following are seven approaches entrepreneurial churches are implementing today that build human and financial capital among materially poor households.

BUILDING HUMAN CAPITAL

John Perkins, the iconic civil rights leader and founder of the Christian Community Development Association, has a well-known mantra: "People need Jesus . . . and a job." Churches can help people build the human capital needed for sustainable employment through job training, networking, and job creation.

Job training. Churches desiring to provide help to un- and underemployed people in their communities do not have to start a ministry from scratch. Two similar national job-training programs offer curricula and training. One is Jobs for Life, headquartered in Raleigh, North Carolina, the other is the Work Life program from the Chalmers Center in Chattanooga.

Four key components mark these programs:

- a biblically based work readiness ("soft skills") training course

- practical workshops on job-search skills (e.g., résumé writing, interviewing)

- support and cheerleading from volunteer champions who attend the classes alongside participants and also offer practical help (e.g., transportation assistance)

- partnerships with employers in the community willing to give graduates from the training program interviews when they have open positions

Jobs for Life is rooted in the conviction that churches need to "flip the list." They note that over 80 percent of churches respond to poverty by offering food, clothing, and emergency cash. In other words, they address the symptoms of the problem. Meanwhile, less than 2 percent focus on employment as their principal strategy for fighting poverty. Un- and underemployment are key reasons why people turn to the church for help. What if over 80 percent of churches nationwide came alongside and assisted supplicants in ways that addressed the root problem? The result would be far less need for that relief assistance and far more dignity for people in need.

In 2016 I led a national evaluation of the Jobs for Life program. During it my colleagues and I identified churches that had achieved particularly high levels of success (high graduation and job placement rates). One was Trinity Baptist Church in Raleigh. Trinity has been offering the Jobs for Life ministry since 2006. It usually fields more than one Jobs for Life class each year and mobilizes an average of fifty volunteers to come alongside participants. Over the years Trinity's program has achieved a graduation rate and a job placement rate of over 75 percent.

We found that successful Jobs for Life sites like Trinity Baptist could point to three key factors that contributed to their high performance.

First, they engaged multiple, talented, engaging instructors from a variety of backgrounds. They work particularly hard to find instructors who possess business or human-resources experience and knowledge. Second, a strong, structured, dedicated leadership team with distinct roles for each member (e.g., recruitment, business liaison, childcare coordinator, class emcee) oversaw these programs. Third, they were highly connected to community resources, such as various social service agencies, community colleges, and rehabilitation centers. In short, they capitalized on their greatest asset: the vocational expertise, experience, and networks of their congregants.

Churches with high job placement rates also had strong student recruitment processes. They spread the word about their classes through a variety of community organizations such as counseling centers, homeless shelters, refugee ministries, community colleges, and prisons. Some encouraged former Jobs for Life class members to invite someone they knew to take the class (and one offered alumni $20 for each referral who graduated the program). Three sites we spoke with had sister churches located in economically distressed neighborhoods that advertised the classes among their neighbors. Churches that used a student application or had an interview process for potential students in place also showed higher job placement rates than those who did not.

Networking: Job clubs. To help people suffering from unemployment or facing career transitions, some churches are offering job club.[8] A job club is simply a gathering of job seekers for mutual support and encouragement.

Typically, it involves networking and some training—usually focused on such topics as the sectors of the local economy offering the best job prospects or the most effective job-searching skills.

Menlo Park Presbyterian Church in the San Francisco Bay Area launched its job club, Career Actions Ministry, in 2008 during the Great Recession. Founder Steve Murata had experienced joblessness, and others in the founding group had also suffered through layoffs. They could empathize with the people in their community who were receiving the dreaded pink slip. "Once you've had that painful experience, you never forget how stressful and really debilitating the [job-search] process can be," Murata says.[9]

Murata felt compelled to launch a support group for people inside and outside the church whose lives were being dislocated by the recession. "The process of looking for a job can feel very isolating," Murata explains. "We wanted to help others going through that." While the church's senior leadership was supportive of the idea, the new job club was "totally a bottom-up effort," he says. It was led by laypeople from the start and continues to be run completely by volunteers.

Menlo Park's ministry has three components: small groups for job seekers, a monthly large-group meeting with speakers addressing various job-search topics and skills, and an online platform called "Career Action" that lists job openings and allows seekers to post résumés.

The ministry partners with the NOVA Job Center in nearby Sunnyvale, California. The Center provides numerous workshops, one-on-one coaching, comprehensive job listings, and skills assessments, among other resources. These are of course all very valuable, but they do not attend to the significant emotional distress job seekers often face. Menlo Park's Job Club does that. The job-search process typically involves many rejections and can go on for months. Murata says, "You need some uplift to allow you to maintain your sense of self-worth and stay positive. The church provides spiritual and emotional support that can cut through the anxiety and depression and give people hope."

A 2014 Department of Labor study reported some 679 job clubs run by faith-based and community-based organizations, many of them congregations.[10] Churches of all different sizes, denominations, and locations host job clubs. Club meeting formats vary, but typically they include

- advice on job searches—what works, what doesn't
- job market news—who is hiring, future openings
- insights from human-resources specialists—how to prepare effective résumés and interviews, understanding hiring practices and employers' needs and expectations, etc.
- guest speakers—learning from subject matter experts
- networking opportunities
- opportunities to share and celebrate success stories
- prayer

In some cases participants in the job clubs end up getting involved in the host church. Murata has seen this happen at Menlo Park and thinks job clubs "are an excellent outreach strategy." Clubs are easy and inexpensive to establish and they address a very practical felt need.

Job creation. Some congregations not only offer job training or job support but seek to create jobs. This is a strategy Overflow Church of Benton Harbor, Michigan, has pursued. Over the past twelve years it has helped to create around forty jobs.

Overflow typically draws about three hundred people on a Sunday. It's a diverse, multiclass congregation that's roughly 40 percent non-White. Pastor Brian Bennett says God's mandate in Jeremiah 29:7 to "seek the peace and prosperity of the city" has inspired leaders to "look for innovative ways to take Jesus beyond the walls of the church and to help our community."[11]

In the early days of planting the church Bennett established an office "right in the heart of the community" and sought to "listen long" to neighborhood residents. "I'd ask them what they thought the greatest need in the community was," he says. "Age didn't matter, ethnicity didn't matter. One hundred percent of the time, over a couple of years of asking that question, the answer was *always* jobs." That's not surprising in a community with an official unemployment rate three times the national rate (and with an unofficial rate that's much higher).

In 2008 Bennett launched Overflow Christian Community Development Association (Overflow CCDA), a sister nonprofit to the church that could oversee the implementation of the congregation's vision of fostering economic renewal. The congregation fully supported the effort. It paid Bennett's salary while allowing him time to serve as the nonprofit's initial executive director as well as their lead pastor.

Overflow CCDA involved other congregations from the start. "When you're hungry and hustling," Bennett laughs, "partnering is a necessity. We could only be strong in collaboration with others." In 2015 Overflow CCDA changed its name to Mosaic CCDA to better capture the multichurch nature of the organization.[12]

The first enterprise Mosaic launched was a resale store. It did very well, generating nearly $10,000 per month by 2011. "On one hand you had people who liked finding good garage sale type bargains and on the other, people who were willing to donate all kinds of used items," says Andrew Robinson, Mosaic's CEO. "It was the first secondhand shop in the neighborhood, and it was a hit." By 2018 the resale store was generating $15,000 per month in profits. It has created between seven and ten jobs (depending on the year), most of them full time.

Mosaic Property Services (MPS) was the second venture. It provides lawn maintenance and snow removal services. Depending on the season, MPS employs twenty to twenty-five people. Ivy Yarbrough, 58, has been working for MPS for several years and credits Mosaic for turning his life around. A native of Benton Harbor, he grew up poor, with seventeen siblings. Jailed for selling drugs, his parole officer referred him to Mosaic for job training and coaching. Yarbrough says the church folks believed in him, and that enabled him to get off drugs.[13]

Mosaic on Campus, the third venture, is the vendor providing meals in the cafeteria at Lake Michigan College's Benton Harbor campus. This enterprise has created one full-time and four part-time jobs. Employees of Mosaic on Campus have the opportunity to become students in the college's degree programs in culinary arts or hospitality management.

Robinson reports that Mosaic has "done well in helping people find entry-level work." To help people find higher-wage jobs, in 2017 Mosaic developed a partnership with Q&A Housing. Their joint venture, called Mosaic Community, partners the two organizations in purchasing dilapidated homes and renovating and selling them. The initiative also engages in home repairs. So far they have renovated and sold one home and are renovating a second one. Eventually, Robinson reports, "We believe any-where from twenty-five to fifty jobs will be created and participants will be able to gain skills in the construction trades." At the same time, the Mosaic Community program is improving the value of some resident property owners' homes and creating opportunities for other residents to become homeowners.

Each of Mosaic's social enterprises is fully self-sustaining and together with Mosaic Resale Store they generate sufficient profits to cover 60 percent of Mosaic CCDA's total budget. The other 40 percent of the roughly $1.2 million budget is raised through grants, contracts, and dona-tions. Overflow Church continues to contribute to the nonprofit's annual budget and mobilizes volunteers to serve both through one-time neigh-borhood projects and as mentor-coaches to residents going through Mo-saic's job-training ministry.[14]

Jobs and job training for youth. Churches can also contribute to their community's economic well-being by investing in young adults. The na-tional unemployment rate for adults ages sixteen to twenty-four averaged 8.8 percent throughout 2019, compared with 3.1 percent for working-age adults. Among African American young adults, it was over 15 percent.[15] Youth unemployment has high personal and social costs. According to the Center for American Progress, workers who are unemployed as young adults earn lower wages for many years "due to foregone work experience and missed opportunities to develop skills."[16]

In Grand Rapids, Michigan, two social enterprises have created jobs for dozens of minority youth: Building Bridges Professional Services and Rising Grinds. Building Bridges' founder, Justin Beene, says he was spurred to act by the fact that youth unemployment in the city was over 25 percent and youth violence was on the rise. Quoting Richard Rohr, Beene says, "If you don't transform your wounds, you will transmit them."[17]

Beene started Building Bridges in 2007 as a small lawn-care business employing a handful of local teens. Of the youth employed, 82 percent had a previous felony or misdemeanor charge and 70 percent had been involved with the foster care system. Today the company has expanded into snow removal, landscaping, home remodeling, and services for seniors. It typically employs twenty-five to thirty individuals (depending on the season), with three-fourths coming from low-income city neighborhoods. The business seeks a quadruple bottom line: they're aiming for economic, social, environmental, and spiritual impact. The young adult employees of Building Bridges go through a life-and-jobs-skills training program, learning money management and anger management, among other skills, while working in the business and being mentored by Christ-followers.

A few years after he started Building Bridges Professional Services, Beene began attending Tabernacle Community Church. He met with his pastor, Artie Lindsey, and asked if the congregation would be interested in partnering with him. Lindsey agreed and the two worked together with a few other community leaders to create the Grand Rapids Center for Community Transformation (GRCCT). The GRCCT is a partnership of Tabernacle, Frontline Church, Bethany Christian Services, and O2, a for-profit business. Its first efforts focused on spreading the word about Building Bridges' mission and helping the enterprise to grow to annual revenue of over $750,000. Congregants from Tabernacle and Frontline who have expertise as lawyers, accountants, human-resources professionals, and insurance agents have provided pro bono counsel to Building Bridges in all these areas.

In 2017 the GRCCT launched a new social enterprise called Rising Grinds Café. This business also follows the model of hiring low-income, high-risk youth and providing them with life-skills training and mentoring, alongside their jobs. Lindsey hopes that youth will grow in leadership, responsibility, and a positive work ethic. He believes some may also acquire business acumen that could enable them to become entrepreneurs while others will mature into business managers.[18] Meanwhile, the café has become a favorite spot of Tabernacle's members.

Creating jobs for youth is not a strategy that needs to be limited to churches serving economically distressed communities. Youth are the future hope of *all* communities. The national youth unemployment rate is regularly much higher than the adult rate. And in every community youth are finding the transition to adulthood very difficult. These realities sparked youth pastor Matt Overton to turn to social-enterprise development as a foundational part of youth ministry.

Seven years ago a group of teens and adults gathered at Overton's home to assist with home renovations on the Overton's fixer-upper.[19] Some of the teens were active in the youth group Overton led at Columbia Presbyterian Church in Vancouver, Washington. Others were more on the fringe. Near the end of the day, Overton realized that the conversations he was having with youth as they wielded hammers and shovels were more relaxed, open, and meaningful than those he often experienced inside the church. The work made the teens contributors, not just receivers. They were being treated as young adults with the ability to handle responsibility—and they liked it. Meanwhile, the remodeling efforts also drew adults from the congregation who hadn't been involved much in the youth ministry or any other church programs. Something had wooed them, and Overton eventually realized what it was. As he told a journalist from *Faith & Leadership*, "I had provided people an outlet to use their natural gifts and talents for a greater social good. It was social entrepreneurship in a nutshell."[20]

The experience got Overton thinking. What if he could start a business that would provide opportunities for youth to learn some job skills and earn money while providing a great context for life-on-life discipleship? "In youth ministry, we attract kids all the time with Cheetos, couches, and games," Overton says. "Why not attract them with jobs and work and life skills?"[21]

Overton gathered eight adults from the congregation as an informal brainstorming team. He included business owners, people with legal and tax experience, and adults he knew would make great mentors. He shared his idea of combining youth ministry with a jobs program. He told them he believed this approach could generate a more engaged faith among both youth and adults at the church. The team—and eventually the church elders—bought the vision and Mowtown Lawn Care was born.

To be a Mowtown employee, youth must complete a series of training workshops. Taught by church members, these cover such topics as employer expectations, goal setting, and personal finance. Teens don't have to be members of the church to be considered for jobs. The first youth were trained and deployed in June 2015.

Mowtown Teen Lawn Care is a for-profit business. Overton used his own money for start-up capital. There's no financial or liability risk for the church. Every six months, a team from the church reviews the company's financials and ensures that the enterprise is advancing the mission of the church. Overton acknowledges that some Christians are skeptical about doing good through doing business. He's committed to overcoming that mindset.

Overton accompanies the teenagers to the job sites and works alongside them. That time, plus the drive time to clients' homes, provides a rich opportunity for mentoring. Overton and his team think up questions to discuss with youth on the job that emerge from the training workshops. He also talks with the teens about their family lives, friends, and schoolwork. Overton is convinced the work offers dignity to the youth while affording natural opportunities for giving advice and correction. He says youth ministries sometimes struggle to provide natural ways for generations to mix. "When adults and students talk about work, money, goals, and life, it creates an easy platform for meaningful conversation and discipleship."[22]

BUILDING FINANCIAL CAPITAL

In addition to building human capital in the ways already described, churches can contribute to their community's flourishing by assisting individuals and their families to build financial capital. Three promising approaches to this are matched saving accounts, microlending, and enterprise pitch competitions.

Matched saving accounts. As noted earlier, most churches respond to poverty by offering short-term income and consumption supports: free food, free clothes, a check to pay the overdue utility bill or rent. Such relief is sometimes needed and appropriate. But often it's nothing but a Band-Aid that helps people muddle through for another month or so.

By contrast, asset-building strategies can help people escape their poverty over time. When a family develops a savings account, it has a buffer against rainy days. And assets can create more wealth, such as when a house increases in value or a stock pays a dividend. Churches can help the working poor build up savings accounts by incentivizing the process through matched savings programs.

Typically, these programs combine financial literacy instruction or coaching with savings incentives. The organization hosting the program determines the level of match—it might be 1:1, 2:1, or even 3:1 for each dollar saved by a participant. Usually, funds are kept in a savings account registered in both the program participant's name and the host organization's name. Access to the funds requires signatures from both parties.

Research shows the positive effects of matched savings programs. For example, an ambitious, randomized 2016 evaluation of such programs by scholars at the Urban Institute concluded that they had contributed to a 9 percent growth in participants' liquid assets (e.g., savings, checking, and money market accounts), a 39 percent decrease in the use of nonbank check-cashing services, and a 34 percent decrease in "hardships related to utilities, housing and health."[23]

Since 2013 North Avenue Presbyterian Church in Atlanta has offered "Faith and Finances," a biblically based financial literacy course developed by the Chalmers Institute, coupled with mentoring and a 1:1 matched savings program. Class graduates can earn up to $1,000 in the months following the program. The church matches every dollar saved with one of its own.

Dion Miller used his savings to pay for truck-driving school. His new commercial driver's license earned him a position with a food-distribution company that paid $1,000 a month more than his previous job. Dion and his wife, Renae, continue to save, working toward their dream of buying their first home.

Two other graduates have used their savings toward college tuition, another bought a used pickup truck, and another replaced the windows on the house he'd purchased at a foreclosure auction. In short, graduates are increasing their human and financial capital. The program also gets people banked, says Matt Seadore, North Avenue's director of mission and ministry. "We had a 90 percent unbanked rate upon entrance to Faith and Finances. We have had nearly a 100 percent success rate with getting participants to open a savings account at a bank or credit union."[24] This cuts down on participants' use of expensive check-cashing services.

Seadore was delighted to repurpose a $15,000 benevolence budget toward the 1:1 savings matches. "We were aware that benevolence monies were not always well-spent," he says.

Matched savings programs also create a context for relationships. As Steve Corbett, coauthor of *When Helping Hurts*, explains, "The process of saving money for an asset purchase, even with match funding, is not quick. . . . This is time that the church and its volunteers can spend loving the individuals in the program as well as their families."[25]

Middle- and upper-class predominantly White churches could also consider getting involved in matched savings ministries as a way of pushing back against historic and contemporary racial injustice in the United States. Many congregants in such churches already have access to wealth-building opportunities through employee benefits like 401(k) accounts. The latter are essentially matched savings programs, with employers contributing the matches. Since low-income earners rarely benefit from such programs, well-off White churches could provide capital grants to underresourced Black churches, enabling them to establish a matched savings program for their members.

Obviously, this approach is not a panacea. But it's one doable, concrete, and proven way that a church can come alongside people long shut out from economic opportunities. As Corbett says of this strategy, "This is not just a nice thing to do. This is promoting justice, which our Father really, really cares about."[26]

Microlending. Microenterprise lending has long been utilized by Christian and secular community-development agencies working in the developing world. Through an initiative called 1K Churches from the Criterion Institute, some US congregations are implementing a similar strategy. The project provides a curriculum that congregational small groups can use to explore biblical teaching on economics. Church members complete the study and then consider ways that they or their church as a whole could participate in redemptive economic investments.

Two churches in Baltimore—Amazing Grace Lutheran Church and First English Lutheran Church—teamed up several years ago to implement microlending. Pastor Gary Dittman of Amazing Grace, which is located in the economically depressed community of McElderry Park, characterizes the church as a "relationship-centered hub." He's proud of how the congregation and community are filled with "resourceful, smart, and innovative" people.[27] The church is committed to listening well, and one thing they have heard is that residents in the neighborhood had entrepreneurial dreams but no access to start-up capital. Dittman reached out to First English, a predominantly White congregation fifteen minutes north, to see about collaborating. First English agreed to provide no-interest loans up to $2,000 to community members, with a repayment period of up to eighteen months. Amazing

Grace recruited a volunteer team of members, called Shepherds, whose job it is to interview loan candidates, hear about their business ideas, and determine the loan amount and repayment schedule. Eventually, Amazing Grace started funding some of the loans too.

The loans have been diverse. One went to a grandmother who had recently taken in her three grandchildren to raise. She used loan funds to secure a vendor license to sell plates of food from a grill in front of her house. Another went to a young man who'd recently been released from prison. He was a licensed electrician but needed funds to buy tools to help him secure employment. Another loan went to a painter from the community who used the funds to purchase equipment enabling him to begin his own painting service.

Criterion Institute calls itself a think tank on finance for social change. Phyllis Anderson directs the 1K Initiative. From prior work she had contacts within the Evangelical Lutheran Church in America (ELCA). When Criterion created the materials and developed implementation guides for different ways congregations could act, ELCA agreed to promote the idea. Anderson estimates that over two hundred churches have utilized the study materials, though far fewer have started a microlending program.[28] Those that do—like Amazing Grace—report that the project has been transformational.

Just north of Baltimore, the Church of the Good Shepherd in Ruxton, Maryland, has also embraced the project enthusiastically. Retired banker Robert Locke, a longtime parishioner, leads the effort.[29] He and nine others from the church completed the 1K Bible study in 2015 and decided they wanted to move forward with a microlending strategy.

The church started making loans in 2016 and to date has lent out $50,000 in fifteen loans. Only $400 from one loan has had to be written off as a loss. Eight have been repaid and the capital recycled; the others are still active. Loans have ranged from $750 to $4,500. To keep things administratively simple, the loans are interest-free. Church of the Good Shepherd's business manager serves as a loan administrator.

A loan committee consisting of Locke, five other congregants, and the church's senior warden reviews each loan request and interviews the applicants. "The face-to-face meetings are the most important thing," Locke says. These allow members to hear the applicant's passion and plan and "get a read on them and their commitment level." Church dollars have helped one woman to expand her small café, enabled a man to start a hauling company, and helped an upholsterer start his own company. That entrepreneur had customers lined up, equipment, and a small building leased. But the facility lacked air conditioning. Locke recalls, "he told the committee he was unwilling to run a literal sweatshop." The man wanted a loan to purchase air conditioners for the space. This loan recipient's business has done so well he has hired two assistants and is paying them $25 per hour.

Good Shepherd initially capitalized the loan fund with $15,000 from its local outreach account. That amount has been recycled twice by repayments from the earliest loans. By being willing to take some risk, this Maryland congregation has put the parable of the talents into action—and multiplied its kingdom investment.

Social enterprise competitions. For nine seasons ABC's *Shark Tank* show has earned top TV viewer ratings. Fans tune in on Friday nights to watch inventors pitch their ideas to a panel of multimillionaire investors. A quick Google search reveals the popularity of pitch competitions, with dozens occurring all over the country. In 2016 I heard about a church version of *Shark Tank* (though an observer dubbed it "dolphin tank" for its much friendlier vibe). In 2017 I had the chance to visit Colonial Church in Edina, Minnesota, and learn about its impressive Innové Project that had given rise to eleven thriving social ventures.

Colonial held its first pitch competition in 2013. That year Leah Porter's Twin Cities Mobile Market was the top winner.[30] Her pitch at Innové won a $37,000 start-up grant from the Innové judges, a $3,000 bonus award from the congregation, and a $250 award from Colonial's Sunday school kids. "I think I'm most proud of that $250 award," Porter says. "It showed us that our pitch was understandable even to kids."[31]

Porter's idea was to convert a city bus into a mobile grocery store and use it to bring fresh meat and produce to residents in the Twin Cities living in food deserts. Minneapolis-St. Paul is the fifth-worst food desert metro area in the United States. That means that thousands of residents lack access to a supermarket within one mile of their homes. Porter, who says she knows what it's like to grow up in a family that struggled to put food on the table, has long had a passion for the issue. While in graduate school she wrote her master's thesis on the problem—and outlined how to address it by using a reconfigured city bus. It was a great idea, and when she floated it with local officials and all sorts of community groups, everyone was enthusiastic. But going from idea to reality required help and investment. "We needed start-up funding," Porter says simply, "and that's just so hard to get."

Other Innové winners have included Exodus Lending, an alternative to payday loan stores; The Sheridan Story, which gets weekend food backpacks into the hands of low-income youth from over one hundred elementary schools; MATOO (Men Against the Trafficking of Others), which has found its niche in the antihuman trafficking space by addressing the demand side; Launch Ministry, which has established a resource center for homeless teenagers in Minneapolis; and HOYO, a small business employing Somali women in the city to make and sell their tasty native meat pastries called sambusas. Other winners have established new initiatives to help the disabled. Two funded entrepreneurs pitched projects with an international focus. All eleven projects were still operating in 2020, and several have grown substantially.

Innové emerged from a lengthy conversation at Colonial that followed the sale of a portion of their land. The sale garnered significant dollars, and the congregation wanted to spend a lot of them on missions. "This is a church that has long had a heart to do good in the community and in the world. Missions is a part of our DNA," former Minister of Mission Brian Jones explains.[32]

Then-Senior Minister Daniel Harrell and Jones wanted to use the money from the land sale on one big initiative rather than many small, diffuse ones. And they wanted something that could engage a large number of congregants in meaningful roles. Harrell proposed hosting a pitch competition. "Minneapolis is like the Silicon Valley of nonprofit entrepreneurship," he says.[33] That, combined with the wealth of marketplace talent he knew existed in Colonial's pews, made a social enterprise competition a good fit.

Indeed, what most excited Harrell about this model was that it would provide practical opportunities for the white-collar professionals in the congregation to be personally engaged in mission, deploying their skills as executives, graphic designers, finance experts, lawyers, and accountants. Testimonies like that of Jeff Siemon were music to Harrell's ears. Siemon, who holds a senior position in finance at General Mills, served as a coach to pitch contender Anna Brelje and her team, which was interested in offering an alternative to payday lending. "Since I work in finance, Anna's project felt like it would be a good fit," Siemon says. "And I just really loved the idea. Payday lending is a huge problem in the community and a really big thing to wrestle with. I was excited by the challenge."[34] He also loved how it made missions so personal. "Just writing a check or giving money in the donation plate is one thing, but actually participating . . . in a more real, tangible way—I thought that was really profound."

During the first competition over 170 of Colonial's roughly 450 regular attenders ended up serving in some capacity. The number was a little smaller the second time around, but the passion ran even deeper. Congregants took it upon themselves to raise about half of the funds that were needed for Innové's second round.

Harrell believes businesses are efficient at allocating time and capital— and that the good some for-profits do can dwarf the social impact of the same amount of money granted to traditional philanthropies. In the end Innové didn't end up funding many for-profit ventures, mainly because most applicants pitched nonprofits. But many of the winners incorporated the discipline of the market in their plans. Porter's Mobile Market, for example, is committed to becoming largely self-sufficient over the next few years through its food sales. She appreciated that the church's approach differed from traditional philanthropy. She says, "Colonial rightly was looking to invest for a return. I hope other churches will follow their lead."

In fact, some churches are. The Innové model has already spread to churches in Texas and Georgia that have held their own pitch competitions.

SUMMING UP

For churches to make a meaningful, sustainable contribution to the economic lives of neighbors in their community, three movements are needed. The first is a movement from relief to longer-term, relational, and holistic investment in the lives of those struggling economically. For too long churches have put most or even all their benevolence resources toward relief. And if we're honest, we've got to admit that we often do so because it's easier.

Handing out food and money to poor people is more convenient and less messy than giving them ourselves, our time, and our talents.

We also sometimes focus on relief assistance because we've bought into a "bigger is better" mentality. When those operating the mercy fund report at year's end that "the church helped one hundred families," everyone can bask in the glow of that seemingly large accomplishment. But if the $10,000 was spent giving $100 to each family, chances are that very few were made better off. Many of those same families will be back again to ask for help. How much better to invest $5,000—plus friendship and support—into two household heads to enable them to get training for a better, higher-paying job or to capitalize a microbusiness that can bring in sustainable revenue.

The second is a shift from a needs-based approach to ministry to an asset-based one. We must start seeing not only the needs of the poor but also their assets. The nineteenth-century Evangelical poverty fighter Octavia Hill used to say that too often churches were ready to *help* the poor but not eager to *know* them.[35] The same critique can be made today. Made in God's image, every person has gifts, talents, and creativity. An asset-based approach resonates better with this truth than does a needs-based approach.

The shift to an assets mentality also involves expanding our imagination about the assets God has placed in our congregations. What he has given *to* us—from musical instruments to multipurpose rooms—is not meant solely *for* us. We are blessed to be a blessing. Living into that requires creative, generous, risk-taking stewardship of the physical and financial assets of the church. God is looking for a return on the capital he has given us. Failing to activate and leverage that capital is like the one-talent steward burying his coin in the ground. The greatest asset God has provided to us for the mission of "flourishing others" is the vocational power sitting in the pews. But this knowledge, skill, and experience are regularly left untapped.

The third shift is one from focusing solely on supplementing people's income to helping them build assets. Churches can help people increase their human capital through training programs of many sorts that increase their marketable skills. We can also encourage their efforts to build their household savings slowly and steadily. We can make financial capital available to fund entrepreneurial dreams that allow our neighbors to deploy their God-given talents and hard work, helping them create sustainable revenue streams. We can assist people in achieving the dream of home ownership or a college education.

These three shifts will require intentionality, humility, sacrifice, risk, and creativity. But, as the stories we've reviewed demonstrate, they are doable. They are also deeply rewarding because they hold the promise of genuine, enduring transformation.

14

THE SUSTAINABLE

FLOURISHING IN THE REALM
OF NATURAL AND PHYSICAL HEALTH

GOOD HEALTH IS A PRECIOUS GIFT often take for granted in the affluent West. The global coronavirus pandemic has awakened us anew to human frailty. This virus, invisible except under a microscope, has run rampant, killing over 5.2 million people as of December 2021. It has devastated economies. It has disrupted huge swaths of our lives—closing schools, curtailing sports events, shuttering businesses, sending millions into the unemployment lines, and moving schools online. We've been afraid because few threats are as scary as those that imperil our health.

Increasingly, experts in both environmental and human health are pointing to the ways that the pandemic is connected to the health of the planet. For example, Aaron Bernstein, director of Harvard C-Change (the University's Center for Climate, Health, and the Global Environment), has argued that "Many of the root causes of climate change also increase the risk of pandemics."[1] He notes, for example, that deforestation creates loss of habitat for animals. These then migrate where they can share germs with other animals and people, increasing the risks for infectious disease.

THE SUSTAINABLE AND HUMAN FLOURISHING

Scientists are telling us that *people health* and *planet health* are inextricably connected. Sociologists with the Thriving Cities Group agree. They note how these intertwined realities of "physical and environmental health can profoundly affect the capacity of individuals to pursue . . . important activities, such as employment, community engagement, and even education."[2]

The deep connection between environmental and human health is a truth that the Bible also affirms. God desires his creation and his children to flourish. Seeking the shalom of our communities involves working to ensure that the natural environment is well-tended and that people have access to the things that promote their holistic health (e.g., nutritious food, green space, medical care, mental health counseling). Indeed, it means recognizing the God-ordained reality that the health of the creation and the health of people go hand in hand.

Some people argue that creation care or "green" concerns are secondary—at best—for Christians. Others dismiss churches working toward these ends as merely catering to contemporary fads. In fact, such congregations are engaged in legitimate labor very much aligned with God's passions and purposes.

The community endowment of the Sustainable encompasses the realm of human and natural health and is concerned with institutions overseeing environmental regulation, public sanitation, public health, and the like. This endowment concerns the management of energy and land, efforts to promote air and water quality, and practices to safeguard public health and make medical care accessible. It is about community residents enjoying such vital goods as safe water, physical and mental health care, safe and healthy food, and clean streets. All of these contribute mightily to human flourishing. God is passionate about these arenas of life and his people throughout history have been pioneers and activists in them.

CREATIONAL INTENT: THE REALM OF THE NATURAL ENVIRONMENT

God loves and delights in his creation. This reality shines through the Scriptures in many ways. The five themes highlighted below provide a good introduction to the Creator's intentions for the natural world he lovingly crafted.

Sabbath: God designed us to live within limits. The first (and arguably most important) biblical principle that illustrates the structure of the Sustainable is that of sabbath ceasing. Genuine shalom requires remembering that God created us as finite beings with limits. This is why sabbath rest is part of the normative rhythm of God's creation. God designed us to need the physical and spiritual ceasing of the sabbath. This makes possible undistracted communion with God and reminds us that we are created *first* for relationship with God, to *be* rather than to *do*.

Sabbath ceasing provides vital guardrails. It protects us against overwork and grants the rejuvenation our bodies, hearts, and minds require for holistic health. It protects us from burnout in a society obsessed with ever-present technology and inundated with the siren song of consumption. Addictions to technology and shopping and the sense of social pressure for constant communication through social media are overloading our brains and overstressing our hearts. They have increased anxiety, depression, and other mental health maladies.

Sabbath ceasing is also something needed for the earth itself to flourish. For example, overconsumption literally trashes the planet while overuse of land depletes its fertility.

Interdependency: God designed human and environmental health to go together. The second theme is that in God's design the shalom of human beings and the shalom of the creation are inextricably bound together. People and the planet exist in a close, mutual relationship. The creation narrative in Genesis reveals that by God's definition of flourishing we humans need the earth and the earth needs us.

Consider the Hebrew word used for humans: *adam.* It is closely tied to the Hebrew word for the ground or earth, *adamah.* God used the dust of the earth combined with his holy breath to make us. And God designed us to be in a mutually dependent relationship with the physical world. We need the earth's waters and crops, and creation needs us to achieve its full potential. Consider Genesis 2:5: "Now no shrub had yet appeared on the earth and no plant had yet sprung up, for the LORD God had not sent rain on the earth and there was no one to work the ground." For nature to flourish, it needs help from God (to send rain) and from humans (to work the ground).

Stewardship: God designed humans to tend and care for the earth. The earth is not ours but the *Lord's* (Ps 24:1). We are trustees, not owners. The interdependent relationship between people and planet shapes the way we are to live into our calling as stewards. The creation accounts in Genesis 1–2 each contain God's commands to human beings to take up the labor of stewarding the creation. In Genesis 1:28 God tells the first humans to "Be fruitful and increase in number; fill the earth and subdue it. Rule over the fish in the sea and the birds in the sky and over every living creature that moves on the ground." In Genesis 2:15 we read that

"The LORD God took the man and put him in the Garden of Eden to work it and take care of it." There are several verbs in these passages: *be fruitful, fill, subdue, rule, work,* and *take care of.* People are charged with ruling creation, but this dominion is to be servant-hearted. As New Zealand clergyman Dick Tripp explains:

> The word '*abad,* translated "work" (in Genesis 2:15) means "to serve." The related noun actually means "slave" or "servant." Though it is the most common Hebrew expression for agricultural labour, it implies the labour is to be undertaken for the sake of the earth—not primarily for the sake of the labourer. It implies that the earth will only bring forth fruit when treated with respect. . . . The word *shamar,* translated "to take care of," suggests watchful care and preservation. It has the connotation of "being vigilant for the sake of another."[3]

Human beings are called by God to tend and care for his created world. We are to develop and multiply its raw materials while also protecting the earth from corruption and pollution.

God designed the nonhuman creation for his glory. It's worth repeating that God deeply loves his creation. In one of the best-known verses of the Bible, we read: "God so loved the world" (Jn 3:16). The Greek word for world there is *kosmos.* The word means "the sum total of everything here and now." This contrasts with the word *oikoumenē,* which means the world of people.[4] God loves *us,* to be sure. He counts humans as more valuable than the sparrows (Mt 10:31). But God also deeply loves and delights in the nonhuman creation.

God created, blessed, and called the earth "good" long before human beings came on the scene. God's first benediction of blessing was over the nonhuman creation. As we consider our stewardship mandate, it's important to remember that the goodness of creation is independent of its utility for humans. The creation has intrinsic goodness because God made it and called it good. It exists for *his* glory. As Job 38:26-27 teaches us, God

> [waters] a land where no one lives,
>   an uninhabited desert,
> to satisfy a desolate wasteland
>   and make it sprout with grass.

Many parts of God's majestic creation are unseen by us mere mortals: the fish and plants in the depths of the oceans and the stars far beyond our galaxies and telescopes. And mysteriously this nonhuman creation is active in praising God. As Psalm 19:1 proclaims, "The heavens declare the glory of God; the skies proclaim the work of his hands." The speech of creation may be inarticulate to us, but it delights God. The earth exists for more than only meeting the needs of human beings.

Not surprisingly, the Scriptures warn us of God's anger toward those who mar and destroy this creation he loves and sustains. Consider the sober words of Revelation 11:18, describing judgment in the end times: "The time has come . . . for destroying those who destroy the earth."

Holistic health: God designed human beings to be healthy and whole. In God's original creation there was no disease, decay, or death. The intricate, complex way God designed the human body is nothing short of wondrous. Consider, for example, how our bodies have their internal cooling system (sweat keeps our temperature down). Or the fact that our blood vessels are helical in shape; this gentle corkscrewing makes the blood flow more evenly, preventing damage from turbulent flow. Or the capacity of the human brain for processing information; the brain has been called "the most complex structure in the universe."[5]

With our exile from the Garden, human beings became subject to sickness and death. But the idea that this is not what God wants for us—that his desire for us is health and wholeness—is indicated in both the Old and New Testaments. In Exodus 15:26 God identifies himself to the Israelites as "the LORD, who heals you." A foundational way God desires to interact with us is as our Great Physician. He tells the Israelites that if they follow in his ways and obey his commands he will keep them from disease. The sentiment is repeated in Deuteronomy 7:14-15 (NKJV). There, God speaks of his love for Israel and his desire for them to follow in his ways so that they might know health and fruitfulness: "There shall not be male or female barren among you or among your livestock. And the LORD will take away from you all sickness."

God's desire for people to experience health is revealed also through his Son, Jesus. Throughout his earthly ministry Jesus compassionately attended to people's physical, emotional, and mental well-being. He healed those afflicted with skin diseases, lameness, blindness, and deafness. He restored sanity to the Gerasene demoniac of Mark 5 and in other instances cast out demons preying mercilessly on individuals. He not only physically healed the woman with a blood hemorrhage (Lk 8:43-48) but by stopping to speak with her, equated her to the socially honored Jairus. He also publicly praised her faith. In so doing he honored her in a way that must have been a balm to her self-esteem—after being an outcast for years—and restored her to community fellowship.

SUMMING UP

The remarkable scene at Lazarus's tomb offers a good synopsis of Jesus' passion for the interrelated realms of natural and human health. In John 11:33, 38 we read that Jesus was "deeply moved" by his friend's death. The word used (*embrimaomai*) can also be employed for the snorting of horses as they prepare to charge an enemy. In humans it refers to anger. In John 11:33 the word *tarassō* is also used, which can be translated as "very agitated." As we know from the Bible's shortest verse, Jesus also wept (Jn 11:35). In Jesus' reactions we see a combination of being angry with and heartbroken over the current deformity of our death-marked world. Here is a clear display of how Jesus feels about things *not* being the way they ought to be in the realm of the Sustainable. As one pastor puts it, Jesus is "angry at sin, sickness, disease, and death for hurting his precious children."[6] Jesus wants a world where death, disease, decay, and pollution no longer exist. He wants this because we were originally made for such a world. Thankfully, to his great praise, we will one day inhabit such a world in the new heavens and new earth.

MALFORMATIONS: THE REALM OF THE NATURAL ENVIRONMENT

The close relationship between people and creation means that human sin has devastating effects on nature. The curse on the earth is the result of human disobedience (Gen 3:17). This theme is echoed in prophetic literature, where we often see a connection between Israel's sins and the barrenness of the land. Zechariah, for example, condemns the Israelites for turning pleasant land into desolate land through their sins of injustice (Zech 7:9-14). Haggai draws a similar connection arising from Israel's failure to prioritize worship of YHWH. He speaks of how the people have left God's temple in "ruins" (Hebrew *harab*) and describes the land as *horeb*, marked by drought (Hag 1:3-11). Isaiah 24:4-5 describes the ruinous ecological consequences of Israel's disobedience, lamenting that the earth "dries up and withers."

The New Testament's most direct commentary on this theme comes in Paul's words in Romans 8:22. There, he discusses how, because of sin, all of creation is "groaning." Because of human disobedience, the material creation is in bondage to futility, corruption, decay, and death (Rom 8:20-21).

We can identify at least three specific malformations of sin that have distorted God's normative intentions for the realm of the Sustainable.

Malformation 1. Acting as though we don't have limits. Mainstream culture in America hates limits. We want to have it all; we want to do it all. Older men don't want to be limited by hair loss; women don't want to be limited by aging. As one contemporary cultural critic has noted, we want compact cars that are spacious and SUVs that are energy efficient. A great deal of our technological innovation goes into pushing the limits. We are overscheduled. We have FOMO (fear of missing out). We want to be everywhere and do everything. We are arrogant because we want godlikeness: we want to get beyond our humanness. But we *are* humans, not gods. We are humans, not machines or superheroes. We cannot do everything. In failing to humbly submit to this reality, we have created unsustainable lives that harm ourselves, our neighbors, and the environment.

Malformation 2. Acting as though only humans matter. Human beings have woefully fallen short of their mandate to care for the creation. Rather than honoring God's ownership of the cosmos, rather than respecting the nonhuman creation he made for his glory, we have too often acted as though we were the only truly important species on the planet. Human greed, expressed in both production models that ignore or discount environmental impact and in out-of-control consumption, has contributed to the creation's groaning.

In *Earthwise: A Guide to Hopeful Creation Care*, the longtime evangelical environmentalist Cal DeWitt notes seven specific degradations of nature: land conversion and habitat destruction, species extinctions, land abuse, resource conversion and wastes and hazards production, global toxification, alteration of planetary energy exchange, and human and cultural abuse.[7] As a result, nature "isn't what it ought to be or what it was created to be. It's alienated, both from us (who were meant to live in harmony with nature, as its directors, or rulers . . .), and from itself."[8]

The effects of these environmental degradations on human health are profound. They include higher rates of tropical disease and cardiorespiratory illnesses stemming from pollution.[9] In July 2020 scientists from the Air Quality Life Index released a study contending that poor air quality is "the greatest risk to human health."[10]

Malformation 3: Acting as though the nonhuman creation matters more than humans. The third kind of malformation arises when the pendulum swings to the opposite side and human well-being is made subservient to that of the nonhuman creation. Radical environmentalist groups like Earth First! and Earth Liberation Front deny God's design for humans to be his rulers (vice-regents) over nonhuman creation. In her article on the religious, scientific, and philosophical underpinnings of radical environmentalism, Bron Taylor writes that such groups seek the overthrow of anthropocentric beliefs and oppose the idea of human superiority.[11] She depicts how some conservationists are inspired by pantheism and animism. They believe the earth is sacred and that industrial civilization is a cancer.[12] Devotees of "deep ecology" within the radical environmentalist camps regard *homo sapiens* as an animal species like any other, says Stanford historian Martin Lewis, and "denounce all humanistic philosophies as inescapably arrogant and ultimately poisonous."[13]

GOD'S LAW: A MEANS OF RE-FORMATION IN THE REALM OF THE SUSTAINABLE

In trying to forge a way forward in addressing these deformations, we can glean wise counsel from the Old Testament. God's instructions to the Israelites in the Old Testament law were designed to mitigate the effects of sin on the health of humans and nonhuman creation.

Sabbath. We've already seen how sabbath rhythm is built into the very structure of creation. Not surprisingly, then, God's instructions about honoring the Sabbath are prominent in the law. Honoring the Sabbath is one of the Ten Commandments. The law required humans and animals to rest every seven days (Lev 23:3) and for fields to lay fallow every seven years (Lev 25:4-5).

A rudimentary public health system. Many biblical scholars have noted how several of the Old Testament regulations formed a kind of rudimentary public health system.[14] Consider, for example, the following:

Sanitation practices. Western Seminary's Jan Verbruggen has compiled a list of hygienic practices included in the law, such as Leviticus 16:4 (ceremonial baths for priests), Leviticus 14:8-9 (those cured of skin diseases required to bathe), Exodus 30:19 (appendages being washed before ceremonial functions), Exodus 19:10 (washing one's clothes before coming before the Lord), Numbers 19:11 (refraining from touching dead bodies, which could spread disease), and Genesis 18:4 (footwashing as a sign of hospitality). The legislation also protected water from the pollution caused by the carcasses of "unclean" species (Lev 11:31-40). God's good law helped the Israelites refrain from practices that could transmit infection.[15] God's law was so practical it even included instructions on toileting (Deut 23:12-13).

Quarantining those with infections. God gave instructions regarding those with skin diseases: while they had a disease, they had to live outside the camp (Lev 13:46).

Limiting sexual relations. (Ex 20:14; Lev 18:6-18, 23; Deut 27:20, 22; 23:17-18). The law prohibited sex outside marriage, sex with animals, incest, and prostitution. Obedience to such regulations would have the positive effect of limiting sexually transmitted diseases.

Use of health inspectors. According to Leviticus 14:43-44 one of the duties of a priest was to serve as a kind of health inspector: "If the defiling mold reappears in the house after the stones have been torn out and the house scraped and plastered, the priest is to go and examine it and, if the mold has spread in the house, it is a persistent defiling mold; the house is unclean."

LOOKING BACK: THE CHURCH AND THE SUSTAINABLE IN HISTORICAL PERSPECTIVE

The saints in ages past were active in both creation care and health care. Christians contributed to strengthening the endowment of the Sustainable by championing certain ideas and attitudes as well as by engaging in specific practices. We'll examine this first regarding creation care and then concerning health care.

Creation care: Christian ideas and attitudes. The Christian church has contributed foundational ideas—such as God's ownership over all things, creation's intrinsic value, and the concept of general revelation—that have positively influenced humankind's interactions with nature.

In the early church the New Testament writers affirmed a strong theology of creation; consider, for example, Colossians 1:16 and Revelation 4:11. They underscored the inherent goodness of God's material creation. As Paul wrote to Timothy, "Everything God created is good, and nothing is to be rejected if it is received with thanksgiving" (1 Tim 4:4-5).

This high view of creation and its trinitarian genesis was the basis for the early church fathers' idea that God reveals himself in both his written Word *and* in "the book of nature." Writing in *Christian History* magazine, Glenn Myers explains:

> Early Christians believed that because the universe was created through the Logos—God's word, logic, reason, and wisdom—creation reflects God's order and character. They engaged in, as they described it, "reading" the book of nature. . . . The most famous figure of early monasticism, Antony (c. 251–356) meditated deeply on God's self-revelation in creation. When asked why he brought no books with him during his hermitage in the Egyptian desert, Antony responded, "My book is the nature of created things. In it when I choose, I can read the words of God."[16]

Christian leaders in medieval times also extolled the Creator and his creation, urging reverent attitudes and practices. German theologian and Dominican Meister Eckhart counseled believers to study the created world for spiritual insights. "Every single creature is full of God," Eckhart taught, "and is a book about God. Every creature is a word of God."[17] The German abbess Hildegard of Bingen delighted in nature, carefully studied the healing properties of plants, and became a practitioner of what today we call homeopathic medicine.[18] But it is the twelfth century's Francis of Assisi who became the most famous environmentally friendly monk. Francis and his "Little Brothers" lived close to the earth and adored all of God's creatures. Francis's famous Canticle of the Creatures praises the Most High God who created "Brother Sun" and "Sister Moon," water, fire, the multitudes of plants, and life-giving mother earth.[19]

While there was less emphasis on these environmental themes during the Reformation era, key leaders like Martin Luther and John Calvin were hardly indifferent. Luther fully embraced the "book of nature" idea, proclaiming that "God writes the gospel not in the Bible alone, but also on trees, and in the flowers and the clouds and stars."[20] While Calvin asserted that "it was chiefly for the sake of mankind that the world was made," he also taught that humankind's dominion should not be seen "as an opportunity for excessive and unbridled consumption."[21] Calvin emphasized humankind's stewardship responsibilities, urging "him who possesses a field [to] endeavor to hand it down to posterity as he received it, or even better cultivated."[22] Calvin's world-affirming theology expressed itself in Geneva in all sorts of practical efforts in health, public sanitation, and safety.[23]

Methodists comprised one of the largest groups of Protestants/Evangelicals in the United States in the mid-nineteenth century, and they displayed a rich appreciation of God's beautiful creation and its healing properties. Organizers of Methodist camp meetings based their selection of locations for these outdoor retreats largely on the basis of how inspiring the landscape was. They believed nature's beauty and the forest's stillness were inspirations to worship.[24] Later in the nineteenth century, Methodist leaders founded clubs to advance "beautification and environmental conservation."[25]

Creation care practices: Sustainable agriculture and conservation. The saints gone before put their ideas into practical actions. The most notable concerned implementing sustainable forms of agriculture and engaging in environmental conservation efforts.

Monks in the early centuries pursued a humble, agrarian life, worshiping the Creator and engaging in gardening, emphasizing humankind's dependence on the creation. Saint Benedict understood work in the gardens, fields, and beehives as not merely necessity but spiritual exercise.[26] Benedict also propounded a gentle attitude toward animals.[27] The Cistercian Order (founded 1098) put Benedict's rule into practice and emphasized cultivation of the land, even draining swamps to reclaim land for farming.[28]

Summing up medieval Christianity's legacy in creation care, historian Ellen Arnold of Ohio Wesleyan University writes:

Almost all medieval saints were connected to local environments and to the protection of God's creation. Medieval saints, scholars, and everyday Christians cared about nature, wrote about nature, and thought deeply about their environment. They recognized the fragility of the earth and valued nature as God's creation. . . . They planted orchards, created massive systems for diverting water resources to run sewage systems, raised fish in artificial ponds to keep steady food supplies, and regulated urban pollution to protect the health of both rivers and people. . . . Medieval land managers developed practices to expand the longevity of natural resources, and to protect the resources they controlled.[29]

Concern for creation was not limited to Western expressions of Christianity. The Orthodox Church, particularly in Ethiopia, deserves mention. There, Christ-followers "made a concerted effort to plant and cultivate trees as part of their congregational space."[30] As Amir Aman Kiyaro reports, "Centuries before forest conservation became a science, the church was preserving trees out of its theology of creation care."[31] To this day the Ethiopian Orthodox Church plays a vital role in addressing deforestation. Researchers say that in the context of the country's general agricultural overdevelopment, without the intervention of the church, "the native trees of Ethiopia would be nearly extinct."[32]

During the Reformation era and beyond, French Huguenots applied their Protestant theology in a practical conservation agenda. The Huguenots believed the poor treatment of forests and fields fueled poverty. They founded schools to teach farming methods imbued with a creation-care ethic.[33] The English Calvinists put similar ideas into action in the seventeenth-century colonies of New England, passing ordinances to preserve wood and soil for future generations and reserving green space for common use. These Puritans saw the world as animated by God's majestic, sustaining, providential care. Respectful stewardship of his creation was the natural response.

Puritan influence (of a sort) continued into the nineteenth century in the activism of Congregationalists, who were leaders in the conservation movement. Environmental historian Mark Stoll contends that it was Congregationalist George Perkins's 1864 book *Man and Nature* that sparked the

American conservation and forest movements.[34] All but one of the heads of the Forest Division (the precursor of the Forest Service) were Congregationalists. The nation's first publicly funded green space, Bushnell Park in Hartford, Connecticut, came into being largely as the result of Congregationalist advocacy led by Reverend Horace Bushnell. Another Congregationalist, Frederick Law Olmsted, designed New York's Central Park and several other national parks.[35]

In the early twentieth century, while fundamentalist Christians were largely withdrawing from cultural engagement in the light of the fundamentalist-modernist controversy, another strand of American Christianity was actively engaging in the conservation of farmland. The Protestant agrarians, writes Kevin Lowe in *Baptized with the Soil,*

> were some of the nation's loudest champions of agricultural conservation. Even after the government's interest waned, soil conservation's religious resources enabled the movement to persist for decades. Protestant agrarians constructed a stewardship ethic that helped contribute to the contemporary language of creation care. In doing so, they helped bring countless Americans into the environmental movement.[36]

CREATION CARE: INSTITUTIONS AND ADVOCACY

In recent decades Christ-followers in the United States and the United Kingdom have taken up a renewed focus on environmental stewardship. The year 1970 saw both the publication of Francis Schaeffer's book *Pollution and the Death of Man* and a resolution by the National Association of Evangelicals that declared, "those who thoughtlessly destroy a God-ordained balance of nature are guilty of sin against God's creation."[37]

A few years later British Evangelical pastor and author John Stott argued for the inclusion of social concern in the 1974 Lausanne Covenant and wrote about the discipline of creation care in his book *The Radical Disciple.* In 1988 at Lambeth XII, the international conference of Anglican bishops, leaders issued a statement asserting that good stewardship of God's earth is a necessary part of Christian discipleship.[38]

In the 1980s and 1990s several Christian institutions dedicated to environmental study and "green" practices emerged. These included the AuSable

Institute for Environmental Studies, established in the United States in 1979 as a center for Christian environmental education; A Rocha, launched in 1983 in Portugal (it now has chapters in nineteen countries); the North American Conference on Christianity and Ecology (launched 1987); and the Evangelical Environmental Network, established in 1993.

The National Association of Evangelicals has issued important statements on creation care in recent years. In 2011 it published "Loving the Least of These: Addressing a Changing Environment" to highlight the connections between environmental problems and international poverty. In October 2015 the NAE issued a "call to action" titled "Caring for God's Creation." It reaffirmed the creation-care principles outlined in the Lausanne Cape Town Commitment, acknowledged the threat posed by climate changes, and called believers to "adopt lifestyles that renounce habits of consumption that are destructive or polluting."[39]

HUMAN HEALTH: CHRISTIAN CONTRIBUTIONS

Christianity's relationship to healthcare goes back to its earliest roots. Individual believers and the church as an institution have been important healthcare providers. Christians have also made important contributions to medical science throughout history.

Voluntary care for the sick. Since Jesus is the Great Physician who brought healing to many—and the apostles Peter and Paul were gifted by the Holy Spirit with power to heal—it is not surprising that care for the sick has been an important aspect of the Christian church from its very earliest days. Followers of the Way were known for their compassion for the poor, hungry, lonely, and sick to the extent that even nonbelievers recognized their sacrificial service.

Clement, a Christian leader in Rome, recorded how the Christian community responded with astounding bravery and compassion during a great plague in the second century in the city of Carthage. There, believers (led by their bishop) were seen on the streets tending to ill victims who'd been thrown out of their homes by pagans. Christ-followers personally tended to these strangers, offering comfort and taking them into their own homes to be nursed.[40]

Organized healthcare and hospitals. Writing in *Christian History*, Gary Ferngren explains that in addition to the merciful works of individual

Christians, "the early church also established organized assistance."[41] Deacons, whose main concern was the relief of physical want and suffering, had a special responsibility to visit the ill and report on their condition to priests. Churches collected alms weekly to help the poor and the sick. In the third century as the church grew, particularly in urban areas, church work became even more institutionalized. The church in Rome divided the city into seven districts and set a deacon over each. These officers and their assistants provided rudimentary care, seeking to relieve patients' suffering.

The earliest hospitals grew out of this long tradition of care for the sick. The best-known and earliest hospital was called the Basileiad, completed in 372 by Basil the Great. Its "live-in staff provided not only aid to the sick, but also medical care in the tradition of Greek medicine."[42] More hospitals, founded by bishops, arose rapidly and spread throughout the eastern Roman Empire such that by the fourth century, "everyone knew what a Christian hospital was."[43]

Guenter Risse, a historian of hospitals, explains that the Christian practice contrasted with that of the Romans. The Romans limited their hospital-like care to soldiers. The Christian hospitals were established instead to cater to "particular social groups marginalized by poverty, sickness, and age."[44] Christians by this point had become so known for the care of the sick that Julian, the pagan Roman emperor who preceded Constantine, wrote in his *Apology* that if the old pagan religion was to succeed, it would need to care for people even better than the ways Christians cared.[45]

During the Middle Ages the church was the most important provider of patient care. For example, in medieval England and Wales it is estimated there were some twelve hundred hospitals, most of them operated by the church. The church also funded the universities where doctors trained.[46]

In the eighteenth century, Christians were at the forefront of the dispensary movement. Dispensaries were a kind of "prototype of general practice" medicine, largely focused on serving the poor in congested, urban neighborhoods.[47] Christ-followers also founded some of the first hospitals in the United States. The practice continued into modern times. In just about any city, one is likely to find a hospital with Christian roots.[48]

Christians were also at the forefront of nineteenth-century efforts to establish or extend healthcare for vulnerable populations. The Salvation

Army (founded 1865), for example, provided medical care for women who'd been reduced to prostitution. Charles West, a Baptist physician, founded the Great Ormond Street Hospital in 1852 in London. It was the first hospital in the United Kingdom specializing in inpatient care for children. A devout Catholic, Louis Braille, invented the Braille system of reading for the blind. The two leading figures in education for the deaf, the Frenchman Roch-Ambroise Cucurron Sicard and the American Thomas Gallaudet were both committed Christ-followers. The first hospice for the dying was founded by the Sisters of Charity in Hackney, England, at the dawn of the twentieth century.[49]

Contributions to medical science. Girolamo Fracastoro, a Christian physician and poet, pioneered the field of epidemiology in the sixteenth century. His research and writing on infectious diseases were the first to suggest that tiny particles could spread contagion from person to person.[50] Educated clergymen in subsequent centuries recognized the connections between health and sanitation and advocated personal and public hygiene.

Martin Luther played an influential role in changing public attitudes toward disease by asserting that most illnesses could be traced to natural explanations rather than black magic. "Luther recommended the use of apothecaries, barbers, physicians, and nurses to cure physical ailments when he ministered to the sick. He recommended fumigation for homes contaminated with the plague and avoidance of unnecessary travel and exposure to different places."[51]

According to the Christian Medical Fellowship, during the Reformation and Renaissance eras multiple Christians made important contributions to the advancement of medical science.[52] For example, William Harvey discovered the circulation of the blood, Jan Swammerdam was the first to observe and describe red blood cells, and Stephen Hales became the first person to measure blood pressure.

Christ-followers have also exerted considerable influence in the field of medical ethics. The godly physician Thomas Browne expanded on the Hippocratic Oath in his seventeenth-century text on medical ethics and whole-person care. Dr. Thomas Percival, an active social reformer of the eighteenth century, wrote the first professional code of ethics for doctors. "From that time onward," the Christian Medical Fellowship explains, "Christian thought has shaped much of the modern profession's ethical conduct, promoting personal integrity, truthfulness and honesty."[53]

SUMMING UP

God created human beings to be whole and to delight in the glories of his creation. History's greatest artists seem to know about that marriage intuitively. Some of the greatest works of Western art, including paintings by Rafael, El Greco, and William Blake, focus on Jesus' healings. Their work tells us God cares about people's health. Some of the greatest musical composers, including Beethoven, Mozart, Mendelssohn, and Haydn, were known as great lovers of nature. Their melodies capture an echo of the beauty and harmony of the original Garden.

One day, in the new creation, the health of humans and the cosmos will be fully restored. Meanwhile, the church of Jesus honors its Lord when it works for the health of people and planet. As we've seen, this is labor that Christians of old took up. In the next chapters, we'll see something of what this work looks like today.

15

A STRATEGY FOR CULTIVATING
THE SUSTAINABLE

COMBAT ENVIRONMENTAL
HEALTH HAZARDS

THE CONGREGANTS OF CHURCH OF THE REDEEMER in Los Angeles are not only attenders of weekly worship services but also are, as one congregant has described, "intimately involved with whatever else is going on in the community, in a holistic way."[1] Members of the church have been instrumental in ridding it of a liquor store that was a hub of criminality, tutoring scores of local schoolchildren, providing homeless women a place to sleep, beautifying the neighborhood, facilitating a drop in crime, and leading Bible studies for the spiritually hungry. From 2014 to 2019 the small church's commitment to love its neighbors led it to accept the role of David in a fight against a Goliath. It took on a multibillion company in an attempt to end toxic oil drilling in its residential community—and won.

One hears plenty about shalom, God's kingdom, and justice—*and* public health and safety—at Church of the Redeemer. This church is a place, says congregant Niki Wong, where "yes, certainly the spiritual health of people matters, but sidewalks and air pollution matter too."

For Richard Parks, one of the church's founders and the head of its sister ministry, Redeemer Community Partnership, the congregation's campaign to shut down the Jefferson drilling site was a way of implementing the Bible's life-giving wisdom. Parks likes to quote Deuteronomy 22:8: "When you build a new house, make a parapet around your roof so that you may not bring the guilt of bloodshed on your house if someone falls from the roof." He says this shows God's concern about the nitty-gritty details of life.[2] Since God cares about people's health and safety, the church should too.

Holistic concern for their neighbors and Church of the Redeemer's strong theology of place have also led the roughly one hundred-member congregation to participate in two major city initiatives to beautify the community and make it safer for bicyclists and pedestrians. These convictions, alongside the church's belief that it is meant to bring a little more heaven to earth, have been the driving forces behind its dogged efforts to end the toxic pollution that flowed from the drilling operations. Its success in doing so owes much to prayer, faith, savvy activism, and the trust it has earned from its neighbors as a result of its faithful, leavening presence over twenty-eight years.

SHUTTING DOWN A DANGEROUS LIQUOR STORE

Like East End Fellowship (see chap. 10), Church of the Redeemer sprang up from the Christian community-development work of young adult believers who had decided to invest in an underserved neighborhood. Richard and a few other new graduates from the University of Southern California and Occidental College moved into South Los Angeles just after the 1992 civil unrest following the acquittal of LAPD officers in the brutal beating of Rodney King. "It was during the crack epidemic. There was tremendous violence, a tremendous amount of fear, and a lot of racial polarization," Richard recalls. "It was a very intense environment."[3] The group rented two homes side by side in the Exposition Park neighborhood.

By God's providence their landlord took to them affectionately when he saw their heart to serve the neighborhood. This man gave the group free use of a building next to their homes. Richard and his friends later used it as a tutoring center. The group's credibility in the neighborhood was solidified, though, as a result of its efforts to shut down Lucky Liquor.

The ugly corner store was the hub of the neighborhood's crime and violence. "Everyone knew that if you wanted to buy drugs, you went to Lucky Liquor," Richard says. "During our first year there were more drive-by shootings there than we could keep track of."

One night when bullets tore through Richard's house, he and his buddies got more angry than scared. The situation was intolerable. They decided to start canvassing their neighbors. "We wanted to listen and see if there was something that we could do together," Richard remembers. They discovered that local moms were afraid to let their little kids play outside. But most of the moms and dads were also working two jobs and overwhelmed with life. Elderly neighbors were scared, and other residents were just wearily resigned. "We found people who frankly did not have hope that things could be any different," Richard explains. "It had been this way for so long."

The young graduates did some research and learned about the city's public nuisance ordinances. With help from their landlord, they rallied local businesses and neighbors and successfully hounded public officials until they shut down Lucky Liquor. Richard explains that the victory that day ended up having ripple effects two decades later. "The day that the doors to the store closed, the gang activity was gone, the violence was gone, the prostitution was gone," he says. "We had known that there was this connection between the chaos in our community and the store, but we had no idea how strong that was." Nowadays a small grocery store called El Rey Market fills the site—and does not sell alcohol.

The experience was transformative. "It ended up introducing us to the idea of community organizing," Richard says. "We forged really wonderful friendships in that time, and we still enjoy the fruits of those friendships today, over twenty-five years later."

The team from Redeemer Community Partnership and Church of the Redeemer used a similar public nuisance ordinance in their battle against the oil company. Niki led the community organizing and says that when she'd talk with neighbors about signing a petition or showing up at a city council meeting, they'd often mention the successful fight against Lucky Liquor.

ORIGINS OF THE CHURCH

Reflecting on Church of the Redeemer's beginnings, Richard says he was not personally trying to start a church. "But when we moved into the neighborhood," he acknowledges, "we really hoped that our life together at some point would involve having a church with our neighbors."

By the early 2000s other young adult Christ-followers desiring to live out Christian community development had moved into the community. These individuals were building relationships and running Bible studies in their homes. They shared a spiritual hunger with their neighbors and parents of kids in the informal tutoring program. They were initially reluctant to start a new congregation since there were so many already in the community. After researching those, however, they discovered that nearly all were commuter churches. "Our friends in the neighborhood didn't necessarily feel welcome there, for a whole host of reasons," explains Richard. "We just realized we needed to start a church here where our friends who were making decisions to follow Jesus could grow."

No one in the group was a trained church planter. Richard committed to raising a new base of support for Redeemer Community Partnership so that tithes that had previously supported the nonprofit could be redirected to the church plant. The team did extensive research and decided to affiliate with the Evangelical Covenant Church. Pasadena Covenant Church, a suburban congregation, generously provided financial and human resources to help sustain the church in its first years. Church of the Redeemer then called a Hispanic minister, Danny Martinez, to serve as the fledging congregation's first pastor.

Theology of place. The church's core group of leaders, Richard says, were committed to a congregation that "would be deeply rooted in the Word, prayer, and shared ministry and accountability. Those things came to characterize our life together; those things were embedded in our DNA from the outset."

Redeemer also sought to be deeply rooted in the neighborhood.

Jennifer Chou Blue joined the church's core team in 2003. She remembers their discussions about a tagline for the congregation. They settled on, "A multi-ethnic family of faith in the community and for the community." Her husband, Kevin, became Church of the Redeemer's second pastor. At the time of this writing, Jen was serving as acting senior pastor.

Anyone from anywhere can attend the church, of course, but only those living within its target neighborhood can be voting members. Jen explains that leaders do not make a strong distinction between members and nonmembers so that all feel welcome. Everyone can attend congregational meetings, and the church budget is shared with all home groups. But there is a core group of individuals living in the geographic parish who've accepted deeper commitments regarding participation in worship, tithing to the church, practicing reconciliation with other members, and living simply in order to give generously to those in need.

As a parish-based congregation, Jen says, "you're affected by the same things that your neighbors are affected by. If you're going to be there and have your kids in the neighborhood schools, the problems of education are *your* children's problems and *your* family's problems. That's where the rubber hits the road on the whole notion of loving your neighbor."[4]

Niki agrees. "Our first motive [in fighting against the oil company] came from our presence," she says. "Our church is called to steward this little section of the earth, and it had a toxic drill site on it."

Bringing heaven to earth. On its website, Church of the Redeemer describes itself as having "a shared concern for the health and well-being for the place to which God has called us." It adds that its hope for the community is for God to transform it "to be more like his kingdom." Jen elaborates:

> We talk a lot about the kingdom of God. We've done a couple sermon series on resurrection and the ushering in of the kingdom here and now. This theology is integrated in everything we do. We pray for God's kingdom to come to our neighborhood [and] it's not pie in the sky. It's about the shalom and the justice of God and the kingdom here and now. Can we really say we're loving our neighbors if these kinds of things [like the drilling] are happening and we just don't care about it?

YOUR NEIGHBOR IS A TOXIC CHEMICAL SITE

Pursuing a community's flourishing includes working for its human and environmental health. The two are vitally connected. According to the World Health Organization, nearly a quarter of all deaths globally are due to preventable environmental factors.[5] Here in the United States the Environmental Protection Agency has noted nine health outcomes, including cancer, asthma, cardiovascular disease, and birth defects, that have been linked to exposure to environmental contaminants.[6]

Poor people and people of color are more likely to live in neighborhoods subjected to environmental hazards such as landfills and toxic waste dumps. In 2016 *Fortune* magazine reported on studies published in the academic journal *Environmental Research Letters* that showed that "the biggest polluters in the U.S.—factories, warehouse and other facilities using toxic substances—are overwhelmingly located in poor, non-white neighborhoods" and that "hazardous waste treatment, storage, and disposal plants also tend to be built in similar low-income, non-white areas."[7] Studies by researchers at the University of Minnesota and Yale University indicate that the poor and minorities are subject to more serious forms of air pollution than are the nonpoor and Whites.[8] The result is that the poor and minorities face greater exposure to pollutants and suffer worse health outcomes. This is the larger context of the environmental injustice that Church of the Redeemer took on in its small neighborhood.

Star-studded LA is, unbeknownst to most, also studded with active oil wells—more than one thousand of them. Many, including the thirty-six oil and gas wells on the Jefferson drilling site, are located in the middle of residential neighborhoods. Kevin Blue says for most of the time Redeemer has been worshiping, participants considered the drilling on Jefferson Boulevard just a nuisance. It was loud and dirty. Only later did they realize it was also dangerous.

In 2014 Richard received an alert by email regarding a city permit for which Freeport-McMorRan, the owner-operator of the Jefferson drill site, was applying. Curious, he looked into the matter and discovered that the company wanted to drill three new wells at the site. According to the permit application he found, the company was asking that the work be allowed to continue 24/7 for as long as two years. The drilling-site owners had also requested that city officials waive any public hearings on the permit.

Richard, Niki, and volunteers from Church of the Redeemer began going door to door, asking neighbors their thoughts about the drilling site. What they learned sobered them. One neighbor talked about plants dying mysteriously. Niki had a plant pathologist from Los Angeles County inspect a group of plants that had all died within a day after a particular operation on the site. He said it looked like they'd died from chemical exposure.

Neighbor Lillian Marenco had experienced years of ear-splitting, metal-on-metal screeching, and diesel and "rotten egg" fumes emanating from the site three doors down from her modest home.[9] She remembered finding a fine oily film covering her car after a particularly active day at the site. Her son grew up with frequent nosebleeds and her husband died from mesothelioma.

She wondered if the site's pollution was a contributor. Other mothers also complained about the frequency of their children's illnesses. They reported kids with asthma, sore throats, and persistent coughing. "The cluster of health impacts [we saw] around the site were very troubling," Richard recalls.[10]

Residents told of their homes being sprayed with oil from leaks at the site and of exhaust fumes billowing from huge trucks labeled with poison warnings, and of how, from their upstairs windows, they saw workers in full hazmat gear on one side of the wall separating the site from family residences, while neighbors in T-shirts and shorts walked their dogs along the other side.

Given the age of the Jefferson drilling site, the oil and gas that had been easy to extract had already been taken out by 2014. Now the site's owners were employing a technique called "acidizing" to get out the rest. In this process thousands of gallons of hydrochloric and hydrofluoric acid are pumped down the well to unstop clogs and dissolve any sediments blocking oil from flowing. No wonder the drill operators were regularly welcoming huge tanker trucks hauling as many as twenty thousand gallons of toxic chemicals to the site.[11] Some of these chemicals, Niki explains, were being stored within ten feet of people's homes. "What really gets me is how many kids live in the area," she told one reporter. "There is an elementary school just two blocks away, seven hundred feet away, from the drill site."[12]

Public health matters. Niki says that Church of the Redeemer embraces creation care but that "the particular messaging in the drill site campaign was focused around health and safety." Neighborhood residents already suffer from the health effects of poverty: lower birth rates, and higher infant mortality rates. "Also," she says, "in this neighborhood you're dealing with residents who have a cumulative burden of negative environmental impacts—light pollution, air pollution, noise pollution—that exact a toll on health."

Church members Nathan and Corissa Pacillas Smith live across the street from the drill site. They've worried about the quality of the air they've been breathing. Niki says they are right to. "The chemicals [used], like hydrochloric acid, methanol—they are known air toxins."[13] Most days Corissa kept the windows closed because of the nasty smells emanating from the site.[14]

For Jen the fight against oil drilling became very personal when the team learned that some of the chemicals being utilized were endocrine disrupters.

"Studies have shown that endocrine disrupters can affect fertility and lead to miscarriages, stillbirths, and birth defects," she explains. "I realized that between four of my friends and myself, who all lived within a half-mile of the drill site, we had suffered eleven miscarriages. The question started to haunt me—what if all of our babies had been lost because of all the endocrine disrupters that were pumped into the ground [and] sprayed into the air?"[15]

Unequal treatment. As the team from Redeemer dug more deeply into the policies and practices of the drilling company, they learned that their neighborhood was being treated far differently than wealthier communities near other drilling sites. On the city's tonier (and Whiter) west side, drilling operators utilized enclosures and electric rigs. Sites were monitored for air quality. Such protections were absent at the Jefferson site. Richard called it "environmental racism."[16]

Months earlier he had met with the director of environmental health and safety and government affairs at Freeport-McMoRan to share his concerns about conditions at the Jefferson site. The company's man mistook Richard for a fellow, privileged Anglo who understood how the world works. As Jen Blue describes, "The director leaned in and said to Richard, 'We aren't talking about the Ritz Carlton at Laguna Nigel, now, are we?'" In other words, since the Jefferson operation was in a community of folks making $30,000 a year versus one where they made near $100,000, the problem wasn't all that important. "It was a chilling window into [their] mindset," Jen laments.

RAISING THEIR VOICES

Church of the Redeemer and Redeemer Community Partnership worked together to continue educating their neighbors and encouraging them to make their concerns known. They organized several public rallies and protest marches, inviting local media and politicians.

Perhaps the most memorable of the events was the children's protest march in 2015. Nearly one hundred kids from Redeemer, another local church, and RCP's tutoring program dressed in yellow and marched around the neighborhood carrying signs reading, "We are not your canaries" and "Don't treat us like canaries in a coal mine."[17] Jen and Kevin Blue's three kids were among them. "Canary Day generated some TV coverage from local stations ABC and NBC," she recalls.

The activity aligned with the church's youth ministries. Jen explains that the children's curriculum provided by the Evangelical Covenant Church "definitely incorporates an emphasis on biblical justice." Richard says the protest march was just another way of expressing discipleship. "We want kids to know that God wants justice, we want them to know they can be change advocates," he told a reporter from the denomination's magazine.[18]

RCP staff and volunteers from the church continued to collect neighbors' stories of the harm drilling was causing. In early 2016 RCP created a community-reporting system whereby neighbors called in to report nuisances experienced from the drill site. Niki sought to learn when the operators planned to do acidizing drops—which typically involved two tankers showing up with some ten thousand gallons of toxic chemicals—so she could lead pop-up protests at those times.

Meanwhile, through monthly updates Niki and Richard kept the congregation informed about the struggle. Church leaders see Redeemer Community Partnership and the church as "two wings of the same bird," Niki explains. RCP is the vehicle through which Church of the Redeemer "lives out its kingdom theology" of bringing foretastes of heaven to earth. Although RCP partners with other churches and agencies, its closest connections are to Church of the Redeemer. At Church of the Redeemer, Richard adds, "there's a tremendous amount of ownership of the work of RCP, and participation, engagement, in that work. . . . A lot of [congregants] probably see it as an extension [of the church]."

In addition to Redeemer's "outside" strategy—garnering media attention and raising public awareness and support—the team also pursued an "inside" strategy, focused on developing relationships with city officials to build political allies in the fight. "We brought city authorities and agency representatives, the city attorney, [and] zoning and public health staff to the neighborhood to see and hear the stories of residents," Niki says. Redeemer also built a strong working relationship with their local city council member Marqueece Harris-Dawson. The councilman and his staff urged the various city departments to support community voices in his district and oppose the oil company.

In the first phase of the fight against the drilling, the church rallied neighbors, many of them people of color, to attend a public hearing of the city planning commission to show their opposition to the expansion permit.

Their voices carried the day. Jefferson drilling-site owner Freeport-McMoRan gave up its expansion plan and later sold the operation to Sentinel Peak Resources.

When Sentinel Peak appealed, RCP worked with Earthjustice, a nonprofit legal firm, to prepare and file a 355-page petition to city officials in 2016 that called on them to enforce its health and safety codes.[19] They used a similar nuisance abatement statute that Richard and his college friends had used to shut down Lucky Liquor. The petition went before LA's City Zoning Administration. The church and RCP worked again to pack the room with community residents to show their support of the petition. "So many community members, many who were Church of Redeemer members, came to the hearing and gave moving and compelling testimony," Niki reported.[20]

The efforts paid off. Commission president Eric Bates was impressed by the turnout. "The community speaking here was very telling and impactful on me," he told a reporter from *Sojourners*.[21] The petition was accepted, and in fall 2017 city officials told Sentinel Peak it had to construct a forty-five-foot-tall enclosure, switch to electric rigs, and install soundproofing—all measures already in place at drill sites in wealthier communities.

Sentinel Peak appealed the decision. At a public hearing of the South Los Angeles Area Planning Commission, they argued that the city's regulatory demands were unduly burdensome. But some seventy residents from the neighborhood were on hand to show their support for upholding the city's actions against Sentinel Peak. The commission did so.

Initially, Sentinel Peak took the matter to court. Shortly thereafter, though, it decided to cease their drilling operations at the Jefferson site rather than attempt to comply with the expensive new regulations. Redeemer's community rejoiced in the news but also wanted to ensure that the company would clean up and not just abandon the site. RCP and its partners met again with city officials to encourage them to monitor Sentinel Peak. In May 2019 city officials told the company it had thirty-six months to close and clean up the site.[22]

David had defeated Goliath.

Today the Redeemer team checks to see that Sentinel Peak is capping the wells and instituting the safety measures it promised. "The company has to submit regular reports to the city on meeting specific goals, and there are big penalties if they don't hit those targets," Niki says. Meanwhile, RCP and the church are listening to their neighbors about the dreams they have for reclaiming the site. At an RCP-hosted community meeting late in 2019, Richard reports, "open park space, affordable housing, and a community center" were the top three suggestions.

LESSONS LEARNED

Several factors contributed to Church of the Redeemer and RCP's victory in its difficult, five-year struggle for justice. One was the Redeemer team's careful and ongoing listening to their neighbors. Niki, Richard, and church volunteers went door to door to every residence along all the blocks surrounding the drill site. Along the way as they heard stories of chronic illness "the injustice became more and more apparent with each resident's story," says Jen. "There is so much power in peoples' stories," Niki adds.[23] Listening at the grassroots level demonstrated to city officials that the church had adequately engaged the community. But even more importantly, she says, it dignifies neighbors by affirming the significance of their experiences.

Patient listening and inviting neighbors into collective action also created hope in residents who had lost heart. Mama Q, a woman who had endured the nearby drilling for thirty years, initially told Niki that there was nothing that could be done about it. She revised her opinion some months later. "Things are changing because you guys are making a lot of noise," she told Niki in 2017. "We just gotta keep praying that God will close this down." Richard affirms the power of community organizing: "I think it's really powerful when you're coming together as a community to change something that could . . . have a transformative, generational impact on children and their families."

A second factor was the team's careful collection of scientific evidence. "We did the research," Richard says simply. God's providence in leading Niki—who holds a master's degree in public health—to Redeemer brought needed technical expertise to the team. She led its efforts to do its homework, gathering data on health impacts from the toxins at the site. Working with other academics, Niki contributed to a study published in 2018 in *The International Journal of Environmental Research and Public Health* that "found a significantly increased rate of asthma in the area surrounding the

Jefferson drill site . . . compared to the broader neighborhood (20.3 percent vs. 9.8 percent)."[24]

Collaborating with other organizations that shared the mission of shutting down the drill site, such as Earthjustice, Stand Together Against Neighborhood Drilling, and the Center for Biological Diversity, was also important. These relationships brought further scientific and legal expertise to the table. Simultaneously, those secular colleagues valued the authority the church brought to the issue. "Having a faith community involved in the struggle reminds city leaders of their moral responsibilities," Maya Golden-Krasner from the Center told a *Sojourners* reporter covering the story.[25]

The most important factors, though, according to Niki, Richard, and Jen, were faith and prayer. RCP's monthly updates at Sunday services were always followed by prayer. Small groups from the church went on neighborhood prayer walks.

Leaders at Church of the Redeemer see the social problems confronting their neighborhood as intertwined with spiritual dynamics. Fighting them necessarily involves spiritual power. "It's not just about a better law . . . though of course we want better laws," explains Jen. "But legal things don't change the heart and spirituality of us as a nation." If there is an animating spirit at work, she continues, things don't just die with better legislation.

This perspective distinguishes the church's social justice work from that carried out by secular groups. "For this church the emphasis has to be more on 'this is actually about God, not just the progressive agenda,'" says Jen. "We're not going to go about doing things exactly the way the progressive agenda does things." So, preachers teach on spiritual warfare. During Lent, parishioners are encouraged to follow prayer guides and liturgies that give focused attention to the inner idolatries that fuel injustice.

Power from the Spirit was also necessary, Richard says, for helping the community to persevere in the kind of faith Jesus wants from his followers: a "faith that can move mountains." Following Redeemer's improbable victory, he summed up in the RCP newsletter:

> Jesus says, "if you have faith as small as a mustard seed, you can say to this mountain, 'Move from here to there,' and it will move. Nothing will be impossible for you" (Matt. 17:20). It is little wonder that an oil company named Sentinel Peak is moving out of our neighborhood.

16

A STRATEGY FOR CULTIVATING THE SUSTAINABLE

ADDRESS FOOD DESERTS

DEATH INTO LIFE: it's one of the central ideas of the Christian faith. Pleasant Hope Baptist Church and its sister ministry, the Black Church Food Security Network (BCFSN), have animated this truth with dirt, seeds, love, and sweat. Their innovative labors have brought literal fruitfulness to food deserts and health where there was once disease.

Pleasant Hope and the BCFSN are led by Rev. Dr. Heber Brown III. At thirty-eight, he's an energetic, prophetic, third-generation African American Baptist preacher in Baltimore, Maryland. His passion for fighting what he calls "food apartheid" stems from his multiple hospital visits to parishioners struggling with conditions brought on or exacerbated by a lack of access to healthy food. Brown's family history includes heart disease and high blood pressure. He remembers calling nine years ago on yet another hospitalized congregant and deciding that he needed to do more than pray. He wanted to address the underlying reasons for his community's poor health outcomes.

Lack of access to fresh, healthy food is one of the most serious challenges of Brown's urban community. According to the Johns Hopkins Center for a Livable Future, 34 percent of Black residents in Baltimore live in food deserts, compared with 8 percent of White residents.[1] The Baltimore City Health Department reports that one in three residents is obese and 12 percent have type 2 diabetes, noting that both conditions disproportionately affect African Americans.[2]

Brown believes that gaining more sway over the community's food supply is the best way of advancing community health. "There's power in having a greater degree of control over your food system," he says, "knowing where your food is coming from [and] how it was grown."[3]

He also believes that the church can be at the center of the solution.

Brown began by suggesting to his flock at Pleasant Hope, where he has served as senior pastor since 2011, that they transform their 1,500-square-foot lawn into a community garden. He assumed that his youth parishioners would be the idea's early adopters, but it turned out the hoary-haired contingent was the first on board. The seniors had experience in gardening, canning, and making jam. They knew how to fashion herb remedies for a variety of ailments, and they remembered the flavor of fresh-from-the-field produce.

The congregation spent funds previously earmarked for landscaping and lawn mowing on new raised beds, seeds, and soil. The new garden was soon producing over one thousand pounds of fresh produce annually.[4] Initially, Pleasant Hope distributed it mainly through their food pantry, supplementing canned goods with highly desired fresh vegetables. Recognizing that simply giving away the produce was not an economically sustainable model, the church began selling a good portion of its harvest through a small monthly farmers' market, plowing the money raised back into the program.

Brown says his flock has readily recognized the value of the gardening initiative from both a practical and spiritual perspective. "Spirituality and agriculture have a deep relationship that is outlined in sacred Scripture and that is practiced in weekly gatherings in worship spaces," Brown says. "I have no problem getting people to buy into this vision."[5]

ECONOMIC EMPOWERMENT

What began as a simple effort to reimagine its land use for community good became what Brown calls a "Soil to Sanctuary pipeline" in April 2015 during the Baltimore Uprising that followed Freddy Gray's funeral.[6] Gray, a twenty-five-year-old Black man, had been critically injured while in police transport and later died. Frustration and despair over years of police abuse boiled over into riots that hit national news. The mayor mandated a curfew and closed the schools—meaning no free lunches for low-income students. Add in shuttered corner stores and the cessation of much public transport, and some inner-city families couldn't find food. Hungry, they started calling

Pleasant Hope Baptist for help. Knowing his own congregation alone could not meet the demand, Brown contacted his farmer friend Aleya Fraser from the Black Dirt Farm Collective and asked her to spread the word about the needs to other producers.

Soon trucks and church vans loaded with produce began rolling into Pleasant Hope's parking lot from farms across the mid-Atlantic region. The church transformed its multipurpose room into a food-distribution center. Volunteers sorted and packed up the produce and loaded it into private vehicles. They set up shop on street corners across the community to get food into the hands of hungry families. After this emergency network had worked for two weeks, Brown realized there was no reason it couldn't become permanent. "We had a system," he says. "We had distribution, production, aggregation sites, all working together."[7]

Brown recognized that marrying supply and demand could bring economic empowerment. Black farmers in Maryland, Virginia, and North Carolina were keen to tap into new markets and Baltimore residents were eager to have access to fresh food. Brown saw that if churches could connect the dots, his community could achieve a sustainable solution.

Leading a charge like this was a natural fit for Pleasant Hope. The congregation has encouraged economic empowerment for years, offering financial literacy workshops to help members and community residents address debt, make financial plans, and learn to gain and manage wealth.

Brown wanted to go beyond charity to self-determination with a sustainable model that addressed one of the root causes of poor health. "We thank God for food pantries, we thank God for soup kitchens, we thank God for food banks," Brown said in a sermon. "But food banks, soup kitchens, and food pantries will not change the underlying conditions that have our community hungry in the first place."[8]

He determined to establish a new pipeline helping farmers to "magnify their presence" in his community.[9] Brown says he's been inspired by civil rights legend Fannie Lou Hamer, who used to argue that if you could feed yourself and your family, nobody could push you around.[10] Brown told local radio station WTOP that he dreams of a day when churches across the country will have markets where "people can come and praise and worship and sing and get a good chunk of the groceries they need for their household at the same time."[11]

Brown began sharing his vision with other African American pastors in the city affected by food apartheid. He encouraged churches to reimagine their assets, turning their land into gardens, their kitchens into healthy cooking demonstration centers, and their parking lots into farmers' markets. Churches are one of the largest land-owning entities in Black communities, he says. "It's a gross waste of resources" when church facilities are used only once a week.[12]

By 2016 Brown had recruited ten churches to the BCFSN. The network helps congregations to establish community gardens on their land, operate pop-up farm stands, and recruit volunteers. Money earned from produce and food product sales during the monthly Soil to Sanctuary Farmers' Market at Pleasant Hope is reinvested in the network. This has enabled the organization to offer $1,000 start-up grants to churches to help them begin growing food onsite at their churches in raised bed gardens.

Pastor Lawrence Rodgers of Westside Church of Christ in Baltimore is an enthusiastic member of the BCFSN. Like Brown, he's seen the deleterious effects of food deserts on his community members' health. It's not right, he says, when "it's cheaper for a person to purchase a cheeseburger than to get a salad." He continues: "Health is a sort of wealth. And your health can affect your social mobility." Rodgers sees Westside's involvement as an "act of social responsibility. As an institution that has the critical resource of land, why not plant a garden to take advantage of that land to feed the folks around us?"[13]

By 2020 the BCFSN had expanded to involve about fifty congregations, mostly but not exclusively in the mid-Atlantic region.

SUPPORTING BLACK ENTERPRISE

The Soil to Sanctuary market at Pleasant Hope sells products from twenty-five growers in the region. Heber Brown himself has made the drive south to purchase thousands of organic, free-range eggs for resale back home. The monthly market at the church has also featured a vegan juicer, bakers, and vending from the Greener Garden, a local, chemical-free urban farm.

Maxine White, who heads the Coalition for Healthier Eating in Bethel, North Carolina, is enthusiastic about her partnership with BCFSN. Her organization works with several local farmers who are now connected to new customers in Baltimore. She says a key motto for her is "The person who controls the food controls the mind and the wellness of the body."[14] The coalition uses its trailers and other food-distribution assets in partnership with BCFSN to get fresh vegetables, meat, eggs, and poultry produced by Black farmers to Black churches.

In 2018 Brown took several BCFSN members on a field trip to Browntown Farms, a fifth-generation Black-owned farm in Warfield, Virginia. The current owners are proud of their legacy but admit that it's been challenging to find affordable ways to market their produce. The connection with the Baltimore network has been a boon. "They've opened up doors and allowed us to hit a market we would not be in otherwise," says Herb Brown Jr. (no relation to Heber Brown). "It's also a point of pride for us that we're sharing our products with people who enjoy and appreciate it and need healthy food."[15] Julius Tillery, a fifth-generation cotton and vegetable farmer in North Carolina, agrees. "Many Black farmers have been burned by planting too much and then not having interested parties wanting to buy their products," he laments. "[The Network] has given black rural farmers confidence that the institution will have their backs when they stretch themselves to plant as much as possible to sell."[16]

Last year, the BCFSN launched a partnership with Master Blend Family Farms, a fourth-generation Black-owned pig farm in North Carolina. The new relationship made it possible to add hormone- and pesticide-free meat to the offerings at the Soil to Sanctuary market. In summer 2020 the network announced another new initiative: the Black Church Supported Agriculture (BCSA) Program. Through it the network will sell boxes packed with produce grown by Black farmers from the Carolinas, Virginia, and other parts of the mid-Atlantic, to church leaders.

VOCATIONAL STEWARDSHIP

The BCFSN project has created new opportunities for congregants at participating churches to deploy their talents. Yvonne Gunn, gardening coordinator at St. Mark's Institutional Baptist Church, reports that "a lot of our church members—especially the kids—have never planted a seed."[17] She and other elders have loved the opportunity to teach the youngsters gardening skills.

A YouTube video advertising an upcoming Soil to Sanctuary cooking demonstration shows Heber Brown with Minnie Little, a twenty-year kitchen volunteer at Pleasant Hope. "It was Sister Minnie who taught me that you don't have to just dump salt on everything," the young pastor laughs. Instead, one can use herbs and spices to add flavor—and eat healthier.[18] Brown has enjoyed watching worshipers come forward to help the movement with their expertise in canning, herbal remedies, and accounting. "The people you need are the people God has already given you," Brown told one reporter in 2019. "Honor the genius that's in your house."[19]

The BCFSN also honors the DNA of Pleasant Hope Baptist Church, where social justice and self-sufficiency are core values. "Social justice was one of the defining characteristics of the prophets and the ministry of Jesus," Brown says. "Therefore, we do not see it as an optional add-on to our understanding of the Christian faith. It is central to who we are as a community."[20] Brown continually keeps the message of serving others in front of his flock. In a blog post in early January 2020, Brown wrote, "New Year's Resolutions far too often are just about me-myself-and-I. But what about our community? Shouldn't we also be thinking, planning, and working collectively to bring about a better day for our families and neighborhoods?"[21]

Brown is justifiably proud of the legacy of the African American church, which has endured despite the fiercest persecutions. The Black church has been the anchor institution in the Black community, he emphasizes.[22] It has been the hub meeting the varied needs of Black families and the birth mother of schools and hospitals. He adds, "From a biblical standpoint, the beginnings of the church as outlined in Acts 2:43-47 also inspire thinking around congregations being proactive and countercultural with respect to caring for one another's needs."[23]

PARTNERSHIPS

This emphasis on self-sufficiency does not preclude healthy partnerships. Where there is shared vision and mutual respect, Brown believes, collaboration can advance the movement. The BCFSN has received grants from the

Maryland-based Town Creek Foundation and the New Visions Foundation in Illinois. Additionally, the Johns Hopkins Community Impact Internships Program has supplied energetic young people as summer interns.[24] In 2019 the Claneil Foundation awarded the BCFSN a four-year, $240,000 "emerging leaders fund" grant.

The BCFSN has also partnered with researchers from Morgan State University and Johns Hopkins University in a project to study the long-term health impacts of the network's initiatives on parishioners in member congregations. The researchers conducted a baseline survey of congregants from six of the churches to identify the prevalence of chronic disease and risk factors for chronic kidney disease. They determined that 54 percent of parishioners had been diagnosed with high blood pressure, 26 percent with high cholesterol, 19 percent with diabetes, and 20 percent with chronic kidney disease. Sixty percent presented with risk factors for chronic kidney disease.[25] The statistics largely matched those of Black residents generally in Baltimore. Researchers plan to repeat their investigation in a few years to see how congregations' participation in the BCFSN and greater access to healthier food will influence health outcomes. Already, though, Darriel Harris, a doctoral student at Johns Hopkins who pastors Newborn Community of Faith Church, has found "early indicators that the fresh food is making a difference in a community where many suffer from illness associated with poverty."[26]

GOOD RESULTS

Since establishing the BCFSN Brown says his congregation's "health IQ has gone through the roof." Additionally, work in the garden has afforded Brown and other adults opportunities to teach participating youth about civil rights pioneers like Vernon Johns, Albert Cleage Jr., and Fannie Lou Hamer, who saw a connection between community-based farming and Black self-determination.[27] These days youth participating in the church's Orita Cross Freedom School learn about environmentalism and nutrition and are encouraged to be activists for positive change in their homes and communities.

And fresh produce isn't the only thing growing at Pleasant Hope these days. Brown reports the Soil to Sanctuary program has even contributed to a bump in church attendance.[28]

17

NEXT STEPS

A ROADMAP FOR THE WORK OF
FLOURISHING YOUR COMMUNITY

In the same way the pilgrim's journey contributes just as much to the
spiritual meaning of pilgrimage as her destination, so the Church's
tending of the earthly peace of Babylon is a participation in her ultimate
enjoyment of shalomic beatitude in the eternal city of God.

NICHOLAS KRAUS,
"JUSTICE AND MERCY CONTENDING FOR SHALOM"

I HOPE THE STORIES—past and present—told herein inspire you for the
part you and your congregation can play in the flourishing of your community. You need not try to replicate what these brothers and sisters have
done. The goal instead is to discern what your assets are, what the issues in
your locality are, and what labors God would have you do.

It's worth noting, though, two critical commonalities among the churches
I have profiled in depth. The first is strong leadership. Don Coleman, Carol
Rienstra, Richard Parks, Leigh Ann Dull, Heber Brown III, David Bailey, Jeff
Greer, and the other pastors and congregational leaders I've highlighted are
people of tremendous vision, energy, perseverance, and faithfulness. They've
taken a long-term view. They've labored in prayer. They've motivated and
mobilized others. They've stood up for truth and justice. And like all good
leaders they've had to endure pain, frustrations, disappointments, and
criticism—and remain committed and hopeful. Leaders of any new initiative for community flourishing will undoubtedly need the same zeal,
prayerfulness, and long-term dedication.

The second is a passion for the kingdom of God and the desire to foretaste
that kingdom come in their cities. These congregational leaders believe in

the comprehensive work of Jesus' redemption. Whether or not they use Abraham Kuyper's language about "every square inch" of the earth being under the lordship of Jesus, they embrace the sentiment. The gospel is to them the power of salvation for not only individuals but institutions, not only persons but places. They believe that the gospel affects *everything*. They believe King Jesus is renewing *all* things and that he has called them to join in that work of renewal. A similar understanding of the gospel of the kingdom is necessary, I believe, to inspire, shape, and sustain any church's vision and action plan for "seeking the peace and prosperity" of its community.

NONNEGOTIABLE PRINCIPLES

There are also at least three foundational principles of community ministry that cannot be ignored if that ministry is to be both faithful and effective.

Relational, holistic ministry. The first is that our ministry among our neighbors must imitate Jesus' way of serving—through relational, holistic ministry. Jesus' compassion was "up close and personal." It was never clinical or brisk. It was a messy love that listened to people's stories, washed feet, and touched lepers. His love was *present*. Jesus healed people one at a time, not in a mass ceremony. God the Father was known among the Israelites as the God of Abraham, Isaac, and Jacob. In other words a God who knows our names, a personal God. And Jesus, God the Son, is just like this. He came near and engaged people on a first-name basis.

Jesus' ministry was not only relational but also holistic. He never treated people as bodies without souls or souls without bodies. Jesus was interested in the whole person: mind, body, affections, will, desires, emotions, experiences, passions, fears, motivations. In *Reconsidering the Full Mission of God*, Dean Flemming describes how Jesus was engaged in being, doing, and telling.[1] This captures Jesus' holistic ministry even better than "word and deed." Jesus both told the good news and lived it.

Asset-based approach. The second nonnegotiable involves embracing an asset-based approach to community ministry. Much current church outreach is conducted from a deficits mentality. It starts with a needs assessment. It focuses on what's wrong and what needs to be fixed. A more biblical approach involves learning not just needs but focusing on the assets of the people and the places we're seeking to influence.

An asset-based approach resonates better with the doctrine of *imago Dei* than does a needs-based approach. The latter can unwittingly demean people we mean to serve or bless by treating them as though they were defined solely by their lack or needs. It can also insidiously fan the flame of our own egos or savior complexes, where we're tempted to believe that we are better than others. The asset-based approach focuses on what's right with a community rather than on what's wrong with it. It directs our attention to the resources already existing in a community. An asset-based approach undercuts paternalism. It remembers that since all people are made in God's image, all have gifts and talents to contribute.

Asset-based ministry is based also on biblical teaching about stewardship. God is a generous provider, and he desires that we steward well *all* the gifts and resources he has given us. We cannot steward well that which we don't recognize we possess. Thus, one of the key tasks of the work of flourishing our communities involves a congregation taking a full inventory of the assets God has granted it. Another involves mapping the assets of the neighborhood or people group the church hopes to serve. We do this so that no available assets are overlooked. Leaving relevant assets untapped simply isn't good stewardship.

Stewarding power faithfully. A third key principle concerns the way we deploy our power. You may be leading a church filled with congregants possessing significant vocational power—people of education, influence, and standing. Or your church itself may be large and well-resourced. Or perhaps the church isn't so big or powerful in the world's estimation, but it possesses street credibility, deep local knowledge, and rich history. Whatever the particular shape of the assets your congregation enjoys, the tendency is to boast in them! Stewarding your power well will require humility and an intentional remembrance of the apostle Paul's warnings about overesteeming gifts and talents. In 1 Corinthians 13, Paul teaches us that gifts are good, but they can't hold a candle to *love.* Our ministry effectiveness depends more on our commitment to try to love well than it relies on our wealth, natural abilities, vocational expertise, local credibility, or rich history. It requires leaders to disciple their congregants in nurturing the mature character—kindness, faithfulness, patience, humility, teachability, and self-control—needed for handling power responsibly.

Moreover, we are called to imitate God's modus operandi with power. How does God steward it? By *sharing* it. God the Father shares authority with us in the cultural mandate, commissioning us as royal priests. Remarkably, this commission is not withdrawn after the fall. God the Son shares his power with his disciples, sending out first the Twelve (Mk 6) and then the Seventy-Two (Lk 10) to preach and heal. Then in John 14:12 Jesus promises even more power through the Holy Spirit to his future disciples (that includes us!) and predicts that we will do "even greater things."

The application of this is that amid power disparities in our broken world, those with relatively more are called to avoid looking down on those with less. This is especially important in any ministry that bridges socioeconomic divides. "We are called to see the poor and the dispossessed as more than just poor, dispossessed, or powerless. We are called to see their potential, their dignity, their latent capacities. We're called to labor *with* them. We do not impose our vocational power *on* them, or even use it *for* them. We are called to bring it *alongside* them."[2]

In short, we are called to do ministry *with*, not *for* or *to* people. This requires embracing both our authority and our vulnerability.[3] It means eschewing paternalism. As we serve humbly as royal priests, we will need to direct our authority in ways that reduce others' vulnerability and restore their own proper authority for positive action in their lives and communities.[4]

THE MAIN TASKS AHEAD

As you move forward in enacting Jeremiah 29:7, you should expect to be involved in six main arenas of work. I will describe these six tasks, but do not offer step-by-step training for them. There's no magic manual for this labor; what I'm offering here is more of a roadmap. As I said at the outset I believe the best way congregations can undertake this work is in the context of a hands-on learning community with other congregations attempting similar local mission.[5] Such learning communities are usually led by veteran coaches knowledgeable in the practices of transformative community ministry.

1. Discipling royal priests. The body of Christ is a royal priesthood. Pastors and congregational leaders begin the work of flourishing the community outside the four walls of the church by first helping Christ-followers to understand and practice this identity within those walls. This involves the ongoing labor of seeking to embody a countercultural social ethic of agape love. This is love empowered by receiving and passing along God's love poured out to us in Christ. The church is a sign of God's reign when we as a body of believers live together in peace, lifting praise to God and honoring him by becoming living sacrifices who practice holiness, reconciliation, radical generosity, humility, and mutual servanthood. These are what N. T. Wright describes as "habits which anticipate the ultimate future" of the consummated kingdom.[6]

As there was for Old Testament Israel, there is a missional aim in this distinctive pattern of life. It is a *witness* to those outside the church, a winsome fragrance capable of attracting people to Jesus. It has that centripetal force. Yet—importantly—the life of the royal priesthood has a wider stage. Israel as a royal priesthood was meant to be "a light for the nations." In the New Testament we see that royal priests are *sent ones* (Jn 20:21). We are called by Jesus to bring "the presence of God into the wider world, carrying forward the mission of declaring God's power and rescuing acts, and beginning the work of implementing the messianic rule of Jesus in all the world."[7] We are to be a centrifugal force in the world too, moving outside in loving service that brings foretastes of renewal.

The church's discipleship work thus looks like nurturing believers as they grow in Christian character (essentially love) and as they reflect God's image in the world. Each believer has opportunities within their spheres of influence to apply the healing, restorative work of priests and the culture-making work of kings. We are agents of flourishing. We're to practice *reigning*—deploying our gifts in loving, sacrificial ways that bring flourishing to others.

In terms of the practical emphasis of this book, this will involve helping people identify the community endowment(s) in which their God-given gifts and daily callings have them laboring. Some will be more involved in the Beautiful, others more involved in the True, still others more engaged in the Prosperous, and so forth. Then, having identified the place(s) God has called them, believers will need help identifying where and how they can add to the good still present in that endowment, resist its deformations, and contribute creatively to needed re-formations. Some efforts will be individual or organic, that is, done by congregants that church leaders support and commission in their spheres of work. Other efforts will be corporate or institutional, that is, done by groups within the church or by the congregation as a whole under a shared vision promoted by church leaders.

2. Preparing for spiritual battle. God is on a mission to restore all things and has invited us to partner with him. God's enemy, Satan, is violently opposed to this work of healing and renewal. We have to be prepared for spiritual warfare. At the heart of such preparation, as the apostle Paul makes clear in his teaching, is prayer. We are to put on the full armor of God (Eph 6:10-20) and to "pray in the Spirit on all occasions" (v. 18). Prayer is vital to every missional journey. It is how we express our reliance on the Holy Spirit's equipping grace. It is how we serve in the strength that God supplies (1 Pet 4:11). It is also "a crucial means by which God's power is unleashed in healing the various forms of brokenness we seek to address in ministries."[8]

New Testament teachings warn us of the reality of evil powers and principalities. Throughout this book I've noted malformations and deformations in the six community endowments. At root these are manifestations of those powers and principalities. The demonic is real, and *it* is the true focus of our battle—not misguided neighbors, corrupt politicians, or a particular political party. Our attempts to reform that which Satan has twisted toward injustice and dehumanization will be opposed in the unseen realm. As Christ-followers who seek to be agents of flourishing we are simultaneously agents of subversion. This is because we are seeking to bring kingdom foretastes into reality, and Jesus' kingdom is subversive. It upends "the world, the flesh, and the devil." Jesus expected and met resistance. He told his followers plainly that they, too, should anticipate it. Thus, our work in trying to advance community flourishing will necessarily involve spiritual disciplines of individual and corporate prayer, fasting, lament, confessing and eschewing idols, and resisting the devil.

3. Conducting a 360-degree inventory: What has God put in your hands? Asset-based ministry starts with a comprehensive inventory of the resources God has placed in your hands.[9] In the asset mapping tool I've helped develop for Made to Flourish, we encourage church leaders to examine five kinds of assets:

- *Human capital:* the vocational power and life experiences of your congregants

- *Current programs:* the ministries that the church offers to members that could potentially be expanded/modified in ways to make them available to nonmembers

- *Financial assets:* the church's annual budget, mercy fund, endowment(s), and its ability to access loan capital

- *Physical assets:* any buildings or facilities owned by the congregation, and their associated features (e.g., kitchens, classroom space, audiovisual equipment, parking lots), its land, and the church's location

- *Relational capital:* church leaders' networks (e.g., connections to local officials, clergy networks, nonprofits, media, employers, and community leaders), church partners from prior and current ministries, and the church's reputation/credibility in the eyes of community residents

The most important asset any church has is its people. It is vital to inventory the skills, vocational expertise, platforms, networks, and influence congregants possess (what in my book *Kingdom Calling* I've called "vocational power").[10] Congregational asset mapping should also involve identifying any clusters of vocational power. For example, one congregation might discover that God has brought an unusual number of businesspeople and entrepreneurs (like Grace Chapel did). Another may find that many congregants are engaged in diverse ways in education (like Marietta Cumberland Presbyterian Church). Such findings may mean that the fellowship is particularly well-positioned to contribute to a certain endowment (as Grace Chapel has in the Prosperous).

4. Assessing the community endowments in your locality. In addition to better understanding what the Lord has put into your hands by mapping the congregation's assets, gaining knowledge of the relative strengths and weaknesses of the six endowments in your context can further help you to discern where your congregation might best deploy those assets. In 2016 the Thriving Cities Group developed a detailed "Citizen's Field Guide" to describe an approach to measuring the health of the six community endowments in a particular community or neighborhood.[11] Their approach involved

identifying some key baseline indicators, gathering demographic information, and conducting interviews with community residents and stakeholders (e.g., leaders of local nonprofit and civic organizations). Figure 17.1
shows the indicators they used for each endowment. To those I've added my
own suggestions of additional or alternative data congregational leaders
could gather.

Endowment	Baseline Indicator	Rationale for the Indicator	Additional & Alternative Indicators
The Good	Residential stability	It's linked to employment, health, finances, relationship stability	Divorce rate; percent fatherless homes; number of nonprofits
The True	HS graduation rate	It's linked to employment, civic participation, crime, physical health	Literacy rates; kindergarten readiness
The Beautiful	Percent vacant properties	It signals crime, lack of community social ties, disinvestment	Number of arts and culture organizations
The Just and Well-Ordered	Levels of violent crime	It's tied to residential stability and a host of physical and mental health issues	Trust levels between residents and police
The Prosperous	Adult labor force participation	It can indicate the number of jobless neighborhood residents who have given up job searching	Number of small businesses in neighborhood; home ownership rates
The Sustainable	Adult obesity	It's linked to multiple chronic illnesses; often linked with poverty	Number of food deserts; pollution measures

Figure 17.1. Thriving Cities baseline indicators by endowment

I realize figure 17.1 could create some anxiety among pastors. You may be
thinking, *I am not a sociologist, an urban planner, or an economist. I don't
know how to go about collecting this kind of data—nor do I see myself having
time to do so!* I have two pieces of good news for you. The first is that you
don't personally have to become an expert. The second is that you may have
some experts sitting in your pews already.

The congregational inventory should help identify members active in
each of the community endowments. These individuals may possess insights into the relative strengths and weaknesses in those endowments. They

may also have relationships with leaders in those endowments with even more insight. Such connections can be tapped to gain knowledge concerning the state of the endowment. Moreover, there may be congregants with data-collecting skills who can be tapped to gather publicly available statistics (like those noted in fig. 17.1). The point is, pastors themselves do not have to become fluent in all this. What they do need to do is embrace the commitment to gaining knowledge about their local context. We expect missionaries to do such work when we send them overseas. *Why would we assume our local ministries could be effective without similar efforts to do our homework?*

5. Discerning God's call: Who are you called to labor alongside? Congregational outreach is typically directed toward

- a particular cause (e.g., fighting payday lending)
- a particular population (e.g., military wives with children whose spouses are away on overseas active duty)
- a particular geography (e.g., the residents in the ten-block Fifeville neighborhood located a five minutes' drive from the church)

In each approach the congregation is hoping to serve a group of main stakeholders. (In the first example, the main stakeholders are people being abused by payday lenders.) There is no right or wrong approach. What your congregation ultimately decides to focus on in local ministry will be influenced by factors like your location, the makeup of the congregation, the networks you're engaged in, denominational initiatives, specific assets in the main stakeholder community that can be built on, the church's history, local partner initiatives, specific opportunities God creates, pressing issues, and insights gleaned from listening prayer, among others.

6. Mapping the community: What assets can be built on? To serve well alongside main stakeholders, an asset-based approach exhorts congregations to take time to get to know these people. It requires actively seeking to discover their gifts rather than being focused *only* on their needs. It involves developing understanding and empathy by listening well.

Given that all people are made in God's image, all have gifts and talents. All are creative in some way. All have been equipped by God for the human vocation of culture making. All are made for interdependent relationships.

Each person is unique and individual, yet each is also made for community and mutuality. The first part of community asset mapping involves discovering the assets possessed by the *individuals* you'll be serving among. This is done through interviewing or surveying individuals in the neighborhood or population group.[12]

Asset mapping will also involve identifying *associational* and *institutional* *assets* in the neighborhood (or within the main stakeholder group). These are the formal and informal value-creating organizations touching on the lives of this group. In a neighborhood-based approach they might include, for example, a residents' association and the local credit union. In a cause or population-group approach, they could include nonprofit organizations providing services to the group or an informal association of entrepreneurs from within the main stakeholder group.

CONCLUSION

Genuine commitment to seeking the peace and prosperity of one's local community involves hard work and substantial time. If you've made it this far through the book, you're clearly the kind of leader willing to make that investment. I'd like to close with two words of encouragement.

First, although difficult, pursuing ministry that genuinely makes a difference is completely plausible and doable. We know this because the church gone before has gone and done it. The strategies these Christ-followers pursued illustrate what I labeled in the introduction of this book as "institutional," "organic," and "partnership-focused" (even if the leaders of that day didn't use such language to describe their activities).

The early church—which, notably, was composed of plenty of people with limited means—exerted outsized influence in Roman society. They saved countless children by engaging in the costly and long-term investment of adoption and saved countless lives by caring for the sick during major plagues. The church in the Middle Ages built institutions like hospitals and homes for the elderly to alleviate suffering. It also spent large amounts of money underwriting great art and artists. Reformation leaders like John Calvin didn't just hand out groceries. They created systems of economic uplift, offering apprenticeships to teenaged orphans and business loans to displaced refugees. African American denominations like the AME fostered mutual aid societies, created credit unions, and built and financed scores of schools. The nineteenth-century British Evangelicals formed political coalitions that led to substantial social reforms, for instance, ending the British slave trade, improving working conditions, and building new housing and public sanitation systems. They also encouraged hundreds of pastors to start Sunday schools, bringing literacy to thousands. Their peers in America likewise organized Christ-followers to implement prison reforms, end child labor, and rescue women from sex trafficking.

In short, the saints who have gone before us contributed in major ways to the peace and prosperity of their cities. Notably, they did it from a variety of social locations, from the margins to the center of culture and places in-between. They did it sometimes with sparse resources and other times with plenty. At all times they did it through rigorous thinking, fervent prayer, strong leadership, long-term commitment, and a willingness to sacrifice and suffer. With the same ingredients we too—as individual believers and corporate churches—can be used by God to influence significant, positive change in our communities. I hope by retrieving the stories of their creativity and commitment within their time periods, I've provided some fodder for our imaginations today. The Jesus whose Spirit inspired them during the challenges they faced is the same Jesus whose Spirit can galvanize us today in facing ours.

Second, we can be encouraged by the promise God offers in Jeremiah 29:7, namely, that in seeking the shalom of others we will experience it ourselves. From a practical perspective the idea that our shalom is linked to our neighbors' well-being isn't so hard to understand. After all, we're living in the same community. If our labors help make that place safer, more beautiful, more prosperous, and healthier for our neighbors, then as residents of that same locale we, too, will experience those benefits.

Yet the verse's promise is somewhat mysterious. The work of fostering shalom for others is laborious and lengthy. It requires sacrifice; it will almost inevitably involve some tears, frustrations, and disappointments. Is that consonant with our shalom?

On this side of the consummated kingdom the answer is yes. Pain and gain go together (as any fitness guru will tell us). Indeed, sometimes the deepest joys are felt because of the sacrifices they required. A deeper sense of satisfaction arises from labor that was hard than from work that was easy.

More than this, though, this promise from God is consistent with a frequent biblical theme: life emerging from death. Jesus taught us that unless a seed goes into the ground and dies it will not bear fruit (Jn 12:24). And he showed us that the cross precedes resurrection.

Our lives as agents of flourishing in communities increasingly suspicious of our faith are built on confidence in the risen Christ. His victory makes it possible for us, exiles though we be, to relate to others in love rather than fear and to offer hospitality rather than hostility to our nonbelieving neighbors. My former pastor Greg Thompson used to say that in the culture war of ideas about who has the best definition of the good society, we need to try to *love* more than we try to *win*. "As we think about what it means to engage the city and to reimagine a civic ecology," Greg says, "we have to remember that our goal is not cultural conquest; it is to seek the common good."[13]

God will have the victory. Jesus is reigning and shall reign. These things are sure and true, an anchor of hope for us amid a society that has wandered so grossly far from authentic shalom. With this hope—and the trustworthiness of God's promise that in the city's shalom we will find our own—we can sacrificially serve our neighbors and show the watching world a glimpse of a way of life that is genuinely alluring.

ACKNOWLEDGMENTS

I AM VERY GRATEFUL to friends and colleagues who conversed with me about the ideas in this book, sharpened my thinking, and offered up prayers. Many thanks to Robert Cunningham, Matt Rusten, Barb Armacost, Ellen Merry, Charlie Self, Luke Bobo, Chuck Proudfit, Chris Robertson, Bryson Davis, Geoff Hsu, Brian Fikkert, David Bailey, Debbie Baldwin, Justin Straight, and Joshua Yates. Thanks also to Sadie Van Vranken who was both a conversation partner and a help with research and transcribing.

Special gratitude goes to Blake Schwarz and Barb McLaughlin, who each read multiple chapters and provided insightful and encouraging feedback. Blake and Barb, I am truly in your debt!

The book would have been impossible without the generous participation of the dozens of interviewees at the churches profiled. I am especially grateful to Mieko Paige, Gabe Coyle, Carol Rienstra, Karen Pearson, Don Coleman, and Chuck Proudfit for helping me connect with others in their churches and organizations.

Several dear friends contributed financially to support me in this book project. I won't name you, but you know who you are, and I hope you know how appreciative I am.

As always, Jay Hein at Sagamore Institute was unstintingly supportive of this work. How fortunate I am to have you, Jay, as a friend and colleague.

NOTES

INTRODUCTION

[1]Paul S. Williams, *Exiles on Mission: How Christians can Thrive in a Post-Christian World* (Grand Rapids, MI: Brazos, 2020), 35.

[2]Timothy Keller, "Counter-Culture for the Common Good," sermon preached at Redeemer Presbyterian Church, New York City, April 3, 2016, www.youtube.com /watch?v=p7XcnJ6K7YA.

[3]The nonnegotiables for community ministry I note in chapter seventeen (relational, holistic ministry; an asset-based approach; and stewarding power faithfully) are equally relevant to overseas ministry. Moreover, I believe that the Human Ecology Framework can be very helpful for congregational leaders engaged in ministry in global cities.

[4]See, for example, the works of Lesslie Newbigin (e.g., *The Open Secret: An Introduction to the Theology of Mission*), Christopher J. H. Wright (e.g., *The Mission of God: Unlocking the Bible's Grand Narrative*), and N. T. Wright (e.g., *Surprised by Hope: Rethinking Heaven, the Resurrection, and the Mission of the Church*).

[5]Michael W. Goheen, *The Church and Its Vocation: Lesslie Newbigin's Missionary Ecclesiology* (Grand Rapids, MI: Baker Academic, 2018), 7.

[6]Christopher J. H. Wright, *The Mission of God: Unlocking the Bible's Grand Narrative* (Downers Grove, IL: IVP Academic, 2006), 51.

[7]Lesslie Newbigin, *The Good Shepherd: Meditations on Christian Ministry in Today's World* (Grand Rapids, MI: Eerdmans, 1977), 67.

[8]Craig G. Bartholomew and Michael W. Goheen, *The Drama of Scripture: Finding Our Place in the Biblical Story*, 2nd ed. (Grand Rapids, MI: Baker Academic, 2014), 232.

[9]Herman Bavinck, "Common Grace," trans. R. C. Van Leeuwen, *Calvin Theological Journal* 24 (1989): 59-61, quoted in Timothy Keller, *Center Church* (Grand Rapids, MI: Zondervan, 2012), 198.

[10]Darrell L. Guder, ed., *Missional Church: A Vision for the Sending of the Church in North America* (Grand Rapids, MI: Eerdmans, 1998), 228, 15, 98.

[11]Wright, *Mission of God*, 62-63.

[12]Albert Wolters, *Creation Regained: Biblical Basis for a Reformational Worldview*, 2nd ed. (Grand Rapids, MI: Eerdmans, 2005), 9.

[13]James Davison Hunter, *To Change the World: The Irony, Tragedy, and Possibility of Christianity in the Late Modern World* (New York: Oxford University Press, 2010), 4.

[14]Gregory Thompson, "The Church in Our Time: Nurturing Congregations of Faithful Presence," *New City Commons*, October 2011, 9-12.

[15]The mission of royal priests involves blessing neighbors far and near, but in this volume I am restricting my focus to local community mission. By doing so I am not saying that this focus trumps our involvement overseas. I believe US churches should be vitally engaged in supporting the global church and sharing our considerable wealth generously in ways that empower materially poor people and victims of oppression abroad.

[16]Yates and his colleagues first developed the framework in 2012 at the University of Virginia's Institute for Advanced Studies in Culture. Yates continues to elaborate the framework at Duke University's Ormond Center for Thriving Congregations and Communities. For a technical articulation of the framework see "Human Ecology and Human Flourishing," Values and Human Flourishing Conference, Yale University, March 24-26, 2017. For a layman's introduction see the Human Ecology video at https://thrivingcitiesgroup.com/whiteboard-video.

[17]I am honored to be part of the training faculty for the MTF/Chalmers Incubator.

[18]David Kinnaman, *unChristian: What a New Generation Really Thinks About Christianity . . . And Why It Matters* (Grand Rapids, MI: Baker, 2007), 11.

[19]The phrase is Charles Taylor's. See James K. A. Smith, *How (Not) to Be Secular: Reading Charles Taylor* (Grand Rapids, MI: Eerdmans, 2014), viii.

1. ALL ABOUT FLOURISHING

[1]Art Lindsley, "The Biblical Definition of Flourishing," Institute for Faith, Work, and Economics, June 6, 2013, https://tifwe.org/the-biblical-definition-of-flourishing.

[2]Much of the introduction to this chapter overlaps with Amy Sherman, "Flourishing: What Is Good for Us?" in *Economic Wisdom for Churches*, ed. Adam Joyce and Greg Forster (Deerfield, IL: Oikonomia Network, 2017). Used by permission.

[3]Miroslav Volf, "Human Flourishing," in *Renewing the Evangelical Mission*, ed. Richard Lints (Grand Rapids, MI: Eerdmans, 2013), 13-30.

[4]Volf, "Human Flourishing," 17.

[5]It's important to look at the *ought* because the *is* certainly seems to show that there's far more misery these days than flourishing. Throughout the world, for example, many of our Christian brothers and sisters suffer persecution and poverty. If flourishing is about personal experiential satisfaction (which Westerners tend to assume requires a certain level of material comfort as well as individual freedom), then plenty of Christ-followers globally are not flourishing. Yet, if you have had the privilege of international travel to

meet some of these believers, as I have had, you've likely noticed that they possessed rich community and a joy not contingent on their external circumstances.

[6]Andy Crouch, *Playing God: Redeeming the Gift of Power* (Downers Grove, IL: Inter-Varsity Press, 2013), 33.

[7]I'm indebted to N. T. Wright, *The Day the Revolution Began* (San Francisco: HarperOne, 2016), 86, for this idea, though his discussion is a little different.

[8]One impediment, though, to diligently obeying those road signs is that it can seem in this fallen world that the unrighteous ignore them and still seem to win the day. David cries out in Psalm 37:35, "I have seen a wicked and ruthless man flourishing like a luxu-riant, native tree." Asaph confessed that he was envious of "the arrogant when I saw the prosperity of the wicked" (Ps 73:3). However, the Bible assures us that the day of the wicked is short. Ultimately, justice will prevail, the evildoer will be undone, and only the good will endure into eternity. Like the writer of Psalm 92, we need to learn to move from our complaints about the temporary triumphs of the wicked to remembering that while "they will be destroyed forever" (v. 7), the righteous "will flourish like a palm tree . . . They will still bear fruit in old age, they will stay fresh and green" (vv. 12-14).

[9]"Well-being . . . for the secularist or non-believer," Dallas Willard has observed, "is a matter of the satisfaction of our natural desires, focused mainly upon our bodies and our social relations." See Willard, "Economic Wisdom and Human Flourishing: Well-being and the Fruits of the Spirit" (lecture, Oikonomia Network's faculty retreat, January 2013), https://oikonomianetwork.org/2013/04/willard-on-wisdom/.

[10]Willard, "Economic Wisdom and Human Flourishing."

[11]Mark Sayers, *Disappearing Church: From Cultural Relevance to Gospel Resilience* (Chicago: Moody Publishers, 2016), 16.

[12]Willard, "Economic Wisdom and Human Flourishing."

[13]See G. K. Beale, *The Temple and the Church's Mission* (Downers Grove, IL: IVP Academic, 2004).

[14]Brian Fikkert and Kelly Kapic, *Becoming Whole: Why the Opposite of Poverty Isn't the American Dream* (Chicago: Moody Publishers, 2019), 138; emphasis added.

[15]Wright, *Day the Revolution Began*, 77-80.

[16]N. T. Wright, *After You Believe: Why Christian Character Matters* (San Francisco: HarperOne, 2010), 76.

[17]Wright, *Day the Revolution Began*, 79.

[18]Wright, *After You Believe*, 81.

[19]N. T. Wright, *How God Became King: The Forgotten Story of the Gospels* (San Francisco: HarperOne, 2012), 73-74.

[20]In another example of God's great mercy, eventually the exiles are brought back from foreign lands and the temple is rebuilt.

[21]Michael W. Goheen, *The Church and Its Vocation: Lesslie Newbigin's Missionary Eccle-siology* (Grand Rapids, MI: Baker Academic, 2018), 32.

[22]Goheen, *Church and Its Vocation*, 32.

[23]Wright, *After You Believe*, 78.

[24]For example, frameworks focusing on individual happiness or well-being, such as "The Flourishing Scale" (see E. Diener et al., "New Measures of Well-Being: Flourishing and Positive and Negative Feelings," *Social Indicators Research* 39 (2009): 247-66) or those limited to economic indicators such as per capita income.

[25]Al Wolters, "Creation," *Comment*, March 1, 2010, www.cardus.ca/comment/article /creation.

[26]Albert Wolters, *Creation Regained: Biblical Basis for a Reformational Worldview*, 2nd ed. (Grand Rapids, MI: Eerdmans, 2005), 16.

[27]Wolters, *Creation Regained*, 32. Wolters believes that since all people are created in God's image, they "have an intuitive sense of normative standards for conduct" (see p. 29).

[28]Wolters, *Creation Regained*, 72-73.

[29]Wolters, *Creation Regained*, 72-73.

[30]Wolters, *Creation Regained*, 75.

[31]See Goheen's postscript in Wolters, *Creation Regained*, 121.

2. THE GOOD

[1]Tim Keller, "NPPB 2018 - Revd Dr Tim Keller - What Can Christianity Offer Our Society in the Twenty-First Century?" Christians in Parliament, YouTube, June 22, 2018, www.youtube.com/watch?v=AkcouxJE6o4.

[2]Keller, "What Can Christianity Offer Our Society?"

[3]Gerhard Lenski, *The Religious Factor: A Sociological Study of Religion's Impact on Politics, Economics, and Family Life* (Garden City, NY: Doubleday, 1961), 309.

[4]Thriving Cities, "Project Brief," Institute for Advanced Studies in Culture, Summer 2015, https://static1.squarespace.com/static/5a0f45fad74cff16c9f6e45e/t/5b858656b8a0 45493d184307/1535477334611/TCP_ProjectBrief_July2015_print+FINAL+7.27 .15+%281%29.pdf.

[5]Thriving Cities, "Citizen's Field Guide," Institute for Advanced Studies in Culture, August 11, 2016, https://static1.squarespace.com/static/5a0f45fad74cff16c9f6e45e/t/5b5 0fa90562fa718f6ca57b1/1532033690754/2016.08.11_Field+Guide.pdf.

[6]Thriving Cities, "Citizen's Field Guide," 53.

[7]Thriving Cities, "Citizen's Field Guide," 53.

[8]Thriving Cities, "Project Brief," 7.

[9]Here we must acknowledge with great lament that all parts of the church have not always defended the essential, God-given dignity of all persons, such as Native Americans and African Americans. Tragically, in some cases church officials were thought leaders arguing *against* the essential equality of all human beings. See Jemar Tisby, *The Color of Compromise: The Truth About the American Church's Complicity in Racism* (Grand Rapids, MI: Zondervan, 2019).

[10]Christopher J. H. Wright, *Old Testament Ethics for the People of God* (Downers Grove, IL: IVP Academic, 2004), 49-50; emphasis added.

[11]Wright, *Old Testament Ethics for the People of God*, 50.

[12]In composing this section, I was aided by the good teaching of Miles Van Pelt, Craig Blomberg, and Thomas Schreiner, "Lecture 9: The Ethics of the Kingdom of God," *Biblical Training*, accessed July 10, 2020, www.biblicaltraining.org/library/ethics-kingdom-god /biblical-theology/van-pelt-blomberg-schreiner. "Almost as much of Jesus' teaching is about how His followers should live, as about what they should believe and how they should think about God's ways with humanity," these theology professors argue.

[13]John Piper, "What Is Love?" *Desiring God*, July 28, 2015, www.desiringgod.org /interviews/what-is-love.

[14]New City Commons, quoted in *MTF Learning Community Core Curriculum: Faculty Guide* (Kansas City: Made to Flourish, 2017), 38.

[15]Van Pelt, Blomberg, and Schreiner, "Ethics of the Kingdom of God."

[16]Andy Crouch, "It's Time to Talk About Power," *Christianity Today*, October 1, 2013, www .christianitytoday.com/ct/2013/october/andy-crouch-its-time-to-talk-about-power.html.

[17]Herbert Schlossberg, *The Silent Revolution and the Making of Victorian England* (Columbus: Ohio State University Press, 2000), 288-89.

[18]Brian Tierney, *The Idea of Natural Rights* (Grand Rapids, MI: Eerdmans, 1997).

[19]Alvin J. Schmidt, *How Christianity Changed the World* (Grand Rapids, MI: Zondervan, 2004), 53.

[20]Schmidt, *How Christianity Changed the World*, 59.

[21]Kevin DeYoung, "The First Sexual Revolution: The Triumph of Christian Morality in the Roman Empire," Gospel Coalition, September 9, 2019, www.thegospelcoalition.org /blogs/kevin-deyoung/first-sexual-revolution-triumph-christian-morality-roman -empire.

[22]Schmidt, *How Christianity Changed the World*, 63.

[23]Schmidt, *How Christianity Changed the World*, 65.

[24]Rodney Stark, *The Rise of Christianity: How the Obscure, Marginal Jesus Movement Became the Dominant Religious Force in the Western World in a Few Centuries* (San Francisco: HarperSanFrancisco, 1997), 104.

[25]"The Impact of Christianity: What If Jesus Had Never Been Born?" *FaithFacts*, accessed January 30, 2020, www.faithfacts.org/christ-and-the-culture/the-impact-of -christianity#Marriage-and-Family.

[26]Peter Brown, *The Body and Society: Men, Women and Sexual Renunciation in Early Christianity* (New York: Columbia University Press, 1988), 148.

[27]M. Cathleen Caveny, "The Order of Widows: What the Early Church Can Teach Us About Older Women and Health Care," *Journal of Christian Bioethics* 11, no. 1 (2005): 11-34.

[28]Caveny, "Order of Widows," 16. Caveny draws here on B. B. Thurston, *The Widows: A Woman's Ministry in the Early Church* (Minneapolis: Fortress Press, 1989), 104-5.

[29]Caveny, "Order of Widows," 17-18.

[30]Eventually, *sati* was outlawed in 1829 by the Christian governor-general William Bentinck. See Evangeline Anderson-Rajkumar, "Ministry in the Killing Fields," *Christian History* 36 (1992).

[31]Nancy A. Hardesty, *Women Called to Witness: Evangelical Feminism in the Nineteenth Century* (Knoxville: University of Tennessee Press, 1999), x.

[32]Keith E. Melder, *Beginnings of Sisterhood: The American Women's Rights Movement, 1800-1850* (New York: Schocken Books, 1977), 39.

[33]Kyle Harper, *From Shame to Sin: The Christian Transformation of Sexual Morality in Late Antiquity* (Cambridge, MA: Harvard University Press, 2016).

[34]Schmidt, *How Christianity Changed the World*, 98.

[35]Schmidt, *How Christianity Changed the World*, 99.

[36]J. P. V. D. Balsdon, *Roman Women: Their History and Habits* (New York: John Day, 1963), 276.

[37]Schmidt, *How Christianity Changed the World*, 111.

[38]Stark, *Rise of Christianity*, 109.

[39]Stark, *Rise of Christianity*, 105.

[40]Susan Mobley, "The Reformation and the Reform of Marriage: Historical Views and Background for Today's Disputes," *Issues in Christian Education* 48, no. 3 (Summer 2015), https://issues.cune.edu/the-lgbt-disputes-teaching-and-practice-in-the -church-2/the-reformation-and-the-reform-of-marriage-historical-views-and -background-for-todays-disputes/.

[41]Mobley, "The Reformation and the Reform of Marriage."

[42]O. M. Bakke, *How Children Became Persons* (Philadelphia: Fortress Press, 2005), 9.

[43]Bakke, *How Children Became Persons*, 260.

[44]Bakke, *How Children Became Persons*, 286.

[45]Bakke, *How Children Became Persons*, 163.

[46]Bakke, *How Children Became Persons*, 163.

[47]David Z. Nowell, *Dirty Faith: Bringing the Love of Christ to the Least of These* (Bloomington, MN: Bethany House, 2014), 74.

[48]Anne E. Lester, "Lost but Not Yet Found: Medieval Foundlings and their Care in Northern France, 1200-1500," *Journal of the Western Society for French History* 35 (2007), https://quod.lib.umich.edu/w/wsfh/0642292.0035.001/—lost-but-not-yet -found-medieval-foundlings-and-their-care?rgn=main;view=fulltext.

[49]Lita Linzer Schwartz and Natalie K. Isser, *Endangered Children: Homicide and Other Crimes* (Boca Raton, FL: CRC Press, 2012), 35.

[50]The Christian adoption movement has made serious mistakes, though, and has been criticized for adopting out children who were not truly orphans. Criticism has led to significant change through which Christian groups have become increasingly engaged in efforts to support destitute families so that they do not place their children in

institutional care. Jedd Medefind of the Christian Alliance for Orphans says that the movement now seeks "to do all possible to preserve and reunify struggling families and to promote local adoption in developing countries." See Kathryn Joyce, "The Trouble with the Christian Adoption Movement," *New Republic*, January 11, 2016, https:// newrepublic.com/article/127311/trouble-christian-adoption-movement.

[51]Sarah Eekhoff Zylstra, "How Foster Care Became a Christian Priority—Just in Time," Gospel Coalition, September 24, 2018, www.thegospelcoalition.org/article/how -foster-care-became-christian-priority-just-time.

[52]Zylstra, "How Foster Care Became a Christian Priority."

[53]Élie Halévy, *The Triumph of Reform 1830–1841*, vol. 3, *A History of the English People in the Nineteenth Century*, trans. E. I. Watkin (New York: Barnes & Noble, 1961), 110.

[54]"Child Labour," National Archives, accessed August 5, 2021, www.nationalarchives.gov .uk/pathways/citizenship/struggle_democracy/childlabour.htm.

[55]Sheena Hastings, "Factory King Who Battled to Free Child Slaves," *Yorkshire Post*, December 12, 2012, www.yorkshirepost.co.uk/news/analysis/factory-king-who-battled -to-free-child-slaves-1-5214596.

[56]"Lord Ashley, Earl of Shaftesbury," *Spartacus Educational*, accessed January 30, 2020, https://spartacus-educational.com/IRashley.htm.

[57]Schlossberg, *Silent Revolution*, 270.

[58]George Kitson Clark, quoted in Schlossberg, *Silent Revolution*, 235.

3. A STRATEGY FOR CULTIVATING THE GOOD

[1]"The Hannahs: A Marriage Healed," Philanthropy Roundtable, accessed February 5, 2020, www.philanthropyroundtable.org/home/programs/culture-of-freedom/the -hannah-s-a-marriage-healed.

[2]Lee Habeeb, "The Incredible Success Story Behind County's Plummeting Divorce Rate Should Inspire Us All," *Newsweek*, July 26, 2019, www.newsweek.com/incredible-success -story-behind-one-countys-plummeting-divorce-rate-should-inspire-us-all-1451188.

[3]Joe Queenan, "Where Good Marriages Go to Die," *Wall Street Journal*, April 4, 2014, www .wsj.com/articles/the-cities-with-the-highest-divorce-rates-1396658920?tesla=y.

[4]"Communio at Work: Divorce Rate Drops 24% in Jacksonville," Communio, accessed February 6, 2020, https://communio.org/impact/communio-at-work-divorce-drops -28-in-jacksonville .

[5]John Stonestreet, "The Church Really Can Strengthen Marriage," *BreakPoint*, December 2, 2019, www.breakpoint.org/the-church-really-can-strengthen-marriage.

[6]W. Bradford Wilcox, quoted in "Communio at Work."

[7]Habeeb, "Incredible Success Story."

[8]W. Bradford Wilcox, Spencer James, and Wendy Wang, "Declining Divorce in Jacksonville: Did the Culture of Freedom Initiative Make a Difference?" Institute for Family Studies, April 2018, 2, https://ifstudies.org/ifs-admin/resources/ifscofjacksonvillereportfinal.pdf.

⁹"Marriage Expert Provides JAX Case Study," Communio, accessed February 6, 2020, https://communio.org/impact/communio-at-work-divorce-drops-28-in -jacksonville.

¹⁰JP DeGance, quoted in Alysse ElHage, "JP DeGance on Jacksonville's Divorce Decline: 5 Questions With Family Studies," Institute for Family Studies, October 18, 2019, https:// ifstudies.org/blog/jp-de-gance-on-jacksonvilles-divorce-decline-5-questions-with -family-studies.

¹¹DeGance, quoted in ElHage, "JP DeGance on Jacksonville's Divorce Decline."

¹²DeGance, quoted in ElHage, "JP DeGance on Jacksonville's Divorce Decline."

¹³DeGance, quoted in ElHage, "JP DeGance on Jacksonville's Divorce Decline."

¹⁴Wilcox, James, and Wang, "Declining Divorce in Jacksonville," 7.

¹⁵Wilcox, James, and Wang, "Declining Divorce in Jacksonville," 8.

¹⁶Benjamin Scafidi, *The Taxpayer Costs of Divorce and Unwed Childbearing: First-Ever Estimates for the Nation and All Fifty States* (New York: Institute for American Values and Georgia Family Council, 2008), 5, https://fluxconsole.com/files/item/441/56084 /Taxpayer-Costs-of-Divorce-and-Unwed-Childbearing.pdf.

¹⁷W. Bradford Wilcox, *Why Marriage Matters: 26 Conclusions from the Social Sciences* (New York: Institute for American Values, 2005), 10-11.

¹⁸W. Bradford Wilcox, "Can We Strengthen Marriage? Lessons from the Culture of Freedom Initiative in Jacksonville, Florida," Jacksonville, Florida, October 18, 2019, www.youtube.com/watch?v=WWngQBQZyUs.

¹⁹W. Bradford Wilcox, telephone interview with the author, March 26, 2020.

²⁰Wilcox, James, and Wang, "Declining Divorce in Jacksonville," 10-11.

²¹Churches are good for marriage. A study by Tyler J. Vander Weele of Harvard, for ex-ample, showed that couples who attend church together have a 47 percent less chance of divorcing. This is due to the sacred view of marriage most churches promote, their preaching against adultery, their marriage-related resources and ministries, and the support couples can gain from each other. See Bob Allen, "Study Links Church Atten-dance with Marriage Stability," *Baptist News Global*, November 29, 2016, https:// baptistnews.com/article/study-links-church-attendance-with-marriage-stability/# .XjxIbWhKhnK.

²²Wilcox, James, and Wang, "Declining Divorce in Jacksonville," 6.

²³This and subsequent quotes except as noted are from the author's telephone interview with Richard Albertson, founder and president, Live the Life Ministries, February 11, 2020.

²⁴DeGance, quoted in ElHage, "JP DeGance on Jacksonville's Divorce Decline."

²⁵Stonestreet, "Church Really Can Strengthen Marriage."

²⁶W. Bradford Wilcox and Alysse ElHage, "How Baptists and Catholics Together Helped Save Thousands of Florida Marriages," *Christianity Today*, October 17, 2019, www .christianitytoday.com/ct/2019/october-web-only/marriage-how-baptists-catholics-helped-florida-couples.html.

[27]This and subsequent quotes except as noted are from the author's telephone interview with Mieko Paige, Marriage and Family Program Manager, Live the Life Ministries, July 9, 2020.

[28]Kiley Crossland, "Fixing the Marriage Crisis," *World*, November 2019, https://world .wng.org/content/fixing_the_marriage_crisis.

[29]John Stonestreet, "Strengthening Marriages Through the Church: An Interview with J.P. DeGance," *BreakPoint*, December 2, 2019, www.breakpoint.org/strengthening -marriages-through-the-church.

[30]DeGance, quoted in Stonestreet, "Strengthening Marriages Through the Church."

[31]DeGance, quoted in ElHage, "JP DeGance on Jacksonville's Divorce Decline."

[32]The information here and subsequent quotes from Wayne Lanier are from the author's telephone interview with Lanier on July 30, 2020.

[33]This and subsequent quotes from Julian are from the video, "Julian Cano: Laying a Foundation for a Healthy Marriage," Philanthropy Roundtable, accessed May 20, 2020, www .philanthropyroundtable.org/home/programs/culture-of-freedom/julians-story.

[34]Scott Grogan, quoted in "Julian Cano: Laying a Foundation for a Healthy Marriage."

[35]Stoica, quoted in "Marriage Expert Provides JAX Case Study."

[36]This and subsequent quotes except as noted are from the author's telephone interview with Barbara Handzel, volunteer leader, Marriage Ministry Team, Resurrection Catholic Church, March 18, 2020.

[37]Scott Braithwaite, quoted in Lauren Hanson, "Premarital Counseling Can Decrease Divorce Rates, Psychologist Says," *Daily Universe*, July 6, 2017, https://universe.byu .edu/2017/07/06/premarital-counseling-can-decrease-divorce-rates-psychologist-says/.

[38]See T. Futris et al., "The Impact of PREPARE on Engaged Couples: Variations by Delivery Format," *Journal of Couple & Relationship Therapy* 10, no. 1 (January 2011): 69-86.

[39]Scott Stanley et al., "Premarital Education, Marital Quality, and Marital Stability: Findings from a Large, Random Household Survey," *Journal of Family Psychology* 20, no. 1 (2006): 117-26.

[40]Jan Johnson, "How Churches Can Be Truly Pro-Family," *Christianity Today*, February 6, 1995, https://janjohnson.org/how-churches-can-be-truly-pro-family/.

[41]Michael J. McManus, "How to Cut the Divorce Rate," *Ethics & Religion*, September 21, 2017, https://ethicsandreligion.com/columns/2017/C1882.htm.

[42]Paul James Birch, Stan E. Weed, and Joseph Olsen, "Assessing the Impact of Community Marriage Policies on County Divorce Rates," *Family Relations* 53, no. 5 (October 2004): 495-503.

[43]"Marriage Is the Most Urgent Gap Ministry for the Church," Communio, accessed August 12, 2020, https://communio.org/facts.

[44]"A Creative Way to Advance Good," *Q Ideas*, accessed August 12, 2020, https://qideas .org/qmoments/a-creative-way-to-advance-good.

[45]W. Bradford Wilcox, telephone interview with the author, March 26, 2020.

[46]JP DeGance, quoted in "A Creative Way to Advance Good."

4. THE TRUE

[1]Tim Rogers, quoted in Jeff Hawes, "Literacy Teacher Actually Employed by a Church," *Associated Press*, March 31, 2018, https://apnews.com/38b07bb550d84b4b97ef79c9dc8 6d2ee.

[2]Rogers, quoted in Hawes, "Literacy Teacher Actually Employed by a Church."

[3]Thriving Cities, "Project Brief," Institute for Advanced Studies in Culture, Summer 2015, https://static1.squarespace.com/static/5a0f45fad74cff16c9f6e45e/t/5b858656b8a04 5493d184307/1535477334611/TCP_ProjectBrief_July2015_print+FINAL+7.27.15+%281 %29.pdf

[4]Daniel Goleman, *Social Intelligence: The New Science of Human Relationships* (New York: Bantam Books, 2006), 4.

[5]Goleman, *Social Intelligence*, 4.

[6]"What Is literacy?" National Literacy Trust, accessed September 17, 2020, https:// literacytrust.org.uk/information/what-is-literacy.

[7]"The Reality of Literacy in America," Barbara Bush Foundation for Family Literacy, accessed September 16, 2020, www.barbarabush.org/why-literacy.

[8]Meghan Cox Gurdon, *The Enchanted Hour: The Miraculous Power of Reading Aloud in the Age of Distraction* (New York: Harper, 2019), xiv.

[9]Donald J. Hernandez, "Double Jeopardy: How Third Grade Reading Skills and Poverty Influence High School Graduation," Annie E. Casey Foundation, 2012, https://eric .ed.gov/?id=ED518818.

[10]Amy Rea, "How Serious Is America's Literacy Problem?" *Library Journal*, April 29, 2020, www.libraryjournal.com/?detailStory=How-Serious-Is-Americas-Literacy -Problem.

[11]Duane Litfin, quoted in Justin Taylor, "10 Ideas Embedded in the Slogan, 'All Truth Is God's Truth,'" Gospel Coalition, May 18, 2015, www.thegospelcoalition.org/blogs /justin-taylor/10-ideas-embedded-in-the-slogan-all-truth-is-gods-truth/.

[12]Cornelius Plantinga Jr., "Educating for Shalom," *Expositions* 9, no. 1 (2015): 80.

[13]Plantinga, "Educating for Shalom," 80-81.

[14]While parents are a child's first educators, others in the covenant community also play a role—and not only in the education of children. Older adult believers are called to invest in younger adult Christians. This idea of intergenerational transfer of wisdom is picked up in the New Testament. For example, in Titus 2:3-5 Paul encourages his protégé to instruct older women to mentor younger ones in the faith. This is not to say that elders are *guaranteed* to be wiser than younger people. Jesus himself upended much conventional thinking about children when he proclaimed that childlikeness was the doorway into his kingdom (Mt 18:3). But the basic assumption of Scripture is that people who love God gain wisdom along the journey of life; therefore, those further along in years have a responsibility to share their lessons learned with the next generation.

[15]Jesus was not only a learner, of course. He was also a teacher. He followed the rabbinic traditions of calling disciples—learners—to himself. He went about teaching and healing (Mt 9:35). He taught the disciples and the crowds and instructed in the synagogues. He mostly talked about the kingdom of God. He also taught about money and leadership and conflict resolution. He also taught by doing. By allowing Mary to sit at his feet and commending her for doing so, he showed that women as well as men are capable of learning. By crossing boundaries of class, religion, and gender, he taught that all people have dignity. Jesus, in sum, was both educated and an educator.

[16]Trent C. Butler, "Education in Bible Times," *Holman Bible Dictionary*, accessed September 14, 2020, www.studylight.org/dictionaries/hbd/e/education-in-bible-times.html.

[17]Brian G. Chilton, "The Education of Jesus of Nazareth," *Christian Post*, May 5, 2019, www.christianpost.com/voices/the-education-of-jesus-of-nazareth.html.

[18]John Oakes, "Were People Literate in the Time of Jesus?" *Evidence for Christianity*, December 4, 2005, https://evidenceforchristianity.org/were-people-literate-in-the-time-of-jesus-r. Oakes reviews the scholarly work of Professor Meir Bar-Ilan, who has estimated the literacy rate was only 1 percent.

[19]If God's kingly rule is understood "only as the history of salvation and the great events of redemption, then indeed it is hard to see the place of wisdom. But once one acknowledges that Yahweh the royal redeemer is also the Creator, a new and richer way of understanding wisdom becomes possible." Craig G. Bartholomew and Ryan P. O'Dowd, *Old Testament Wisdom Literature: A Theological Introduction* (Downers Grove, IL: InterVarsity Press, 2011), 290-91.

[20]Craig G. Bartholomew and David J. H. Beldman, eds., *Hearing the Old Testament: Listening for God's Address* (Grand Rapids, MI: Eerdmans, 2012), 330.

[21]Abraham Kuyper, quoted in Dennis Johnson, "Spiritual Antithesis: Common Grace, and Practical Theology," Westminster Seminary California, January 1, 2002, https://wscal.edu/resource-center/spiritual-antithesis-common-grace-and-practical-theology.

[22]Herman Bavinck, *Reformed Dogmatics*, vol. 2, *God and Creation*, trans. John Vriend (Grand Rapids, MI: Baker, 2004), 209-10.

[23]Francis A. Schaeffer, *Escape from Reason*, in *The Francis A. Schaeffer Trilogy: Three Essential Books in One Volume* (Wheaton, IL: Crossway, 1990), 218.

[24]Timothy Keller, "Late Modern or Post-Modern?" Gospel Coalition, October 6, 2010, www.thegospelcoalition.org/article/late-modern-or-post-modern.

[25]Keller, "Late Modern or Post-Modern?"

[26]Jean-François Lyotard, *The Postmodern Condition: A Report on Knowledge* (Minneapolis: University of Minnesota Press, 1984), xxiv.

[27]Carlos Aguilar et al., "The Antimoderns," *Christianity Today*, November 13, 2000, www.christianitytoday.com/ct/2000/november13/7.74.html.

[28]Timothy Keller, "A Biblical Critique of Secular Justice and Critical Theory," *Life in the Gospel*, August 2020, https://quarterly.gospelinlife.com/a-biblical-critique-of-secular-justice-and-critical-theory.

[29]Nicole Baker Fulgham, *Educating All God's Children: What Christians Can—and Should—Do to Improve Public Education for Low-Income Kids* (Grand Rapids, MI: Brazos, 2013), 15.

[30]Robert Hanna et al., "Comparable but Unequal," Center for American Progress, March 11, 2015, www.americanprogress.org/issues/education-k-12/reports/2015/03/11/107985/comparable-but-unequal.

[31]Linda Darling Hammond, "Unequal Opportunity: Race and Education," Brookings Institution, March 1, 1998, www.brookings.edu/articles/unequal-opportunity-race-and-education.

[32]Alana Semuels, "Good School, Rich School; Bad School, Poor School," *Atlantic*, August 25, 2016, www.theatlantic.com/business/archive/2016/08/property-taxes-and-unequal-schools/497333.

[33]Ted Williams III, "Why Should Christians Care about Public Education?" *Capital Commentary*, June 22, 2012, www.cpjustice.org/public/capital_commentary/article/546.

[34]"Public Schools: Christians Are Part of the Solution," Barna Group, August 26, 2014, www.barna.com/research/public-schools-christians-are-part-of-the-solution.

[35]"Public Schools: Christians are Part of the Solution."

[36]Jemar Tisby, "Public Education Is a Matter of Biblical Justice," *Equip*, February 11, 2020, www.equip.org/article/christians-and-public-education-a-matter-of-biblical-justice.

[37]Tisby, "Public Education Is a Matter of Biblical Justice."

[38]"History of Publishing: Books in the Early Christian Era," *Britannica*, accessed November 14, 2020, www.britannica.com/topic/publishing/Books-in-the-early-Christian-era.

[39]*Britannica*, "History of Publishing."

[40]Harvey J. Graff, *The Legacies of Literacy* (Bloomington: Indiana University Press, 1987), 30.

[41]Richard Gawthorpe and Gerald Strauss, "Protestantism and Literacy in Early Modern Germany," *Past & Present* 43, no. 1 (August 1984): 31-55.

[42]Karen Stetina, "What the Reformation Did and Didn't Do for Women," Good Book Blog, October 31, 2017, www.biola.edu/blogs/good-book-blog/2017/what-the-reformation-did-and-didn-t-do-for-women.

[43]Robert Woodberry, "The Missionary Roots of Liberal Democracy," *American Political Science Review*, May 2012, 249-51.

[44]Robert Woodberry, quoted in Andrea Palpant Dilley, "The Surprising Discovery About Those Colonialist, Proselytizing Missionaries," *Christianity Today,* January 8, 2014; emphasis added.

[45]"Religion and Education Around the World," Pew Research Center, December 13, 2016, www.pewforum.org/2016/12/13/religion-and-education-around-the-world.

[46]Rodney Stark, *The Victory of Reason: How Christianity Led to Freedom, Capitalism, and the Western Success* (New York: Random House, 2007), xi.

[47]Tertullian, quoted in Stark, *Victory of Reason*, 7.

[48]Stark, *Victory of Reason*, 32.

[49]David Sorkin, *The Religious Enlightenment: Protestants, Jews and Catholics from London to Vienna* (Princeton, NJ: Princeton University Press, 2008), 3.

[50]Ulrich L. Lehner, "Review of David Sorkin's *The Religious Enlightenment: Protestants, Jews and Catholics from London to Vienna*," *Theology Faculty Research and Publications*, January 1, 2012, 160.

[51]"The Epistle of Ignatius to the Philadelphians," in *The Ante-Nicene Fathers*, ed. Alexander Roberts and James Donaldson (Grand Rapids, MI: Eerdmans, 1981), 1:81.

[52]W. M. Ramsay, *The Church in the Roman Empire Before A.D. 170* (London: Hodder & Stoughton, 1893), 245.

[53]Alvin J. Schmidt, *How Christianity Changed the World* (Grand Rapids, MI: Zondervan, 2001), 173, 176.

[54]Schmidt, *How Christianity Changed the World*, 177.

[55]Schmidt, *How Christianity Changed the World*, 179.

[56]Peter Y. DeJong, "Calvin's Contribution to Christian Education," *Calvin's Theological Journal* 2, no. 2 (November 1967): 200.

[57]Harvey J. Graff, *The Legacies of Literacy* (Bloomington: Indiana University Press, 1987), 162-63.

[58]Semuels, "Good School, Rich School."

[59]Herbert Schlossberg, *The Silent Revolution and the Making of Victorian England* (Columbus: Ohio State University Press, 2000), 205.

[60]Schmidt, *How Christianity Changed the World*, 180-85.

[61]Schlossberg, *Silent Revolution*, 207.

[62]"Friedrich Froebel Created Kindergarten," *FroebelWeb*, accessed September 15, 2020, www.froebelweb.org.

[63]Jacques Le Goff, *Medieval Civilization* (New York: Barnes & Noble, 2000), 120.

[64]George M. Marsden, "The Soul of the American University," *First Things*, January 1991, www.firstthings.com/article/1991/01/the-soul-of-the-american-university.

[65]"College and Universities with Religious Affiliation," encyclopedia.com, September 14, 2020, www.encyclopedia.com/education/encyclopedias-almanacs-transcripts-and-maps/colleges-and-universities-religious-affiliations. The encyclopedia estimates roughly 1,000 faith-related universities and colleges. Of these, 65 are Jewish, 5 are Islamic, and 4 are Buddhist.

[66]B. Denise Hawkins, "Echoes of Faith: Church Roots Run Deep Among HBCUs," *Diverse*, July 31, 2012, https://diverseeducation.com/article/17259.

[67]John Sibley Butler, *Entrepreneurship and Self-Help Among Black Americans*, rev. ed. (Albany, NY: SUNY Press, 2005), 92. Butler also collected information on the Afro-American Baptists. By 1909 that denomination was supporting 107 schools of varying education levels and had established property worth over $600,000.

[68]William E. Montgomery, *Under Their Own Vine and Fig Tree: The African-American Church in the South, 1865–1900* (Baton Rouge: Louisiana State University Press, 1993), 148-52.

[69]"Institutions of Higher Education," African Methodist Episcopal Church, accessed August 6, 2021, http://ame-church.com/directory/institutions-of-higher-education.

[70]Mark Ward Sr., "Knowledge Puffs Up: The Evangelical Culture of Anti-Intellectualism as a Local Strategy," *Sermon Studies* 4, no. 1 (2020).

[71]Mark A. Noll, "The Evangelical Mind Today," *First Things*, October 2004, www.firstthings.com/article/2004/10/the-evangelical-mind-today.

[72]Noll, "Evangelical Mind Today."

[73]Jonathan Merritt, "Alan Jacob's Antidote to Christian Anti-Intellectualism," *Religion News Service*, October 11, 2017, https://religionnews.com/2017/10/11/alan-jacobs-christians-think.

[74]See Jemar Tisby, *The Color of Compromise: The Truth About the American Church's Complicity in Racism* (Grand Rapids, MI: Zondervan, 2019), 145. It should be noted that some scholars question whether the correlation between the rise of private school enrollment with the period of public school desegregation was linked to racism. They contend that additional factors—such as the Supreme Court's 1962 ruling to end prayer in public schools, the introduction of sex education in the classrooms, and the disruptions of busing—also played a role.

5. A STRATEGY FOR CULTIVATING THE TRUE

[1]Samuel Freedman, "Help from Evangelicals (Without Evangelizing) Meets the Needs of an Oregon Public School," *New York Times*, August 9, 2013, www.nytimes.com/2013/08/10/us/help-from-evangelicals-without-the-evangelizing.html.

[2]"BeUndivided," YouTube, February 12, 2013, www.youtube.com/watch?v=UfrSH9lnaRc.

[3]Samuel Smith, "Gang-Infested Portland School Revitalized by Church Program; Pastor Challenges America's 300,000 Churches to Help Nation's Troubled Public Schools," *Christian Post*, February 12, 2015, www.christianpost.com/news/gang-infested-portland-school-revitalized-by-church-program-pastor-challenges-americas-300000-churches-to-help-nations-troubled-public-schools.html.

[4]Smith, "Gang-Infested Portland School Revitalized."

[5]Kevin Palau, *Unlikely: Setting Aside our Differences to Live Out the Gospel* (New York: Howard Books, 2015), 88-91.

[6]"7 Years Later," *Vimeo*, accessed August 6, 2021, https://vimeo.com/146085703.

[7]All the statistics in this paragraph except where noted are from "The Condition of Education: May 2020," National Center for Education Statistics, accessed October 13, 2020, https://nces.ed.gov/programs/coe.

[8]"Low-Income and Minority Students Continue to Lag in High School Graduation Rates," *Fortune*, May 3, 2017, https://fortune.com/2017/05/03/high-school-graduation-rates-minorities.

[9]Ke Wang et al., *Indicators of School Crime and Safety: 2019* (Washington, DC: US Department of Education, 2020), 43.

[10]Wang, *Indicators of School Crime and Safety*, iv.

[11]Wang, *Indicators of School Crime and Safety*, 50.

[12]Sarah Mervosh, "How Much Wealthier Are White School Districts Than Nonwhite Ones? $23 Billion, Report Says," *New York Times*, February 27, 2019, www.nytimes.com/2019/02/27/education/school-districts-funding-white-minorities.html.

[13]Charles M. Payne, *So Much Reform, So Little Change: The Persistence of Failure in Urban Schools* (Cambridge, MA: Harvard Education Press, 2008), 192.

[14]Reggie McNeal, "Follow These 6 Tips for Successful School Partnerships," City Gospel Movements, accessed September 18, 2020, https://citygospelmovements.org/resource/partner.

[15]Nancy Mitchell, telephone interview with the author, October 18, 2019. Mitchell was serving as executive director of Caring for Kids at the time of the interview.

[16]Cathy Lorino, school social worker, Rushton Elementary School, telephone interview with the author, November 4, 2020.

[17]"America After 3 PM: Afterschool Programs in Demand," Afterschool Alliance, October 2014, www.afterschoolalliance.org/documents/AA3PM-2014/AA3PM_Key_Findings.pdf.

[18]"Principals and After-School Programs: A Survey of PreK–8 Principals," National Association of Elementary School Principals, August 2001, 12, https://files.eric.ed.gov/fulltext/ED465212.pdf.

[19]Amy L. Sherman, "Literature Review for the Barnhill Family Foundation," Sagamore Institute, 2020.

[20]This and subsequent quotes are from Cynthia Wallace, executive pastor, Bible Center Church, telephone interview with the author, November 3, 2020.

[21]This and subsequent quotes are from Kerri Clauser, telephone interview with the author, November 23, 2020.

[22]Tacumba Turner, manager, Oasis Farm and Fishery, telephone interview with the author, November 10, 2020.

[23]"Common Core's Orphaned Subjects: Music and the Arts," Best Schools, March 23, 2020, https://thebestschools.org/magazine/finearts.

[24]Jessica Hoffmann Davis, quoted in Mary Tamer, "On the Chopping Block, Again" *Harvard Ed. Magazine*, Summer 2009, www.gse.harvard.edu/news/ed/09/06/chopping-block-again.

[25]Rosa Ramirez and *National Journal*, "Arts Educational Programs Help Minorities, Low-Income Youth," *Atlantic*, November 21, 2012, www.theatlantic.com/politics/archive/2012/11/arts-educational-programs-help-minorities-lower-income-youth/429552.

[26]"Numerous studies, including those by James S. Catterall, professor at UCLA Graduate School of Education and Information Studies, find that regular participation in fine arts classes raises SAT scores by an average of 91 points and improves coordination between hemispheres of the brain." See "Common Core's Orphaned Subjects."

[27]"The Wesley Academy of Music," First United Methodist Church, accessed June 9, 2020, www.fumcfrankfort.org/wesley-academy-of-music.

[28]Larry Gordon, "Mentoring's Promise and Limits," *Atlantic*, December 14, 2016, www.theatlantic.com/education/archive/2016/12/why-some-mentors-fail/510467.

[29]Gordon, "Mentoring's Promise and Limits."

[30]Karen Pearson, executive director, Kids Hope USA, personal correspondence to the author, September 21, 2020.

[31]Steven Gutierrez, "The Impact of School-Based Mentoring on Student Achievement and School Engagement in Elementary Aged At-Risk Students: Implications for Leadership" (EdD thesis, University of Houston, May 2012), vi-vii.

[32]This and all subsequent quotes are from Lisa Douglas, Kids Hope director, Marietta Cumberland Presbyterian Church, telephone interview with the author, October 2, 2020.

[33]Brad Griffin, "Through the Zone," Fuller Youth Institute, June 12, 2006, https://fulleryouthinstitute.org/articles/through-the-zone.

[34]"Blue Nile Passage, Inc.," Abyssinian Baptist Church, accessed October 2, 2020, https://abyssinian.org/connect/affiliates/blue-nile-passage-inc.

[35]"Boys' Rite of Passage," Allen Temple Baptist Church, accessed October 3, 2020, www.allen-temple.org/ministries/community-care/boys-rite-of-passage.

[36]"Boys' Rite of Passage."

[37]"Welcome to Daughters of Imani Page," First Community AME Church, accessed October 3, 2020, www.fcame.org/daughters-of-imani.html.

[38]"College Enrollment Rates," National Center for Education Statistics, accessed September 30, 2020, https://nces.ed.gov/programs/coe/pdf/coe_cpb.pdf.

[39]See Paul Fain, "Wealth's Influence on Enrollment and Completion," *Inside Higher Ed*, May 23, 2019, www.insidehighered.com/news/2019/05/23/feds-release-broader-data-socioeconomic-status-and-college-enrollment-and-completion.

[40]Emily Tate, "Graduation Rates and Race," *Inside Higher Ed*, April 26, 2017, www.insidehighered.com/news/2017/04/26/college-completion-rates-vary-race-and-ethnicity-report-finds.

[41]Jon Marcus, "New Figures Suggest Community College Grad Rates Higher Than Thought," *Hechinger Report*, August 6, 2013, https://hechingerreport.org/new-figures-suggest-community-college-grad-rates-higher-than-thought.

[42]Emery Ailes III, quoted in Ellie Ashford, "Church Partnerships Promote Community Engagement," *Community College Daily*, February 14, 2020, www.ccdaily.com/2020/02 /church-partnerships-promote-community-engagement.

[43]Timothy Beard, quoted in Ashford, "Church Partnerships Promote Community Engagement."

[44]Jill Barshay, "Behind the Latino College Degree Gap," *Hechinger Report*, June 18, 2018, https://hechingerreport.org/behind-the-latino-college-degree-gap.

[45]Barshay, "Behind the Latino College Degree Gap."

[46]Kevin Barry, "Local Church Partners with Northwest University to Help Hispanic Students Complete Their College Degrees," *News5Cleveland*, December 2, 2019, www .news5cleveland.com/a-better-land/local-church-partners-with-northwest-university -to-help-hispanic-students-complete-their-college-degrees.

[47]Barry, "Local Church Partners with Northwest University."

[48]Karen Zeigler and Steven A. Camarota, "67.3 Million In the United States Spoke a Foreign Language at Home in 2018," Center for Immigration Studies, October 29, 2019, https://cis.org/Report/673-Million-United-States-Spoke-Foreign-Language -Home-2018#:~:text=Based%20on%20analysis%20of%20newly,the%20entire %20population%20of%20France.

[49]All information about CrossPoint Alliance Church's ESL program comes from the church's website (crosspointakron.org/esl) and the author's telephone interview with Bruce Lyman, pastor for international ministries, CrossPoint Alliance Church, September 29, 2020.

6. THE BEAUTIFUL

[1]Cody C. Delistraty, "The Beauty-Happiness Connection," *Atlantic*, August 15, 2014, www.theatlantic.com/health/archive/2014/08/the-beautyhappiness-connection /375678.

[2]Anthony O'Hear, *Philosophy in the New Century* (London: Continuum, 2001), 102.

[3]Thriving Cities, "Citizen's Field Guide," August 11, 2016, https://static1.squarespace.com /static/5a0f45fad74cff16c9f6e45e/t/5b50fa90562fa718f6ca57b1/1532033690754 /2016.08.11_Field+Guide.pdf.

[4]"What Is Placemaking?" Project for Public Spaces, accessed October 21, 2020, www.pps .org/article/what-is-placemaking.

[5]Anna Marazuela Kim et al., "Thriving Cities Endowment Brief: The Beautiful," Thriving Cities, accessed August 7, 2021, www.academia.edu/14896884/Brief_on_the_Beautiful _as_an_Endowment_of_Thriving_Cities.

[6]Eric O. Jacobsen, *The Space Between: A Christian Engagement with the Built Environment* (Grand Rapids, MI: Baker Academic, 2012), 14.

[7]Kim et al., "Thriving Cities Endowment Brief."

[8]"Why the Arts Matter," National Endowment for the Arts, September 23, 2015, www .arts.gov/stories/blog/2015/why-arts-matter. This article by staff at the National

Endowment for the Arts offers a couple dozen thoughtful reasons and undoubtedly there are even more.

[9]William A. Dyrness, *Visual Faith: Art, Theology and Worship in Dialogue* (Grand Rapids, MI: Baker Academic, 2001), 99.

[10]Makoto Fujimura, "The Function of Art," *Faith & Leadership*, May 9, 2011, https://faithandleadership.com/makoto-fujimura-function-art.

[11]Kyle Strobel, "Embracing contemplation with Kyle Strobel," *Think Biblically* (podcast), September 5, 2019, www.biola.edu/blogs/think-biblically/2019/embracing-contemplation.

[12]See Paul Evdokimov, *The Art of the Icon: A Theology of Beauty*, trans. Steven Bigham (Redondo Beach, CA: Oakwood Publications, 1990), 2.

[13]Andrew Cuneo, "Beauty Will Save the World—But Which Beauty?" *In Pursuit of Truth: A Journal of Christian Scholarship*, May 18, 2009, www.cslewis.org/journal/beauty-will-save-the-world-but-which-beauty.

[14]Given that God is an artist, it's not surprising that the Bible, his own Word, is conveyed through multiple literary forms: prose, story, poetry, and song. We see all of these on display throughout the Old Testament, particularly in the Wisdom literature. God even spoke to his people via the medium of drama. In Ezekiel 4:1-4, God gives his prophet instructions for enacting the forthcoming siege of Jerusalem. He tells Ezekiel to use clay to draw pictures and fashion miniature siegeworks and battering rams to depict his coming judgment against his wayward people. Jesus was artistic in his teaching style, employing vivid word pictures, metaphors, and symbols. He made frequent use of the parable, which is itself a literary art form that requires—like much visual art—contemplation. Peter Enns writes, "Speaking in parables is indeed similar to an artist's craft. Neither are systematic, logical arguments aimed at intellectual persuasion. Rather, they create impressions, whole new worlds of meaning intended to turn old worlds on their heads. Further, they do not always clarify, but actually can by design obscure a deeper reality. To apprehend that deeper reality, one must—like a patron facing a timeless painting—continue to seek, ponder, and meditate on what is being said. . . . Parables were Jesus' canvas for 'painting' a new vision for what life in his kingdom should look like." Peter Enns, "Jesus the Artist," BioLogos, September 28, 2012, https://biologos.org/articles/jesus-the-artist.

[15]Hans Urs von Balthasar, quoted in Gregory Wolfe, "The Wound of Beauty," *Image Journal* 56, https://imagejournal.org/article/the-wound-of-beauty.

[16]Peter Enns, "Jesus the Artist."

[17]John of Damascus, *Defense Against Those Who Oppose Holy Images*, quoted in Dan Graces, "#202: John of Damascus for Icons," Christian History Institute, accessed October 21, 2020, https://christianhistoryinstitute.org/study/module/john-of-damascus.

[18]Philip G. Ryken, *Art for God's Sake: A Call to Recover the Arts* (Phillipsburg, NJ: P&R, 2006), 42.

[19]Francis A. Schaeffer, *Art and the Bible* (Downers Grove, IL: InterVarsity Press, 2006), 90.

[20]Schaeffer, *Art and the Bible*, 90.

[21]Cornelius Plantinga, Jr., *Not the Way It's Supposed to Be: A Breviary on Sin* (Grand Rapids, MI: Eerdmans, 1995), 10.

[22]One thing that is not precisely a malformation but that is a tension concerns the relationship between the beautiful and the prosperous. In the fallen world, we face difficult choices and proximate outcomes. We can imagine property developers coming to an economically distressed community with a proposal to open a strip mall. The plans may not be particularly beautiful. (How many truly beautiful strip malls have you seen in your lifetime?) Do residents and leaders jump on the opportunity to have new businesses (and goods and services and jobs and tax-paying corporate citizens) in the neighborhood or decline the proposal because of the hit it will take in the realm of the Beautiful? There are no easy answers.

[23]N. T. Wright, *Broken Signposts: How Christianity Makes Sense of the World* (San Francisco: HarperOne, 2020), 93.

[24]Joshua LaRock, quoted in a video produced by Trinity Grace Church in New York City several years ago. Unfortunately, there's no longer a link to the video.

[25]Theodore F. Wolff, "Creating Art: It Takes More Than Just Individual Expression," *Christian Science Monitor*, February 24, 1982, www.csmonitor.com/1982/0224/022400.html.

[26]Wolff, "Creating Art."

[27]This and subsequent quotes except as noted are from Jeremiah Enna, founder of Culture House, telephone interview with the author, November 2, 2020.

[28]Daniel Siedell, "Altars to an Unknown God: Modern Art for Modern Christians," *Image* 59, accessed December 4, 2020, https://imagejournal.org/article/altars-unknown-god.

[29]Siedell, "Altars to an Unknown God."

[30]Jeffrey Spier, *Picturing the Bible: The Earliest Christian Art* (New Haven, CT: Yale University Press, 2007).

[31]Annemarie Weyl Carr, "Jeffrey Spier, Picturing the Bible: The Earliest Christian Art," *CAA.Reviews*, March 12, 2008, www.caareviews.org/reviews/1092#.X5CniNBKhnI.

[32]"Christian Art: c150–2000," *Christian Art*, accessed October 1, 2019, www.visual-arts-cork .com/christian-art.htm#christianart.

[33]"Christian Art," *Medieval Chronicles*, accessed October 21, 2020, www.medievalchronicles .com/medieval-art/christian-art.

[34]William Anderson, *The Rise of the Gothic* (Salem, NH: Salem House, 1985), 57.

[35]"Christian Art."

[36]"The Role of Beauty," Ligonier Ministries, accessed October 6, 2020, www.ligonier.org /learn/devotionals/role-beauty.

[37]Camille Paglia, "Religion and the Arts in America," *Arion* 15, no. 1 (Spring–Summer 2007): 9, www.bu.edu/arion/files/2010/03/Paglia-Religion-and-the-Art.pdf.

[38]Donald J. Grout et al., *History of Western Music* (New York: W. W. Norton, 2005), 30.

[39]Paul Henry Lang, *Music in Western Civilization* (New York: W. W. Norton, 1997), 85.

[40]Lang, *Music in Western Civilization*, 84.

[41]Edward Dickinson, *Music in the History of the Western Church* (Freiburg im Breisgau, Germany: Outlook Verlag, 2020), 76.

[42]John Bortslap, "Classical Music and Christianity," accessed October 22, 2020, http://johnborstlap.com/classical-music-and-christianity/.

[43]Homer Ulrich and Paul Pisk, *A History of Music and Musical Style* (San Diego: Harcourt, Brace & World, 1963), 26.

[44]"The Theology and Place of Music in Worship," Reformed Church in America Commission on Worship, accessed October 24, 2020, www.faithward.org/the-theology-and-place-of-music-in-worship.

[45]"Religious Music in the Later Renaissance," *Encyclopedia.com*, accessed October 22, 2020, www.encyclopedia.com/humanities/culture-magazines/religious-music-later-renaissance.

[46]"Religious Music in the Later Renaissance."

[47]Keith D. Lilly, *Urban Life in the Middle Ages, 1000–1450* (London: Red Globe, 2002), 10.

[48]Keith D. Lilly, "Cities of God? Medieval Urban Forms and Their Christian Symbolism," *Transactions* 29, no. 3 (September 2004): 296.

[49]Philip Bess, "Why I Take Architecture Students to Flanders," *Notre Dame Magazine*, April 29, 2016, https://magazine.nd.edu/stories/why-i-take-architecture-students-to-flanders.

[50]"Henry Roberts," *Oxford Reference*, accessed October 21, 2020, www.oxfordreference.com/view/10.1093/oi/authority.20110803100423905.

[51]Heather Sharps, "Elizabeth Gaskell and Sir James P. Kay-Shuttlesworth-A Literary Relationship," *Gaskell Society Journal* 11 (1997): 15-24.

[52]Octavia Hill, *Colour, Space, and Music for the People* (London: Kegan Paul, Trench, 1884), 89-90.

[53]"Octavia Hill: Her Life and Legacy," National Trust, accessed October 21, 2020, www.nationaltrust.org.uk/features/octavia-hill-her-life-and-legacy.

[54]"Horace Bushnell," Bushnell Park Foundation, accessed October 21, 2020, www.bushnellpark.org/about-2/history-2/horace-bushnell.

[55]Tony Carnes, "Central Park: The Largest Religious Art Work in New York City," *Journey Through NYC Religions*, June 17, 2019, https://nycreligion.info/central-park-largest-religious-art-work-york-city-part-2-series-god-nyc-gardens.

[56]Eric O. Jacobsen, "The New Urbanism," Baylor University, accessed October 24, 2020, www.baylor.edu/ifl/christianreflection/CitiesandTownsArticleJacobsen.pdf.

[57]Jacobsen, "New Urbanism."

[58]R. Bruce Stephenson, "John Nolen's Legacy for New Urbanism," *View* 1 (Summer 2014): 9.

[59]Robert Beevers, *The Garden City Utopia: A Critical Biography of Ebenezer Howard* (London: Palgrave Macmillan, 1988), 23.

[60]Philip Bess, *Till We Have Built Jerusalem: Architecture, Urbanism, and the Sacred* (Wilmington, DE: Intercollegiate Studies Institute, 2006), 94.

[61]Kathleen Curran Sweeney, "Building Jerusalem: Christianity and the New Urbanism," *Public Discourse*, March 30, 2017, www.thepublicdiscourse.com/2017/03/18681.

[62]Philip Bess, quoted in Conor B. Dugan, "City of God, City of Man," *Humanum* 3 (2013), https://humanumreview.com/articles/city-of-god-city-of-man.

[63]On a positive note, the past fifty years have seen a resurgence in attentiveness to the arts among (some) Evangelicals. In the 1960s and 1970s, Francis Schaeffer and Hans Rookmaaker "challenged believers to emerge from their cocoons and engage the culture, including in the arts" (Eric Gorski, "A Cultural Renaissance for the Christian Evangelical Art World," *Seattle Times*, August 4, 2007, www.seattletimes.com/news /a-cultural-renaissance-for-the-evangelical-christian-art-world). Today one can find centers for art and theology on seminary campuses, conferences on Christianity and the arts, platforms encouraging arts patronage (e.g., the By/For Project), serious Christian reflection on art (e.g., the journal *Image*), networks of academics interested in the arts (e.g., the Society for the Arts in Religious and Theological Studies), and professional guilds such as Christians in the Visual Arts and Christians in the Theatre Arts.

[64]N. T. Wright, *Surprised by Hope: Rethinking Heaven, the Resurrection, and the Mission of the Church* (New York: HarperOne, 2008), 231-32.

[65]Richard B. Hays, "Why Should We Care About the Arts?" *Faith & Leadership*, August 1, 2011, https://faithandleadership.com/richard-b-hays-why-should-we-care-about-arts.

[66]Hays, "Why Should We Care About the Arts?"

[67]Hays, "Why Should We Care About the Arts?"

[68]Denis Haack, "Review of *Visual Faith: Art, Theology & Worship in Dialogue* (William A. Dyrness, 2001)," Ransom Fellowship, July 7, 2007, https://ransomfellowship.org/article /visual-faith-art-theology-worship-in-dialogue-william-a-dyrness-2001.

[69]William A. Dyrness, quoted in Haack, "Review of *Visual Faith*."

[70]Zahnd, *Beauty Will Save the World* (Lake Mary, FL: Charisma House, 2012), xv.

7. A STRATEGY FOR CULTIVATING THE BEAUTIFUL

[1]This and subsequent quotes except as noted are from Gabe Coyle, campus pastor, Christ Community Church–Downtown Campus, telephone interview with the author, October 17, 2020.

[2]Tom Nelson is also the founder of the national pastors' network Made to Flourish.

[3]"Artistic Expressions: Explore Kansas City's Dynamic Art and Gallery Culture," *Visit KC*, accessed December 8, 2020, www.visitkc.com/visitors/things-do/arts-and-culture /art-galleries-kc.

[4]This and subsequent quotes except as noted are from Leigh Ann Dull, then-director, Four Chapter Gallery, telephone interview with the author, November 3, 2020.

[5]Formerly Campus Crusade for Christ, CRU is an interdenominational Christian ministry focused on connecting college students and others to Jesus Christ.

[6]Kelly Kruse, "My Iron Heart," *Kelly Kruse,* accessed December 7, 2020, www.kellykrusecreative.com/my-iron-heart.html.

[7]This and subsequent quotes except where noted are from Kelly Kruse, telephone interview with the author, November 17, 2020.

[8]Kelly Kruse, "My Iron Heart."

[9]This and subsequent quotes except as noted are from Jeremiah Enna, founder of Culture House, telephone interview with the author, November 2, 2020.

[10]This and subsequent quotes except as noted are from Tyler Chernesky, former associate pastor at Christ Community Church–Downtown, telephone interview with the author, October 28, 2020.

[11]This and subsequent quotes except as noted are from Sara Forsythe, volunteer director, Mission Adelante Summer Arts Camp, telephone interview with the author, November 4, 2020.

[12]Tom Nelson, personal correspondence with the author, December 20, 2020.

[13]Tom Hoopes, "Why Beauty Will Save the World and Why That's Good News Even Today," *Aleteia,* September 24, 2018, https://aleteia.org/2018/09/24/why-beauty-will-save-the-world-and-why-thats-good-news-even-today.

[14]"Home page," Proximity Project, accessed December 10, 2020, www.proximityprojectinc.com.

[15]"Home page."

[16]The project was called "Amnesia Therapy: Remembering the Future." It was done by members of a nontraditional, nondenominational church in Houston's Pleasantville neighborhood called Awakenings Movement. See Eric Harrison, "A Pastor Seeks to Revive Houston's Memory with Art," *Faith & Leadership,* June 3, 2013, https://faithandleadership.com/pastor-seeks-revive-houstons-memory-art.

[17]Lockerbie Central United Methodist Church in Indianapolis began showing documentary films more than ten years ago, inviting community members to attend and discuss issues raised. This led over time to a partnership with local artists and community advocates to create the "Earth House Collective." It is a community center located inside the church building that features a coffee shop as well as a live performance stage and seating.

[18]Mission Church in Lancaster, Pennsylvania, https://mission-church.com/.

8. THE JUST AND WELL-ORDERED

[1]Bob Linthicum, *Transforming Power: Biblical Strategies for Making a Difference in Your Community* (Downers Grove, IL: InterVarsity Press, 2003), 20-21.

[2]Guian McKee, "The Just and Well-Ordered," Thriving Cities Endowment Brief, accessed August 9, 2021, https://static1.squarespace.com/static/5a0f45fad74cff16c9f6e45e

/t/5b4faa0d562fa744561340a9/1531947534349/Endowment-Brief-The-Just-and-Well
-Ordered.pdf.

[3]Andy Crouch, *Playing God: Redeeming the Gift of Power* (Downers Grove, IL: Inter-
Varsity Press, 2013), 13.

[4]Crouch, *Playing God*, 51.

[5]Timothy Keller, *Generous Justice: How God's Grace Makes Us Just* (New York: Penguin,
2010), 3.

[6]Keller, *Generous Justice*, 4.

[7]Nicholas Wolterstorff, *Justice: Rights and Wrongs* (Princeton, NJ: Princeton University
Press, 2010), 75-76.

[8]Keller, *Generous Justice*, 10.

[9]Keller, *Generous Justice*, 11.

[10]Tim Keller, "The Beauty of Biblical Justice," *byFaith*, October 26, 2010, emphasis added,
https://byfaithonline.com/the-beauty-of-biblical-justice. Wolterstorff makes a similar
argument in *Justice: Rights and Wrongs*.

[11]Christopher J. H. Wright, *New International Biblical Commentary: Deuteronomy*
(Peabody, MA: Hendrickson, 1996), 261.

[12]Tim Keller, "What Is Biblical Justice?" *Relevant*, August 23, 2012, https://relevantmagazine
.com/god/what-biblical-justice.

[13]Bruce K. Waltke, *A Commentary on Micah* (Grand Rapids, MI: Eerdmans, 2007), 391.

[14]Barbara Armacost and Peter Enns, "Crying Out for Justice: Civil Law and the Prophets,"
in *Law and the Bible: Justice, Mercy and Legal Institutions*, eds. Robert F. Cochran Jr.
and David VanDrunen (Downers Grove, IL: InterVarsity Press, 2013), 127-28.

[15]Howard Zehr and Ted Grimsrud, "Rethinking God, Justice, and Treatment of Offenders," *Journal of Offender Rehabilitation* 35, no. 3/4 (Fall 2002): 259-285, https://
peacetheology.net/restorative-justice/rethinking-god-justice-and-treatment-of
-offenders/.

[16]Zehr and Grimsrud, "Rethinking God, Justice, and Treatment of Offenders,"
emphasis added.

[17]Friedrich Nietzsche, quoted in Crouch, *Playing God*, 46.

[18]"Structural Racism," Urban Institute, accessed December 12, 2020, www.urban.org
/features/structural-racism-america. Defending the reality of structural racism in
America is beyond the scope of this book. To learn about it, see for example Michelle Alexander, *The New Jim Crow: Mass Incarceration in the Age of Colorblindness*,
10th anniv. ed. (New York: New Press, 2020); Richard Rothstein, *The Color of Law:
A Forgotten History of How Our Government Segregated America* (New York: Liv-
eright, 2017); C. Vann Woodward, *The Strange Career of Jim Crow* (New York:
Oxford University Press, 2002); Isabelle Wilkerson, *Caste: The Origins of our Dis-
contents* (New York: Random House, 2020); Jemar Tisby, *The Color of Compromise:
The Truth About the American Church's Complicity in Racism* (Grand Rapids, MI:

Zondervan Reflective, 2019); Derrick Darby and John L. Rury, *The Color of Mind: Why the Origins of the Achievement Gap Matter for Justice* (Chicago: University of Chicago Press, 2018); John Hoberman, *Black and Blue: The Origins and Consequences of Medical Racism* (Berkeley: University of California Press, 2012); and Paul Ortiz, *An African American and Latinx History of the United States* (Boston: Beacon Press, 2018).

[19]Bill Bishop, *The Big Sort: Why the Clustering of Like-Minded America is Tearing Us Apart* (New York: Houghton Mifflin, 2008), front matter.

[20]Joshua Yates, "Human Flourishing and the Urban Possibilities for our Grandchildren," Headliner Lecture, Institute for the Study of Human Flourishing, University of Oklahoma, December 8, 2016, www.youtube.com/watch?v=XFFj-vHYpYo.

[21]Charles Murray, "Is White, Working Class America 'Coming Apart'?" National Public Radio, February 6, 2012, www.npr.org/2012/02/06/146463384/is-white-working-class -america-coming-apart.

[22]Nicholas Krause, "Justice and Mercy Contending for Shalom: Towards an Anglican Social Theology," (unpublished paper, Restoration Arlington, Arlington, Virginia, January 2019), 10, http://restorationarlington.org/wp-content/uploads/2019/01/Justice -and-Mercy-Contending-for-Shalom.pdf.

[23]Oliver O'Donovan and Joan Lockwood O'Donovan, eds., *From Irenaeus to Grotius: A Sourcebook in Christian Political Thought 100–1626* (Grand Rapids. MI: Eerdmans, 1999), 46-47.

[24]Thomas Hughson, "Social Justice in Lactantius's *Divine Institutes*: An Exploration," in *Reading Patristic Texts on Social Ethics: Issues and Challenges for Twenty-First Century Christian Social Thought,* eds. Johan Leemans, Brian J. Matz, and Johan Verstraeten (Washington, DC: Catholic University of America Press, 2011), 185-205.

[25]Hughson, "Social Justice in Lactantius's *Divine Institutes*," 198.

[26]David A. Skeel Jr. and William J. Stuntz, "Christianity and the (Modest) Rule of Law," *Faculty Scholarship at Penn Law* 82 (2006): 812.

[27]Christopher Collins, "Alfred's Doombook: The Anglo-Saxon Foundations of Magna Carta," *Litera Scripta* (blog), December 2, 2019, www.law.ua.edu/specialcollections /2019/12/02/alfreds-doombook-the-anglo-saxon-foundations-of-magna-carta.

[28]Philip Jenkins, "How Christian Views Have Shaped Criminal Justice System [*sic*]," *Ethics Daily,* May 10, 2018, https://ethicsdaily.com/how-christian-views-have-shaped -criminal-justice-system-cms-24859.

[29]John Hamond, "The Origins of Restraint," *GoodFaithMedia,* accessed January 16, 2020, www.historynet.com/the-origins-of-restraint.htm.

[30]Hamond, "The Origins of Restraint."

[31]"At the Roots of Methodism: Wesley fought for Prison Reform," Illinois Great Rivers Conference, January 25, 2012, www.igrc.org/newsdetail/41831.

[32]"At the Roots of Methodism."

[33]David Fraccaro, "How an ID Card Helps Build Trust Between Immigrants and Law Enforcement," *Faith & Leadership,* February 7, 2017, https://faithandleadership .com/david-fraccaro-how-id-card-helps-build-trust-between-immigrants-and-law -enforcement.

[34]Fraccaro, "How an ID Card Helps Build Trust."

[35]Luke Bobo and Samuel L. Feemster, "A Practical Way to Build Trust Between Police and the Community," *City Gospel Movements,* December 21, 2017, https:// citygospelmovements.org/resource/a-practical-way-to-build-trust-between-police -and-the-community/.

[36]Joel Johnson, senior pastor, Westwood Community Church, Skype interview with the author, July 21, 2014.

9. A STRATEGY FOR CULTIVATING THE JUST: ADVANCE RESTORATIVE JUSTICE

[1]"Criminal Justice Facts," Sentencing Project, accessed February 29, 2020, www .sentencingproject.org/criminal-justice-facts.

[2]Bruce Western and Becky Pettit, "Collateral Costs: Incarceration's Effect on Economic Mobility," Pew Charitable Trusts 2010, www.pewtrusts.org/~/media/legacy/uploadedfiles /pcs_assets/2010/collateralcosts1pdf.pdf.

[3]Ashley Nellis, "The Color of Justice: Racial and Ethnic Disparity in State Prisons," Sentencing Project, June 14, 2016, www.sentencingproject.org/publications/color-of -justice-racial-and-ethnic-disparity-in-state-prisons.

[4]Mariel Alper et al., "2018 Update on Prisoner Recidivism," US Department of Justice, May 2018, www.bjs.gov/content/pub/pdf/18upr9yfup0514.pdf.

[5]Andrew Mead, copastor, Church of the Servant, telephone interview with the author, March 31, 2020.

[6]This and subsequent quotes are from the author's telephone interview with Peter Vander Meulen, June 16, 2020.

[7]Andrew Mead, quoted in Emily Joy Stroble, "Celebrating 10 Years of Worship and Welcome in Basic English," *The Banner,* June 14, 2019, www.thebanner.org/news/2019/06 /celebrating-10-years-of-worship-and-welcome-in-basic-english.

[8]This and subsequent quotes, except as noted, are from the author's telephone interview with Troy Rienstra, May 21, 2020.

[9]"Agenda for Synod 2005," Christian Reformed Church, 558, www.crcna.org/sites /default/files/2005_agenda.pdf.

[10]This and subsequent quotes, except as noted, are from the author's telephone interview with Carol Rienstra, March 2, 2020.

[11]This and subsequent quotes, except as noted, are from the author's telephone interview with Rich Rienstra, July 2, 2020.

[12]Personal email to the author from Bob Arbogast, pastor, Celebration Fellowship, July 2, 2020.

[13]Ben Van Houten, "Mission Behind Bars," *The Banner*, August 13, 2012, www.thebanner.org /together/2012/08/mission-behind-bars.

[14]"Alpha Inspires Brothers in their Faith," *Celebration Fellowship Newsletter*, Fall 2015, www.churchoftheservantcrc.org/wp-content/uploads/2015/10/CF_Fall_2015 _Newsletter_email-24.pdf.

[15]Chris Meehan, "Called Forth into New Life," *The Banner*, September 30, 2016, www .thebanner.org/together/2016/09/called-forth-into-a-new-life.

[16]"Dave Koetje, newly appointed CEO of Celebration Fellowship," *Celebration Fellowship Newsletter*, Fall 2015, www.churchoftheservantcrc.org/wp-content/uploads/2015/10 /CF_Fall_2015_Newsletter_email-24.pdf.

[17]Barb Leegwater, quoted in Meehan, "Called Forth into New Life."

[18]This and subsequent quotes, except as noted, are from the author's telephone interview with Jimmy Erickson, June 25, 2020.

[19]David Rylaarsdam, quoted in Jon Gorter, "Prison Ministry Degree Program Reflects Restorative Justice," *Calvin Chimes*, February 26, 2015, https://calvinchimes .org/2015/02/26/prison-ministry-degree-program-reflects-restorative-justice/?_ga=2 .80490206.876192769.1592231046-76545612.1591910299.

[20]Lois M. Davis et al., "Evaluating the Effectiveness of Corrective Education: A Meta-Analysis of Programs that Provide Education to Incarcerated Adults," RAND Corporation, 2013, www.rand.org/pubs/research_reports/RR266.html.

[21]Kary Bosma, director of operations, Calvin Prison Initiative, personal correspondence with the author, July 2, 2020.

[22]Matt Kucinski, "A Familiar Game, A New Outcome," Calvin University, October 15, 2019, https://calvin.edu/news/archive/a-familiar-game-a-new-outcome.

[23]This and subsequent quotes except where noted are from the author's telephone interview with Todd Cioffi, director, Calvin Prison Initiative, July 8, 2020.

[24]Logan T. Hansen, "Living Water Ministry Halfway Houses 'Inappropriately Located,' township attorney says," *MLive*, July 13, 2018, www.mlive.com/kentwood/2018/07 /living_water_ministry_halfway.html.

[25]This and subsequent quotes, except as noted, are from the author's telephone interview with Jimmy Erickson, June 25, 2020.

[26]This is the name COS gave the program. The original name from Summer Institute of Linguistics and American Bible Society is "Healing the Wounds of Trauma." Information is available at www.traumahealinginstitute.org.

[27]Carol Rienstra, telephone interview with the author, January 21, 2020.

[28]"Faith," Safe & Just Michigan, accessed August 10, 2021, www.safeandjustmi.org /partners/faith; emphasis added.

[29]Carol Rienstra, quoted in Greg Chandler, "Michigan Church Hosts 'Speaking of Restorative Justice, What Shall We Do?'" *The Banner*, May 18, 2018,

www.thebanner.org/news/2018/05/michigan-church-hosts-speaking-of-restorative
-justice-what-shall-we-do.

[30]David LaGrand, quoted in Chris Meehan, "Restorative Justice Allows Victims and Offenders to Meet," Christian Reformed Church, October 21, 2015, www.crcna.org
/news-and-views/restorative-justice-allows-victims-and-offenders-meet?utm
_source=CRC+News&utm_campaign=171cf99ebf-CRC+News+%7C+October+21
%2C+2015&utm_medium=email&utm_term=0_468bc4c3c9-171cf99ebf-51818442.

[31]David LaGrand, "Restorative Justice: A Better Way," *The Banner*, May 6, 2019, www
.thebanner.org/features/2019/05/restorative-justice-a-better-way.

[32]LaGrand, "Restorative Justice."

[33]Chris Becker, quoted in Rachel Van Gilder, "Program Aims to Keep Kent Co. Kids Out
of Court," Wood TV, February 12 2018, www.woodtv.com/news/kent-county
/program-aims-to-keep-kent-co-kids-out-of-court.

[34]Becker, quoted in Van Gilder, "Program Aims to Keep Kent Co. Kids Out of Court."

[35]Safe and Just Michigan was formerly called the Citizens Alliance on Prisons and
Public Spending.

[36]Barbara Wieland, "Safe and Just Michigan's Top 10 for Criminal Justice Reform in
Michigan," Safe & Just Michigan, December 19, 2019, www.safeandjustmi.org/2019/12/19
/safe-just-michigans-top-10-for-criminal-justice-reform-in-2019.

[37]Troy Rienstra, "Let the Revolution of the Heart and Mind Begin," *Prisoners in Christ*
(blog), March 1, 2013, https://prisonersinchrist.org/let-the-revolution-of-the-heart
-and-mind-begin.

[38]Bryan Stevenson, *Just Mercy: A Story of Justice and Redemption* (New York: Spiegel &
Grau, 2015), 17.

[39]"The World as We Know It," Cru Press, February 2012, www.cru.org/content/dam/cru
/legacy/2012/02/IJM-Social-Justice-Bible-Studies-Revised.pdf.

[40]Bethany Hoang, Stephanie Summers, and Bethany Jenkins, "The Pursuit of Biblical
Justice," Gospel Coalition, accessed August 10, 2021, www.thegospelcoalition.org
/course/the-pursuit-of-biblical-justice/#course-introduction.

[41]"What Is Outrageous Justice?" Prison Fellowship, accessed August 10, 2021, www
.prisonfellowship.org/about/justicereform/landing-pages/outrageous-justice.

[42]Gary Fields and John R. Emshwiller, "As Arrest Records Rise, Americans Find Consequences Can Last a Lifetime," *Wall Street Journal*, August 18, 2014, www.wsj.com
/articles/as-arrest-records-rise-americans-find-consequences-can-last-a-lifetime
-1408415402.

[43]"A Survey of Christian Perceptions on Incarceration and Justice Reform," Prison Fellowship, October 2019, www.prisonfellowship.org/wp-content/uploads/2020/01
/Prison-Fellowship-Christian-Barna-Polling-Results-2019.pdf.

10. A STRATEGY FOR CULTIVATING THE JUST:
BE A RECONCILING COMMUNITY

[1]This and subsequent quotes, except where noted, are from the author's telephone interview with Iesha Williams, June 20, 2020.

[2]This and subsequent quotes, except where noted, are from the author's interview with Don Coleman, then lead pastor, East End Fellowship, November 12, 2019, Richmond, VA.

[3]This and subsequent quotes are from the author's telephone interview with Percy and Angie Strickland, June 30, 2020.

[4]Amy Julia Becker, "The New School Choice Agenda," *Christianity Today*, April 9, 2012, www.christianitytoday.com/ct/2012/april/school-choice.html.

[5]Corey Widmer, quoted in Becker, "New School Choice Agenda."

[6]This and subsequent quotes, except where noted, are from the author's telephone interview with Lawson Wijesooriya, founding elder, East End Fellowship, April 23, 2020.

[7]Mary Kay Avula, quoted in Becker, "New School Choice Agenda."

[8]"Divided by Design: Findings from the American South," E Pluribus Unum, October 2019, 76, www.dividedbydesign.org/static/report-09da5f2905801cb7265cb94c5eee7ee7.pdf.

[9]Tom Perriello, "Tackling the Racial Wealth Gap," *Medium*, February 24, 2017, https://medium.com/tom-for-virginia/tackling-the-racial-wealth-gap-959ff8e0131c.

[10]Corey Widmer, quoted in "About Us," East End Fellowship, http://www.eastendfellowship.org/about-us. Corey is former copastor of East End Fellowship.

[11]John Perkins, quoted in Becker, "New School Choice Agenda."

[12]Corey Widmer, "Want to be Multiethnic? Get Ready for Discomfort," *Thin Places* (blog), August 25, 2014, www.christianitytoday.com/amyjuliabecker/2014/august/want-to-be-multiethnic-get-ready-for-discomfort.html.

[13]This and subsequent quotes, except as noted, are from the author's interview with Elena Aronson, November 13, 2019, Richmond, VA.

[14]This and subsequent quotes, except as noted, are from the author's interview with David Bailey, executive director, Arrabon, November 13, 2020, Richmond, VA.

[15]See, for example, Jennifer Harvey, *Dear White Christians: For Those Still Longing for Racial Reconciliation* (Grand Rapids, MI: Eerdmans, 2014).

[16]James K. Smith, *Desiring the Kingdom* (Grand Rapids, MI: Baker Academic, 2009).

[17]This and subsequent quotes, except as noted, are from the author's telephone interview with Erin Rose, then-pastor of worship and teaching, East End Fellowship, April 17, 2020.

[18]Various alumni of the internship program have formed the band Urban Doxology. Visit www.urbandoxology.com.

[19]Andy Crouch, "Being Culture Makers: An Interview with 'StudentSoul,'" Andy Crouch, January 2007, https://andy-crouch.com/articles/being_culture_makers.

11. THE PROSPEROUS

[1]"Project Brief," Thriving Cities, Summer 2015, https://static1.squarespace.com /static/5a0f45fad74cff16c9f6e45e/t/5b858656b8a045493d184307/1535477334611/TCP _ProjectBrief_July2015_print+FINAL+7.27.15+%281%29.pdf.

[2]Tom Nelson, *The Economics of Neighbor Love* (Downers Grove, IL: InterVarsity Press, 2017), 9.

[3]For an excellent discussion of this point, see Brian Fikkert and Kelly Kapic, *Becoming Whole: Why the Opposite of Poverty Isn't the American Dream* (Chicago: Moody Publishers, 2019).

[4]See Gregory Fairchild, Ben Alexander, and Alison Elias, "The Prosperous," Thriving Cities, accessed March 2, 2020, https://static1.squarespace.com/static/5a0f45fad74cff16c9f6e45e /t/5b4fa9b2f950b726398934ed/1531947443761/Endowment-Brief-The-Prosperous.pdf.

[5]Nelson, *Economics of Neighborly Love*, 31-32.

[6]Scripture contains over four hundred references to God's heart for the poor.

[7]Elizabeth Howell, "How Many Stars Are There in the Universe?" *SPACE.com*, May 31, 2014, www.space.com/26078-how-many-stars-are-there.html.

[8]This theme of abundance is repeated in descriptions of the new heavens and new earth. There too there will be no hunger or thirst (Rev 7:16; Is 49:10). In the midst of the new Jerusalem, the tree of life will bring forth ceaseless fruit each month (Rev 22:2). The prophet Amos foretells the day "when the reaper will be overtaken by the plowman / and the planter by the one treading grapes. / New wine will drip from the mountains / and flow from all the hills" (Amos 9:13). And in the world to come, even that which was barren will be fruitful. The desert will "blossom as a rose" (Is 35:1 KJV). "Instead of the thorn shall come up the fir tree, / and instead of the brier shall come up the myrtle tree" (Is 55:13 KJV). We will experience a fertility beyond imagining.

[9]Michael Sean Winters, "Review: Cloutier's 'The Vice of Luxury,'" *National Catholic Reporter*, accessed November 14, 2020, www.ncronline.org/blogs/distinctly-catholic/review -cloutiers-vice-luxury.

[10]Nelson, *Economics of Neighbor Love*, 29.

[11]John Bolt, *Economic Shalom: A Reformed Primer on Faith, Work, and Human Flourishing* (Grand Rapids, MI: Christian's Library Press, 2013), 28-29.

[12]Jeff Van Duzer, *Why Business Matters to God* (Downers Grove, IL: InterVarsity Press, 2010), 41-42.

[13]Michael Rhodes and Robby Holt, *Practicing the King's Economy* (Grand Rapids, MI: Baker, 2018), 86-87.

[14]There are some signs this is beginning to change. On August 19, 2019, the Business Roundtable released a new statement on the purpose of the corporation, signed by over 180 CEOs. They pledged to lead their enterprises in ways that would benefit all their stakeholders—not just the shareholders but also "customers, employees, suppliers, and communities" ("Business Roundtable Redefines the Purpose of a Corporation to

Promote 'An Economy that Serves All Americans,'" Business Roundtable, August 19, 2019, www.businessroundtable.org/business-roundtable-redefines-the-purpose-of-a-corporation-to-promote-an-economy-that-serves-all-americans). In October 2020, *Fortune* magazine published an essay declaring Friedman's doctrine dead and calling for universal adoption of the Public Benefit Corporation for large corporations (Colin Mayer, Leo E. Strine Jr., and Jaap Winter, "50 Years Later, Milton Friedman's Shareholder Doctrine Is Dead," *Fortune,* September 13, 2020, https://fortune.com/2020/09/13/milton-friedman-anniversary-business-purpose).

[15]For example, Michael Sandel, *What Money Can't Buy: The Moral Limits of Markets* (New York: Farrar, Straus & Giroux, 2012).

[16]See, for example, William T. Cavanaugh, *Being Consumed: Economics and Christian Desire* (Grand Rapids, MI: Eerdmans, 2008).

[17]See, for example, Peter H. Lindert and Jeffrey G. Williamson, *Unequal Gains: American Growth and Inequality Since 1700* (Princeton, NJ: Princeton University Press, 2016), and Pablo Mitnik and David B. Grusky, "Economic Mobility in the United States," Pew Charitable Trusts, July 2015, www.pewtrusts.org/~/media/assets/2015/07/fsm-irs-report_artfinal.pdf.

[18]Rhodes and Holt, *Practicing the King's Economy*, 58.

[19]Rhodes and Holt, *Practicing the King's Economy*, 58-59.

[20]Rhodes and Holt, *Practicing the King's Economy*, 60.

[21]"The Sabbath Year and the Year of Jubilee (Leviticus 25)," Theology of Work Project, accessed September 2, 2020, www.theologyofwork.org/old-testament/leviticus-and-work/the-sabbath-year-and-the-year-of-jubilee-leviticus-25.

[22]Eventide Funds (www.eventidefunds.com/) and Praxis Mutual Funds (www.praxismutualfunds.com/) are two good examples.

[23]Rhodes and Holt, *Practicing the King's Economy*, 130.

[24]Rhodes and Holt, *Practicing the King's Economy*, 131.

[25]Rhodes and Holt, *Practicing the King's Economy*, 151.

[26]Lauren M. Johnson, "A Los Angeles Church Is Paying Off $5.3 Million of Medical Debt in Its Community," *CNN*, December 24, 2019, www.cnn.com/2019/12/24/us/church-medical-debt-payoff-trnd/index.html.

[27]See, for example, C. K. Prahalad, *The Fortune at the Bottom of the Pyramid: Eradicating Poverty Through Profits* (London: Pearson, 2013); and Mark Cheng, "How Business Can Lift People out of Poverty," *Forbes*, March 21, 2014, www.forbes.com/sites/ashoka/2014/03/21/how-business-can-lift-people-out-of-poverty-4-insights-from-the-worlds-best-social-entrepreneurs/#11f9f026a95b.

[28]Maxim Pinkovskiy and Xavier Sala-i-Martin, "Parametric Estimations of World Distribution of Income," National Bureau of Economic Research, October 2009, www.nber.org/papers/w15433.

[29]"Decline of Extreme Global Poverty Continues but Has Slowed: World Bank," World Bank, September 19, 2018, www.worldbank.org/en/news/press-release/2018/09/19 /decline-of-global-extreme-poverty-continues-but-has-slowed-world-bank.

[30]Michael E. Porter and Mark R. Kramer, "Creating Shared Value," *Harvard Business Review*, January-February 2011, https://hbr.org/2011/01/the-big-idea-creating-shared-value.

[31]Mayer, Strine Jr., and Winter, "50 Years later, Milton Friedman's Shareholder Doctrine Is Dead."

[32]"Our Mission: Advancing Redemptive Entrepreneurship," Praxis, accessed October 16, 2020, https://praxislabs.org/mission-and-model#:~:text=REDEMPTIVE%20STRATEGY %20is%20designing%20%26%20leading,the%20renewal%20of%20all%20things .&text=REDEMPTIVE%20OPERATIONS%20establishes%20processes%2C%20culture ,within%20and%20beyond%20the%20venture.

[33]Interestingly, based on scholarship from Reta Halteman Finger, it seems likely that the early Jerusalem congregation thought creatively about how to sustain their community over time. Rather than only imagining people selling some asset and then buying food for the week, "We should picture them perhaps, liquidating Barnabas's farm to purchase livestock in Jerusalem or tools for a new olive oil-press operation in the city" (Reta Halteman Finger, quoted in Rhodes and Holt, *Practicing the King's Economy*, 171-72).

[34]Phillip J. Long, "Acts 20:1-5—The Collection for the Saints," *Reading Acts*, April 7, 2011, https://readingacts.com/2011/04/07/acts-201-5-the-%E2%80%9Ccollection-for -the-saints%E2%80%9D.

[35]"Money in Christian History: A Gallery of Church Fathers," *Christian History* 14 (1987): www.christianitytoday.com/history/issues/issue-14/money-in-christian-history -i-gallery-of-church-fathers.html.

[36]"Money in Christian History."

[37]"Money in Christian History."

[38]Leland Ryken, "That Which God Hath Lent Thee: The Puritans and Money," *A Puritan's Mind*, accessed January 17, 2020, www.apuritansmind.com/stewardship /rykenlelandpuritansandmoney.

[39]Ryken, "That Which God Hath Lent Thee."

[40]Ryken, "That Which God Hath Lent Thee."

[41]Ryken, "That Which God Hath Lent Thee."

[42]As scholar Demetrios Constantelos observes, "In contrast to the non-Christian world, Christianity removed boundaries and broke down racial and ethnic fences, proclaiming that 'there is neither Jew nor Greek, there is neither slave nor free, there is neither male nor female' but all are one in Christ Jesus (Gal. 3:38). The practice of philanthropy by the early Church went beyond care for its own to care for Jews, Greeks, and Romans" (Demetrios J. Constantelos, "Origins of Christian Orthodox *Diakonia*: Christian Orthodox Philanthropy in Church History," *Agape-Biblia*, accessed August 12, 2021, www

.agape-biblia.org/orthodoxy/Seek_the_Welfare_of_the_City/Origins%20of%20Orthodox %20Christian%20Diakonia.pdf).

[43]Peter Brown, *Through the Eye of the Needle: Wealth, the Fall of Rome, and the Making of Christianity in the West, 350–550 AD* (Princeton, NJ: Princeton University Press, 2012).

[44]Nicholas Krause, "Justice and Mercy Contending for Shalom: Toward an Anglican Social Theology," (unpublished paper, Restoration Arlington, Arlington, Virginia, January 2019), http://restorationarlington.org/wp-content/uploads/2019/01/Justice -and-Mercy-Contending-for-Shalom.pdf.

[45]Brown, *Through the Eye of the Needle*, 79.

[46]Brown, *Through the Eye of the Needle*, 75.

[47]Herbert Schlossberg, *The Silent Revolution and the Making of Victorian England* (Columbus: Ohio State University Press, 2000), 156-57.

[48]See David Hall, ed., *Welfare Reformed: A Compassionate Approach* (Phillipsburg, NJ: P&R, 1994), 133-64.

[49]Matthew Bishop and Michael Green, *Philanthrocapitalism: How Giving Can Save the World* (New York: Bloomsbury Press, 2008), 23.

[50]Michael Mollat, *The Poor in the Middle Ages: An Essay in Social History* (New Haven, CT: Yale University Press, 1986), 38.

[51]Glenn Sunshine, "The Church and the Poor: Historical Perspectives," Institute for Faith, Work, and Economics, June 6, 2012, https://tifwe.org/part-7.

[52]J. W. Brodman, *Charity and Religion in Medieval Europe* (Washington, DC: Catholic University Press, 2009).

[53]Vic George, *Major Thinkers in Welfare: Contemporary Issues in Historical Perspective* (Bristol, UK: University of Bristol Policy Press, 2010), 74.

[54]Adam Hamilton, "The Foundry in London: Two Sides of the Gospel," *Adam Hamilton* (blog), September 19, 2014, www.adamhamilton.org/blog/the-foundry-in-london-two -sides-of-the-gospel/#.V4oGk7grI2x.

[55]Schlossberg, *Silent Revolution*, 181-83.

[56]Marvin Olasky, *The Tragedy of American Compassion* (Wheaton, IL: Crossway, 1992), 7, 10, 13.

[57]C. Eric Lincoln and Lawrence H. Mamiya, *The Black Church in the African American Experience* (Durham, NC: Duke University Press, 1990).

[58]Alex D. Colvin and Darron D. Garner, "Social Work and the African American Church: Using a Collaborative Approach to Address Service Delivery," paper presented at the NACSW Convention, Raleigh-Durham, NC, 2010.

[59]Sunshine, "Church and the Poor."

[60]See Hall, ed., *Welfare Reformed*, 133-64.

[61]Schlossberg, *Silent Revolution*, 156-85.

[62]Schlossberg, *Silent Revolution*, 181-83.

[63]Jessica Gordon Nembhard, *Collective Courage: A History of African American Cooperative Economic Thought and Practice* (University Park: Penn State University Press, 2014), 33.

[64]Nembhard, *Collective Courage*, 302.

[65]Hamilton, "Foundry in London."

[66]Schlossberg, *Silent Revolution*, 183.

[67]"The National Baptist Convention, Inc.: Entrepreneurship, Education, and Faith," *This Far by Faith*, accessed August 15, 2020, www.pbs.org/thisfarbyfaith/journey_3/p_7.html.

[68]Elias Camp Morris, quoted in "The National Baptist Convention, Inc."

[69]Nembhard, *Collective Courage*, 41.

[70]Juliet E. K. Walker, *The History of Black Business in America: Capitalism, Race, Entrepreneurship*, vol. 1, *To 1865*, 2nd ed. (Chapel Hill: University of North Carolina Press, 2009), 111-12.

[71]Phillip E. Gipson, "Empowering the Black Community: Faith-Based Economic Development," (master's thesis, University of North Texas, August 2001), http://citeseerx.ist .psu.edu/viewdoc/download?doi=10.1.1.458.1392&rep=rep1&type=pdf.

[72]Hazel Trice-Edney, "AME Church Leaders Cite Economic Empowerment as 2015 Goal," *Northstar News Today*, January 21, 2015, http://triceedneywire.com/index .php?option=com_content&view=article&id=5044:ame-church-leaders-cite-black -economic-empowerment-as-2015-goal&catid=54&Itemid=208.

[73]Hazel Trice-Edney, "AME Church and Black Banks Launch New Partnership for Black Wealth," *Black Enterprise*, July 19, 2018, www.blackenterprise.com/ame-church-and -black-banks-launch-new-partnership-for-black-wealth. AME congregations have also birthed numerous large and small community-development corporations in the United States, including in Los Angeles, the Ward Economic Development Corporation (out of Ward AME) and the South Los Angeles Community Development and Empowerment Corporation (out of First AME); in Miami, BAME CDC (out of Greater Bethel AME); in Atlanta, St. Philip CDC (out of St. Philip AME); and in New York City, Allen AME Community Development Corporation (out of Allen AME Church), to name a few. These CDCs have built thousands of units of affordable housing, reclaimed vacant properties, sponsored job-training programs, incubated new businesses, and financed major commercial real estate developments (e.g., strip malls and grocery stores) to revitalize economically distressed communities.

[74]"History of the National Baptist Convention," National Baptist Convention, accessed August 15, 2020, www.nationalbaptist.com/about-nbc/our-history.

[75]"Housing Commission," National Baptist Convention USA, accessed August 15, 2020, www.nationalbaptist.com/departments/ministries-commissions/housing-commission.

[76]"NBC, USA, Inc. Partners with the USDA to Increase Agricultural Awareness and Participation," National Baptist Convention, February 8, 2016, www.nationalbaptist.com /nbc-usa-inc-partners-usda-increase-agricultural-awareness-participation.

[77] Andrew Billingsley, *Mighty Like a River: The Black Church and Social Reform* (Oxford: Oxford University Press, 1999). He notes that Black Methodists and Baptists have been more involved in such activities than congregations in the Church of God in Christ denomination.

[78] C. H. Caldwell and L. M. Chatters, "Church-Based Support Programs for Elderly Black Adults: Congregational and Clergy Characteristics," in *Handbook on Religion, Spirituality and Aging*, ed. M. A. Kimble et al. (Minneapolis: Augsburg Fortress, 1995).

[79] E. Eng and J. W. Hatch, "Networking Between Agencies and Black Churches: The Lay Health Advisor Model," *Journal of Prevention and Intervention in the Community* 10 (1991): 123-46.

[80] John Sibley Butler, *Entrepreneurship and Self-Help Among Black Americans*, rev. ed. (Albany: State University of New York Press, 2005), 86.

12. A STRATEGY FOR CULTIVATING THE PROSPEROUS: REDEEM BUSINESS FOR COMMUNITY GOOD

[1] This and subsequent quotes, except where noted, are from Pete West, executive director, Self Sustaining Enterprises, telephone interview with the author, September 17, 2020.

[2] This and subsequent quotes, except where noted, are from Jeff Greer, senior pastor, Grace Chapel, telephone interview with the author, September 16, 2020.

[3] This and subsequent quotes, except as noted, are from Chuck Proudfit, elder, Grace Chapel, telephone interview with the author, September 16, 2020.

[4] Jeff Greer and Chuck Proudfit, *Biznistry: Transforming Lives Through Enterprise* (Mason, OH: P5 Publications, 2013), loc. 229, Kindle.

[5] See Michael E. Porter and Mark R. Kramer, "Creating Shared Value," *Harvard Business Review*, January–February 2011, https://hbr.org/2011/01/the-big-idea-creating-shared-value.

[6] West interview, August 7, 2018.

[7] West interview, September 17, 2020.

[8] This and subsequent quotes, except as noted, are from Kevin Schweiger, Marketplace Minister, telephone interview with the author, October 1, 2020.

[9] Mike Breen and Steve Cockram, *Building a Discipling Culture*, 2nd ed. (Greenville, SC: 3DM, 2011).

[10] Greer and Proudfit, *Biznistry*, loc. 391.

[11] Greer and Proudfit, *Biznistry*, loc. 391.

[12] West interview, August 7, 2018.

[13] Stuart M. Butler and Carmen Diaz, "'Third Places' as Community Builders," Brookings Institution, September 14, 2016, www.brookings.edu/blog/up-front/2016/09/14/third-places-as-community-builders.

[14] In the wake of the coronavirus pandemic, the gyms have had to cut some staff.

[15] Greer interview, March 18, 2019.

[16] Greer, interview, September 16, 2020.

[17] Greer, interview, March 18, 2019.

[18] Greer and Proudfit, *Biznistry*, loc. 1333.

[19]Jeff Greer and Chuck Proudfit, "Biznistry: 'What If' We Took a New Approach?" *Outcomes*, Fall 2016, 30, https://outcomesmagazine.com/app/uploads/2017/08/OC_Fall-2016.pdf.

13. A STRATEGY FOR CULTIVATING THE PROSPEROUS: DEPLOY ASSETS TO BUILD ASSETS

[1]The terms *relief*, *rehabilitation*, and *development* are used to describe the three main programmatic responses to poverty in *When Helping Hurts*.

[2]"Why Assets Matter," Corporation for Enterprise Development, 2013, https://prosperitynow .org/files/PDFs/financial_capability_planning_guide/WhyAssetsMatter_2013updates.pdf.

[3]Michael Sherraden, *Assets and the Poor: A New American Welfare Policy* (New York: M. E. Sharpe, 1991).

[4]"The essential insight from Sherraden's work," writes *Prosperity Now*'s Ethan Geiling, "was that assets can matter economically, socially and psychologically in ways that income alone does not. More recent research has reinforced this insight: that income—by itself—is necessary, but not sufficient, to allow families to escape poverty, achieve financial stability and move up the economic ladder." Geiling reports that research has shown that assets can create a financial buffer to help low-income households weather emergencies, promote economic mobility for single mothers, increase success in the labor market, and improve the likelihood of attending and succeeding in college (Ethan Geiling, "An Overview of Asset-Building Research," *Prosperity Now*, January 12, 2012, https://prosperitynow.org/blog/overview-asset-building-research).

[5]A decade ago, recognizing his contribution to innovative thinking, *Time* magazine named Sherraden one of the "2010 *Time* 100," the magazine's list of the most influential people in the world. (See Jessica Martin, "Impact of *Assets and the Poor* Grows 20 Years After Its Release," *Source*, December 13, 2011, https://source.wustl.edu/2011/12/impact -of-assets-and-the-poor-grows-20-years-after-its-release.)

[6]Duke University's National Congregations Study, for example, found that the most common way churches offer aid to the poor is through free food. (See Mark Chavez and Allison Eagle, "Religious Congregations in 21st Century America," Duke University, National Congregations Study 2015, 22.) An earlier national survey, the Faith Communities Today (FACT) initiative of the Hartford Institute for Religion Research, found that over 80 percent of congregations engaged in financial benevolence, which typically involves assistance with rent, utilities, or medical bills ("A Quick Question: Over 80% of US Congregations Help Those in Need: True or False?" Hartford Institute for Religion Research, accessed October 10, 2020, http://hirr.hartsem.edu/research /quick_question15.html).

[7]According to 2011 census data, the net worth of the average US Black household is $6,314, compared with $110,500 for the average White household (Nicholas Kristoff, "When Whites Just Don't Get It," *New York Times*, August 30, 2014). According to scholars at the Brookings Institution, in 2016 the typical White family had a net worth of $171,000 while the typical Black family had a net worth of $17,150 (Kriston McIntosh

et. al., "Examining the Black-White Wealth Gap," Brookings Institution, February 27, 2020, www.brookings.edu/blog/up-front/2020/02/27/examining-the-black-white -wealth-gap/). Economists at the Federal Reserve Bank of Cleveland explain that this gap is "the consequence of many decades of racial inequality that imposed barriers to wealth accumulation either through explicit prohibition during slavery or unequal treatment after emancipation." These included such things as legally mandated segregation in schools, discrimination in the job market, and redlining "which reduced access to capital in black neighborhoods." (See Dionissi Aliprantis and Daniel R. Carroll, "What Is Behind the Persistence of the Racial Wealth Gap?," Federal Research Bank of Cleveland, February 2, 2019, www.clevelandfed.org/newsroom-and-events /publications/economic-commentary/2019-economic-commentaries/ec-201903-what -is-behind-the-persistence-of-the-racial-wealth-gap.aspx.)

[8]The material from this section of the book overlaps with Amy L. Sherman, "One Way Churches Can Implement Economic Wisdom," *Common Good*, August 28, 2018, www .madetoflourish.org/resources/job-clubs-one-way-churches-can-implement-economic -wisdom.

[9]This and subsequent quotes are from Steve Murata, telephone interview with the author, July 11, 2018.

[10]John Trutko et al., "Formative Evaluation of Job Clubs Operated by Faith- and Community-based Organizations: Finding from Site Visits and Options for Future Evaluation," Department of Labor, Chief Evaluation Office, May 2014, www.dol.gov/sites /dolgov/files/OASP/legacy/files/FINAL_REPORT_formative_evaluation_job_clubs _operated_faith_cbo.pdf.

[11]This and subsequent quotes are from Brian Bennett, pastor, Overflow Church, telephone interview with the author, June 5, 2019.

[12]Its ties to Overflow remain strong. Bennett serves as board president. The current CEO of Mosaic, Andrew Robinson, serves on Overflow Church's leadership team and is part of the regular rotation of preaching pastors for the congregation.

[13]Ivy Yarbrough, telephone interview with the author, June 18, 2019.

[14]Several years ago Mosaic's leaders started implementing the Jobs for Life job-life skills training program. The team had realized through its experience with the social enterprises that many neighbors needed a combination of classroom training, mentoring/ coaching, and on-the-job training if they were going to succeed in mainstream workplaces. "Through much trial and error," Bennett says, "we've created something that is Christ-centered, people-focused, operationally more sustainable, and not bound to typical grant cycles." Since 2014 Mosaic's program has graduated nearly 350 individuals, 139 of which have been employed in the social enterprises to hone their on-the-job skills. A majority of these have gone on to mainstream jobs in the community. Overall, program leaders report an impressive 85 percent job placement rate among graduates.

[15]"Youth Unemployment in the United States, January-June 2019," *Mathematica*, January-June 2019, www.google.com/url?sa=t&source=web&cd=&ved=2ahUKEwi2puez1rjyA hVqFTQIHdR3B_0QFnoECAMQAQ&url=https%3A%2F%2Fwww.mathematica .org%2F-%2Fmedia%2Fpublications%2Fpdfs%2Flabor%2F2019%2Fsff-subgroups.pdf %3Fla%3Den&usg=AOvVaw1alAyWviuuzkVhBFCb0GDM.

[16]Sarah Ayres Steinberg, "The High Cost of Youth Unemployment," Center for American Progress, April 5, 2013, www.americanprogress.org/issues/economy/reports/2013/04 /05/59428/the-high-cost-of-youth-unemployment.

[17]Justine Beene, quoted in "Bridges," *Vimeo*, 2016, https://vimeo.com/192781531.

[18]Luke Bobo, "How a Church's Café Provides Job Training to At-Risk Youth," Made to Flourish, November 28, 2017, www.madetoflourish.org/resources/how-a-churchs-cafe -provides-job-training-to-at-risk-students.

[19]Much of the material in this and the next four paragraphs overlaps with Amy Sherman, "Racial Wealth Gaps and What Your Church Can Do About It," Sagamore Institute, May 17, 2019, https://sagamoreinstitute.org/racial-wealth-gaps-and-what-your-church -can-do-about-it.

[20]Matt Overton, quoted in Marc Covert, "Mowtown Teen Lawn Care Is a Social Enterprise Offering a New Model for Youth Ministry," *Faith & Leadership*, May 3, 2016, https:// faithandleadership.com/mowtown-teen-lawn-care-social-enterprise-offering-new -model-youth-ministry.

[21]Overton, quoted in Covert, "Mowtown Teen Lawn Care."

[22]Matt Overton, "How Social Enterprise Has Changed My Congregation and Me," *Faith & Leadership*, November 14, 2017, https://faithandleadership.com/matt-overton-how -social-enterprise-has-changed-my-congregation-and-me.

[23]Gregory Mills et al., "Building Savings for Success: Early Impacts from the Assets for Independence Program Randomized Evaluation," Urban Institute, December 2016, viii, www.urban.org/sites/default/files/publication/86146/building_savings_for_success.pdf.

[24]Matt Seadore, director of mission and ministry, North Avenue Presbyterian Church, telephone interview with the author, March 21, 2019.

[25]"Why Should God's People Start Matched Savings Programs?" Chalmers Center, 2018, https://chalmers.org/wp-content/uploads/2018/11/ida-matched-savings-and -gods-people.pdf.

[26]Steve Corbett, quoted in "Foundations for Matched Savings" (video), Chalmers Center, accessed April 2, 2019, https://chalmers.org/matched-savings-ida-toolkit.

[27]Gary Dittman, "Congregational Stories: Extending Healing in East Baltimore," Criterion Institute, December 12, 2017, https://criterioninstitute.org/resources/extending -healing-in-east-baltimore.

[28]Phyllis Anderson, project lead, 1K Churches, Criterion Institute, telephone interview with the author, November 21, 2017.

[29]Information on Church of the Good Shepherd's microlending program is from the author's telephone interview with Robert Locke, August 16, 2018, and from Robert Locke, "Congregational Stories: Lending, Learning, Leading," Criterion Institute, February 13, 2018, https://criterioninstitute.org/resources/people-of-god-lending-learning-leading.

[30]Much of this section overlaps with Amy L. Sherman, "How One Church Launched 11 Social Ventures," *Green Room* (blog), March 30, 2018, https://greenroomblog.org/2018/03/30/how-one-church-launched-11-social-ventures/?share=google-plus-1.

[31]This and subsequent quotes are from Leah Porter, Founder, Twin Cities Mobile Market, interview with the author, Edina, Minnesota, April 27, 2017.

[32]This and subsequent quotes are from Brian Jones, (then) minister of missions, Colonial Church, interview with the author, Edina, Minnesota, April 27, 2017.

[33]This and subsequent quotes are from Daniel Harrell, (then) senior pastor, Colonial Church, Edina, Minnesota, April 27, 2017.

[34]This and subsequent quotes are from Jeff Siemon, congregant, Colonial Church, Edina, Minnesota, April 27, 2017.

[35]James L. Payne, ed., *The Befriending Leader: Social Assistance Without Dependency, Essays by Octavia Hill* (Sandpoint, ID: Lytton Publishing, 1997), 67.

14. THE SUSTAINABLE

[1]Aaron Bernstein, quoted in "Coronavirus, Climate Change, and the Environment: A Conversation on COVID-19 with Dr. Aaron Bernstein," Harvard C-CHANGE, accessed July 4, 2020, www.hsph.harvard.edu/c-change/subtopics/coronavirus-and-climate-change.

[2]"Citizen's Field Guide," Thriving Cities, August 11, 2016, https://static1.squarespace.com/static/5a0f45fad74cff16c9f6e45e/t/5b50fa90562fa718f6ca57b1/1532033690754/2016.08.11_Field+Guide.pdf.

[3]Dick Tripp, "Biblical Mandate for Caring for Creation: Part I," *Exploring Christianity*, February 4, 2016, http://christianity.co.nz/2016/02/biblical-mandate-for-caring-for-creation-part-i.

[4]Tripp, "Biblical Mandate for Caring for Creation."

[5]Mark Cosgrove, *The Brain, the Mind, and the Person Within: The Enduring Mystery of the Soul* (Grand Rapids, MI: Kregel Academic, 2018), 13.

[6]J. Scott Duvall, "Angry at Death: Reading John 11," *Intersections*, January 24, 2017, https://everydaybioethics.org/intersections/angry-death-reading-john-11.

[7]Calvin B. DeWitt, *Earthwise: A Guide to Hopeful Creation Care*, 3rd ed. (Grand Rapids, MI: Faith Alive Christian Resources, 2011), 41-60.

[8]Tim Keller, "Creation's Groans Are Not Meaningless," Gospel Coalition, July 15, 2015, www.thegospelcoalition.org/article/creations-groans-are-not-meaningless.

[9]"Why Should Christians Care for Creation?" BioLogos, accessed November 21, 2020, https://biologos.org/common-questions/why-should-christians-care-for-creation.

[10]Patrick Galey, "Air Pollution 'Greatest Risk' to Global Life Expectancy," *AQLI*, July 28, 2020, https://aqli.epic.uchicago.edu/news/air-pollution-greatest-risk-to-global-life-expectancy.

[11]Bron Taylor, "The Tributaries of Radical Environmentalism," *Journal for the Study of Radicalism* 2, no. 1 (2008): 28.

[12]Taylor, "Tributaries of Radical Environmentalism," 39.

[13]Martin W. Lewis, *Green Delusions: An Environmentalist Critique of Radical Environmentalism* (Durham, NC: Duke University Press, 1994), 28.

[14]James Florence and Annette Florence, "Historical Roots of Public Health," PowerPoint presentation, Liberty University, 2018, https://slideplayer.com/slide/14333804. See also Jan Verbruggen, "Health and Healthcare in Ancient Israel," *Transformed*, October 28, 2013, https://transformedblog.westernseminary.edu/2013/10/28/health-and-healthcare-in-ancient-israel-2.

[15]Gerhard F. Hasel, "Health and Healing in the Old Testament," *Andrews University Seminary Studies*, 21, no. 3 (Autumn 1983): 191-202, www.andrews.edu/library/car/cardigital/Periodicals/AUSS/1983-3/1983-3-01.pdf.

[16]Glenn E. Myers, "The Heavens Declare the Glory of God," *Christian History*, 10-11, accessed December 23, 2019, https://christianhistoryinstitute.org/magazine/issue/creation-care.

[17]Meister Eckhart, quoted in Myers, "Heavens Declare the Glory of God," 15.

[18]Hildegard of Bingen, quoted in Myers, "Heavens Declare the Glory of God," 12.

[19]Francis of Assisi, "The Canticle of the Creatures," *Appleseeeds*, accessed January 1, 2020, www.appleseeds.org/canticle.htm.

[20]Martin Luther, quoted in Joe Ware, "Environgelicals: Reclaiming Environmentalism from the New Age Movement," *Premier Christianity*, December 2015, www.premierchristianity.com/home/environgelicals-reclaiming-environmentalism-from-the-New-Age-movement.

[21]John Calvin, quoted in Jason Foster, "The Ecology of John Calvin," *Reformed Perspectives* 7, no. 51 (December 18–24, 2005), https://thirdmill.org/magazine/article.asp?link=http:%5E%5Ethirdmill.org%5Earticles%5Ejas_foster%5Ept.jas_foster.calvin.ecology.html&at=The%20Ecology%20of%20John%20Calvin.

[22]John Calvin, quoted in Mark Stoll, "The Environment Was a Moral Issue Long Before Pope Francis," *HuffPost*, July 3, 2015, www.huffpost.com/entry/the-environment-was-a-mor_b_7716102.

[23]Jerry Pillay, "The Church as a Transformation and Change Agent," *HTS Theological Studies* 73, no. 2 (2017), www.scielo.org.za/scielo.php?script=sci_arttext&pid=S0259-94222017000300025.

[24]Donald J. Kohrs, "Methodism in America," in "Chautauqua: The Nature Study Movement in Pacific Grove, California," 2015, 71-73, https://seaside.stanford.edu/Chautauqua.

[25]Kohrs, "Methodism in America," 71-73.

[26]Kohrs, "Methodism in America," 12.

[27]Robert White, "A Burning Issue: Christian Care for the Environment," Jubilee Centre, December 27, 2019, https://www.jubilee-centre.org/cambridge-papers/a-burning-issue -christian-care-for-the-enviornment-by-robert-white.

[28]Shane Murray, "Dig Reveals Secrets of 'Green' Monks," *Irish Times*, August 4, 2009, www.irishtimes.com/news/dig-reveals-secrets-of-green-monks-1.712438.

[29]Ellen Arnold, "Pope Francis and the Traditions of Medieval Environmentalism," June 22, 2015, www.thismess.net/2015/06/pope-francis-and-traditions-of-medieval.html.

[30]Jennifer Powell McNutt, "An Unsung Inspiration for the Protestant Reformation: The Ethiopian Church," *Christianity Today*, August 2020, www.christianitytoday.com /history/2020/august/unsung-inspiration-for-protestant-reformation-ethiopian -chu.html.

[31]Amir Aman Kiyaro, "Churches Are Saving Ethiopia's Last Remaining Native Trees," *Christianity Today*, August 12, 2019, www.christianitytoday.com/ct/2019/september /ethiopian-orthodox-christians-deforestation-creation-care.html.

[32]McNutt, "Unsung Inspiration."

[33]Stoll, "Environment Was a Moral Issue."

[34]Stoll, "Environment Was a Moral Issue."

[35]Stoll, "Environment Was a Moral Issue."

[36]Kevin M. Lowe, *Baptized with the Soil: Christian Agrarians and the Crusade for Rural America* (New York: Oxford University Press, 2015), 141.

[37]"NAE Issues Calls to Action on Creation Care," National Association of Evangelicals, October 20, 2015, www.nae.net/nae-issues-call-to-action-on-creation-care.

[38]David Calderwood, "Voice in the Wilderness: Historical Christian Attitudes to the Environment and the Emergence of A Rocha," *Environment and Nature in New Zealand* 3, no. 2 (December 2013), www.environmentalhistory-au-nz.org/2013/12/voice-in-the -wilderness-historical-christian-attitudes-to-the-environment-and-the-emergence-of -a-rocha.

[39]National Association of Evangelicals, "NAE Issues Calls to Action on Creation Care."

[40]"The Christian Contribution to Medicine," Christian Medical Fellowship, Spring 2000, www.cmf.org.uk/resources/publications/content/?context=article&id=827.

[41]Gary Ferngren, "Healing the City," *Christian History*, accessed November 21, 2019, https://christianhistoryinstitute.org/magazine/article/healing-the-city.

[42]Christian Medical Fellowship, "Christian Contribution to Medicine."

[43]Christian Medical Fellowship, "Christian Contribution to Medicine."

[44]Guenter B. Risse, *Mending Bodies, Saving Souls: A History of Hospitals* (Oxford: Oxford University Press, 1999), 59.

[45]Christian Medical Fellowship, "Christian Contribution to Medicine."

[46]"Developments in Patient Care," *BBC Bitesized*, accessed January 3, 2020, www.bbc .co.uk/bitesize/guides/z27nqhv/revision/1.

[47]Christian Medical Fellowship, "Christian Contribution to Medicine."

[48]There are over seven hundred faith-based hospitals in the United States today. Consider, for example, Wake Forest Baptist Medical Center in Winston-Salem, NC; Presbyterian Hospital Albuquerque; Episcopal Hospital in Philadelphia; Bethany Brethren Hospital, Chicago; IU Health Methodist Hospital and Ascension St. Vincent Hospital in Indianapolis; St. John's Episcopal Hospital in Far Rockaway, NY; Methodist Dallas Medical Center; Presbyterian/St. Luke's Medical Center and St. Joseph's Hospital in Denver; and Mississippi Baptist Medical Center in Jackson.

[49]St. Joseph's Hospice was founded in 1905. See www.stjh.org.uk/about-us/our-history/.

[50]Christian Medical Fellowship, "Christian Contribution to Medicine."

[51]Peter Saunders, "Medicine and the Reformation," Christian Medical Fellowship, Autumn 2017, www.cmf.org.uk/resources/publications/content/?context=article&id=26701.

[52]Christian Medical Fellowship, "Christian Contribution to Medicine."

[53]Christian Medical Fellowship, "Christian Contribution to Medicine."

15. A STRATEGY FOR CULTIVATING THE SUSTAINABLE: COMBAT ENVIRONMENTAL HEALTH HAZARDS

[1]This and all other quotes, except where noted, are from the author's telephone interview with Niki Wong, (then) director of policy and organizing, Redeemer Community Partnership, February 10, 2020.

[2]Bob Smietana, "God, Guns and Oil," *Christianity Today*, August 18, 2017, www.christianitytoday.com/ct/2017/september/god-guns-oil-los-angeles-church.html.

[3]This and all subsequent quotes, except where noted, are from the author's telephone interview with Richard Parks, February 13, 2020.

[4]This and subsequent quotes, except as noted, are from the author's telephone interview with Jennifer Chou Blue, interim pastor, Church of the Redeemer, March 10, 2020.

[5]A. Pruss-Ustun et al., *Preventing Disease Through Healthy Environments* (Geneva, Switzerland: WHO, 2006).

[6]"Disease and Conditions," Environmental Protection Agency, accessed October 2, 2020, www.epa.gov/report-environment/disease-and-conditions.

[7]Erik Sherman, "If You're a Minority and Poor, You're More Likely to Live Near a Toxic Waste Site," *Fortune*, February 4, 2016, https://fortune.com/2016/02/04/environmental-race-poverty-flint.

[8]Emily Badger, "Pollution Is Segregated, Too," *Washington Post*, April 15, 2014, www.washingtonpost.com/news/wonk/wp/2014/04/15/pollution-is-substantially-worse-in-minority-neighborhoods-across-the-u-s; and Cheryl Katz, "People in Poor Neighborhoods Breathe More Hazardous Particles," *Scientific American*, November 1, 2012, www.scientificamerican.com/article/people-poor-neighborhoods-breate-more-hazardous-particles.

[9]Susan Abram, "How These Neighbors Took on the Oil Company in the Backyard and Won," *HuffPost*, July 27, 2019, www.huffpost.com/entry/oil-drill-site-protest-california_n_5d391la0e4b004b6adbab9c6.

[10]Richard Parks, quoted in Redeemer Community Partnership, "The Jefferson Drill Documentary," accessed August 19, 2020, http://makejeffersonbeautiful.weebly.com /documentary.html.

[11]Smietana, "God, Guns and Oil."

[12]Smietana, "God, Guns and Oil."

[13]Niki Wong, quoted in, Redeemer Community Partnership, "Jefferson Drill."

[14]Smietana, "God, Guns and Oil."

[15]See Jennifer Chou Blue, "Deborah's Song," in *Voices Rising: Women of Color Finding and Restoring Hope in the City*, ed. Shabrae Jackson Krieg and Janet Balasiri Singletary (Pomona, CA: Servant Partners, 2018), 71-94.

[16]Richard Parks, quoted in Abram, "How These Neighbors Took on the Oil Company."

[17]Stan Friedman, "Covenanters Help Lead Fight Against L.A. Neighborhood Oil Wells," *Covenant Companion*, May 5, 2017, https://covenantcompanion.com/2017/05/05 /covenanters-help-lead-fight-against-l-a-neighborhood-oil-wells.

[18]Richard Parks, quoted in Friedman, "Covenanters Help Lead Fight."

[19]Friedman, "Covenanters Help Lead Fight."

[20]Parks, quoted in Friedman, "Covenanters Help Lead Fight."

[21]Eric Bates, quoted in Megan Sweas, "Fighting for the Right to Breathe," *Sojourners*, June 2018, https://sojo.net/magazine/june-2018/fighting-right-breathe.

[22]Bob Smietana, "Urban Oil Well to Be Shut Down, Cleaned Up After Pressure from LA Activists," *Religion News Service*, June 4, 2019, https://religionnews.com/2019/06/04 /urban-oil-well-to-be-shut-down-cleaned-up-after-pressure-from-la-faith-activists.

[23]"There Ain't Nothin' You Can Do, Baby Girl," *Servant Partners* (blog), December 14, 2017, www.servantpartners.org/post/there-ain-t-nothin-you-can-do-baby-girl.

[24]Sweas, "Fighting for the Right to Breathe."

[25]Sweas, "Fighting for the Right to Breathe."

16. A STRATEGY FOR CULTIVATING THE SUSTAINABLE: ADDRESS FOOD DESERTS

[1]"1 in 4 Baltimore Residents Live in a Food Desert," Johns Hopkins Center for a Livable Future, June 10, 2015, https://clf.jhsph.edu/about-us/news/news-2015/1-4-baltimore -residents-live-food-desert.

[2]"Community Health Assessment," Baltimore City Health Department, September 20, 2017, https://health.baltimorecity.gov/sites/default/files/health/attachments/Baltimore %20City%20CHA%20-%20Final%209.20.17.pdf.

[3]Heber Brown III, "Black Church Food Security Update," YouTube, Black Church Food Security Network, October 8, 2017, www.youtube.com/watch?v=L6SEpHV9LmM&lis t=PLIZWFn4di5spi8Kxsgpebn4Zq66JGXtxr&index=6.

[4]Edie Gross, "A Network of Black Farmers and Black Churches Delivers Fresh Food from Soil to Sanctuary," *Faith & Leadership*, May 28, 2019, https://faithandleadership.com /network-black-farmers-and-black-churches-delivers-fresh-food-soil-sanctuary.

[5]Heber Brown III, quoted in Rachel Nania, "I Wanted to Do More for People Than Just Pray: Pastor Blends Faith, Farms to End Food Insecurity in Black Churches," WTOP Radio, February 4, 2019, https://wtop.com/lifestyle/2019/02/i-wanted-to-do-more -for-people-than-just-pray-pastor-blends-faith-farms-to-end-food-insecurity-in -black-churches.

[6]Some of the material in this and the next two sections overlaps with Amy L. Sherman, "How Churches Are Helping in Food Deserts," *Common Good*, January 8, 2020, www .madetoflourish.org/resources/beyond-charity-how-churches-are-helping -food-deserts.

[7]Heber Brown III, quoted in Kendall Vanderslice, "Reverend Dr. Heber Brown and the Black Church Food Security Network," *Good Food Jobs* (blog), October 9, 2018, www .goodfoodjobs.com/blog/reverend-dr-heber-brown-and-the-black-church-food -security-network.

[8]Heber Brown III, quoted in Adelle Banks, "Black Church Food Security Network Brings Fresh Food to Baltimore," *Christian Century*, May 8, 2018, www.christiancentury.org /article/news/black-church-food-security-network-brings-fresh-food-baltimore.

[9]Gross, "Network of Black Farmers and Black Churches."

[10]Heather Clark, "Freedom Fighters," *Put an Egg on It*, June 24, 2029, www.putaeggonit .com/blog/2019/6/17/freedom-farmers2.

[11]Heber Brown III, quoted in Nania, "I Wanted to Do More for People."

[12]Brown, quoted in Nania, "I Wanted to Do More for People."

[13]Lawrence Rodgers, quoted in "Pastor Lawrence Rodgers: Westside Community Church," YouTube, August 7, 2017, www.youtube.com/watch?v=Z828COkhMPM&lis t=PLIZWFn4di5spi8Kxsgpebn4Zq66JGXtxr&index=5&t=0s.

[14]Maxine White, quoted in Leilani Clark, "Black Churches, Powerful Cultural Forces Set Their Sights on Food Security," *Civil Eats*, July 9, 2018, https://civileats. com/2018/07/09/black-churches-powerful-cultural-forces-set-their-sights-on-food -security.

[15]Heber Brown Jr., quoted in Gross, "Network of Black Farmers and Black Churches."

[16]Julius Tillery, quoted in Clark, "Black Churches, Powerful Cultural Forces."

[17]Yvonne Gunn, quoted in Heber Brown III, "St. Mark's Institutional Baptist Church Garden," Black Church Food Security Network, August 7, 2017, www.youtube.com/wa tch?v=qXJBzpPFINY&list=PLIZWFn4di5spi8Kxsgpebn4Zq66JGXtxr&index= 4&t=0s.

[18]Heber Brown III, quoted in "From the Church Kitchen: Interview with Minnie Little," Black Church Food Security Network, July 31, 2018.

[19]Brown, quoted in Gross, "Network of Black Farmers and Black Churches."

[20]Heber Brown III, "Becoming More of Who We've Always Been," Pleasant Hope Baptist Church, April 30, 2019, www.pleasanthope.org/single-post/2019/04/30/Becoming -More-Of-Who-Weve-Always-Been.

[21]Heber Brown III, "New Year's Resolutions Must Consider Community Too," Pleasant Hope Baptist Church, December 27, 2019, www.pleasanthope.org/single-post /2019/12/27/New-Years-Resolutions-Must-Consider-Community-Too.

[22]Heber Brown III, quoted in Vanderslice, "Reverend Dr. Heber Brown and the Black Church Food Security Network."

[23]Brown, "Becoming More of Who We've Always Been."

[24]Gross, "Network of Black Farmers and Black Churches."

[25]"Diving into Data," A BCFSN Facebook Live Stream event hosted by Heber Brown III with Laurice Howell of Morgan State University and Darriel Harris of Johns Hopkins University, June 17, 2019, www.facebook.com/BlackChurchFSN/videos/891626864530478.

[26]Darriel Harris, cited in Adam MacInnis, "Baltimore Pastor Sees Long-Term Solution to Food Insecurity: Black Church Farms," *Christianity Today*, August 3, 2020, www .christianitytoday.com/news/2020/august/food-security-hunger-covid-protests-black -church-farm.html.

[27]Gross, "Network of Black Farmers and Black Churches."

[28]Nania, "Growing Faith and Food at Black Churches."

17. NEXT STEPS

[1]Dean Flemming, *Recovering the Full Mission of God: A Biblical Perspective on Being, Doing and Telling* (Downers Grove, IL: IVP Academic, 2013).

[2]Amy L. Sherman, *Kingdom Calling: Vocational Stewardship for the Common Good* (Downers Grove, IL: InterVarsity Press, 2011), 139.

[3]Andy Crouch, *Strong and Weak: Embracing a Life of Love, Risk and Flourishing* (Downers Grove, IL: InterVarsity Press, 2016), 11.

[4]Crouch, *Strong and Weak*, 35, 66-67.

[5]Some resources for finding learning communities and coaching include Made to Flourish (https://www.madetoflourish.org/), The Chalmers Center (https://chalmers.org/), Good Cities (https://goodcities.net/), Ormond Center (https://ormondcenter.com/community -craft-collaborative), Seed to Oaks (https://seedtooaks.com/), Missions 3.0 (http:// sattalks.org/missions-3-0-for-churches/), and Communities First Association (https:// www.cfapartners.org/).

[6]N. T. Wright, *After You Believe: Why Christian Character Matters* (San Francisco: HarperOne, 2010), 91.

[7]Wright, *After You Believe*, 86.

[8]Charles Self, personal correspondence with the author, October 23, 2020.

[9]Tools and coaching on mapping your congregational assets are available from Made to Flourish (madetoflourish.org).

[10]See Sherman, *Kingdom Calling*.

[11]"Citizen's Field Guide," *Thriving Cities*, August 6, 2011, https://static1.squarespace.com /static/5a0f45fad74cff16c9f6e45e/t/5b50fa90562fa718f6ca57b1/1532033690754 /2016.08.11_Field+Guide.pdf.

[12]A variety of tools are available to help with this. Three good sources include the Chalmers Center (https://chalmers.org/), Made to Flourish (www.madetoflourish .org/), and Communities First Association (www.cfapartners.org/).

[13]Greg Thompson, quoted in Jeff Haanen, "Six Ways to Live as Christians in the City," *For the Life of the World* (blog), accessed January 25, 2016, www.letterstotheexiles .com/6-lessons-living-christians-city.

MADE TO FLOURISH
A PASTORS' NETWORK FOR THE COMMON GOOD

The pastoral work you are called to do plays an important role in nurturing human flourishing and furthering the common good. We want to be a helpful resource as you faithfully equip your congregation to be followers of Jesus in all dimensions of life.

That's why we exist. Made to Flourish is a nationwide membership organization that equips pastors with a deeper understanding of the essential connection between Sunday faith and Monday work. Our goal is to help empower you to lead flourishing churches. As congregants begin to understand the intrinsic value of their daily work to God, it completely transforms their perspective on their work and how they do it.

Membership is free—we exist solely to provide you with relationships and resources to strengthen your ministry. We do this through a monthly newsletter, a resource-filled website, national events, online workshops and webinars, and city networks where you can meet with other local pastors.

By becoming a member, you will receive a welcome kit with several core faith-and-work resources, be connected to a city network, and receive special access to our events, seminars, and online learning opportunities.

WILL YOU JOIN WITH US TODAY?

Apply for the network at **madetoflourish.org/apply**.

For more written, video, and audio resources,
visit us at **madetoflourish.org**. You can also stay in touch by
following us on Twitter (**@madetoflourish**) and liking us on
Facebook (**facebook.com/MTFpastor**).

MADE TO FLOURISH

10901 Lowell Ave, Ste 130 | Overland Park, KS 66210
info@madetoflourish.org | www.madetoflourish.org

MADE TO FLOURISH RESOURCES

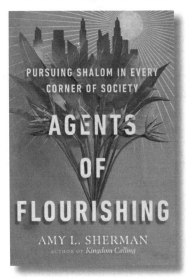

Agents of Flourishing
978-1-5140-0078-6

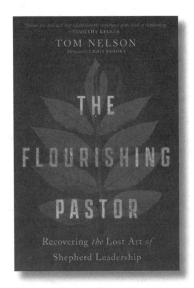

The Flourishing Pastor
978-1-5140-0132-5